AIC EDUCATION US COLLEGE G
CHINESE STUDENTS

AIC佳桥 中国校友说美国名校

佳桥教育科技（北京）有限公司◎编著

知识产权出版社
全国百佳图书出版单位

图书在版编目（CIP）数据

AIC 佳桥中国校友说美国名校. 第一辑 / 佳桥教育科技（北京）有限公司编著. —北京：知识产权出版社，2017. 6

ISBN 978-7-5130-4791-3

Ⅰ. ①A… Ⅱ. ①佳… Ⅲ. ①高等学校—介绍—美国 Ⅳ. ①G649. 712. 8

中国版本图书馆 CIP 数据核字（2017）第 046103 号

内容提要

本书是专为中国学生设计制作的美国大学选校指南。基于 AIC 佳桥教育的内部研究、专有数据库，及对在校就读的中国学生进行的问卷调查，本书详细介绍了在 US News 美国最佳大学排名（US News Best Colleges Ranking）上排名前 50 的部分美国综合性大学和文理学院，如学校的基本信息、学术机会、职业发展、校园人文环境、录取难度等，为计划申请美国顶尖大学本科项目的中国学生提供了绝佳的第一手资料，可以很好地帮助学生在申请开始前找到适合自己的学校，做到有的放矢。

责任编辑：刘琳琳　　**责任出版**：刘译文

AIC 佳桥中国校友说美国名校（第一辑）

佳桥教育科技（北京）有限公司　编著

出版发行：知识产权出版社有限责任公司	**网　　址**：http：//www. ipph. cn
社　　址：北京市海淀区西外太平庄 55 号	**邮　　编**：100081
责编电话：010-82000860 转 8390	**责编邮箱**：susan-lin886@ 163. com
发行电话：010-82000860 转 8101/8102	**发行传真**：010-82000893/82005070/82000270
印　　刷：北京嘉恒彩色印刷有限责任公司	**经　　销**：各大网上书店、新华书店及相关专业书店
开　　本：710mm×1000mm　1/16	**印　　张**：25
版　　次：2017 年 6 月第 1 版	**印　　次**：2017 年 6 月第 1 次印刷
字　　数：350 千字	**定　　价**：58. 00 元

ISBN 978-7-5130-4791-3

致　谢

如果没有许多人的努力和帮助，本书是不可能完成的。

特别感谢助理编辑余冰见对中文译稿的审校，和对本书出版工作的沟通协调。

特此感谢 Charlene Hsiao，高悦，曾睿睿，Adhiraaj Anand，Bryce Heatherly，Kam Yan，Francis Miller，Xander Robinson，Brianna Posadas，Katie Odhner，Jonathan Hsieh，Andy Blake，Ma Jing，Nicholas Daen，Rose Filler，Alena Shish 等的努力工作。

感谢佳桥教育管理团队张晨、萧永正、颜培、史鑫、汤加易及李莹的支持和帮助。

感谢在美国各地的佳桥校友及他们的朋友的慷慨分享。不仅如此，他们还积极地邀请了更多的同学参与了我们的问卷调查。你们是最棒的，本书是为你们而创作的！

Acknowledgements

This book wouldn't have been possible without the contributions of many. Would like to thank the following people in particular:

James Bingjian Yu (Assistant Editor), Charlene Hsiao, Gao Yue, Ruirui Zeng, Adhiraaj Anand, Bryce Heatherly, Kam Yan, Francis Miller, Xander Robinson, Brianna Posadas, Katie Odhner, Jonathan Hsieh, Andy Blake, Ma Jing (Dido), Nicholas Daen, Rose Filler, Alena Shish and many others...

The leadership team at AIC Chen Zhang, Stephen Siu, Pei Yen, Xin Shi, Malo Tang, Karen Li.

And the awesome AIC alumni across the US and their friends, who have shared generously and gotten their peers involved to provide candid feedback on what they think of their colleges. This book is for you guys!

序　　言

一、引言

在过去的十年间，中国赴美留学的人数暴增。从2006年的62582人，增长到2016年的328547人，增长了4倍多[1]。去美国读大学是一个重要的人生决定，是人生中一项重要的投资，需要长期的规划和投入，英语学习就更不用说了。然而，目前中国读者（家长、学生、升学顾问、学校老师）接触到的中文的申请指导材料基本上直接翻译自英语读物，但这些读物主要是为美国读者创作的。许多申请美国大学的美国学生本身就可以从父母身上获得很多经验，而这些经验是不易被“翻译”的。即使有些美国的孩子父母是移民，但由于他们从小在美国生活、长大，也耳濡目染了许多美国社会的规范，同时他们的许多老师和升学顾问也正是他们要申请的大学的校友。此外，现有公开的录取统计数据也往往无法反映出中国学生入学竞争的激烈程度。例如，大学官网和一些大学排名机构，如《美国新闻和世界报道》，公布的是全部被录取学生的SAT分数分布范围（有时不把体育生统计在内）。但国际学生通常只占到全部学生人数的10%左右，且国际学生之间也有很多不同。例如，被哥伦比亚大学录取的美国学生SAT I分数的中位数通常低于2200，但我们的经验告诉我们，对于中国学生来说，这个数值大约是2310。因此，我们希望通过本书消除文化差异所带来的影响，指出在申请过程中对美国人来说是“显而易见”，但对中国人却并非如此的一些道理；同时提供一些中国读者想知道的申请信息。无论从质量上还是数量上来说，这些信息对他们决定申请哪所大学都是非常有帮助的。申请适合自己的大学不但能够让录取几率最大化，而且可以充分利用学校提供的资源，有利于个人在求学期间的顺利成长和毕业后的发展。

我们发现因为信息缺乏，许多中国的家长和学生对美国大学的了解并不多，很多学生在申请时只知道盯准“常春藤联盟”大学。我们理解大家对常春藤联盟大学的好感，但对于留学领域的真正专业人士而言，这让我们知道中国家长和学生对美国大学还有很多不了解的地方。有些学校，如哈维·穆德学院，约翰·霍普金斯大学和塔夫茨大学虽然不属于常春藤联盟，但都拥有极高的声誉和严苛的学生选拔机制。此外，大学之间的教育理念、办学文化也大相径庭。例如，布朗大学的课程设置是灵活开放的，而哥伦比亚大学采取的则是核心课程设置，代表了两种截然不

[1] 数据来源：http://www.iie.org/Research-and-Publications/Open-Doors/Data/Fast-Facts#.WLk86VV97IU

同的教育理念。因此，或许有学生对两种教育环境都喜欢，都能够适应，但更多的学生则更适合其中的一种。对一个美国人来说，就好像说他既支持共和党，又支持民主党一样；对于中国人来说，就像说您既喜欢甜豆腐脑，也喜欢咸豆腐脑。

我们知道，许多中国人对于美国大学的了解，包括学校名气，主要来源于上一波留学热潮时留学美国的中国人，但当时的留学生主要就读的是美国大学的研究生院。因此，他们对美国只提供本科阶段教育的文理学院知之甚少。这里我们要感谢佳桥的合作伙伴——美国顶尖文理学院中国巡展的努力。他们邀请了美国顶尖文理学院的招生官来中国和学生、家长交流，增加他们对文理学院的了解。本书介绍了更多文理学院提供的资源，如很多文理学院会和大型研究型大学合作，为它们的学生提供更多的如在工程方面的学习项目。

尽管申请美国顶尖大学的中国学生数量在不断增长，但大学未来提供给中国学生的录取名额不可能比现在增加多少。首先，不是每个学生都适合哈佛这样的顶尖大学；其次，就算适合，也不可能都被录取。所以，更多地了解美国大学变得更加重要。我们相信美国的高等教育系统会继续提供优质、独特的教育，即便其中很多学校不为家长、学生所熟知。我们相信中国家长和学生将会认识到这些事实，只是时间问题。除顶尖名校外，还有很多培养了大量社会各领域人才的大学值得我们去了解。我们希望本书不但可以帮助您发现这些大学，而且可以帮助您顺利拿到录取通知。

二、关于佳桥教育

佳桥教育是中国第一家聘请美国顶尖名校毕业生在中国提供大学申请咨询服务的教育公司。目前，佳桥在美国新泽西州和中国的北京、上海、深圳、杭州、成都和西安六大城市设有公司和分公司。但在现代高科技的帮助下，拥有 12 年运营经验的佳桥所服务的学生已遍布中国广州、南京、沈阳、昆明、郑州、大连、武汉等各大城市和部分国家及地区，如美国、英国、（中国）香港、新加坡、印度和加拿大。12 年来，共有超过 2500 名的佳桥学生毕业于或正在就读美国顶尖大学。

佳桥以关心学生的成长和让学生学有所长而自豪。我们不以大学录取结果来衡量我们的成功，我们关注的是佳桥校友在大学期间和毕业后所取得的成就。我们骄傲的是从佳桥的学生中走出了 16 位企业家、3 位作家和数百名在顶尖研究生院，如哈佛大学设计学院、哥伦比亚大学法学院和知名公司，如 Uber、谷歌、微软和高盛，追寻自己职业梦想的佳桥人。

2015 年，佳桥出版了《你离哈佛并不远》一书，帮助中国学生了解美国的大学、大学的录取过程，同时给学生在申请和求学过程中寻找人生方向提供建议。麻省理工学院前中国区总面试官蒋佩蓉亲自为该书作了序。

2010 年，立足于内部研发，佳桥出版了《38 所常青藤》一书，力图进一步帮助行业了解美国大学不同的教育体系。这本书厘清了一些对美国大学的误解，尝试让家长和学生不再只关注大学的排名。

2009 年，佳桥创作出版了《我如何进哈佛》。这本书是佳桥和另一机构合作编纂的佳桥第一本书的延续。

2007 年，我们编著了《你也能进哈佛》。该书是中国大陆最早关于美国高等学校教育和申请的原创书籍之一，在当时的市场上引起了很大的反响（被认为是 2008 到 2010 年间业内最有指导意义的著作之一）。

同时，佳桥陆续为学生制作了《大学生存指导手册》和近 20 期校友通讯（季刊），为佳桥校友提供最新的关于专业、职业生涯规划等方面的建议，以及介绍发生在佳桥的新鲜事。

2012 年，佳桥开启了年度“大学博览会”活动，邀请各大名校的佳桥在读校友分享有关大学学习和生活的第一手资讯。同时邀请嘉宾发表演讲，如佳桥教育创始人兼 CEO 张晨、麻省理工学院前工学院副院长、国际项目主任和机械工程系 Skolkovo 基金会教授俞久平（Dick K. P. Yue）。

在过去 12 年的实践和研发中，通过真实的学生案例和校友反馈，我们一直在不断优化对大学所关注学生特质的定性分析，同时密切跟踪大学不断变化的对于录取的定量要求，如标准化考试分数。经过观察，我们发现了名校在录取上的很多有趣的变化。我们不但要与您分享我们作为专业留美咨询专家的发现，而且我们要与您分享正在名校就读的佳桥校友的集体智慧和丰富经历。佳桥知道教育对中国的重要性，能为中国家庭服务也是我们的莫大荣幸。因为您的支持，才有了我们的发展壮大，才有了我们的也许是美国顶尖名校中最大的中国校友网络。和您们分享一些我们的先发优势和成功的果实，我们感到自豪。

三、《AIC 佳桥中国校友说美国名校》有什么与众不同

《AIC 佳桥中国校友说美国名校》是第一本专门为中国学生设计制作的本科选校指南。本书中所有内容均为佳桥原创。在内部研究、专有数据库及对在本书中介绍的学校就读的中国学生分别进行了问卷调查的基础上，我们创作了本书。在创作本书时，我们也注意到了一些不适用于中国读者的地方，并对此作了调整。例如多样性，对美国人来说意味着国际学生的数量，但对中国学生来说则意味着一所学校里亚洲/亚裔学生的数量。又比如说，美国人更习惯于去远离城市的地方（美国人通常称之为“城郊”）生活居住，但中国学生通常会不喜欢交通或者周边设施不够方便的地方。因此，在本书中我们不仅列出了每所学校的具体位置，还注明了学校离最近的大城市的距离。

未来我们还会继续推出对更多学校的介绍。

以下是本书的一些独特亮点：

1. 招生官具体联系方式

列出中国地区招生官或区域（如大中华区）招生主管的姓名和电子邮箱。毫无疑问，这些招生官会审阅您的申请资料，对中国学生申请时遇到的问题最为熟悉。大多数情况下，在海外中学就读的中国学生由主管学校所在地区的招生官负责。

备注：中国地区招生官联系方式可能会有变动

2. 学校地址

除学校的具体地址外，也会注明离学校最近的大城市以及往返城市和学校之间的主要交通方式和大约花费的时间。

3. 学生人口分布

- 国际学生比例
- 亚洲/亚裔学生比例

4. 佳桥校友录取情况

- 录取比例
- SAT 阅读成绩中位数
- SAT 数学成绩中位数
- SAT 写作成绩中位数
- SAT 总分中位数
- TOEFL 成绩中位数

备注：根据学校关于 SAT 分数的具体政策，取单次最高分或拼分最高分的中位数（满分为 2400）。请见本书附录 1 新旧 SAT、新 SAT 与 ACT 官方换算表。

5. 有无助学金

以佳桥学生申请经验为依据统计。

6. 学生对学校的评价

特别提醒，本部分的评价非常主观，就像同一碗面不同人品尝起来会有不一样的反应，评价学校也是如此。即便两个学生对同一所学校都有较好的评价，如果给学校打分的话，4 分为最高分，他们会选择 3 分，2. 8 分还是 3. 5 分呢？尽管主观评分有一定的局限，我们仍然认为分享佳桥校友的校园体验是有必要的。虽然个人观点不一定总是对的，也仅代表一家之言，但仍不失为一个有趣和有用的参考。以下评分都以 4 分为满分，4 分代表了最高评价。

- 安全：校园够安全吗？您觉得有多安全？
- 有趣：您觉得学校有趣吗？

- 生活成本：日常开销是否太高？
- 中国食物：学校（内）附近可以吃到中餐吗？好吃吗？
- 交通便利：学校附近的交通是否便利？
- 酒吧和俱乐部：您给学校（附近）的酒吧和俱乐部打多少分？
- 超市/便利店选择：日常食品、生活用品的质量怎么样，品种多吗？
- 周边就业市场：是否容易获得实习、志愿者或任何接触真实社会的机会？
- 是否需要车：买车对出行或生活是否必需？
- 总评：整体来说，您的评价是什么？

7. 气候

之所以加入对学校所在地区的气候概况介绍，是因为学生和家长对美国的环境不是特别熟悉。此外，一般学生自己查找的时候，会发现在美国温度的度量采取的是华氏温度，而不是摄氏温度，其他很多度量单位也是如此。我们按中国人的习惯做了换算，帮您省掉许多麻烦。

8. 从中国出发的航班

本书提供了从国内大城市到美国的航班信息。到美国后如何去学校的信息（包括乘飞机、穿梭巴士、的士或者火车）也有提供。

备注：因为交通线路会随时更新，请在动身前确认最新信息。

四、关于大学的选择

第一辑选校指南并没有涵盖所有的学校，包括一些知名大学如耶鲁大学、威廉姆斯学院及宾夕法尼亚大学。我们正在核实一些数据，继续做相关研究，计划在后续的系列书籍中推出对更多学校的介绍。未来我们会加大努力，邀请除佳桥校友外的更多学生加入进来，为大家介绍更多大学、更多信息。提前谢谢您的理解！

五、本书是如何编著的

在过去的三年，我们对数百位中国留学生进行了问卷调查。尽管信息并不是全部来自于佳桥校友，但所有的受访对象在受访时均为正在美国高校就读的中国留学生。受访者都来自中国，一小部分在海外读的高中。虽然中国国内学生和海外高中学生在录取数据上会有一些差异，但由于样本人数足够多，我们认为这些差异不会影响到相关数据的参考价值。同时因为我们的学生来自中国各大城市和其他部分国家及地区，我们认为地理位置也不会影响到我们信息的准确性。

本书中的数据更新至 2016 年 4 月，大学排名为《美国新闻和世界报道》2014—2015 年度的美国大学排名。

六、本书的格式

每所学校介绍由 8 大类信息组成：

1. 学校的基本信息

一些基本信息，如学校地址、网站、招生官的姓名和电子邮件。

2. 信息速览

学生感兴趣的关键信息，主要是一些统计数据，如学生人口分布、有本科项目的学院、类似的大学、录取数据、学校周边环境、气候、交通等。

3. 最佳匹配点分析

最适合这所大学的是哪一类型的学生（匹配对学生申请和入学后的表现非常重要）。

4. 学术机会

- 学科体系设置
- 受欢迎的专业
- 学术强项
- 学术文化氛围
- 学术资源
- 课程难易程度（例如，拿“A”有多容易）

5. 职业发展

- 学校为学生职业发展提供的资源和支持
- 学生就业时进入的主要公司或机构

6. 校园人文环境

- 校园活力
- 校园活动的丰富性
- 校园文化
- 社交压力
- 多样性

7. 录取难度

根据佳桥学生的申请经验，指出学校在录取考核学生时重要的定量或定性标准。

8. 需要考虑的事情

简要总结可能喜欢或者不喜欢这所学校的学生类型。

七、如何使用本书

本书中的学校按英文字母顺序排列。

另，本书中的部分信息似乎和其他地方的信息不一致，而书中内容也会出现“自相矛盾”之处。这里需要解释说明一下。

您可能会发现书中的一些评级和其他地方的信息不一致。举例来说，您也许了解到某大学称他们对国际学生采取与需求无关（Need-blind）的政策，这意味着他们会无条件满足申请学生的助学金（Financial Aid）要求，无论金额多少；申请助学金不会影响到录取。但本书仍说在这所大学获得经济资助的可能性很低。这是我们从中国学生实际申请经验中得到的结论，尽管可能不是完全正确。

书中内容的“自相矛盾”。例如您可能读到“因为靠近波士顿，巴布森学院的学生们拥有足够的实习和工作机会”，但在“学生为学校所在地区打分”部分，学生对周边就业市场的评价并不高。这里可能是受访学生因某些原因，如没有车或不知道这些信息，没能够积极主动地利用好这些机会。又比如某一所大学有足够的资源，学生们的课外活动和社交活动丰富多彩，但受访学生对此并不认同，也没有觉得在学校的生活有多愉快。可能的原因很多，也许是学生之前生活的地方比这所学校更有意思，又也许是学生所习惯的娱乐方式在学校里找不到，再或者是这个学生没有找到自己认为有趣的朋友圈。因受访的学生数量总体比较可观，这种极个别的情况产生的影响可以忽略不计，但主观印象和实际情况有所不同是有可能的。

八、奖学金/助学金信息

九、评级（根据“学生为学校所在地区打分”部分的得分进行排名）

附录 2 排名表里的大学均获得了至少一个受访学生给予的 4 分（满分）好评。

十、最后的备注

尽管我们的团队已经尽了最大的努力来确保本书中不出现错误，但错误总是难免的，特别是对于这样一本全新的书来说。如果您在阅读本书时发现了错误，请发送邮件到 **info@jq-edu.com** 告诉我们，我们将非常感激。无论您是喜欢还是讨厌本书，我们都希望收到您的宝贵意见。只有这样，我们才能在以后把本系列的书籍做得更好。

开始享受您的阅读之旅吧！

李章源（Johnny Lee）

《AIC 佳桥中国校友说美国名校》主编

Preface

1) Introduction

The number of Chinese international students attending US colleges has more than quintupled in the past decade, from 2006 to 2016. Applying and attending US colleges and universities is a major life and investment decision, requiring numerous years of planning and dedication, let alone English preparation. Yet, many resources available to the Chinese audience (parents, students, counselors, school officials) are direct translations of existing materials in English, which were created for an American audience. Many American students that apply to American colleges and universities are children of parents who have attended American colleges and universities, thus have a higher knowledge base that is not easily transferrable with simple language translation. Even those children in the US whose parents are immigrants, for example, have natural exposure to American societal norms simply by growing up and living in the US, with access to many teachers and guidance counselors who are alumni of the schools high school students are applying to. Moreover, the statistics available publicly currently do not reflect just how competitive it is for an international Chinese student to gain admissions. For example, SAT score ranges contained in school websites and rankings like the US News and World Report apply for the entire school (sometimes there are exceptions, such as for athletes). However, international applicants make up typically approximately only 10% of the student population, and there is great variance among international students. For example, the median SAT I score for Columbia for an American student would be in the low 2200, but for a Chinese international student, our experience tells us that it is approximately 2310. This guide aims to not only bridge this cultural gap by highlighting some aspects that may be "obvious" to Americans but otherwise not-so to us in China, but also goes a step further in providing information that a Chinese audience would like to know and are helpful for deciding a school in both qualitative and quantitative terms. Having a good fit with the school is not only important for maximizing chances of getting in, but also finding an environment where you can maximize your chance of thriving and succeed beyond college.

Due to a lack of information specific to the Chinese student experience and catering to China's situation, we find many parents and students in China are still uninformed about

US colleges and universities, with many seeking only to attend the Ivy League. We understand the perception continues to remain favorable for the Ivy League schools, but such statements are one of the easiest ways for true experts in our field to know how much you don't know. For example, Harvey Mudd College, Johns Hopkins University, Tufts University are not a part of the Ivy League, but are very rigorous and highly-regarded universities. Moreover, the educational philosophies, thus cultures, of the institutions are also very unique. For example, Brown University, which offers an open curriculum and Columbia University, which offers a Core Curriculum, could not be more different in their philosophies. Thus, while there may be some students who could fit both the educational environments, many will fit more closely with one, not the other. To an American, it's almost like saying that you support both Republicans and Democrats. To a Chinese, it's perhaps akin to saying that you like both sweet tofu curd and salty tofu curd.

We understand that many of the Chinese audience's familiarity with US colleges, including perceptions of prestige, are informed by the institutions the earlier wave of Chinese students attended, many of which attended American graduate schools. Thus, familiarity with liberal arts colleges, which only offer undergraduate education, remain less well-known. We applaud recent efforts by our valued educational partner, the China LAC Tour, which brings admissions officers of top US liberal arts colleges to China to increase familiarity of Chinese parents and students to these top-notch schools. The Guidebook reveals more of the types of resources liberal-arts colleges offer through partnerships with larger research universities that may offer a broader curriculum such as in engineering.

Despite the ever-increasing demand of Chinese students to attend the best institutions of higher education in the US, the number of seats open to Chinese international students will likely not increase much more than is currently available. First of all, not everyone is fit to attend Harvard. Secondly, even if fit, not everyone can attend. Thus, it becomes even more important to know more about US colleges and universities. We believe the American higher education system continues to provide a unique and compelling education. Just because some of them are not as well known in China today, the facts don't change. We believe perception will catch up with the truth. It's only a matter of time. There are some fine gems that have educated some of the world's finest scholars, leaders, innovators, contributors spanning all spectrums of society for decades. This guide will help you not only find them, but we hope also help you get in.

2) About AIC

AIC Education is the first education company in China to provide college admissions consulting services employing graduates of top US colleges and universities on-the-ground in China. We operate in New Jersey and in six cities across China from Beijing, Shanghai, Shenzhen, Hangzhou, Chengdu, Xian, but in reality, through over twelve years of operating experience and top-notch technology, serve students both across China (including Guangzhou, Nanjing, Shenyang, Kunming, Zhengzhou, Dalian, Wuhan) and the world (including high schools in the US, UK, Hong Kong (China), Singapore, India, Canada). Our presence is not limited to our physical locations. We have worked with over 2,500 alumni who all have attended or currently attend the top US colleges and universities.

We pride ourselves in our care for student growth and expertise, and measure our success not based on college admissions results, but on alumni achievement in college and beyond. We boast [16] entrepreneurs, [3] published authors, and hundreds who are building their careers whether at top graduate schools such as Harvard Graduate School of Design, Columbia Law School or companies like Uber, Google, Microsoft, Goldman Sachs.

In 2015, we published "*You Are Not Far from Harvard*", which shows how to understand US colleges, the admissions process, as well as providing advice about how to find direction in life before and during college. The book's forward was written by Rossana Lin, the former MIT head of interview for China region.

In 2010, we published "*The* 38 *Ivies*", which, based on internal research and development, seeks to further help the market understand the different education systems adopted by US colleges. This book dispels misconceptions about US colleges, and seeks to drive the attention of parents and students away from superficial rankings.

In 2009, we authored "*How I Got Into Harvard*", which is a continuation in the series of AIC's first book published under an organization AIC formerly partnered with.

In 2007, we authored "*You Too Can Get Into Harvard*", which is one of the first original books in China on US college education and admissions, having a significant impact on the market at the time (informally known as one of the leading books in the industry from 2008-10).

We have also produced for our students a College Survival Guidebook and over 16 alumni quarterly magazines that keep our alumni updated with the latest on majors, career advice, and happenings at AIC.

In 2012, we started an annual college fair, which brings together various alumni attending the colleges to share first-hand experience of what the experience is like. Past guest speakers have included Chen Zhang, AIC's Founder and CEO, and Dick Yue, Skolkovo Foundation Professor of Mechanical Engineering, Director of International Programs, and former Associate Dean of Engineering at Massachusetts Institute of Technology.

Through our past 12 years of operations, research and development, we have continually refined these qualitative traits, both with real student cases and alumni feedback, and kept track of the ever-changing quantitative admissions requirements like test scores. We have observed some very interesting behavior at some top colleges and we want to share with you some of not only our findings as admissions consulting experts, but also the collective wisdom and experiences of actual AIC alumni that are attending these colleges and universities. We understand how important education is to this nation, and we consider it an extreme privilege to serve Chinese families. We owe our geographic scale and alumni network, likely the largest among top US colleges, to your support. It gives us great pride to share with you some of the fruits of our first-mover advantage and our success.

3) What is AIC Education US College Guide for Chinese Students

AIC Education US College Guide for Chinese Students is the first-ever guidebook for US colleges and universities written for the Chinese international student. Unlike many peers in our industry, our findings are based on propriety, original research. Based primarily on feedback from Chinese international students, hailing from across China (and even the world) attending the particular college and our own internal research and proprietary database, we provide a perspective that already adjusts for assumptions that may not apply to a Chinese audience. For example, diversity to an American may mean the number of students that are international students, but for a Chinese student, may mean the number of non-Asians including Asian Americans. Moreover, while Americans may be more used to being in environments further away from cities (the "suburbs" as Americans would call it), Chinese students may find the absence of cosmopolitan amenities more difficult to accept. Thus, we have noted not only where the school is located, but how far it is from a major city.

For future editions, we will expand the range of schools to the top 70, 100, and beyond.

Below are the following unique highlights of our guidebook:

i. Admissions Officer Contact details

Where available, the China admissions officer's name and email address, otherwise known as the Territory Manager, which covers China are provided. Students who are applying from overseas high schools, will, in most cases, be covered by a separate Territory Manager. The China admissions officer will almost certainly review your application and be most familiar with any questions you may have about applying as a Chinese international student.

Note: China admissions officer information may change.

ii. Location

Instead of simply including the address of the school, the closest major city and approximate time it takes to get there by car are included.

iii. Student population demographics

- The percentage of international students is provided
- The percentage of Asian American/ Asians is provided

iv. Admissions Statistics of AIC alumni Applicants that got admitted

- Percentage of AIC applicants accepted
- Median SAT I Critical Reading score
- Median SAT I Math score
- Median SAT I Writing score
- Median SAT I Composite score
- Median TOEFL score

Note on methodology: Provided median of super-score or highest score in single-sitting depending on school-specific admissions policy. Used old SAT conventions. Please see Appendix 1 *for Score Conversion chart to New SAT and to ACT*

v. Financial Aid Availability

Based on experience of AIC students applying.

vi. What Students Say

This section deserves word of caution because it is fairly subjective. The same bowl of noodles could taste good to one student, but less good to another. And even if both students rate it very good, would they consider it a 3.0 out of 4.0 or a 2.8 or 3.5? Despite obvious limitations in subjectivity, we still think it would be useful to share what AIC students thought of their college environment. Perceptions are not always true and can vary depending on the individual, nevertheless can be a fun and useful metric when taken with a grain of salt and in context of a broader set of information. All metrics out of scale of 4. 0, where 4.0 is the best rating.

- Safety: How safe is campus? How safe do you feel?
- Fun: How fun is your campus?
- Expensive: How expensive are living costs?
- Chinese food: Is good Chinese food readily accessible? Is it any good?
- Transportation: How convenient is it to get around?
- Bars and Clubs: How do you rate the bars and clubs in and around campus?
- Market/Grocery options: How are the quality and quantity of grocery options?
- Surrounding Job Market: Is it easy to get internships, volunteer opportunities and any real-world experience?
- Necessity of Car: Is it necessary to have a car to get around and enjoy life?
- Overall: What is your overall experience?

vii. Climate

Climate is included because parents and students may be less familiar with America. Moreover, when you look this information up yourself, you'll find that measuring conventions Americans use can be different such as using Fahrenheit not Celsius, inches, not meters. We have saved you the hassle!

viii. Transportation from China

Transportation options from major Chinese cities are provided including airplane, shuttle, taxi, or train options where available

Note: as transportation routes may change at any time, with new routes forming all the time, we advise you to double check before booking trip.

4) How the Colleges were selected

The First Edition Guidebook doesn't contain all colleges and universities, with some notable absences such as Yale University, Williams College, and the University of Pennsylvania. We are still verifying data and research and plan to release in the next edition along with an expanded range of colleges. As we move through making improvements for the Second Edition, we hope to increase both scope and depth of participation, widening scope beyond just AIC alumni and thereby include a greater variety of colleges and greater variety of information. We thank you in advance for your understanding!

5) How the College Guide was compiled

Over the past three years, we surveyed hundreds of Chinese international students. While not all information comes from AIC alumni, all survey respondents are Chinese international students attending the university at the time of survey. Respondents come from all over China, with a minority coming from high schools abroad. While there can be some difference in admissions statistics for applicants from China and abroad, the sample size is large enough where we didn't feel this difference skewed meaningfulness of the averages. Also, because we have a national presence in China and work with Chinese international students across the world, we do not think our information is skewed by geography.

All information in the Guidebook is current as of April 2016. Thus, the US News and World Report Rankings used are 2014-15.

6) The Format

Each school profile is divided into eight major categories:

i. School Basic Information

Basic information such as address, website, name of admissions officer and email

ii. At a Glance

Key information of interest, mainly statistics, such as regarding the school, student population, admissions, environment, similar schools, climate, transportation

iii. Best Fit Analysis

The type of student that best fits the school (important for both admissions and student performance)

iv. Academic Opportunities

- Structure of academic programs
- Popular majors
- Academic strengths
- Academic Culture
- Academic Resources
- Competitiveness of Curriculum (e.g. how easy to get an "A")

v. Career Development

- Career development opportunities and support
- Major employers

vi. Campus Social Environment

- Vibrancy of campus environment
- Various options on campus
- Student Culture
- Social Pressure
- Diversity

vii. Selectivity

Any important pointers for applicants whether quantitative or qualitative in criteria based on past AIC applicants

viii. Things to Consider

Quick summary of types of students that may or may not like the school

7) How to use the Guidebook

The Guidebook is ordered alphabetically.

Some areas of the Guidebook may seem contradictory to information sources externally, but also internally i.e. within the document itself.

External Contradictions: You may find that some of quantitative ratings (out of 4.0 scale) may be inconsistent with some of the information in the text. For example, you may read that a college professes that it is internationally need-blind, meaning they will meet the financial need of international students regardless of the amount of that need. They may also say that asking for aid will not affect your chances of admissions. The Guidebook may still say that Financial Aid Availability is low at this school. Because we look at practice, while this may not be completely true, we believe it to be the case based on our experience for Chinese international students.

Internal Contradictions: In the text of the Guidebook, it may say that Babson has a lot of access to internships and activities due to proximity to Boston, but our "What Students Say..." section may not reflect a high mark in Surrounding Job Market. There could be several reasons including the students that responded to survey weren't proactive to take advantage of those opportunities for whatever reason, such as they didn't have a car or maybe didn't know about them. Another example could be that a college has numerous activities and a vibrant social life, but for whatever reason, survey respondents didn't agree and were not having fun at their school. Again, there are many potential reasons such as the respondent comes from a place that is considered more fun, thus college pales in comparison. Or the respondent is used to a certain way of having fun that is not as readily available. Or a respondent may not have yet found the friend circle he or she considers fun. The number of respondents we have gotten smoothens out for such individual unique circumstances, but it's possible that perception and reality may be different.

8) Scholarship/Financial Aid Information

9) Ratings (Rankings by metrics in "What Students Say...")

Colleges included in Appendix 2 reflect at least one respondent that provided a 4-star (out of 4) rating for the category.

10) Final Remarks

Despite our team's best efforts to ensure no errors occurred, mistakes can happen to the best of us, especially for a new product.If you find any, kindly feel free to write to us at [**info@jq-edu.com**]. Regardless of whether you love the Guidebook or hate it, we would love to hear back from you on what you found useful and areas we can improve to make the Guidebook more informative.

Enjoy!

***AIC Education US College Guide for Chinese Students*, Editor-in-Chief**

Johnny Lee

目　录

中文版

英文版

中文版

阿姆赫斯特学院

地址：220 SOUTH PLEASANT STREET，AMHERST，MA 01002
网址：WWW.AMHERST.EDU
中国招生官：无
招生办公室电话：413-542-2328
招生办公室邮箱：ADMISSION@AMHERST.EDU
附近主要城市：波士顿，阿姆赫斯特学院距波士顿近150公里，可以通过穿梭巴士或者“小飞侠”巴士（Peter Pan Bus Lines）到达

最佳匹配点分析

在文理学院排名中，阿姆赫斯特学院与威廉姆斯学院一直轮流坐头把交椅。目前，阿姆赫斯特学院暂居第二。阿姆赫斯特学院位于阿姆赫斯特镇上，小镇坐落在麻省（马萨诸塞州）的群山之中，距离波士顿近150公里车程。虽然只是一个小镇，阿姆赫斯特还是为学生们提供了包含艺术品商店和众多餐厅在内的充满活力的环境。作为五院联盟的一员，阿姆赫斯特学院的学生也可以选择在曼荷莲学院、马萨诸塞大学阿姆赫斯特分校、史密斯学院，或者汉普郡学院上课并享受它们的资源。许多教授来到阿姆赫斯特唯一的目的就是教学和指导学生，给学生们构建一个严格的学术环境。近些年来，学校在社会经济和种族上都尽力让校园更多元化，然而，自我隔离在校园中依然很常见。

信息速览	
US News[①]文理学院排名	2
学校位置	东北
学校类型	私立
周边环境	乡村

本科学生情况	
学生总数	1785 (2014)
申请人数	8478 (2014)
录取率	14% (2014)
男女学生比例	51/49
国际学生百分比	10%
亚裔美国人百分比	14%

你可能还想考虑以下学校	
威廉姆斯学院	哈佛大学
布朗大学	普林斯顿大学
达特茅斯学院	明德学院

学术机会

寻求声名显赫的精英本科教育的学生会在阿姆赫斯特如鱼得水。学校的课堂通常很小，平均大约 16 人的小型课堂一直是学校的骄傲。一位佳桥的校友说："所有教过我的和正在教我的教授都非常容易接近，他们每周都有至少四小时的办公室时间，另外预约时间见面也很容易。" TYPO（Take Your Professor Out）项目，也就是"约见教授"，是阿姆赫斯特学院出资让学生与教授在晚饭时间见面的项目。阿姆赫斯特学院共有 38 个专业，其中最热门的是经济（16%）、英语（11%）和心理（11%），其他优势学科还有政治科学、生物，以及法律、法理和社会思潮。五院联盟让阿姆赫斯特的学生有了在可持续发展研究、佛学研究，以及亚洲、太平洋、美国研究等领域取得专业证书的机会。因为阿姆赫斯特学院没有核心课程或者通识教育的要求，学生们在课程规划上很灵活，可以自主设计跨学科课程。研究在本科生中很常见。学生也有可能获得许多类似于学院院长夏季研究项目（Dean of the Faculty Summer Research Program）或者霍华德•休斯奖学金（Howard Hughes Fellowship）的项目资助。

职业发展

阿姆赫斯特学院的学生数量少于 2000 人，对于每个个体的特别关注让这所学校甚为骄傲。每位本科生在到来之初就会有一位大一学生顾问，目的在于引导学生发现他们意向专业中的职业机会。专业顾问会在学生选定专业的时候分配给学生。Pathways 是一个阿姆赫斯特学院校友和在校学生之间的指导项目，在有相似职业规划的校友和学生之间形成合作关系。阿姆赫斯特实习选择项目（ASIP，Amherst Select Internship Program）独家为本校学生服务，为他们促成由阿姆赫斯特学生家长、校友和朋友提供的实习机会。大约 80% 的阿姆赫斯特毕业生计划（或考虑）继续攻读硕士或博士学位，但是阿姆赫斯特的校友在毕业后直接进入竞争激烈的公司方面也很成功。在 2013 年的毕业生中，教育（18.5%）、金融服务（16%）和卫生保健（16%）是三个最受欢迎的领域。阿姆赫斯特校友工作的热门公司包括麦肯锡、贝恩（Bain & Company）和基石咨询公司（Cornerstone Consulting Group）等。

① 美国有多个机构对大学进行排名，其中最有影响力的就是由《美国新闻和世界报道》（*The US News and World Report*）发布的美国大学排名，即 US News 排名。

校园人文环境

因为在校园中可能遇见每一个学生，所以请准备好加入一个高度亲密的集体。一位佳桥的校友说，有些时候阿姆赫斯特“太小了”，也因此不像研究型大学那样能吸引到演讲人。认识所有在阿姆赫斯特的中国国际学生非常容易，但是他们不一定会结成一个小团体。学生们总会自我隔离地分为几个团体：富裕的学生、运动员、国际生和少数族裔。当然，人群中也有例外。在阿姆赫斯特的学生通常都很友好、有合作精神，但是也常常有一种沉浸于自我世界的范儿。对于一个小学校来说，一位佳桥校友表示：“派对很大”。除五院联盟的社会活动之外，“阿姆赫斯特每月都会举办一些正式的活动，每两周就有一些大型派对。”阿姆赫斯特镇也会举办酒吧品酒活动，许多这样的活动就发生在学校周边。

录取难度

被阿姆赫斯特录取的学生通常有很强的领导能力，在高中阶段也高度参与了课外活动。通常只有屈指可数的名额留给中国学生，想申请的学生需要做好面对强烈竞争的准备。

需要考虑的事情

你会喜欢阿姆赫斯特，如果……

- 你想要得到所有教授的个性化的关注
- 你想要利用五院联盟的所有机会
- 你的梦想是成为一名教育家、银行家，或者咨询顾问

你会不喜欢阿姆赫斯特，如果……

- 你更喜欢一个不是那么精英主义的学生群体
- 你没有准备好面对新英格兰刺骨寒冷的冬天

佳桥校友录取情况

录取比例	14.3%
SAT 阅读成绩中位数	760
SAT 数学成绩中位数	800
SAT 写作成绩中位数	760
SAT 总分中位数	2320
TOEFL 成绩中位数	115

财政情况

全年学费	50562 美元 (2015—2016)
经济资助可能性	非常低

学生为学校所在地区打分

安全	4
有趣	3
生活成本	2
中国食物	2
交通便利	3
酒吧和俱乐部	1
超市 / 便利店选择	1
周边就业市场	1
是否需要车	3
总评	3

*满分 4 分

气候

年平均气温范围	1℃ ~14℃
年平均降水量	128cm
年平均湿度	75.9%
年平均降雪量	182cm

从中国出发的航班

学生们可以从北京、上海或者香港乘直飞航班到波士顿洛根国际机场（BOS，Logan International Airport）。之后乘两个小时的穿梭巴士或者的士到达校园。

巴布森学院

地址：231 FOREST STREET，BABSON PARK，MA 02457
网址：WWW.BABSON.EDU
中国招生官：CHERYL BORDEN
招生官邮箱：CBORDEN@BABSON.EDU
招生办公室电话：781-239-5522
附近主要城市：波士顿

最佳匹配点分析

作为创业研究（Entrepreneurial Studies）学科的发源地，巴布森学院在商科教育领域十分有名。它的校友和教师包括丰田集团总裁和首席执行官、家得宝（Home Depot）集团的共同创立人，以及福特汽车的董事等。有创业精神、努力想在商界崭露头角的学生会喜欢学校不拘泥于课堂内的动手学习方式。当然，他们也需要接受新英格兰寒冷的冬天和竞争激烈的商业环境。

学术机会

巴布森的旗舰本科项目是创业研究，该项目已经连续17年被US News评为同类项目第一名。虽然所有学生的专业都是商业，但是学生们可以选择不同的主攻方向，且巴布森大约半数的课程是通识教育类课程。每门课学生不多，都由教授亲自执教，且标准严格。许多教授也会用案例分析的方式进行教学，让学生们通过一系列角色扮演和模拟活动学习课本中的概念。在第一年的管理基础和创业课程中，学生小组会获得高达3000美元的资金来开展和实施自己的商业计划。

职业发展

巴布森学院距离波士顿仅有20分钟车程，所以学生们可以享受充足的实习和工作机会。另外，学生们只在周一到周四上课，这样他们可以一边读书，一边开始自己的职业生涯。每年在校园内有超过150个校友活动和多种创业支持项目，如巴布森校友支持创业项目（BASE，Babson Alumni Supporting Entrepreneurs），给予了巴布森学生充分的与杰出校友交流和建立联系的机会。在毕业后的规划方面，93%的2013届毕业生开始了工作（25%在金融领域，19%在市场营销方向，14%在业务拓展类），6%的学生在半年之内开始了硕士或者博士的学习。

校园人文环境

巴布森学院的学生给旁人的通常印象是富裕的预科生（preppy），穿着学院风套装去上课的学生并不少见。当美国大部分高等学校的学生在政

信息速览

US News 排名	无[①]
学校位置	东北
学校类型	私立
周边环境	郊区

本科学生情况

学生总数	2107 (2014)
申请人数	6199 (2014)
录取率	28% (2014)
男女学生比例	53/47
国际学生百分比	27%
亚裔美国人百分比	15%

你可能还想考虑以下学校

宾夕法尼亚大学	东北大学
波士顿学院	纽约大学
波士顿大学	

佳桥校友录取情况

录取比例	45%
SAT 阅读成绩中位数	610
SAT 数学成绩中位数	780
SAT 写作成绩中位数	670
SAT 总分中位数	2060
TOEFL 成绩中位数	105

财政情况

全年学费	46784 美元 (2015—2016)
经济资助可能性	非常低

① 该校属于商学类专业院校（Specialty Schools）。因同类的学校数目不多，US News 没有对此类学校进行排名。

学生为学校所在地区打分

安全	4
有趣	2
生活成本	3
中国食物	1
交通便利	2
酒吧和俱乐部	2
超市 / 便利店选择	2
周边就业市场	1
是否需要车	4
总评	2

*满分 4 分

气候

年平均气温范围	-4℃~21.7℃
年平均降水量	121cm
年平均湿度	70%
年平均降雪量	127cm

从中国出发的航班

从北京、上海或者香港有到达波士顿洛根国际机场（BOS, Logan International Airport）的直飞航班。学生可以乘公交、火车或者的士到校园。

治上偏自由时，《菲斯克指南》（Fiske Guide）开玩笑说巴布森学院是“在麻省一个可以骄傲地称自己为共和党人的学校”，虽然学生们在政治上并不活跃。虽然并不是一个种族非常多样化的学校，但 85% 的学生住在校园里，为整个学校营造了一种亲密的社区感，校园内社交活动十分丰富。联谊会（Greek life）[①]在校园中存在但是并不广泛，只有 19% 的女同学和 17% 的男同学参加，学生们更喜欢在周末乘坐免费巴士到波士顿去。虽然学生不多，巴布森学院仍有接近 100 个学生俱乐部和组织，中国学生会也有大约 100 名成员。

录取难度

从标准化考试分数上来看，巴布森学院并不是最挑剔的；但是整体来说，巴布森学院其实很挑剔，别掉以轻心。除非你很优秀，能够轻松地进入前 15 的大学，否则还是多做一些准备比较明智，如果你喜欢这所学校的话。

需要考虑的事情

你会喜欢巴布森学院，如果……

- 你对商业非常感兴趣
- 与理论学习比起来，你更喜欢实践
- 你在竞争激烈的环境中可以茁壮成长

你会不喜欢巴布森学院，如果……

- 你痛恨冷天气
- 你希望大学里具有种族多样性
- 你希望探索商业外的其他学科

① Greek life，意为“希腊生活”，是美国大学特有的一种社团活动，包括兄弟会（fraternity）、姐妹会（sorority）等，通常以 1—3 个希腊字母为组织命名。本书中统一译为“联谊会”。

波士顿学院

地址：140 COMMONWEALTH AVENUE，CHESTNUT HILL，MA 02467
网址：WWW.BC.EDU
中国招生官：PETER CARUSO
招生官邮箱：PETER.CARUSO@BC.EDU
招生办公室电话：617-552-3100
附近主要城市：波士顿

最佳匹配点分析

1863 年，耶稣会建立了波士顿学院。从那时开始，波士顿学院就作为一个与耶稣会和天主教有联系的学校而存在。校园里 70% 的学生都信仰天主教，但新来的学生也不必为此感到不安，因为他们不需要皈依天主教。不过学生们需要与年降雪超过 30 天的严寒搏斗。想寻找商业方面指导的学生会特别喜欢这所大学，因为波士顿学院的相关项目排名在前十之列。另外，波士顿学院有一系列要求较为严格的核心课程，以鼓励学生们获取更全面的知识。

学术机会

作为一所宗教学校，学生需要上一门神学课来满足核心课程的要求。不过，许多学生都认为这门课对于理解宗教中的哲学十分有益，也从来不会有被强迫之感。除了博雅

信息速览

US News 大学排名	30
学校位置	东北
宗教联系	罗马天主教
学校类型	私立
周边环境	城市

本科学生情况

学生总数	9100 (2015)
申请人数	29486 (2015)
录取率	29% (2015)
男女学生比例	53/47
国际学生百分比	6%
亚裔美国人百分比	10%

有本科项目的学院①

莫里西文理学院（Morrissey College of Arts and Sciences）

林奇教育学院（Lynch School of Education）

卡罗尔管理学院（Carroll School of Management）

康纳护理学院（Connell School of Nursing）

伍兹高等研究院（Woods School of Advancing Studies）

你可能还想考虑以下学校

塔夫茨大学	弗吉尼亚大学
威廉和玛丽学院	圣母大学
维拉诺瓦大学	乔治城大学

教育（Liberal Arts）的基础课程之外，学生还必须学习文学、自然、历史、哲学、社会科学、数学、艺术和文化多样性方面的课程。所有的大一学生都会参加写作研讨会，而大四学生需要完成一门大学顶点课程（University capstone 是美国大学为大三、大四学生开设的一门综合性课程。学生在其中反思自己之前所学，也为将来的职业发展奠定基础）。另外，学生也可以通过波士顿学院本科生研究项目（Boston College Undergraduate Research Program）或者夏季研究机遇项目（Summer Research Opportunities）得到研究机会。对于需要经济资助的学生，本科生研究学者项目（Undergraduate Research Fellows Program）可以让学生通过研究换取资助。

波士顿学院有四所专业学院。其中卡罗尔管理学院和康纳护理学院都很难转入，但文理学院通常来说录取标准比较宽松。波士顿学院最强的项目包括化学、经济、英语、金融、政治学、物理和历史。在拥有八个图书馆和大量纸质和电子书籍的波士顿学院，相信每个人都会学到很多知识。

职业发展

大约 22% 的学生会继续攻读硕士或博士学位，其中 26% 的学生选择教育学，19% 选择法学。立即开始全职工作的学生大概占全体毕业生的 60%。在波士顿，实习机会一应俱全。大多数毕业生毕业后进入会计、金融服务、护理和教育行业（如 Teach for America②）。最佳雇主包括四大会计师事务所、银行和 Teach for America。学校的职业中心会帮助学生和校友与雇主及其他校友建立联系。

① 文理学院只提供本科阶段的教育，学校提供的学术项目均为本科项目。

② 美丽美国，美国最领先的非营利性教育机构之一。

校园人文环境

波士顿学院无论是从地理上、种族上还是宗教上都不是一个非常平衡的学校：大约 72% 的学生来自麻省，而 70% 的学生信仰天主教。本科生中只有 141 人是中国学生，这意味着学生会有充分的空间在美国这个大熔炉里感受不同的文化。不同的学生组织能给学生们与志同道合的人探索和发展他们兴趣的机会。波士顿学院不允许联谊会存在，也尽力保持一个严肃的校园环境，但是派对和未成年人饮酒（美国的合法饮酒年龄是 21 岁）仍然存在。不过，超过 21 岁的学生可能会在城市里或者附近的学校找到丰富的夜生活。话虽如此，许多学生仍能在宿舍里、志愿者项目中，或者其他课外活动中找到亲密的朋友。

人们可以很容易地通过着装和对运动的热爱分辨出波士顿学院的学生。当你看到一群学生穿着他们最喜欢的体育队伍的运动衫在校园里晃来晃去，或者是许多你的同龄人为校内比赛做准备时，不要惊讶。

虽然波士顿学院不在波士顿的市中心，但是学生们可以选择方便的公共交通进城，而波士顿绝对不会让你失望。因为在美国历史中独特的地位和这座城市对体育的痴迷，波士顿有种类繁多的娱乐活动和让人感到深受启发的地方。

录取难度

波士顿学院通常会录取 SAT 成绩在 2100~2200 而且在高中做过很多志愿服务的学生。大约 82% 的录取新生高中时成绩居年级前 10%。

需要考虑的事情

你会喜欢波士顿学院，如果……

佳桥校友录取情况

录取比例	26%
SAT 阅读成绩中位数	680
SAT 数学成绩中位数	800
SAT 写作成绩中位数	725
SAT 总分中位数	2140
TOEFL 成绩中位数	109

财政情况

全年学费	46670 美元 (2015—2016)
经济资助可能性	非常低

学生为学校所在地区打分

安全	3
有趣	3
生活成本	4
中国食物	3
交通便利	3
酒吧和俱乐部	4
超市 / 便利店选择	3
周边就业市场	3
是否需要车	2
总评	4

*满分 4 分

气候

年平均气温范围	-4℃ ~23℃
年平均降水量	120.7cm
年平均湿度	69.8%
年平均降雪量	125.7cm

从中国出发的航班

学生可以乘坐从北京、上海或者香港起飞到波士顿洛根国际机场（BOS，Logan International Airport）的直飞航班。机场距离学校约有 35 分钟车程。

- 橄榄球、篮球和曲棍球是你的第二语言，或者你想要找到一个有强大体育项目的学校
- 你认为将来你会在金融方面有所成就
- 你希望能接触到城市的资源但是又不想在城市的中心

你会不喜欢波士顿学院，如果……

- 你不想让你的周围有大量信仰天主教的学生
- 你很担心成为少数族裔
- 你不喜欢下雪和寒冷的冬日

波士顿大学

地址：233 BAY STATE ROAD，BOSTON，MA 02215
网址：WWW.BU.EDU
中国招生官：SAMANTHA FIFIELD
招生官邮箱：SFIFIELD@BU.EDU
招生办公室电话：617-353-2300
附近主要城市：波士顿

最佳匹配点分析

波士顿大学位于波士顿中心地区，而波士顿是麻省（及新英格兰地区）的文化中心，为学生提供了丰富的社交和学术机会。波士顿大学的排名在全美大学中一路攀升，它在US News的排名在过去几年中上升了十位，因此也成为越来越多中国留学生的心仪选择。波士顿大学完全融入了充满活力的波士顿，愿意放弃传统校园的学生应该来这里。如果你不介意被新英格兰严酷的冬天层层包裹，并且对金融、管理、教育或者电影研究有强烈的兴趣，那么在波士顿大学你就会有无限的机会为未来做好准备。

信息速览

US News 大学排名	41
学校位置	东北
学校类型	私立
周边环境	城市

本科学生情况

学生总数	16496 (2014)
申请人数	54757 (2015)
录取率	32% (2015)
男女学生比例	40/60
国际学生百分比	24.4%
亚裔百分比	14.8%

有本科项目的学院

文理学院（College of Arts & Sciences）
传播学院（College of Communication）
工程学院（College of Engineering）
艺术学院（College of Fine Arts）
综合研究学院（College of General Studies）
萨金特卫生与康复科学学院（College of Health and Rehabilitation Sciences: Sargent College）
弗雷德里克 S. 帕蒂全球研究学院（Frederick S. Pardee School of Global Studies）
管理学院（Questrom School of Management）
教育学院（School of Education）
酒店管理学院（School of Hospitality Administration）

你可能还想考虑以下学校

福坦莫大学	东北大学
纽约大学	凯斯西储大学

学术机会

作为全美最大的私立大学之一，波士顿大学超过 90% 的大一课程学生数都少于 25 人，这点可能让很多打算申请的学生颇为惊讶。拥有 10 个不同的学院，每个学院对通识教育都有独特的要求，波士顿大学为学生提供了多样化的学术项目和课程。波士顿大学最有名的本科学院之一是传播学院，它为学生们进入电影电视、新闻、大众传媒、广告和公共关系领域打下了良好基础。该院的校外研究项目——洛杉矶实习项目（Los Angeles Internship Program）为学生提供在好莱坞制片人身边实习一学期的机会。总体来说，波士顿大学着眼于把学生学习的领域和他们想要从事的工作联系起来，拥有专业经验让学生们在毕业之后更容易找到工作。在波士顿大学学习工程、计算机和商业的学生经常会和同学们竞争以获得好成绩，特别是在人数超过 300 人的初级课程上。

职业发展

波士顿大学是准备进入职场学生的一个上佳之选，因为它在美国东海岸拥有强大的校友网络。但波士顿大学校友网的影响远远超出了它所在的区域。在 2012 年，由纽约时报与其国际版共同发起的调查显示，波士顿大学的全球市场就业情况在全美大学中排名第七，仅次于哈佛大学、耶鲁大学、斯坦福大学、麻省理工学院、哥伦比亚大学和普林斯顿大学。波士顿大学毕业生的平均起薪是每年 46000 美元，而他们在职业生涯中期的平均薪酬是每年 90000 美元。波士顿大学校友会管理的职业咨询网络（Career Advisory Network）是校友们参与的一个为学生们提供职业建议的志愿者项目，帮学生解决常见的问题，比如如何在感兴趣的领域起步、职业对于社交生活的影响，以及是否应该继续攻读研究生等问题。波士顿大学有 51 个国际校友组织，在国际校友中间颇有影响。大学的职业发展中心（The Center for Career Development）会在本科生和校友寻找实习和工作的过程中提供帮助。

校园人文环境

波士顿大学的社交魅力主要在于波士顿市能够提供给年轻人无限的机会。这座城市历史悠久，有许多著名的历史景点和蕴涵丰富的博物馆可供发掘。波士顿对于使用虚假身份证明进入酒吧和俱乐部有严格的限定，所以 21 岁及以下的学生只能在联谊会派对和公寓派对中展开社交。对于已经达到合法饮酒年龄的学生来说，Landsdowne 街是喜欢俱乐部的学生们的通常选择，但更随意的酒吧 / 俱乐部是像 Middle East，Phoenix Landing 和 Venu 这样的地方。与其他美国高校相比，波士顿大学在体育上并没有占完全的主导地位，但一位佳桥校友表示，在国家大学体育协会的一级锦标赛中，波士顿大学的曲棍球是最受欢迎的。波士顿市为学生们提供了足够多观看职业体育赛事的机会，最突出的项目包括棒球、橄榄球和篮球。许多佳桥校友都在大量的中国国际生群体中找到了安全感。一位佳桥校友说，波士顿中国城里的几家正宗中国菜馆慰藉了大家的思乡之情。波士顿大学有超过 500 个学生组织，大家在其中可以与志同道合的同龄人一起探索和追求自己的兴趣。

录取难度

因为波士顿大学在最近几年声名鹊起，它的录取率直线下滑。波士顿大学不同的学院在录取时的竞争激烈程度很不一样，但是来自中国的学生通常需要超过 1900 分的 SAT 成绩来为自己谋得一席之地。

佳桥校友录取情况

录取比例	39.7%
SAT 阅读成绩中位数	590
SAT 数学成绩中位数	770
SAT 写作成绩中位数	665
SAT 总分中位数	1995
TOEFL 成绩中位数	104

财政情况

全年学费	47422 美元 (2015—2016)
经济资助可能性	非常低

学生为学校所在地区打分

安全	3
有趣	3
生活成本	4
中国食物	3.5
交通便利	4
酒吧和俱乐部	1.5
超市 / 便利店选择	2
周边就业市场	2.5
是否需要车	2
总评	3

*满分 4 分

气候

年平均气温范围	–3℃ ~23℃
年平均降水量	122.4cm
年平均湿度	69.8%
年平均降雪量	129 cm

从中国出发的航班

从北京、上海和香港都有直达波士顿的航班。学生可以从洛根国际机场（BOS，Logan International Airport）乘坐穿梭巴士或出租车到学校。根据交通状况和交通工具的不同，从机场到学校需要 15~50 分钟。

需要考虑的事情

你会喜欢波士顿大学，如果……

- 你对管理、金融、教育或者电影有特殊的兴趣
- 你有自我驱动力，并且非常主动
- 你在竞争激烈的城市环境中如鱼得水

你会不喜欢波士顿大学，如果……

- 你希望身处一个传统的大学校园，而不是一个与城市融于一体的学校
- 你认为小型的课堂胜过一切
- 你不愿意忍受寒冷的冬季

布兰迪斯大学

地址：415 SOUTH STREET，WALTHAM，MA 02454
网址：WWW.BRANDEIS.EDU
中国招生官：无
招生办公室电话：781-736-3500
招生办公室邮箱：ADMISSION@BRANDEIS.EDU
附近主要城市：波士顿，公交车或者火车 20~30 分钟到达

最佳匹配点分析

我们一开始想说："如果你不是犹太人，不要申请。"但是实际上，布兰迪斯的学生在政治倾向上偏自由、开放、敢于直言。所以我们或许应该说：如果你不是自由主义者，或者你并不热心政治，不要申请。你需要性格开朗，并且有很强的适应性才能融入一个主体是白人和犹太人的学生群体。另外，如果你奉行"努力工作，尽情玩耍"的原则，那布兰迪斯大学可能无法帮助你实现第二点。如果你想要成为一名教师，或者你喜欢波士顿和纽约，请选择布兰迪斯。

学术机会

布兰迪斯大学的办学宗旨是让学生体验到最好的大学教育，所以所有的课程都由教授执教。在布兰迪斯，最热门的专业包括化学、生物和经济。说到学术严谨，一位中国

信息速览

US News 大学排名	34
学校位置	东北
学校类型	私立
周边环境	郊区

本科学生情况

学生总数	3729 (2014)
申请人数	10004 (2014)
录取率	35% (2014)
男女学生比例	43/57
国际学生百分比	18%
亚裔美国人百分比	12.8%

有本科项目的学院

文理学院（College of Letters and Sciences）

布兰迪斯国际商学院（Brandeis International Business School）

你可能还想考虑以下学校

塔夫茨大学	波士顿学院
埃默里大学	波士顿大学
纽约大学	布朗大学

学生说："实际上课程非常难。"为了在学业上帮助学生，布兰迪斯大学从本科生中选出了一批精于学业的罗斯福学者（Roosevelt Fellows）为同学们选择课程提供咨询。除此之外，学生们还可以向布兰迪斯本科生学习小组（BUGS，Brandeis Undergraduate Group Study）咨询，寻求同伴的指导。想要将来当老师的学生们可以考虑布兰迪斯大学排名很高的教育项目。对于国际学生来说，入口项目（Gateway Program）值得推荐，它包括帮助学生提高英语熟练程度的强制性暑假课程和学期内每周的写作指导，可以帮助学生更好地过渡。

职业发展

布兰迪斯毕业生的最佳雇主包括美林证券（Merrill Lynch）、大通曼哈顿银行（Chase Manhattan）、高盛投资银行、德意志银行（Deutsche Bank）、Teach for America 以及 Peace Corps①。在毕业前的六个月内，58% 的毕业生获得了聘用，36% 的人得到了毕业生职位（graduate position，大多存在于金融行业中的培养毕业生的职位），还有 4% 的毕业生仍在寻找工作。卫生保健、教育、服务行业、金融服务，以及咨询业都是最吸引学生的行业。很多学生在毕业之前就已经有至少三次实习的经历，这证明了学校职业中心的能力和学生自己的雄心。一位佳桥校友骄傲地说道："布兰迪斯大学在纽约和波士顿都有完美的校友网络。"

校园人文环境

"顺便提一句，犹太人无处不在"，一位佳桥的校友说，从布兰迪斯毕业的同学很难不注意到这一点。大约 50% 的学生是犹太人，21% 的学生是少数族裔，18% 的学生是国际生，学校中女生占大多数。值得注意的一点是，布兰迪斯大学是无宗派的，而且排他性会被人鄙视，这也许解释了为什么联谊会在校园中被禁止。关于派对，一位中国学生

① 和平护卫队，是一个由美国联邦政府管理的美国志愿者组织。组织使命包括三个目标：提供技术支持，帮助美国境外的人了解美国文化，帮助美国人了解其他国家的文化。

说:“只有 60% 的学生会参加派对，我们不是一个派对学校，”他又说道“我们在图书馆和美术馆里面开派对。”饮酒现象并不普遍，但是体育活动非常常见。该学生表示体育活动场所“非常非常大，像我们的科学楼一样。”尤其是足球场地。学校提供了很多课外活动，包括学生自己运营的电视台和广播。学校提供免费穿梭巴士到各种活动的中心——波士顿。作为犹太信仰的一部分，学生高度重视社会工作和社区服务。献血、支教、为少数族裔工作，和为无家可归者建造庇护所都是常见的活动，许多布兰迪斯大学的学生都参与其中。与波士顿地区其他大学相比，该校的中国国际学生群体并不是那么强大。

录取难度

行动主义和社区（community）服务方面很被招生委员会看重。布兰迪斯大学的录取竞争很激烈，但是与波士顿地区其他一些大学（比如哈佛大学和麻省理工学院）相比激烈程度要小些。想要来这所大学的学生 SAT 成绩至少需要 2100 分。

需要考虑的事情

你会喜欢布兰迪斯大学，如果……

◆ 你对非本国的文化很感兴趣，尤其是源于美国东海岸的文化

◆ 你比较勤快，不介意在附近区域的短途往返

你会不喜欢布兰迪斯大学，如果……

◆ 你认为专属俱乐部是大学经历里面有趣的一部分

◆ 你希望快速简洁地接近一个文化熔炉

◆ 你害怕同性恋

佳桥校友录取情况

录取比例	26.5%
SAT 阅读成绩中位数	645
SAT 数学成绩中位数	785
SAT 写作成绩中位数	685
SAT 总分中位数	2040
TOEFL 成绩中位数	106

财政情况

全年学费

47702 美元 (2015—2016)

经济资助可能性　低

学生为学校所在地区打分

安全	4
有趣	2
生活成本	2
中国食物	3
交通便利	3
酒吧和俱乐部	1
超市 / 便利店选择	2
周边就业市场	3
是否需要车	4
总评	4

*满分 4 分

气候

年平均气温范围	−5℃ ~22℃
年平均降水量	119.4cm
年平均湿度	68.4%
年平均降雪量	129.6cm

从中国出发的航班

从北京、上海和香港出发都有直飞航班到达波士顿洛根国际机场（BOS，Logan International Airport），之后开车 30 分钟即可到达校园。

布朗大学

地址：75 WATERMAN STREET，PROVIDENCE，RI 02912
网址：WWW.BROWN.EDU
中国招生官：PANETHA OTT
招生官电话：401-863-2378
招生官邮箱：PANETHA_OTT@BROWN.EDU
附近主要城市：普罗维登斯；距离波士顿不到 1 小时车程，距离纽约 3 小时

最佳匹配点分析

在八所常青藤学校里，布朗大学以它在学术和社交方面的自由氛围而著称。总的来说，布朗大学为拥有全国最快乐的学生而骄傲，每个人都能在这里找到自己的一席之地。然而，未来的学生也应该考虑自己是否喜欢一年中大半时间的阴雨和寒冷天气。如果你喜欢课程设置明确的大学，也许其他学校会更适合你，因为布朗的课程是出了名的开放。

学术机会

1969 年，布朗创立了“新课程”，向学生们介绍跨学科的大学课程：学生们有上任何课程而选择通过 / 不通过的权利，成绩的等级划分不再存在，成绩单上也不再有加号、减号或者“无学分”。毋庸置疑，这让学生在学业规划上有了更多的灵活性。学生可以设计自己的专业，也不用再担心上的课程是否满足通识教育要求。但是，这也让选择并进入热门课程变得更困难了。学生们表示

教授们在上课时既细心又引人入胜。布朗大学顶尖的本科项目包括生物、历史、国际关系、英语文学和政治科学。布朗只有不到 20% 的课堂有 50 个或以上的学生，这为学生的本科教育打下了坚实的基础。因为学校距离罗德岛设计学院很近，学生们也可以在那里上课。如果学生们想要更深入地在罗德岛设计学院学习，他们可以选择为期五年的布朗 / 罗德岛设计学院联合培养项目。

信息速览

US News 大学排名	14
学校位置	东北
学校类型	私立
周边环境	城市

本科学生情况

学生总数	6320 (2015)
申请人数	30396 (2015)
录取率	9.5% (2015)
男女学生比例	48/52
国际学生百分比	11.6%
亚裔美国人百分比	12.9%

有本科项目的学院

文理学院（The College）

工学院（School of Engineering）

你可能还想考虑以下学校

哈佛大学	普林斯顿大学
康奈尔大学	塔夫茨大学
达特茅斯学院	

职业发展

大约 65% 的本科生在大学毕业之后进入职场，另有 22% 的学生选择继续深造。许多学生选择攻读医学方面的专业学位，法律和教育紧随其后。对于选择进入职场的学生来说，商业、教育、医药、艺术、政府部门，以及传媒都是对他们有吸引力的热门行业。

因为普罗维登斯是罗得岛州的首府，许多学生在政府部门找到了实习。那些对政府工作不感兴趣的学生也不必担心，众多知名公司也会在布朗大学招揽人才。常见的招聘方包括贝恩、高盛、谷歌、哈佛大学、摩根士丹利、Peace Corps，Teach for America 和微软。布朗大学在美国东海岸有强大的校友网络，但是它在国际上的影响力比起哈佛、耶鲁来说稍逊一筹。

校园人文环境

美国白人占校园学生的多数，亚裔学生以 13% 的比例居于第二，不过绝大多数学生不会因为自己的种族或者民族感到不安。97% 的学生来自外州，12% 的学生是国际学生。与其他类似的录取难度较大学校的学生相比，布朗的学生更加有合作精神也更加放松。另外，他们在政治上也更加活跃，尤其是在社会正义问题上。联谊会在学生群体中影响不大，只有 12% 的男同学和 4% 的女同学参加。布朗大学有超过 400 个学生社团，主题从校内篮球到无伴奏合唱应有尽有。饮酒在学生中间很流行，而且布朗大学一直以一些风格过分活泼的派对出名。普罗维登斯不是纽约那样的拜金城市，但是它仍然有许多文化活动而且是一个学生漫步的安全天堂。

佳桥校友录取情况

录取比例	12.6%
SAT 阅读成绩中位数	710
SAT 数学成绩中位数	800
SAT 写作成绩中位数	720
SAT 总分中位数	2180
TOEFL 成绩中位数	112

财政情况

全年学费	50224 美元 (2016—2017)
经济资助可能性	非常低

学生为学校所在地区打分

安全	3.5
有趣	2
生活成本	3
中国食物	1
交通便利	2
酒吧和俱乐部	1.5
超市 / 便利店选择	1
周边就业市场	1.5
是否需要车	2
总评	3

*满分 4 分

气候

年平均气温范围	1℃ ~20℃
年平均降水量	125.5cm
年平均湿度	76.03%
年平均降雪量	103.2cm

从中国出发的航班

没有来往中国的直飞航班，学生们必须通过转机才能来到西奥多•弗朗西斯•格林纪念国家机场（PVD，Theodore Francis Green Memorial State Airport）。机场距离布朗大学有 15 分钟的穿梭巴士车程。

录取难度

布朗大学选择学生非常严格，而且一般来说它不会录取太多来自中国的学生。在美国学习的国际学生更有可能进入这所常青藤学校，你的艺术气息或者古灵精怪也很有可能帮你忙。

需要考虑的事情

你会喜欢布朗，如果……

- 你希望探索不同的学术领域
- 医学院是你的梦想
- 你想要去一所像文理学院那样的大学同时又希望这所学校是享誉全国的常青藤。

你会不喜欢布朗，如果……

- 你需要大城市的活跃氛围；
- 你不能容忍古怪的人物或者事情。

布林莫尔学院

地址：101 N MERION AVE，BRYN MAWR，PA 19010
网址：WWW.BRYNMAWR.EDU
中国招生官：JENNIFER KEEGAN
招生官电话：610-526-7877
招生官邮箱：JKEEGAN@BRYNMAWR.EDU
附近主要城市：费城，乘坐 SEPTA 火车需 20 分钟

最佳匹配点分析

乘短途火车可以从布林莫尔学院到达费城市中心。“布林莫尔”在威尔士语中的本意是“大山”，它的校园经常被评为美国最美丽的大学校园之一。实际上，学院的 M. Carey Thomas 图书馆已被认定为美国国家历史名胜。因为学校的学生总数只有一千多人，年轻的女性在这里会得到很多世界著名教授在学术上的帮助。布林莫尔的政治氛围十分自由，甚至偏激进。许多学生都参与到了社会激进活动中。在布林莫尔，超过三分之一学生的专业都是数学或者自然科学，希望在自然科学、科技、工程和数学（STEM）等相关领域就职的学生应该考虑这所女校。

学术机会

在毕业生选择攻读博士的学生人数排名中，布林莫尔位居全美前十，学生们对

信息速览

US News 文理学院排名	25
学校位置	东北
学校类型	私立
周边环境	郊区

本科学生情况

学生总数	1300
申请人数	2700（过去四年平均）
录取率	39.9%（过去四年平均）
男女学生比例	0/100
国际学生百分比	24%
亚裔百分比	14%

你可能还想考虑以下学校

巴纳德学院	哈弗福德学院
韦尔斯利学院	史密斯学院
斯沃斯莫尔学院	曼荷莲学院

待学业非常认真。然而，作为贵格会机构荣誉准则的一部分，同学之间不能谈论成绩。这项规定也减少了本科生学习时的竞争感。虽然布林莫尔的文科专业在数量上与其他文理学院比起来十分有限，但是它在自然科学上的水平大大超越了其他学院。每年大约有3%的毕业生是物理专业的，这个数字是美国女大学毕业生平均值的50倍。布林莫尔学院与哈弗福德学院以及斯沃斯莫尔学院结成了三校联盟，后两者都曾经是男校。作为贵格会联盟的一部分，学生们也可以在宾夕法尼亚大学选修课程。另外，与加州理工学院合作的3-2项目让对工程感兴趣的学生可以选择大学的前三年在布林莫尔完成应用科学课程，后两年在加州理工学院学习工程。一个新的名为360°的跨学科项目让学生们有机会学习来自人文和自然科学领域两个或三个专业的一系列课程，用多种方法去解决现实世界中的问题。

职业发展

布林莫尔的职业培训项目（Extern Program）给了学生们在决定选择职业领域之前尝试不同道路的机会。在寒假或者春假，该项目支持学生们在不同岗位上接受两天到两周的培训。布林莫尔的招聘项目（Recruiting Program）鼓励雇主来到布林莫尔校园面试毕业生和暑期实习生。布林莫尔的毕业生们选择的道路多种多样，多数在学术界和教育界。2012年的毕业生中，有人去了伦敦政经学院或北卡罗来纳州立大学读博士；有人去了旧金山或者亚特兰大为Teach for America 工作；也有人选择了Green Corps。《华尔街日报》将布林莫尔学院排在了为法学院、医学院、商学院输送学生数量最多的文理学院榜单的前十名。

校园人文环境

布林莫尔推行接纳和包容的文化，校园非常多样化。“我们学校有大量的国际学生，我们在学校里也扮演了重要的角色。这里有来自亚洲、欧洲、非洲和南美洲的国际学生。”一位佳桥校友写道。学校里大半的学生都是有色人种学生或者国际学生。一位佳桥校友表示，布林莫尔的体育活动乏善可陈：“我们的队伍通常非常小。”布林莫尔小城富足又安全，但是除了几个昂贵的精品店和星巴克咖啡之外没有什么可以提供给学生们。不过从布林莫尔小镇到费城坐火车只要 22 分钟，在那里学生们就可以尝试城市里的多彩生活了。虽然布林莫尔的小镇没有太多夜生活，但是学生们仍有一些选择。一位佳桥校友评论道："50% 的派对都充满了三校（布林莫尔学院、哈弗福德学院、斯沃斯莫尔学院）的学生。派对当然是有的，但是我不认为会有某些大学的派对那么盛大。"传统是该学校身份不可或缺的一部分，学校致力于让本科生融为一体并且培育一种社区感。比如说，在每学期第一周课程结束之后就会举行游行夜(Parade Night)，在这一天大学第一年新生会与大三学姐结对，而后者会引导前者度过两年的学校生活。

录取难度

虽然布林莫尔的本科生人数不多，但是其中国际学生占相当比例，而且学校对来自中国的国际学生尤其友好。SAT 超过 2000 分的学生被录取的概率更大一些。

需要考虑的事情

你会喜欢布林莫尔学院，如果……

- 你是一位对物理、数学或者外国语言感兴趣的年轻女性
- 你在国际学生很多的学校感到比较舒适
- 你以学习为重而且思想独立
- 你乐于挖掘传统

你会不喜欢布林莫尔学院，如果……

- 你是个男生。即使你有 SAT 满分的成绩和治愈癌症药品的专利，你也不会被录取
- 你希望加入一个有出名文科项目的文理学院
- 你希望在学校周围有许多社交选择

佳桥校友录取情况

录取比例	35.4%
SAT 阅读成绩中位数	670
SAT 数学成绩中位数	795
SAT 写作成绩中位数	710
SAT 总分中位数	2115
TOEFL 成绩中位数	110

财政情况

全年学费

46030 美元 (2015—2016)

经济资助可能性　较低

学生为学校所在地区打分

安全	3.5
有趣	2.5
生活成本	2
中国食物	2.5
交通便利	3
酒吧和俱乐部	2
超市 / 便利店选择	2.5
周边就业市场	1.5
是否需要车	2.5
总评	2.5

*满分 4 分

气候

年平均气温范围	-2℃ ~24℃
年平均降水量	116.9cm
年平均湿度	71.72%
年平均降雪量	49.8cm

从中国出发的航班

中国到费城没有直达航班，学生需转机一次才可到达费城国际机场（PHL，Philadelphia International Airport）。从机场开车或者坐火车到达布林莫尔市需大约半小时。

加州理工学院

地址：1200 EAST CALIFORNIA BOULEVARD，PASADENA，CA 91125
网址：WWW.CALTECH.EDU
中国招生官：JANN LACOSS
招生官电话：626-395-6343
招生官邮箱：JLACOSS@CALTECH.EDU
附近主要城市：洛杉矶，坐公交车需要两个小时，开车 20 分钟

最佳匹配点分析

如果你希望以后赚很多钱，你应该来这里，加州理工毕业生的起薪中位数是全美最高的，但前提是你认为自己有足够的能量、乐观精神和毅力挺过四年严苛的学术训练。如果你准备进入研究生院并且读一个理科博士的话，你也应该从加州理工开始。对知识的好奇心和开放的心态能帮助你享受在这个独一无二的学校的美好时光。

学术机会

为了"喂饱"新一代年轻天才们，加州理工提高了课程的标准——有时候甚至到了让人难以忍受的程度，绝对不要低估课程的难度。光是核心课程就有 30 门之多，学生们在这个不大的学校里经常会感到巨大的压力。同时，学校用众多的学术机会，包括夏季本科生研究项目（SURF，Summer Undergraduate Research Fellowship）等方式来奖励学生们。学生们可以选择和教授合作或者开展他们自己的项目并且获得一定的报酬。一位

校友说："只要给教授写电子邮件就可以了。很容易找到做研究的机会。"大部分学生每年夏天都会参加这个项目，而且很多学生连续几年做同一个项目。一位佳桥的校友分享道："教授们都很友好，但是他们也非常忙。"另外，和本科生经常在一起工作又住得很近的研究生也经常和他们指导的本科生建立亲密而有益的关系。加州理工有六大学科体系，生物与生物工程、化学与化学工程、工程与应用科学、地质与行星科学、人文和社会科学，及物理、数学和天文学。大约 20% 的学生会修两个专业。即使没修两个专业，学生们仍然会有很大的学习压力。为了缓解学术压力，加州理工在第一年采取通过／不通过的打分制度。一位佳桥校友说："学术环境以合作为主。大家都一起做作业，很多人在做完自己的事情之后也会帮助别人。"加州理工与西方学院（Occidental College）以及艺术中心设计学院（Art Center College of Design）都有合作，学生们可以在以上两个学校上课并得到加州理工的学分。

信息速览

US News 大学排名	10
学校位置	西海岸
学校类型	私立
周边环境	郊区

本科学生情况

学生总数	1001 (2014)
申请人数	6507 (2015)
录取率	9% (2015)
男女学生比例	54/46
国际学生百分比	7%
亚裔美国人百分比	38%

你可能还想考虑以下学校

斯坦福大学　哈维·穆德学院
麻省理工学院
加州大学伯克利分校
卡内基梅隆大学

职业发展

加州理工不公布毕业生的数据，但学生们估计多达 50% 的毕业生在毕业之后选择继续攻读研究生。许多顶级咨询和技术公司，比如贝恩（Bain）、艾意凯咨询（LEK Consulting）、微软、英伟达公司（Nvdia）、甲骨文公司（Oracle）和辉瑞制药（Pfizer）都很看重加州理工学生们的能力。校友网络虽然小，但是十分有用。但也有一位中国国际学生吐露："大多数工作都是在学术界的，因此没有太多来自社会上的机会。"但是，加州理工的 TecherLink 项目通过实习和工作机会将在校学生和校友联系起来，目前为止十分成功。因为其靠近硅谷，加州理工的毕业生可以顺利地从大学生活过渡到工作中，在初创技术公司开启自己的职业生涯。

校园人文环境

学校的社交生活围绕着各个住宿学院展开。七所学院各有自己的风格、社区、建筑、派对和传统等。毋庸置疑，同一住宿学院的学生之间的关系异常牢靠，他们彼此帮助、勇敢面对严酷的学术环境。合作和社区感对于学生们的幸福感至关重要，尤其是像加州

佳桥校友录取情况

录取比例	22.2%
SAT 阅读成绩中位数	740
SAT 数学成绩中位数	800
SAT 写作成绩中位数	785
SAT 总分中位数	2310
TOEFL 成绩中位数	116

财政情况

全年学费
43710 美元 (2015—2016)
经济资助可能性 低

学生为学校所在地区打分

安全	3.5
有趣	3
生活成本	2.5
中国食物	3
交通便利	1
酒吧和俱乐部	2
超市 / 便利店选择	2
周边就业市场	2
是否需要车	4
总评	3

*满分 4 分

气候

年平均气温范围	13℃ ~25℃
年平均降水量	59.6cm
年平均湿度	79.9%
年平均降雪量	0cm

从中国出发的航班

从首都国际机场、上海浦东国际机场或者香港国际机场出发都有直飞航班到达洛杉矶。从洛杉矶国际机场（LAX，Los Angeles International Airport）到学校开车需要 35 分钟。

理工这样的学校。本科生们熬夜到非常晚，一起聊天、在宿舍楼里面闲逛或者做作业。第一年结束之后可以搬出宿舍楼，但是 95% 的学生都选择继续和室友们住在一起。中国留学生群体不用担心自己在这里不适应。虽然加州理工有一部分学生不擅长社交，但是他们总能在加州理工开放又特殊的学生群体里找到适合自己的社群。在学生群体中，大约 38% 的学生是亚裔，9% 是拉丁美裔，2% 是非洲裔美国人，13% 是国际学生，34% 是白人。

中国留学生表示："加州理工的派对非常无聊。学校里面的亚裔和犹太人相当多。"

录取难度

被录取的学生都是全球科学和数学方面的精英。国际奖项、竞赛上的成就，以及在工程方面的创新发明非常重要，这些被认为是一个合格的申请者应当拥有的。

需要考虑的事情

你会喜欢加州理工学院，如果……

- 你认为一个大家彼此认识的小社区棒极了
- 你从五岁甚至更小就知道自己要学习科学或技术

你会不喜欢加州理工学院，如果……

- 你希望有广泛的约会选择
- 你希望在一个美国大城市里生活
- 你对于学术压力很大的环境感到厌倦

卡尔顿学院

地址：1 N COLLEGE ST.，NORTHFIELD，MN 55057
网址：WWW.CARLETON.EDU
中国招生官：CHARLIE COGAN
招生官电话：507-222-4190
招生官邮箱：CCOGAN@CARLETON.EDU
附近主要城市：明尼阿波利斯，开车需要 1.5 小时

最佳匹配点分析

作为美国中西部最出色的文理学院之一，卡尔顿学院在本科生培养上倾注了极大的心血。典型的“卡尔”（卡尔顿学生的绰号）都热爱学术，但不是“学霸”或热爱竞争。分数膨胀现象存在，但不严重，佳桥校友表示只有“大约 20% 的学生得到 A”。卡尔顿的学生都拥有足够的幽默感和与人协作的意愿。卡尔顿学院的强势专业主要集中在自然科学方面，特别是生物、化学和地质学。如果你希望有朝一日成为博士的话，来这里吧，卡尔顿学院的学生成为博士的比例全美排第六。

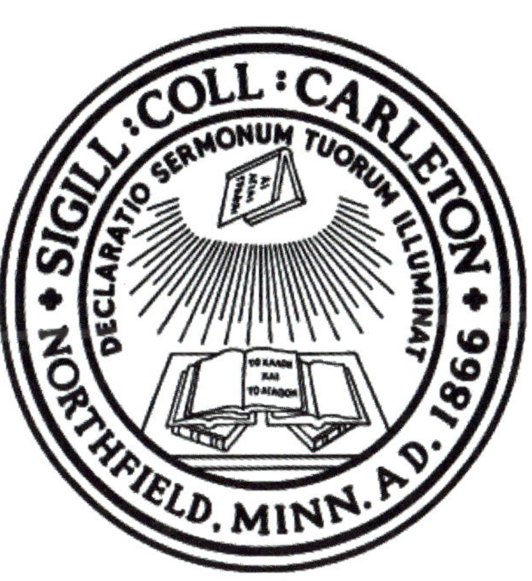

信息速览

US News 文理学院排名	8
学校位置	中西部
学校类型	私立
周边环境	乡村

本科学生情况

学生总数	2014 (2015)
申请人数	6722 (2015)
录取率	20.6% (2015)
男女学生比例	47/53
国际学生百分比	10.3%
亚裔美国人百分比	8.4%

你可能还想考虑以下学校

戴维森学院	马卡莱斯特学院
威廉姆斯学院	塔夫茨大学

学术机会

卡尔顿学院实行三学期制，每个学期上三门课。因为每个学期只有十个星期，课程通常都进行得很快，且要求严格。卡尔顿学院的核心课程十分广博，涉及多个学科。如果你已经明确了自己的专业并且对其他方面都不感兴趣的话，那这些核心课程可能会是个累赘。虽然在卡尔顿得到 A 并不容易，但是学生们从喜爱教学的教授身上获益良多。佳桥校友称赞教授们“在课堂之外也非常容易接近，无论是讨论学术问题还是个人的困惑。”这里评价教授的标准是看他们是否能向学生解释清楚他们的所思所想和学生们对他们是否在意。与美国的许多文理学院相似，卡尔顿的课堂很小，学校也夸耀自己的学生 / 教师比例是 9:1。一位佳桥校友说：“课堂很小，你觉得自己在一个非常亲密的集体中，你对周围的人也所知甚多”，但是有些时候“从能提供的课程上来看卡尔顿太小了。”虽然卡尔顿不是美国最国际化的文理学院之一，但是 70% 的学生会参加校外学术活动。在物理科学方面的研究机会很充足，每年夏天系里和教授个人共提供 50 到 60 个学生与教授合作的研究职位。

职业发展

在卡尔顿学院，学生们发现因为教授都很容易接近，所以获得在相关专业研究的机会也比较容易。大多数学生认为他们在毕业之后不会从事与咨询或者财经相关的工作。一位佳桥校友听说“学生们在毕业之后不会选择光鲜的职业，好多学生会接着读研究生院。”卡尔顿学院的职业中心提供多种平台供学生们发掘自己的兴趣。比如校外实习让学生们“可以在校友工作的地方与他们一起工作，给学生们高质量的观察时间和实践经验。”卡尔沙发（Couches-for-Carls）项目让在校生和校友在寻找工作的过程中可以找到由校友提供的免费住宿的地方。

校园人文环境

卡尔顿学院被大家认为是能吸引杰出人才而不是精英主义者的地方。一个学生提到卡尔顿时说学校“在智识方面非常多元化，每个人都非常友好。”这所文理学院在运动上并不是非常有名，但是男子和女子飞盘队在竞赛方面战绩颇丰，在 2001 年、2009 年和 2011 年的全国锦标赛上获得了冠军。在这样一个联系紧密的小社区中，传统是卡尔顿校园人文环境不可或缺的一部分。在众多传统中，冬天在户外冰场上玩冰上扫帚球、春天纪念一位名叫 Rotblatt 的棒球投手的节日和冬季中旬舞会是这所学院最受瞩目的几个活动。明尼苏达州诺斯菲尔德（Northfield）提供的校外娱乐项目并不多，所以学生们只能在校内社交。卡尔顿学院没有兄弟会或者姐妹会，所以派对并不是生活的一大部分。“学生们只在周末参加派对，也没有同伴压力去参加派对。”一位佳桥校友说。

录取难度

卡尔顿学院录取学生时精挑细选，但是它不在最挑剔的学校之列，而且与类似学校相比，它对中国学生算是格外友好的。在录取上，他们有过不看学生成绩，而是更多发掘学生的天赋和特质的先例。但录取的过程并不是那么“容易”，学校有其“独特”的录取方式。

需要考虑的事情

你会喜欢卡尔顿学院，如果……

- 有比较小、能培养人能力的课堂对你的学习环境至关重要
- 你希望有一个充满创造力并且奇特的环境

你会不喜欢卡尔顿学院，如果……

- 你希望进入咨询或者金融行业
- 你不希望忍受寒冷的冬天

佳桥校友录取情况

录取比例	12.9%
SAT 阅读成绩中位数	730
SAT 数学成绩中位数	800
SAT 写作成绩中位数	760
SAT 总分中位数	2290
TOEFL 成绩中位数	114

财政情况

全年学费

48987 美元 (2015—2016)

经济资助可能性　低

学生为学校所在地区打分

安全	4
有趣	2
生活成本	2
中国食物	2
交通便利	1.5
酒吧和俱乐部	2
超市 / 便利店选择	1
周边就业市场	2
是否需要车	2.5
总评	3

* 满分 4 分

气候

年平均气温范围	-10℃ ~23℃
年平均降水量	80.4cm
年平均湿度	78.28%
年平均降雪量	93.2cm

从中国出发的航班

明尼阿波利斯国际机场（MSP，Minneapolis International Airport）距离学校开车需要一个小时。没有从中国出发的直达航班。

卡内基梅隆大学

地址：5000 FORBES AVE，PITTSBURGH，PA 15213
网址：WWW.CMU.EDU
中国招生官：无
招生办公室电话：412-268-2082
招生办公室邮箱：UNDERGRADUATE-ADMISSIONS@ANDREW.CMU.EDU
附近主要城市：匹兹堡

最佳匹配点分析

作为一所著名的研究型大学，卡内基梅隆大学在许多学术领域都表现出色。从艺术与人文到生物技术和计算机科学，能够承受得了课业负担的学生在这里能获得一份良好的教育，学会如何利用课堂知识解决现实社会中的问题。

学术机会

卡内基梅隆大学致力于为学生们提供一种“通识－职业”教育：既不忽视通识教育的重要性，也强调培养抢手的技术能力。为了达到上述目的，跨学科的课程设置非常普遍。佳桥校友们表示课程通常都要求颇高，尤其是与数学和自然科学相关的领域，不过课程内容也没有困难到“不可能学会”。他们同时觉得“课堂上学生的人数刚好，每一位学生都能得到足够的关注。”大多数课程都是由教授执教的，在办公时间也很容易接触到他们。一位佳桥校友提到：“研究生助教提供的习题课（session）对理解课程是非常有益的。”卡内基梅隆大学最强的学科包括：计算机科学、工程、音乐和戏剧。本科生的研究资金来源多种多样，包括支付研究费用的拨款（grants）、夏季项目的研究经费（fellowships）和支持学生们在学术会议上做报告的奖金（awards）。“遇见智慧头脑”（Meeting the Minds）研讨会每年五月召开，旨在庆祝整个校园本科生研究的成果。

职业发展

得益于学校与匹兹堡市中心的近距离，学生们可以在学年内以及暑期在学校附近找到实习和工作机会。职业培训中心会提供许多资源供学生们探索不同的机会。另外，卡内基梅隆大学与谷歌、脸书、IBM 以及其他许多公司都有合作，帮助学生和校友得到在这些公司工作和实习的机会。虽然许多毕业生都在科技领域工作，但仍有一部分人选择了去其他领域，如教育、艺术、咨询和工程。2013 年，27% 的毕业生毕业之后选择了继续完成研究生或博士教育。

校园人文环境

因为卡内基梅隆大学在艺术、人文和自然科学方面都有优秀的学术科目，所以来到这里的学生背景各不相同，有各种各样的兴趣。不过，正如一个佳桥校友指出的：“我们学校的戏剧狂人就像科技呆子一样多，但是他们互不来往。”学术上同样有丰富的多样性，但是各个小圈子之间也没有交集。佳桥的学生们还说“有很多来自不同文化背景的学生”，这样一来很多中国学生在这里并不觉得自己是少数族裔。匹兹堡市中心离学校只有 20 分钟公交车车程，在那里学生可以找到很多校园外的活动，酒吧、俱乐部、音乐会和戏剧表演一应俱全。因为大多数学生都非常关注

信息速览

US News 大学排名	23
学校位置	东北
学校类型	私立
周边环境	城市

本科学生情况

学生总数	5800 (2015)
申请人数	36131 (2015)
录取率	16.2% (2015)
男女学生比例	54/46
国际学生百分比	20%
亚裔美国人百分比	31%

有本科项目的学院

工程学院（College of Engineering）
艺术学院（College of Fine Arts）
迪特里希人文与社会科学学院（Dietrich College of Humanities & Social Sciences）
泰珀商学院（Tepper School of Business）
梅隆自然科学学院（Mellon College of Science）
计算机科学学院（School of Computer Science）
约翰•海因茨学院（H. John Heinz Ⅲ College）

你可能还想考虑以下学校

哥伦比亚大学　康奈尔大学
哈佛大学　约翰•霍普金斯大学
麻省理工学院　西北大学

佳桥校友录取情况

录取比例	33.6%
SAT 阅读成绩中位数	680
SAT 数学成绩中位数	800
SAT 写作成绩中位数	720
SAT 总分中位数	2200
TOEFL 成绩中位数	110

财政情况

全年学费

49610 美元 (2015—2016)

经济资助可能性　　非常低

学生为学校所在地区打分

安全	3
有趣	2
生活成本	2
中国食物	2
交通便利	2
酒吧和俱乐部	2
超市 / 便利店选择	2
周边就业市场	3
是否需要车	4
总评	3

* 满分 4 分

气候

年平均气温范围	−3℃ ~23℃
年平均降水量	93.8cm
年平均湿度	79.85%
年平均降雪量	45.8cm

从中国出发的航班

从中国出发无直达匹兹堡的航班，学生们需要转机一次。从匹兹堡国际机场（PIT，Pittsburgh International Airport）学生们可以选择出租车、租车、公交车或者穿梭巴士到学校。驾车大约需要半小时，公共交通大约需要 1.5 小时。

学术，校园里的社交场景相对缺乏。用一位佳桥校友的话来说：“我们并不在学期里开派对。”虽说如此，仍然有 11% 的男生和 12% 的女生加入了联谊会。

录取难度

卡内基梅隆大学并不容易申请，特别是热门专业，如计算机科学。但好的一面是，它给你足够的空间去展现你自己。不是标准化考试高手，但综合素质很全面的学生可以考虑这所大学。

需要考虑的事情

你会喜欢卡内基梅隆大学，如果……

- 你希望接受为工作做准备的教育
- 你对工程、计算机科学、音乐或者戏剧感兴趣
- 你希望在校园外有大量的社交活动

你会不喜欢卡内基梅隆大学，如果……

- 你希望校园内有活跃的社交场面
- 你在寻找一个完整的学生群体
- 你希望不仅仅把注意力放在学术上

凯斯西储大学

地址： 10900 EUCLID AVE，CLEVELAND，OH 44106
网址： WWW.CASE.EDU
中国招生官： DREW CRAWFORD，MEGAN GOODMAN
招生官邮箱： DREW.CRAWFORD@CASE.EDU，MEGAN.GOODMAN@CASE.EDU
招生办公室电话： 216-368-4450
附近主要城市： 芝加哥，开车大约需要 4 小时

最佳匹配点分析

凯斯西储大学由凯斯理工学院和西储大学两校合并而成，它有实力雄厚的技术教育，在人文学科方面也表现出众。虽然它不像卡内基梅隆大学那样出名，但是凯斯西储大学可以提供与其相似的教育，且从以往数据来看录取也要容易一些。

学术机会

所有学生在大学四年里都会参加通识教育与奖学金研讨会项目（SAGES，Seminar Approach to General Education and Scholarship program）。这个项目给了学生在小型的研讨会课堂锻炼批判性思维和写作能力的机会。据一位佳桥校友说，学校的课程颇为严格，但是还可以把握，在办公时间也可以很容易地接触到教授们。凯斯西储大学特别引人注目的专业包括生物医学工程、高分子科学、护理学和音乐。预科计划学者项目（Pre-professional Scholars Program）也会提前给符合

信息速览

US News 大学排名	37
学校位置	中西部
学校类型	私立
周边环境	城市

本科学生情况

学生总数	5121 (2015)
申请人数	22821 (2015)
录取率	36% (2015)
男女学生比例	55/45
国际学生百分比	11%
亚裔美国人百分比	20%

有本科项目的学院

凯斯工学院（Case School of Engineering）
文理学院（College of Arts and Sciences）
弗朗西斯·佩恩·伯顿护理学院（Frances Payne Bolton School of Nursing）
威瑟海德管理学院（Weatherhead School of Management）

你可能还想考虑以下学校

俄亥俄州立大学
卡内基梅隆大学
密西根大学
约翰·霍普金斯大学
华盛顿大学圣路易斯

标准的法学院、社会工作学院、医学院或者牙医学院的学生有条件录取的机会。在本科生研究方面，凯斯西储的资源项目（SOURCE，Support of Undergraduate Research & Creative Endeavors）为学生们提供了许多选择，在校内帮助教授们做项目，或利用附近机构资源丰富的优势（例如克利夫兰美术馆、自然博物馆和植物园）做个人项目。

职业发展

克利夫兰地区工程与医药公司众多，学生们在寻找实习的过程中几乎没有困难。因为学校离一些艺术和历史区域也很近，其他行业的工作或实习机会也不难得到。实习课程项目（Practicum Program）给文理学院和管理学院的学生提供长达 14 周全职带薪实习的机会。令人难以置信的是 2013 届毕业生中有 42% 选择继续读研究生或博士生。毕业之后选择立即工作的毕业生们都集中在工程、信息技术、商业和护理领域。虽然凯斯西储大学的校友网络并不特别出名，但是学校的学生和校友还是有机会从校友职业网络（Alumni Career Network）那里得到建议。

校园人文环境

凯斯西储大学紧张的学习氛围和学生们热爱合作的环境互为补充。不管是一起做作业，还是在期末考试周的半夜尖叫（Midnight Scream），合作总是被特别强调。学生通常会被认为是书呆子，但是佳桥校友表示大家的兴趣还是非常广泛的。学校在克利夫兰市意味着学生们可以接触到许多校外活动，即便联谊会（吸引了 28% 的男生和 31% 的女生）以及其他的学生组织通常都会在校内举行活动。学生们坐公交车有优惠，但是佳桥校友说还是有车比较方便，特别是如果你想去芝加哥或其他城市的话。学生群体非常活跃，有 55% 的学生参加校内体育赛事。体育赛事通常不会吸引学生们太多的注意，但对阵卡内基梅隆大学的橄榄球赛还是会吸引一大批追随者。

录取难度

凯斯西储大学不要求额外的申请文书，且提供提早行动（Early Action）申请，于是很多学生将这所优秀的学校作为一个“出气筒”。申请者很多，但能被录取的却很少。即便是很优秀的学生，收到推迟录取通知或是拒信也是很正常的事。

需要考虑的事情

你会喜欢凯斯西储大学，如果……

- 你希望在本科期间就开始做研究
- 你对工程或者医学预科很感兴趣
- 你非常享受合作的环境

你会不喜欢凯斯西储大学，如果……

- 你更喜欢一个人工作 / 学习
- 你希望校内有非常强的体育文化
- 你不想在城市里生活

佳桥校友录取情况

录取比例	19.3%
SAT 阅读成绩中位数	640
SAT 数学成绩中位数	800
SAT 写作成绩中位数	690
SAT 总分中位数	2130
TOEFL 成绩中位数	106

财政情况

全年学费	44156 美元 (2015—2016)
经济资助可能性	非常低

学生为学校所在地区打分

安全	2
有趣	2
生活成本	2
中国食物	2
交通便利	1
酒吧和俱乐部	2
超市 / 便利店选择	1
周边就业市场	3
是否需要车	4
总评	2

* 满分 4 分

气候

年平均气温范围	-3℃ ~23℃
年平均降水量	106.2cm
年平均湿度	78.48%
年平均降雪量	151cm

从中国出发的航班

从中国到克利夫兰没有直达航班，学生们需要先在芝加哥转机。在到达克利夫兰霍普金斯国际机场（CLE，Cleveland Hopkins International Airport）之后，学生们需要坐一段短途火车再加上一段汽车才能到学校。

克莱尔蒙特麦肯纳学院

地址：500 E 9th STREET，CLAREMONT，CA 91711
网址：WWW.CMC.EDU
中国招生官：CONOR FRITZ
招生官邮箱：CFRITZ@CMC.EDU
招生办公室电话：909-621-8088
附近主要城市：洛杉矶，到学校 40 分钟车程。

最佳匹配点分析

有志成为商业领袖、对公共事务感兴趣，并且希望得到全面通识教育的学生最适合入读克莱尔蒙特麦肯纳学院。在酒精面前感到不自在的学生应远离该校。虽然学生们不会感受到必须饮酒的压力，但派对在这里特别广泛而且是社交的一大部分。作为克莱蒙特学院联盟的成员，克莱尔蒙特麦肯纳学院把亲密的校园氛围和丰富的资源结合在了一起。如果你希望体验文理学院的智识氛围并且在毕业后做商业相关的工作，你应该来这里。

学术机会

如果你希望得到“实用的”通识教育，你应该考虑克莱尔蒙特麦肯纳学院，《华尔街日报》把这所学校排在向法学院、商学院和医学院输送学生最多的十所学校榜单上。有将近 30% 的学生学习经济专业，其他热门专业还包括政府研究、商业和国际关系。

学院提供加速综合自然科学系列项目（AISS，Accelerated Integrated Science Sequence），该项目允许大一学生选择一系列快速的自然科学科目。但这个项目是为真正对自然科学有激情的学生设计的，因为它要求学生们每个星期上 13 小时的课程（星期五要上 5 个小时）。总体来说，学生们表示学校的自然科学项目并不是特别强，但学校和斯科里普斯学院以及匹泽学院共享自然科学项目。

学生们都乐于合作，极少互相比较成绩，不过一个佳桥校友表示这里的学生骨子里“非常喜欢竞争”。

72% 的学生会和教授一起做研究，所以研究机会非常丰富。所有的课程都是由教授执教的，一位佳桥校友反映教授们“非常容易接近”。虽然克莱尔蒙特麦肯纳学院是一所小学校，但它有非常多的资源，因为它属于克莱尔蒙特联盟。除本校的 33 个专业和 8 个系列之外，学生们还可以从姐妹校的 2000 多门课程中选课。

信息速览

US News 文理学院排名	9
学校位置	西海岸
学校类型	私立
周边环境	郊区

本科学生情况

学生总数	1328 (2015)
申请人数	7152 (2015)
录取率	9.8% (2015)
男女学生比例	51/49
国际学生百分比	16.6%
亚裔美国人百分比	10.3%

你可能还想考虑以下学校

波莫纳学院　匹泽学院
西方学院　斯科里普斯学院
斯坦福大学

职业发展

受访的佳桥校友表示，克莱尔蒙特麦肯纳学院的学生十分专注，在学习上以就业为导向。在参加调查的 2013 届毕业生中有 87% 的毕业生在毕业之前完成了至少一次实习。在 2013 年，学院资助了 146 项夏季实习（大部分是在非营利机构）。48% 的受访毕业生在毕业前 6 个月之内找到了全职工作，还有 13% 进入了研究生院。常见的职业选择包括咨询（21%）、投资银行（13%）、会计（13%）、金融（10%）、自然科学 / 技术（10%），以及教育 / 非营利行业（10%）。另有 15% 的学生在商业和政府 / 法律界找到了工作。学生中也丝毫不缺乏理想主义者，2013 届毕业生中有 9 位获得了富布莱特奖学金（Fulbright Scholarship）。

校园人文环境

克莱尔蒙特麦肯纳学院的学生在用生命开派对。虽然校园里没有联谊会，但是宽松的饮酒政策和大量有主题的派对（比如说蒙特卡洛大师赛、超级英雄）为学院的派对赢得了五校联盟中最大、最精心准备的派对的名声。学生们的社交生活主要在校园附近展

佳桥校友录取情况

录取比例	15.2%
SAT 阅读成绩中位数	710
SAT 数学成绩中位数	800
SAT 写作成绩中位数	680
SAT 总分中位数	2170
TOEFL 成绩中位数	105

财政情况

全年学费

48800 美元 (2015—2016)

经济资助可能性 非常低

学生为学校所在地区打分

安全	4
有趣	3
生活成本	2
中国食物	2
交通便利	3
酒吧和俱乐部	1
超市 / 便利店选择	1
周边就业市场	1
是否需要车	3
总评	3

*满分 4 分

气候

年平均气温范围	11℃ ~25℃
年平均降水量	58.7cm
年平均湿度	81.87%
年平均降雪量	0cm

从中国出发的航班

从中国有直达航班到洛杉矶国际机场（LAX，Los Angeles International Airport）。在不堵车的情况下，机场距离学校约 45 分钟车程（因此开车大概需要一个小时到一个半小时之间）。

开（94% 的学生住在校内），因为克莱尔蒙特镇虽然拥有很多时装店、餐馆、电影院和冰淇淋店，但是还没有足够的活力和面积被称为大学城。虽然克莱尔蒙特麦肯纳的学生对政治十分敏感，但是他们不自负，而且对彼此非常接纳。学生们在种族上很多样化（3% 的非洲裔美国人，8% 的西班牙裔和 10% 的亚裔），在政治观点上也是如此。不过在性取向和宗教上缺乏多样性。国际学生占学生总数的 17%，中国学生（2014 年有 22 位中国学生入学）超过 50 名，是国际学生中最大的一个群体，所以他们并不会感到孤单。通常来说这里的学生在与不同背景的人交往的过程中做得很好。Marian Miner 厨师神殿（Marian Miner Cook Athenaeum）每周四天请名人来做演讲，让学生们在享受美味晚餐的同时进行智识上的辩论。

录取难度

和其他克莱尔蒙特联盟的学校一样，克莱尔蒙特麦肯纳录取的门槛很高。SAT 分数在 2280 分以下的学生几乎不可能被录取。拥有领导经验并且经历均衡的学生更受学校青睐。

需要考虑的事情

你会喜欢克莱尔蒙特麦肯纳学院，如果……

- 你想进入一个文理学院，但是又希望学校有职前教育的氛围
- 你享受全年 T 恤 / 人字拖的打扮
- 你在与不同背景的学生打交道的过程中感到很自如

你会不喜欢克莱尔蒙特麦肯纳学院，如果……

- 你希望体验联谊会生活
- 你更希望不在校园里度过你的大部分时间

威廉玛丽学院

地址：116 JAMESTOWN ROAD，WILLIAMSBURG，VA 23187-8795
网址：WWW.WM.EDU
中国招生官：DEBORAH BASKET
招生官电话：757-221-4223
招生官邮箱：DLBASK@WM.EDU
附近主要城市：华盛顿特区，坐 AMTRAK 火车需要 2 小时

最佳匹配点分析

如果你想进入这所全美第二古老的大学，你最好做好面对严格学术标准的准备，这些标准在过去 300 多年的实施过程中被不断完善。以模糊公立大学和私立大学的界限出名，威廉玛丽学院是严肃对待学术的学生们的避风港。如果你在寻找更喧嚣的乐趣，那么你不应该在此停留。研究机会对于有志于此的学生们来说非常丰富，尤其是在 STEM（Science，Technology，Engineering，Mathematics 科学、技术、工程与数学）领域。希望在这里见到很多中国国际学生，或者是任意一国国际学生的同学们的愿望恐怕要落空了。不过，如果你希望住在美国历史里，可能在全美没有几个地方比威廉斯堡更适合了。

信息速览

US News 大学排名	34
学校位置	中部大西洋地区
学校类型	公立
周边环境	郊区

本科学生情况

学生总数	6301 (2015)
申请人数	14952 (2015)
录取率	34.5% (2015)
男女学生比例	44/56
国际学生百分比	5.7%
亚裔美国人百分比	8.2%

有本科项目的学院

文理学院（Programs in Arts and Sciences）

梅森商学院（Mason School of Business）

教育学院（School of Education）

你可能还想考虑以下学校

乔治城大学　塔夫茨大学

波士顿学院　弗吉尼亚大学

北卡罗来纳大学教堂山分校

学术机会

与某些综合性大学不同的是，威廉玛丽学院非常强调四年的本科教育。这一点通过小型课堂和学校提供的难度颇高的课程可以看出。在这里最热门的专业包括商业、管理、营销、生物和心理。佳桥的校友说："所有的课程都是由教授执教的，他们都很容易接近"，而且"课程很少按照百分比评分。在数学和自然科学课上得到 A 并不难，不过在人文学科上就很不容易。"带着一点逗趣的主观，学生们表示学校学术严格的名声不是无中生有。虽然如此，学生们并不认为学校的气氛压抑，"这里的学生们都很聪明而且有合作精神。我们有时候会组成学习小组，在考试之前进行复习。"作为一所出名的研究型大学，学生们可以获得参加一流研究项目的机会。

职业发展

学校里梅森商学院的声誉颇佳，有多达 87% 的学生在毕业前的几个月内就找到了工作。总体来看，有 64% 的学生在毕业之后直接参加了工作。常见的雇主有 AmeriCorp①，彭博（Bloomberg）、博思艾伦咨询公司（Booz Allen Hamilton）、中情局（CIA）、IBM，精锐媒体（MediaVest）、Peace Corps，Teach for America，德勤、毕马威、安永和普华永道。威廉玛丽的校友网络不像东岸私立学校那样强大，而且佳桥的学生们告诉我们大多数学生都来自华盛顿特区或者弗吉尼亚。学校表示本校学生获得博士的比例大于任何其他公立大学。

校园人文环境

作为一所公立大学，威廉玛丽学院主要为弗吉尼亚的学生服务，所以绝大多数学生都来自本州。只有大约 5% 的学生来自其他国家，而 60% 的学生是白人。虽然没能提供

① 美国志愿队，美国的一个从事公益服务的组织，其成员在美国横跨东西海岸的 25000 多个地方提供服务，服务内容有提升教育、提供救灾服务、促进经济机会、帮助退役军人和军人家属、保护环境和扩大卫生服务等。

种族多样性，但是学校宽松的饮酒政策弥补了这点不足，可能是为了让来自不同文化的学生能够自由交往。不过学生们从来不会滥用这种自由，佳桥的校友透露："没有喝酒的压力，在我们学院里有一些人会喝酒，但不是很多。"联谊会吸引了 25% 的男生和 29% 的女生，不过它并没有太强的存在感。毒品在校园内是绝对禁止的。

在校园之外，威廉斯堡是一个很昂贵的旅游小镇，在营业时间之外没有太多乐趣，学生们更倾向于在校园内的活动。佳桥校友建议学生们买一辆车。

录取难度

作为一所公立大学，威廉玛丽学院不在除弗吉尼亚之外的美国各州或者其他国家招收太多学生。学生的 SAT 大多在 2000 到 2250 之间，被录取的学生都是他们高中的活跃领袖。

需要考虑的事情

你会喜欢威廉玛丽学院，如果……

- 你希望和美国白人交朋友
- 你在寻找酒吧场景
- 你希望在华盛顿特区实习或者工作
- 学习、考试和学术探索对你来说非常重要

你会不喜欢威廉玛丽学院，如果……

- 你希望遇见来自世界各地的人们
- 你不想参与到定义这个学校的种种传统中

佳桥校友录取情况

录取比例	29%
SAT 阅读成绩中位数	675
SAT 数学成绩中位数	800
SAT 写作成绩中位数	725
SAT 总分中位数	2140
TOEFL 成绩中位数	109

财政情况

全年学费

35122 美元 (2015—2016)

经济资助可能性　非常低

学生为学校所在地区打分

安全	4
有趣	1.5
生活成本	1.5
中国食物	2
交通便利	2
酒吧和俱乐部	1.5
超市 / 便利店选择	1.5
周边就业市场	1.5
是否需要车	4
总评	2.5

* 满分 4 分

气候

年平均气温范围	3℃ ~26℃
年平均降水量	114.7cm
年平均湿度	74.65%
年平均降雪量	22.9cm

从中国出发的航班

从中国没有直达威廉斯堡的航班。学生可直飞华盛顿杜勒斯国际机场（IAD，Dulles International Airport），然后乘 AMTRAK 火车到达威廉斯堡。

哥伦比亚大学

地址：1130 AMSTERDAM AVENUE，NEW YORK，NY 10027
网址：WWW.COLUMBIA.EDU
中国招生官：EDWARD TRUONG
招生官邮箱：ET2416@COLUMBIA.EDU
招生办公室电话：212-854-2522
附近主要城市：纽约（哥伦比亚大学在曼哈顿）

最佳匹配点分析

我们很难找到不喜欢哥伦比亚大学的学生，特别是这所大学出色的多样性和显著的地理优势。总体来说，我们听到的唯一抱怨是附近的地区可能有一点危险和吵闹。大多数学生对于他们征服充满干劲、快速向前的纽约市的能力充满信心，不过纽约并不适合每一个人。对于学术认真或者不太确定自己专业的学生们会发现哥伦比亚非常适合他们，但是如果你已经有了明确的学术目标，那么哥伦比亚的核心课程可能会拖慢你的步伐。

学术机会

作为全美录取难度排名第四的大学，哥伦比亚大学尽其所能确保学生在进入大学以后能够很好地适应这里的生活。学校特别出色的学科有英语、历史、政治科学、经济、生物、音乐、戏剧和机械工程，并且对于核心课程的设置一直保持了严格的标准。学生们需要花两年时间去完成这些要求，其中包括两个学期的自然科学、对于现当代文明、文学以及人文科学的理解。这所常春藤学校拥有自己的教授评分系统，为学生们提供许多研究机会。用一位佳桥校友的话来说，哥伦比亚大学的气氛是“追求智识发展而不是为工作做准备。”哥伦比亚保持了亲密的学习氛围，中国学生们表示说“研究生只会教复习课。执教小型研讨课的教授都极易接近而且特别热心，他们有针对学生的办公时间，不过你如果在其他时间和他们交流他们也非常乐意。”这里的工程学院因其交叉学科研究而出名，覆盖的领域有生物工程和纳米技术。虽然为了获得优质教育的学费非同一般，但这是值得的。

信息速览

US News 大学排名	4
学校位置	东北
学校类型	私立
周边环境	城市

本科学生情况

学生总数	8613 (2015)
申请人数	36250 (2015)
录取率	6.1% (2015)
男女学生比例	53/47
国际学生百分比	16%
亚裔美国人百分比	17%

有本科项目的学院

哥伦比亚学院（Columbia College）
哥伦比亚工程与应用科学学院（Columbia School of Engineering and Applied Sciences）

你可能还想考虑以下学校

哈佛大学　普林斯顿大学
纽约大学　宾夕法尼亚大学
达特茅斯学院

职业发展

除了强调通识教育，哥伦比亚大学也提供给学生足够的机会让他们着眼于未来的发展。学校会组织学生参与优秀公司的人际交流会和校内面试，如摩根大通和领英（LinkedIn）。对于那些对学术感兴趣的学生，从纽约市的研究机构得到实习机会并不困难。在 2013 届毕业生中，58.3% 的学生开始了工作，20% 确认会在毕业后的六个月内进入研究生院。在选择工作的学生中，55.7% 年薪超过了 50000 美元，更有 30.8% 的年起薪超过了 70000 美元。学生们会在全球最好的 10 所学校里选择研究生院。选择加入企业工作的学生会进入金融服务、咨询、计算机、教育、研究、法律服务、互联网与电子商务，以及传媒领域。哥伦比亚大学学生的常见雇主包括埃森哲咨询公司（Accenture）、摩根大通、花旗集团、谷歌、哥伦比亚大学和美国银行。哥伦比亚大学拥有美国最强大的校友网络之一，它向校友提供一系列服务，包括使用哥伦比亚职业辅导网络（Columbia Career Coaches Network）。

校园人文环境

佳桥的校友分享说：“在课堂上、讲座上、派对上以及各种学生活动里面你总能见到新人，所以感觉学校很大。不过当你意识到你所有的朋友都被以某些方式联结在一起的

佳桥校友录取情况

录取比例	17.3%
SAT 阅读成绩中位数	740
SAT 数学成绩中位数	800
SAT 写作成绩中位数	795
SAT 总分中位数	2310
TOEFL 成绩中位数	115

财政情况

全年学费

50526 美元 (2015—2016)

经济资助可能性 低

学生为城市打分

安全	3
有趣	4
生活成本	3
中国食物	3
交通便利	4
酒吧和俱乐部	4
超市 / 便利店选择	4
周边就业市场	2.5
是否需要车	1
总评	4

*满分 4 分

气候

年平均气温范围	-2℃ ~24℃
年平均降水量	122cm
年平均湿度	66%
年平均降雪量	38.1cm

从中国出发的航班

从中国可以选择从北京国际机场、上海浦东国际机场或者香港国际机场直飞肯尼迪国际机场（JFK，John F. Kennedy International Airport）。从机场到学校的公共交通需要大约 40 分钟。

时候，学校又变得很小了。”所以最后，感觉哥伦比亚就像是一个小学校。中国学生认为哥伦比亚非常多样化（是所有常春藤学校里面最多样化的），这所学校不知不觉地接纳了所有人。52% 的学生群体是少数族裔。

在纽约市有很多事情可做，就像是人们对这里的期望一样。不过中国学生暗示：“我们离哈勒姆区还是有一点近。”大概有 10% 的女生和 10% 的男生参加联谊会，不过如果你志不在此就不用注意这些。哥伦比亚大学有很多自己的传统，比如说有机化学之夜（Orgo Night），在期末考试周的前一天（也是有机化学考试的前一天），学校的行进乐队会在半夜冲进图书馆，用一个小时的演奏打断所有严肃的学习。另外，哥伦比亚的新晋企业家社团（CORE，Columbia Organization of Rising Entrepreneurs）每年都会举办各种活动和竞赛，来激发学生们的灵感和创业动力。

录取难度

录取的竞争难以想象地激烈，因为哥伦比亚是全美最难录取的大学之一。SAT 超过 2300 分也不能保证绝对录取，学生们在提交的申请中应该表现出对在纽约市学习的极大兴趣。

需要考虑的事情

你会喜欢哥伦比亚大学，如果……

- 你希望接触到来自世界各地的文化
- 你喜欢充满艺术气息的活动，参观博物馆和看剧对你来说很有吸引力
- 你希望以后进入金融领域

你会不喜欢哥伦比亚大学，如果……

- 任意的危险都会让你感到害怕
- 你认为在你的专业之外探索课程就是浪费时间

康奈尔大学

地址：144 EAST AVENUE，ITHACA，NY 14853
网址：WWW.CORNELL.EDU
中国招生官：无
招生办公室电话：607-255-5241
招生办公室邮箱：ADMISSIONS@CORNELL.EDU
附近主要城市：纽约，乘坐大巴需要 4 小时

最佳匹配点分析

对于中国留学生来说，康奈尔大学是一个可以为他们提供 7 个本科学院选择的全面的大学。在社交和学术上积极主动的学生会在这里得到最大的发展。学校校园很大，因此参加学校社团组织对于拓展和壮大自己的社交网是非常重要的。不论你是爱好运动，喜欢交朋友还是派对迷，在这里都能找到属于自己的圈子。但是务必谨记：这里的课业负担有时会让人觉得喘不过气，拖延症患者会感到无所适从。据佳桥校友反映“伊萨卡市距其他城市至少要两个小时，所以这里确实会缺少很多大城市元素，但这是一个美丽的地方。”另外康奈尔的冬天非常寒冷，所以来到之前请务必准备你最暖和的冬衣。

学术机会

在 US News 上排名第 15 的康奈尔大学提供非常具有挑战性的学术课程，学校的“杀

信息速览

US News 大学排名	15
学校位置	东北
学校类型	私立
周边环境	郊区

本科学生情况

学生总数	14315 (2015)
申请人数	41907 (2015)
录取率	14.9% (2015)
男女学生比例	48/52
国际学生百分比	10%
亚裔美国人百分比	16%

有本科项目的学院

农业和生命科学学院（College of Agriculture and Life Sciences）
建筑、艺术和规划学院（College of Architecture, Art, and Planning）
文理学院（College of Arts and Sciences）
工程学院（College of Engineering）
酒店管理学院（School of Hotel Administration）
人类生态学学院（College of Human Ecology）
工业和劳工关系学院（School of Industrial and Labor Relations）

你可能还考虑以下学校

杜克大学	哈佛大学
普林斯顿大学	斯坦福大学
耶鲁大学	宾夕法尼亚大学

手期末考试”也很出名。基础课通常由研究生助教协助上课，但是学生们说教授也非常容易接近。康奈尔热门的专业包括生物、酒店管理和经济学。一些佳桥校友会觉得学校太大了，但某些专业性较强的学院的学生则反映他们的师生比例非常完美。文理学院的学生可以充分利用康奈尔大学广泛的课程设置和学业要求，他们三分之二的课程是自己专业以外的选修。因为康奈尔被外界所知的学生自杀率，学生们很容易从学校获得优质的心理辅导服务。同时学校也为那些想要发展自己研究项目的学生提供很多资源。

职业发展

大部分的康奈尔毕业生会在毕业初即获得一份工作，其中很多人都从金融界开始。据职业网站的统计数据显示，54% 的学生选择一毕业就直接开始工作，另外有 30% 会选择追求更高层次的教育。近年来，学生反映找到工作非常容易。康奈尔的职业中心在帮助毕业生锁定工作方面成效斐然，它将寻找当地和外地的工作需求分开进行管理。佳桥校友说“学生们之间关系密切，校友都非常愿意为我们提供工作机会。”

校园人文环境

康奈尔大学拥有出色的多元文化群体，中国留学生在这里不愁找不到国内或者其他国家的学生交朋友。2012 年学校的中国本科留学生人数是 341 人。很多佳桥校友表示他们周围的朋友中有一半来自中国。一个学生说道：“我们有来自世界各地的同学、不同的信仰，选择专业和辅修也很多样化。”学校里有很多人支持同性恋群体，从这一点可以看出学校的开放性。佳桥校友说一般情况下“学校有很多派对，经常在周末举办”。冰上曲棍球和橄榄球在康奈尔最受欢迎。学校拥有 500 多个学生组织，每天校园内都有各种活动。20% 到 25% 的学生参加了联谊会，但是这不占社交生活的主导地位。因为学校看重饮食文化，所以“食物选择非常多样化，但是中国食物选择比较少”。

录取难度

康奈尔的工程学院是相对更难录取的一个学院。比较而言，其他学院能接受的 SAT 成绩在 2100 分到 2300 分之间。

需要考虑的事情

你会喜欢康奈尔大学，如果……

- 你喜欢橄榄球和冰上曲棍球
- 你对商科、酒店管理、工业关系、工程学或者人类生态学感兴趣
- 你期待大部分的社交活动发生在校园内
- 你希望接近一个中国留学生社区
- 你寻求种族多元化

你会不喜欢康奈尔大学，如果……

- 你讨厌寒冷的气候
- 你希望待在一个美国大城市
- 你希望学校的课堂有小型的亲密氛围
- 你不喜欢为就业而学习的学习氛围

佳桥校友录取情况

录取比例	12%
SAT 阅读成绩中位数	730
SAT 数学成绩中位数	800
SAT 写作成绩中位数	770
SAT 总分中位数	2290
TOEFL 成绩中位数	114

财政情况

全年学费	49116 美元 (2015—2016)
经济资助可能性	非常低

学生为学校所在地区打分

安全	3.5
有趣	3
生活成本	3
中国食物	2.5
公共交通	2
酒吧和俱乐部	2
超市 / 便利店选择	2
周边就业市场	3
是否需要车	3
总评	3

＊满分 4 分

气候

年平均气温范围	-6℃ ~21℃
年平均降水量	94.8cm
年平均湿度	77.99%
年平均降雪量	124.1cm

从中国出发的航班

从中国有到达纽约的直达航班。学生们到达肯尼迪国际机场（JFK，John F. Kennedy International Airport）之后可以乘坐大巴到伊萨卡，大概需要 4 个小时。

达特茅斯学院

地址：6016 MCNUTT HALL，HANOVER，NH 03755
网站：WWW.DARTMOUTH.EDU
中国招生官：BECKY SABKY
招生办公室邮箱：可以在 HTTPS：//ADMISSIONS.DARTMOUTH.EDU/CONTACT-US 页面给招生办公室写邮件
招生办公室电话：603-646-2875
附近主要城市：波士顿，开车需要两个半小时

最佳匹配点分析

那些想要申请常青藤大学，又期待一个小型文理学院学习氛围的学生们可以选择达特茅斯学院。达特茅斯学院位于新罕布什尔州和佛蒙特州交界处的一个只有 11000 人的小镇。学校致力于本科教育，将密切的课堂氛围和充足的研究机遇很好地结合在了一起。学校的核心课程要求高，但选择和安排很灵活。这里冬天漫长寒冷，社交场景不多见，学生们更多的是被他们对学术的热爱、对自然力量的折服，以及很多很多的啤酒凝聚在一起。

DARTMOUTH
VOX CLAMANTIS IN DESERTO
1769

学术机会

达特茅斯学院的“达特茅斯计划”非常出名，它是学校创新的一个季度制学制体系，在整体上决定着学校的学制步调和学术精神。学生们需要在学校度过 12 个学期，其中大

一和大四的秋季、冬季和春季学期以及大二之后的夏季学期是必须在校园里度过的；学生们可以自由选择什么时候在学校度过其余的5个学期。这种灵活性赋予了学生一年的自由时间，他们可以通过实习、志愿服务项目或者实地研究来获得完整的工作经验。从另一方面看，这种学制也有劣势，那就是课程进行得相当快，每三个月就要有一次期末考试。学校的通识教育要求非常广泛，因此学生们可以获得全面的综合教育。最热门的专业有经济学、政府研究、历史和工程。说到学习环境，达特茅斯为学生们创造了通力协作的氛围。据一个佳桥校友反映“教授通常都非常容易接近”，所有接受调查的学生都表示学校的课堂规模刚刚好。达特茅斯学院的学生做任何事情都专注而又充满激情，因此不管汉诺威市多么缺乏活力，达特茅斯的学生群体都能用他们活跃的智识来弥补这一点。

信息速览

US News 大学排名	12
学校位置	东北
学校类型	私立
周边环境	乡村

本科学生情况

学生总数	4307 (2015)
申请人数	20507 (2015)
录取率	10.9% (2015)
男女学生比例	51/49
国际学生百分比	8.9%
亚裔百分比	14.9%

有本科项目的学院

文理学院（Undergraduate College）

塞耶工程学院（Thayer School of Engineering）

你可能还考虑以下学校

杜克大学　波士顿学院

宾夕法尼亚大学　西北大学

乔治城大学

职业发展

达特茅斯学院历史悠久，但历久弥新。它的毕业生中有170人曾在美国国会服务，它在《财富》杂志培养出最多500强CEO的大学排行榜上排名第4。拥有如此强大的校友网，2012届毕业生中超过60%的学生在毕业前6个月内得到聘用就不足为奇了。毕业生的就业领域主要分布在金融、教育和咨询领域，健康/科学、艺术/传媒和技术类工作共占25%。大部分的毕业生选择继续留在东北或者中部大西洋沿岸城市工作，但也有很多毕业生在华盛顿特区、芝加哥以及加州和得克萨斯州一些热门大城市就业。继续读研究生院也是一个普遍的选择，11%的毕业生目前已经就读研究生项目，还有64%的毕业生打算在毕业五年内继续深造。达特茅斯学院的学生中也不乏理想主义者，学校一直位居小型院校Peace Corps志愿者产出排名前20。

校园人文环境

《动物屋》这部描绘大学派对疯狂生活和恶作剧的经典美国电影，就是以达特茅斯学院昔日疯狂的联谊会生活为灵感来源创作的。近年来，达特茅斯学院永无休止的派对名

佳桥校友录取情况

录取比例	10.3%
SAT 阅读成绩中位数	735
SAT 数学成绩中位数	800
SAT 写作成绩中位数	780
SAT 总分中位数	2310
TOEFL 成绩中位数	118

财政情况

全年学费	48120 美元 (2015—2016)
经济资助可能性	非常低

学生为学校所在地区打分

安全	3
有趣	2
生活成本	3
中国美食	1
公共交通	1
酒吧和俱乐部	1
超市 / 便利店选择	1
周边就业市场	2.5
是否需要车	2.5
总评	2

*满分 4 分

气候

年平均气温范围	-9℃ ~20℃
年平均降水量	104.1cm
年平均湿度	81.06%
年平均降雪量	182cm

从中国出发的航班

学校和机场之间有机场巴士，也有公交车直接开往洛根国际机场（BOS，Logan International Airport）和曼彻斯特波士顿区域机场（MHT，Manchester-Boston Regional Airport）。洛根国际机场距离学校开车要两个半小时，有从中国直达的航班；曼彻斯特机场距离学校一个半小时车程，没有从中国直达的航班。

声已经有所减缓。即便如此，因为学校的饮酒政策非常宽松，汉诺威又是一个不能提供太多娱乐项目的乏味小镇，联谊会生活仍然占学校的主导地位。对于那些厌倦了派对或者对派对不感兴趣的学生们来说，达特茅斯远足俱乐部（Dartmouth Outing Club）也是一个非常好的选择，它吸引了众多学生，也是非常重要的一个社交媒介。

达特茅斯学院的学生有时候会被看作是千篇一律的白人预备学校学生、派对狂，以及保守的老男孩关系网受益者。但在今天，达特茅斯学院是一个进步和多元的地方（尽管自我隔离比较普遍）。在这里你可以找到各种类型的学生，但是他们普遍都热爱户外运动、踏实，而且信奉“努力学习，尽情玩耍”的原则。所有接受调查的佳桥校友都反馈说他们的朋友中中国留学生的比例不到 30%，每年入学的中国学生都少于 10 人。对达特茅斯学院感兴趣的学生来到这里后应当做好融入多样化群体的心理准备。

录取难度

达特茅斯录取的中国学生非常有限，没有 2200 分的 SAT 成绩几乎不可能被录取。在美国高中的学习经历可能会对申请有利，因为学校会更加认可美国高中的成绩标准。

需要考虑的事情

你会喜欢达特茅斯，如果……

- 你热爱户外活动
- 你非常关注自己的职业发展

你会不喜欢达特茅斯，如果……

- 城市生活是你对美国的最大憧憬
- 排外的联谊会生活会让你望而却步
- 一个人人都认识彼此的社区让你感到窒息

戴维森学院

地址：209 RIDGE ROAD，DAVIDSON，NC 28035
网址：WWW.DAVIDSON.EDU
中国招生官：KAYE-LANI LAUGHNA
招生官邮箱：KALAUGHNA@DAVIDSON.EDU
招生办公室电话：800-768-0380
附近主要城市：夏洛特，乘坐巴士或者开车需要 20 分钟

最佳匹配点分析

因为和长老会的深厚渊源，戴维森学院非常重视服务和诚信，这一点在学校的荣誉制度上得到了很好的体现。学校的考试可以是自行安排、无人监考的。荣誉制度同时指导着学校的学术、社交生活以及参与率达到 85% 的社区服务。那些追求卓越和全面教育的学生会在戴维森学院受益匪浅，它的人文艺术核心课程是学校本科课程的基石。令人遗憾的是戴维森的地理位置。那些希望找一个大名鼎鼎不用每次提到学校名字都要跟人解释一番的学生肯定不会喜欢这里。

学术机会

戴维森的学生以努力学习和工作为傲。亲密的课堂氛围、平易近人的教授和受到足够敬畏的诚信准则塑造了学生的求知欲和学校的互信氛围。戴维森的人文艺术核心课程要求学生在文学、艺术、历史、宗教和哲学方面各修一门课程，同时修三门数学或者自

信息速览

US News 文理学院排名	9
学校位置	中部大西洋
学校类型	私立
宗教归属	长老会
周边环境	乡村

本科学生情况

学生总数	1950 (2015)
申请人数	5382(2015)
录取率	22.2% (2015)
男女学生比例	49/51
国际学生百分比	5.9%
亚裔百分比	6.2%

你可能还想考虑以下学校

圣约翰学院	维克森林大学
达特茅斯学院	范德比尔特大学

然科学课程以及两门社会科学课程。想要从事研究项目的学生也可以找到很多机会，这些研究项目通常都包含在课程中。在 2012 年，有 243 名学生参加了一学期的独立研究项目。学校课程设置比较均衡，热门专业有政治、英语和心理学，一些自然科学类专业，像生物和化学也很受欢迎。另外，戴维森还提供与哥伦比亚大学和华盛顿圣路易斯大学合作的工程类文学学士－理学学士（BA-BS）学位课程。总的来说，70% ~ 80% 的学生渴望走出北卡州，他们会在毕业前选择国外学习项目。另外一点不足是很多学生抱怨学校近年来的评分标准越来越严，导致学习环境更加严苛。

职业发展

戴维森野猫队是该校学生的真实写照，80% 的学生最终会取得硕士或者博士学位。最近一届毕业生中，有 44% 得到了全职工作，18% 参与到研究或者服务类项目中，还有 20% 选择继续深造。拥有超过 60% 的校友捐赠率，戴维森的学生们都非常忠诚并以母校为傲。超过四分之一的学生毕业后会选择待在北卡州，尽管有 12% 现在住在国外。

校园人文环境

直到今天，戴维森的学生依旧以上层白人和美国南部居民为主（46.5% 的学生来自美国东南部各州），学校的政治氛围也倾向于保守。不过戴维森依然是开放和欢迎外来群体的，国际学生虽然只占学生群体的 6%，但是他们都倾向于融入美国人中去。种族多样性是校园里最热门的话题，经常出现在校报头条和各种讨论中。

兄弟会和由女生组成的饮食俱乐部（分别有 35% 和 40% 的参与率）确立了学校社交生活的基调。戴维森的学生也懂得如何利用周末放松自己，不管是参加派对，还是参加联合董事会举办的各种活动。社交生活基本全是在校园里进行，一个只有 7100 人口的小镇本身就是“精致”的缩影。因此也有学生抱怨派对总是重复没有新意。对于另外一些学生来说，夏洛特是一个较近的能够提供更多休闲娱乐的不错的去处。另外，默特尔海滩（Myrtle Beach）和滑雪斜坡距离学校都只有几个小时车程，也可以作为一种选择。

录取难度

戴维森学院在中国的知名度不是很高，因此申请的人数比较少。同样，录取的人数也非常少，录取的竞争很激烈。戴维森学院比较看重学生的课外活动成就以及批判性思维和反省的能力。

需要考虑的事情

你会喜欢戴维森学院，如果……

◆ 你寻找的是一个拥有紧密联系的大学社区环境，并且希望教授对学生的关注度非常高

◆ 你不知道怎么洗衣服（唯一一所提供免费洗衣服务的大学！）

你会不喜欢戴维森学院，如果……

◆ 如果有人问"戴维森是哪个大学"，你会觉得受到了冒犯

◆ 你希望找一个有着大量中国留学生的学校（并且很容易就想念中国食物）

佳桥校友录取情况

录取比例	23.1%
SAT 阅读成绩中位数	660
SAT 数学成绩中位数	790
SAT 写作成绩中位数	700
SAT 总分中位数	2150
TOEFL 成绩中位数	110

财政情况

全年学费

46966 美元 (2015—2016)

经济资助可能性　非常低

学生为学校所在地区打分

安全	4
有趣	2
生活成本	3
中国食物	2
交通便利	2.5
酒吧和俱乐部	1
超市 / 便利店选择	1
周边就业市场	1.5
是否需要车	3
总评	2.5

*满分 4 分

气候

年平均气温范围	4℃ ~26℃
年平均降水量	113.8cm
年平均湿度	78.13%
年平均降雪量	9.7cm

从中国出发的航班

夏洛特·道格拉斯国际机场（CLT，Charlotte Douglas International Airport）距离学校30分钟车程，可以打车从机场前往学校。没有从中国出发的直飞航班。

杜克大学

地址：2138 CAMPUS DRIVE，DURHAM，NC 27708
网址：WWW.DUKE.EDU
中国招生官：SOLOMON ENOS
招生官电话：919-684-0175
招生官邮箱：SOLOMON.ENOS@DUKE.EDU
附近主要城市：北卡州首府罗利（达勒姆到达罗利需要三十分钟，在杜克大学和北卡教堂山大学之间有免费往返巴士可以搭乘）

最佳匹配点分析

持续稳居全美高校排名前 10，杜克大学一直以来都是全美最顶尖高校中保持“学校精神”的冠军。位于著名的“北卡研究三角区”，杜克大学的三一文理学院和普拉特工程学院给学生的是无可比拟的学术机遇。联谊会生活和对篮球的热情造就了杜克学生们的卓越成就和务实精神，同时他们又是非常具有竞争力和雄心的一群人。

Duke UNIVERSITY

学术机会

杜克的电子和生物医学工程专业实力雄厚，文理学院的生物学、神经科学、经济学和公共政策专业也非常强大。作为全美篮球名校，体育竞技精神弥漫整个校园。杜克大学的学术环境不可避免地受此影响，竞争异常激烈。一个普拉特工程学院的佳桥校友说，在杜克想要拿到 A 是“非常困难的”。杜克的这种竞争氛围成为学生们规划自己学习的动力，大家的时间安排都非常紧凑。83% 的本科生都会修双专业、辅修其他专业，或者获得某项认证证书。学校也向学生们提供了很多独特的交叉学科的学习机会，学生们还可以根据自己的兴趣设计专业。因为学校在生命科学和工程学方面的优势，杜克大学为学生们提供了很多在校内外跟随世界知名教授做研究的机会。对健康科学感兴趣的学生一定不要错过杜克，学校附近的机构提供众多医学研究方面的机会。从事研究的学生还有机会获得杜克大学创立的一些研究项目，如 TGen-Duke 生物医学未来项目（TGen-Duke Biomedical Futures Program）和霍华德·休斯研究基金（Howard Hughes Research Fellows）的资金资助。

信息速览

US News 大学排名	8
学校位置	南部
学校类型	私立
周边环境	郊区

本科学生情况

学生总数	6485 (2015)
申请人数	31186 (2015)
录取率	11% (2015)
男女学生比例	50/50
国际学生百分比	10%
亚裔百分比	22%

有本科项目的学院

三一文理学院（Trinity College of Arts and Sciences）

普拉特工程学院（Pratt School of Engineering）

你可能还想考虑以下学校

北卡罗来纳大学教堂山分校

哈佛大学　普林斯顿大学

莱斯大学　弗吉尼亚大学

职业发展

杜克大学附近的医学中心为药理学和生物化学专业的学生提供了工作机会。尽管杜克大学引以为傲的是它优秀的医学预科和健康科学，以及名声在外的工程项目，但实际上很多杜克毕业生却是在竞争激烈的金融服务和咨询领域就业。2012 年对杜克大学大四学生的调查报告显示，该届毕业生进入这两个领域的比例分别是 15.5% 和 12.1%，且大多在纽约就业，几乎占到了该届毕业学生人数的四分之一。杜克还为本科生举办多样性的社交晚宴（Diversity Networking Dinner）活动，满足一些希望加强自己机构多元化的雇主的要求，邀请如黑石集团（BlackRock）、加拿大皇家资本市场（RBC Capital Markets）和摩根大通这样的金融巨头参与其中。专家走进校园（Fannie Mitchell Expert-in-Residence）系列讲座鼓励富有成就的专家通过建立导师体系为杜克大学的学生提供关于职业方面的知识和咨询服务。

校园人文环境

杜克大学的国际生和美国学生群体都颇为多元化，白人只占学生总数的 50% 多一点。一个佳桥校友说杜克真的“非常多元化，学校有如此多来自不同国家和地区的国际学生。”

佳桥校友录取情况

录取比例	12%
SAT 阅读成绩中位数	730
SAT 数学成绩中位数	800
SAT 写作成绩中位数	765
SAT 总分中位数	2275
TOEFL 成绩中位数	115.5

财政情况

全年学费

49498 美元 (2015—2016)

经济资助可能性 非常低

学生为学校所在地区打分

安全	2.5
有趣	2
生活成本	3
中国食物	2
交通便利	3
酒吧和俱乐部	2
超市 / 便利店选择	2
周边就业市场	2.5
是否需要车	3.5
总评	3

*满分 4 分

气候

年平均气温范围	3℃ ~26℃
年平均降水量	115.4cm
年平均湿度	77.87%
年平均降雪量	10.6cm

从中国出发的航班

罗利达勒姆国际机场（RDU, Raleigh-Durham International Airport）距离学校仅 25 分钟车程。杜克在假期提供往返学校的摆渡车，也可以搭乘出租车。没有从中国出发的直飞航班到这里。

但是，不同背景的学生倾向于成立自己的小圈子。从社交层面讲，杜克学生信奉“好好学习，尽情玩乐”，这也符合学校的“冠军文化”氛围。杜克的两个主要社会活动都围绕男子篮球队——也就是大家熟知的蓝魔（Blue Devils）展开，学校的联谊会生活也非常惹人注目。很多学生会去众人皆知的“K-ville”安营扎寨，以期进入一些知名度高的篮球比赛（杜克大学的篮球队主教练“老 K 教练”Michael Krzyzewski 也是美国国家篮球队的教练，他执教杜克大学多达 30 年。在 2011 年 11 月 16 日，他成为 NCAA 篮球历史上获胜场数最多的主教练（903 场））。与其他一些精英学校相比，杜克大学的派对生活让人刮目相看，你有机会一周四天都能参加提供酒水的派对。大约 27% 的男生参加了兄弟会，42% 的女生参加了姐妹会。

录取难度

申请人数逐年递增，近几年每年有一千多名中国学生申请杜克大学，但杜克大学每年只提供三十多个新生名额给中国学生。

需要考虑的事情

你会喜欢杜克大学，如果……

- 竞争激烈的学术氛围会让你热血沸腾
- 你有学习健康科学或工程学的强烈愿望

你会不喜欢杜克大学，如果……

- 你更喜欢亲密、协作的学习氛围

埃默里大学

地址：201 DOWMAN DR，ATLANTA，GA 30322
网址：WWW.EMORY.EDU
中国招生官：SCOTT ALLEN
招生官邮箱：SCOTT.ALLEN@EMORY.EDU
招生办公室电话：404-727-6036（EMORY COLLEGE），770-784-8328（OXFORD COLLEGE）
附近主要城市：亚特兰大

最佳匹配点分析

作为一所拥有数个预科项目的中型大学，埃默里大学向来是中国留学生的热门选择。位于美国发展速度最快的城市之一——亚特兰大的郊区，埃默里大学可以提供给学生大量的校内外机会，不论是在社交、学术还是职业方面。尽管学校传统上会吸引大量的美国南方学生，但是学校的多元化和政治活跃性，以及对于世界事务的高度参与意识还是非常出名的。

学术机会

埃默里大学共分为九个学院，每个学院有自己的录取程序。埃默里大学的学生前两年在埃默里文理学院或者牛津学院学习，后两年再选择进入戈伊苏埃塔商学院、内尔霍格森伍德拉夫护理学院，或者埃默里文理学院。对商科感兴趣的学生应该认真考虑该校，因为录取的学生可以选择大二后申请商学院为期两年的项目，并且可以得到在亚特兰大

信息速览

US News 大学排名	21
学校位置	南部
学校类型	私立
周边环境	城市

本科学生情况

学生总数	7803 (2015)
申请人数	20462 (2015)
录取率	23.6% (2015, 埃默里学院) 37.5% (2015, 牛津学院)
男女学生比例	44/56
国际学生百分比	18.5%
亚裔百分比	19%

有本科项目的学院

埃默里文理学院（Emory College of Arts and Sciences）

牛津学院（Oxford College）

戈伊苏埃塔商学院（Goizueta Business School）

内尔·霍格森·伍德拉夫护理学院（Nell Hodgson Woodruff School of Nursing）

你可能还考虑以下学校

杜克大学　弗吉尼亚大学

西北大学　范德比尔特大学

华盛顿圣路易斯大学

市区金融公司实习的机会。真正想要尝试拿到戈伊苏埃塔商学院录取的学生要知道该学院素有埃默里大学最难申请项目的名声。一个在埃默里大学学习商科的佳桥校友说“拿到 A 真的非常难，商学院采用按照百分比评分的打分政策，只有 10% 的学生能拿到 A。”大二后学生也可以另外申请转学到护理学院。护理学院以及化学和生物专业的学生都可以从埃默里大学与疾病控制中心（CDC，Center of Disease Control）的良好关系中获益。申请埃默里大学的学生可以选择在亚特兰大的主校区，也可以选择先在距离主校区仅 40 英里的牛津学院进行两年的通识学习，在这里学习氛围更加亲密，之后再过渡到学校的主校区进行学习。埃默里大学的专业学科像医学预科和法律预科都有着非常好的声誉，对工程感兴趣的学生可以加入学校与佐治亚理工合作的双学位项目，该项目的学生可以获得埃默里的本科学位和佐治亚理工的工程学本科或者研究生学位。

职业发展

一般来说，埃默里大学的学生非常关注毕业后的职业发展。一个佳桥的校友说在埃默里“如果你去学校的职业中心，很容易就能找到工作机会。”埃默里同诸多亚特兰大地区机构的合作关系是它最吸引学生的一面。除了可以提供在疾病控制中心半工半读（work-study，国际学生不适用）、实习和做志愿者的机会外，全球健康学者项目（Global Health Residency Scholars Program）还可以提供给学生们在全球范围内保健领域实习的机会。另外，只要学生符合国际项目中心（Center for International Programs Abroad）列出的一些要求，学生在国外的实习就可以转成学分。埃默里大学的学术调查和研究项目（SIRE，Scholarly Inquiry and Research at Emory）可以为对研究感兴趣的学生提供资助，而夏季本科研究经历项目（SURE，Summer Undergraduate Research Experience）让学生可以在导师指导下进行研究，并可以在夏天结束时在研讨会上演讲。最近一个关于埃默里大学 2013 届毕业生的调查显示 43% 的学生毕业后进入了研究生院和专业学院，26% 的学生直接选择就业。其他的一些学生则选择国外的志愿者服务或者毕业后实习。

校园人文环境

关于埃默里大学最令学生不安的一点可能是“学校精神”的缺乏。一个佳桥校友说“学校里体育真的不大流行”，本科生在这里找不到生活焦点。不过，一些佳桥校友也会觉得埃默里是一个“ 派对学校”，因为你可以找到“任何类型的派对”。大约四分之一的男生和女生参加到联谊会生活中。兄弟会举办的几个大型活动也排在学年内，但是学生们也会在校外寻找派对机会。他们会涌入亚特兰大市区享受城市丰富的酒吧和俱乐部生活，学校有便捷的往返巴士穿梭于市区与学校间。尽管埃默里商学院的学生以“竞争”而闻名，整个埃默里大学的学生群体给人的印象是悠闲，但是“个性鲜明”以及“职业导向的”。另外，可持续性和环境保护在这里非常受重视，很多学生致力于改变生活方式以保护环境。

录取难度

埃默里大学算是 US News 全美大学排名前 20 中最好录取的一所大学了。申请牛津学院更容易被录取，分数相对低的学生可以选择这里，毕业时获得的也是埃默里大学的学位。建议学生两个校区同时申请。

需要考虑的事情

你会喜欢埃默里大学，如果……

- 你喜欢美食！亚特兰大有太多非常棒的各

佳桥校友录取情况

录取比例	13.4%
SAT 阅读成绩中位数	670
SAT 数学成绩中位数	795
SAT 写作成绩中位数	690
SAT 总分中位数	2130
TOEFL 成绩中位数	111

财政情况

全年学费

45700 美元 (2015—2016, 埃默里学院)

41000 美元 (2015—2016, 牛津学院)

经济资助可能性 低

学生为学校所在地区打分

安全	3
有趣	2.8
生活成本	2.5
中国食物	2.5
公共交通	2
酒吧和俱乐部	2
超市 / 便利店选择	2
周边就业市场	2
是否需要车	4
总评	2.8

*满分 4 分

气候

年平均气温范围	5℃ ~26℃
年平均降水量	133.4cm
年平均湿度	76.12%
年平均降雪量	2.5cm

从中国出发的航班

从学校乘坐出租车或者公共巴士需 30 分钟到一个小时到达亚特兰大哈茨菲尔德·杰克逊国际机场（ATL，Hartsfield-Jackson International Airport）。从中国没有到亚特兰大的直达航班。

种餐馆可供选择

- 你希望在校内和校外都有最完美的机会
- 你更喜欢种族多元化程度高的学校

你会不喜欢埃默里大学，如果……

- 你寻找的是拥有很多学校荣耀的大学
- 你想要找一个在美国其他地区也拥有很强大校友网的学校

乔治城大学

地址：37th AND O STREETS，NW，WASHINGTON，DC 20007
网址：WWW.GEORGETOWN.EDU
中国招生官：VANESSA J. KREBS
招生官邮箱：VJK5@GEORGETOWN.EDU
招生办公室电话：202-687-3600
附近主要城市：华盛顿特区

最佳匹配点分析

位于美国首府华盛顿特区较为富裕的地区，乔治城大学拥有世界上最富影响力的城市所能提供的数不尽的各种资源，这注定会给学生独特的大学体验。乔治城大学的学生可以近水楼台地获得各种政府机构、非政府组织和哥伦比亚特区附近商业公司的实习机会。拥有全美顶级的外交学院，乔治城大学吸引了全球众多对外交学和政治学感兴趣的顶尖人才，最主要的是学校还有匹配的强势语言项目助力。同样地，校园本身也是很多政治言论和活动的聚焦地。然而不幸的是，近年来，来自中国大陆的学生已经非常难以在该校谋得一席之地了。

学术机会

近年来乔治城大学在美国 US News 上的排名持续攀升，这一点不足为奇。乔治城大学一直因其是华盛顿特区的学术发电厂而骄傲。学校的有利位置使得乔治城大学能够在

信息速览

US News 大学排名	21
学校位置	中部大西洋地区
学校类型	私立
宗教联系	罗马天主教
周边环境	城市

本科学生情况

学生总数	7595 (2014)
申请人数	19478 (2015)
录取率	17% (2015)
男女学生比例	45/55
国际学生百分比	13.7%
亚裔百分比	9.2%

有本科项目的学院

乔治城学院（Georgetown College）

沃尔什外交学院（Walsh School of Foreign Service）

麦克多诺商学院（McDonough School of Business）

护理与健康研究学院（School of Nursing and Health Studies）

你可能还想考虑以下学校

杜克大学	波士顿学院
宾夕法尼亚大学	康奈尔大学
圣母大学	弗吉尼亚大学

各个领域招募到顶级教授，特别是在涉外事务、国际交流和商业方面。此外，乔治城大学还吸引了一大批外交官和国家元首（包括前校友比尔·克林顿）在学年期间来校园进行演讲。学校的拉菲克·B·哈里里大楼（Rafik B. Hariri Building）于2009年完工，是麦克多诺商学院最新的建筑。这座大楼拥有最先进的设备和讲演厅，同时向本科生和研究生开放，在过去的几年里也见证了商学院排名的持续上升。很多通识性的课程，像化学入门和微观经济学入门都非常受大一新生的欢迎，常常人满为患，但是大二、大三以及大四的课程通常以密切的小组讨论形式进行。

职业发展

乔治城大学最强大的校友网分布在东海岸，特别是华盛顿特区和纽约大都会地区，在旧金山和洛杉矶地区也有一些乔治城大学的校友。乔治城大学四个本科学院的很多学生毕业后都会在咨询和金融领域找到工作。与很多中型规模的美国大学一样，乔治城大学也会邀请顶尖银行机构，如花旗银行和高盛投资公司，到校举行招聘会。考利职业中心（Cawley Career Education Center）为学生们提供与职业服务专家进行模拟面试的机会，让学生们了解如何在面试中表现出自己最佳的一面。另外，也有很多校友毕业后选择进入专业学院继续深造。

校园人文环境

尽管起源于耶稣会，但乔治城大学接受有不同信仰的学生的申请，不过它在录取过程中确实会考虑学生的宗教信仰。另外，作为一所耶稣会学校，联谊会生活以及相关的活动是禁止出现在校园内的。因此，学生们一般是在大一宿舍里，通过学校200多个合作课程俱乐部，以及相关活动中认识和结交朋友。

在热门的社团组织中，举办社交活动比较出色的有The Corp（一个由学生运营的公司）、乔治城校友及学生联邦信用合作社（Georgetown University Alumni & Student Federal

Credit Union），以及一些较大的校内俱乐部和校队（它们在维持学校运动精神方面发挥着重要作用）。在冬天和春天，学生们会支持自己的国家一级篮球队 Georgetown Hoyas 的各种赛事，乔治城大学篮球队一度产生过多位 NBA 专业球员。

距离华盛顿特区的喧闹繁华和市中心如此近，学生们拥有得天独厚的优势享受周边的各种酒吧和餐馆。很多这些休闲场所距离学生的住地步行就能到达，非常方便。

尽管乔治城大学有着广泛的国际学生群体，但是近年来经常被冠以培养了很多"势利眼"的名声。很多学生自诩为来自美国东北部的富裕家庭，有些甚至坚称这些精英主义者参与的很多独家派对和酒吧活动最终会主宰学校的社交场景。

录取难度

乔治城大学不是那么相信中国学生的成绩单（之前出现过多起伪造成绩单的丑闻），因此，录取的中国学生也很少。近年来他们开始增加在中国的录取名额，但今后的录取态势难以预测。

需要考虑的事情

你会喜欢乔治城大学，如果……

- 你希望去一个拥有很多荣耀的学校，特别是在篮球方面
- 你对国际关系、外交事务或者外交学感兴趣
- 你对学年内的实习机会有兴趣

你会不喜欢乔治城大学，如果……

- 一想到"学院派"（preppiness）风格你就会感到难堪
- 你更喜欢一个安静的乡村格调的校园。虽然不是纽约，但是华盛顿特区还是有一些吵闹

佳桥校友录取情况

录取比例	27%
SAT 阅读成绩中位数	770
SAT 数学成绩中位数	800
SAT 写作成绩中位数	710
SAT 总分中位数	2200
TOEFL 成绩中位数	109

财政情况

全年学费

48048 美元 (2015—2016)

经济资助可能性　　非常低

学生为学校所在地区打分

安全	2.5
有趣	3
生活成本	4
中国食物	2.5
交通便利	3.5
酒吧和俱乐部	3
超市 / 便利店选择	3
周边就业市场	3
是否需要车	1.5
总评	3

*满分 4 分

气候

年平均气温范围	0℃ ~25℃
年平均降水量	107cm
年平均湿度	76.56%
年平均降雪量	44.5cm

从中国出发的航班

从北京有直飞航班到达华盛顿杜勒斯国际机场（IAD，Dulles International Airport），但机场到学校的交通不是特别方便。

佐治亚理工学院

地址：225 NORTH AVE NW，ATLANTA，GA 30332
网址：WWW.GATECH.EDU
中国招生官：ANDREA JESTER
招生官邮箱：ANDREA.JESTER@ADMISSION.GATECH.EDU
招生办公室电话：404-894-4154
附近主要城市：亚特兰大

最佳匹配点分析

尽管也提供人文学科教育，并且拥有出色的建筑和管理学相关专业，但佐治亚理工学院最为人们所熟知的还是其大名鼎鼎的工程类专业。学校位于亚特兰大市中心，拥有优越的地理位置。如果学生们愿意接受这里闷热的夏季、紧张的课业负担，以及不是完全安全的城市环境，那么他们在这里可以接受到顶尖的技术教育。

学术机会

佐治亚理工学院的课业以充满挑战出名，很多学生需要五年才能拿到学位。佳桥的校友也对这点表示认同，认为佐治亚理工学院的课程相当难，但是如果努力学习也是可以把控的。他们说有些课程是由助教来上课的，特定的一些入门课程，像微积分和计算机科学的上课人数都非常多，但是通过办公时间会面、邮件甚至 Skype 的方式都能很容易地接触到教授。由于学校实行的是按照百分比评分的政策，加上学业压力本身就很大，所以竞争还是非常激烈的。本科生也有不少参加研究项目的机会，学校的佐治亚理工研究所（Georgia Tech Research Institute）会为大约40%的研究项目提供资金支持。佐治亚理工学院为学生们提供了十种交叉学科的学习项目，同附近主要的大学也有合作项目，比如同埃默里大学的3-2合作办学项目。

职业发展

坐落在亚特兰大这样的大都市中心，又是众所周知的名校，佐治亚理工学院为学生们提供了相当丰富的实习和工作机会。学校的本科生合作教育项目（Undergraduate Cooperative Education Program）尤其出名。这是一个五年的项目，参加该项目的学生在不同学期可以选择在学校学习或全职工作，从而可以在完成本科学位学习的同时获得有价值的工作经验。佐治亚理工学院的校友们以地区或者相同的兴趣为基础建立了强大的校友网络，校友组织为校友提供终生职业指导。

校园人文环境

佐治亚理工学院的学生深谙努力学习、尽情娱乐的道理，他们会利用周末尽情放松，疏解平时学习的压力。一位佳桥校友说，校园里有很多联谊会举办的派对可以参加（兄弟会和姐妹会分别吸引到学校23%的男生和29%的女生）。学校的体育赛事也吸引到不少学生的关注，尤其是佐治亚理工学院的橄榄球队和篮球校队。得益于亚特兰大市中心的有利位置，学生们有非常丰富的校外活动和娱乐项目可以挖掘。但是需要提醒的是，学生们需要特别注意自身安全，因为学校周边的一些地方并不是特别安全，车辆盗窃和持械抢劫事件时有发生。但是总体说来，佳桥校友反映学校大部分时候还是让人感到安全的。至于多样性，佳桥校友表示校园的多样性还是令人满意的，他们经常会和不同国家、不同文化背景的同学合作完成课堂项目。

信息速览

US News 大学排名	36
学校位置	南部
学校类型	公立
周边环境	城市

本科学生情况

学生总数	15142 (2015)
申请人数	27270 (2015)
录取率	32% (2015)
男女学生比例	65/35
国际学生百分比	11%
亚裔美国人百分比	19.8%

有本科项目的学院

建筑学院（College of Architecture）
计算机学院（College of Computing）
工程学院（College of Engineering）
理学院（College of Sciences）
舍勒商学院（Scheller College of Business)
伊万·艾伦文理学院（Ivan Allen College of Liberal Arts）

你可能还考虑以下学校

杜克大学　埃默里大学
密歇根大学　弗吉尼亚理工大学

佳桥校友录取情况

录取比例	19%
SAT 阅读成绩中位数	640
SAT 数学成绩中位数	800
SAT 写作成绩中位数	695
SAT 总分中位数	2135
TOEFL 成绩中位数	106

财政情况

全年学费

45972 美元 (2015—2016)

经济资助可能性 无

学生为学校所在地区打分

安全	2
有趣	3
生活成本	1
中国食物	3
交通便利	2
酒吧和俱乐部	2
超市 / 便利店选择	3
周边就业市场	3
是否需要车	4
总评	3

*满分 4 分

气候

年平均气温范围	5℃ ~26℃
年平均降水量	133.4cm
年平均湿度	76%
年平均降雪量	2.5cm

从中国出发的航班

从中国没有直达亚特兰大的航班。学生需要转机才能到达。到达离学校最近的哈兹菲尔德—杰克逊国际机场（Hartsfield-Jackson International Airport）后，学生可以搭乘火车或者的士到达学校。

录取难度

很多没有进入莱斯大学、康奈尔大学、麻省理工学院、约翰•霍普金斯大学等顶尖工程学院的学生，往往把佐治亚理工学院作为他们的中间档或保底学校。注意，由于申请者越来越多，佐治亚理工学院已经开始拒绝一些优秀的申请者了，现在你也许需要将它列为你的梦想学校了。

需要考虑的事情

你会喜欢佐治亚理工学院，如果……

- 你想要去一个团队精神非常强的学校
- 你对工程学非常感兴趣
- 你想在城市生活

你会不喜欢佐治亚理工学院，如果……

- 你不喜欢炎热的气候
- 你想要同教授保持亲密的关系
- 你不想要一个竞争激烈的环境

哈佛大学

地址：86 BRATTLE STREET，CAMBRIDGE，MA 02138
网址：WWW.HARVARD.EDU
中国招生官：无
招生办公室电话：617-495-1551
招生办公室邮箱：学生可以在 HTTPS：//COLLEGE.HARVARD.EDU/CONTACT-US 上提出问题、查看答案
附近主要城市：波士顿，从市中心搭乘出租车或者地铁只要十分钟时间

最佳匹配点分析

哈佛大学是最优秀的人才与最渴望知识的头脑相会的地方。那些想要见识学术界名人的学生毋庸置疑应该来这里，而那些想要得到更多教授关注的学生则可能需要另寻他处。这里到处是金钱和高级俱乐部，学生们来到这里应当学会超然物外，或者做好充分准备融入其中。那些想要进入金融行业的学生会发现哈佛的校友网非常有用。

学术机会

在哈佛，你很难不充满动力，因为你身边是 21 世纪最聪明的一群人。这里的教授成就卓著，甚至助教也都硕果累累，学生们对他们充满敬畏。但是想要抓住一个与这些令人敬仰的教授见面的机会还是颇为困难的。不过学校安排有学术建议时间，架起了教授和学生之间沟通的桥梁。成绩膨胀现象可能存在，学生们可以很容易地拿到 B+，而 A 和 C 却不易拿到。

信息速览

US News 大学排名	2
学校位置	东北
学校类型	私立
周边环境	城市

本科学生情况

学生总数	6700 (2014)
申请人数	37307 (2015)
录取率	5.6% (2015)
男女学生比例	53/47
国际学生百分比	12.2%
亚裔美国人百分比	21.3%

有本科项目的学院

工程和应用科学学院（School of Engineering and Applied Sciences）
哈佛本科学院（Harvard College）

你可能还考虑以下学校

普林斯顿大学　达特茅斯学院
耶鲁大学　宾夕法尼亚大学
哥伦比亚大学

哈佛的东亚研究项目广受赞誉，但是它显然不是唯一一个课程丰富又充满创新的专业。很多系都有非常现代化的设施，可以为它们的学生提供丰富的资源。像视觉艺术系就为学生们提供免费的美术用品，摄影工作室则总是向学生们开放。对生物感兴趣的学生在哈佛有 5 个小方向可以选择，这样学生们就可以学得更加专一。学校还设置了一个数学 55 课程，该课程将 4 年的数学课程压缩到一年来学习，这些都充分显示了学校为求知若渴的学生们提供了多么广泛的选择空间。交叉登记（Cross-registration）可以让学生们有机会在麻省理工学院上课。学习的过程是专为那些爱冒险的学生们设计的。注册课程前学生们有一周的课程筛选时间，Q-guide 会提供往届学生的评价参考。哈佛大学的校友捐赠额全美排名最高（尽管普林斯顿大学的人均捐赠数额最多），这意味着学校提供给学生的资源是源源不断的。

职业发展

从对 2013 届毕业生的调查数据来看，61% 的学生毕业后即被聘用，18% 选择继续攻读研究生。在被雇佣的学生中 16% 选择了咨询行业，15% 选择了金融领域。哈佛大学本科阶段没有商科专业的事实并没有阻挡它的毕业生进入这些领域。想要留在东海岸的中国留学生可以在那里找到一大批哈佛校友。工程和技术领域专业毕业生也收入颇丰。

当被问到 10 年内的职业发展前景的时候，有 20% 的学生想要在健康领域有所建树，11% 想要在艺术和娱乐行业发展，9% 希望在政府部门工作。哈佛毕业生的平均年薪是 60000 美元。校友非常活跃，每隔五年会回母校重聚。

校园人文环境

大概没有人会对波士顿充满文化和激情的环境感到不满，市区距离学校所在的剑桥仅十分钟路程。多达 80 个学校的学生们会在周末涌向波士顿，所以周边的小镇都会有足够多的事情可以做。但是马萨诸塞州关于饮酒的法律非常严格，因此不要试图携带伪造的身份证明买酒。另外，在冬天，这里也很难看到太阳。

哈佛的住宿体系不是典型的大学模式，但是却非常紧密地将学生们联系在一起。大一新生会在开学初期被分配好住宿，但是到了大二他们就可以自行决定接下来的三年与哪八个人住在一起。每个人都喜欢住在校内，而且真的每个人都住在校内，不过宿舍和设施会相对古老一些。

尽管不像一些州立大学那样派对盛行，但是饮酒也是非常热门的一项娱乐活动。在被调查的 2013 届大四学生中，25% 的学生每周饮酒超过两次，只有 9% 表示从不饮酒，7% 每月会喝一次。在同一批学生中，有 38% 表示吸过大麻，25% 表示偶尔为之，16% 表示尝试过更加刺激的毒品类化学物。哈佛大学不承认正式的联谊会，但一些非官方的联谊会群体还是存在的。在剑桥，Finals Clubs 是闪光灯的聚焦点。这些俱乐部是哈佛大学的一些非常排外的秘密俱乐部，他们会邀请大二和大一的学生参加考验期（punch season），这些学生会受到俱乐部成员的考核以决定是否有资格入会。这些俱乐部有时候也会举办一些学校非会员学生可以参加的派对活动，俱乐部的成员中有 10% 的男性和 5% 的女性会参加。排外是很多哈佛大学俱乐部的通性，不止 Finals Clubs 是这样。多样化在校园里不成问题，因为 6% 的学生群体是非洲裔美国人，21% 是亚裔，8% 是西班牙裔，还有 12% 的国际学生。学生的思想大多都自由开放。

录取难度

作为全美最顶尖的院校之一（正如 US News 显示的那样），每年只有不到 6% 的申请者会被录取，被录取的中国学生更是寥寥无几。没有保证你录取的魔法公式。

佳桥校友录取情况

录取比例	4.8%
SAT 阅读成绩中位数	770
SAT 数学成绩中位数	800
SAT 写作成绩中位数	800
SAT 总分中位数	2370
TOEFL 成绩中位数	116

财政情况

全年学费

45278 美元 (2015—2016)

经济资助可能性 高

学生为学校所在地区打分

安全	3.5
有趣	3
生活成本	3
中国食物	3
交通便利	4
酒吧和俱乐部	3
超市 / 便利店选择	3
周边就业市场	3.5
是否需要车	1
总评	4

*满分 4 分

气候

年平均气温范围	-3℃ ~23℃
年平均降水量	122cm
年平均湿度	69.8%
年平均降雪量	129cm

从中国出发的航班

学生们可以选择从首都国际机场、浦东国际机场或者香港国际机场直飞波士顿洛根国际机场的航班。打车从波士顿洛根国际机场到学校 (BOS, Logan International Airport) 只需 15 分钟。

需要考虑的事情

你会喜欢哈佛大学，如果……

- 当教授太忙的时候，你能独立学习。
- 你喜欢波士顿周边地区
- 对于你来说，学术成就要比娱乐声望更重要

你会不喜欢哈佛大学，如果……

- 你喜欢社交生活更加丰富的学校
- 温和的气候条件是你考虑大学的一个因素
- 你不喜欢寒冷的气候

哈维 · 穆德学院

地址：KINGSTON HALL，301 PLATT BOULEVARD，CLAREMONT，CA 91711
网址：WWW.HMC.EDU
中国招生官：PETER OSGOOD
招生办公室电话：909-621-8011
招生官邮箱：POSGOOD@HMC.EDU
附近主要城市：洛杉矶，乘火车从洛杉矶国际机场到达哈维 • 穆德学院约 45 分钟

最佳匹配点分析

哈维 • 穆德学院是那种可以接收任何类型学生的学校，但是未必所有学生都喜欢这里。拥有不同爱好、性情，和古怪之处的学生在这里都会如鱼得水；但是如果你的思想不够开放，那么不要来这里。哈维 • 穆德学院的宗旨是培养数学家、科学家和工程师。通过哈维 • 穆德学院涵盖人文学科和社会学科的综合教育，他们非常清楚自己对世界将要产生的影响。不管你是希望通过学术，还是职业途径在科学道路上取得成就，哈维 • 穆德学院都不会令你失望。不过如果你对学习 STEM 学科不是那么认真，那么就不要选择哈维穆德。

学术机会

哈维 • 穆德学院只有六个专业（物理、数学、工程、化学、生物、计算机科学）和三个联合专业（数学与生物、计算机科学与数学、数学与计算生物学），简单得一分钟就能记住。但这种简单很具有迷惑性，这点从一个普通的“穆德人”（Mudders，哈维 • 穆德学院的学生总是骄傲地这样称呼自己）毕业前需要完成的课程上就能看出来。核心课

信息速览

US News 文理学院排名	14
学校位置	西海岸
学校类型	私立
周边环境	郊区

本科学生情况

学生总数	815 (2015)
申请人数	4119 (2015)
录取率	13% (2015)
男女学生比例	54/46
国际学生百分比	13%
亚裔美国人百分比	20%

你可能还考虑以下学校

麻省理工学院
罗斯霍曼理工学院
加州理工学院
卡内基梅隆大学
莱斯大学
富兰克林•欧林工程学院

程要求学生必须在数学、科学和工程领域选择三分之一的课程，同时另三分之一必须是人文学科、艺术和社会科学方面的课程。在哈维•穆德学院的历史上仅有 7 个学生曾经拿到过 4.0 的 GPA，成绩膨胀在这里根本不存在。每个哈维•穆德的学生都有参加研究的经历，大部分都完成了学校独有的实践项目（Clinic Program）或者毕业生论文。Clinic Program 是学校的标志性项目，大部分集中在工程、计算机、物理和数学领域。参加该项目的学生会合作完成一个由公司给出的项目。通常这些公司之后会从这些项目组里招聘自己需要的人才。由于在校学生人数不多，所有的教授都会记住你的名字甚至其他的事情，不管你是不是他们班里的学生。每年夏季都会有 200 名学生参与研究项目。另外因为哈维•穆德学院是克莱尔蒙特联盟（Claremont Consortium）的成员之一，所以学生们可以自由选修其他联盟学院的课程。

职业发展

据说哈维•穆德学院的毕业生拥有全美最高的起薪。大约 63% 的学生毕业后选择工作，30% 选择继续硕士或博士教育，4% 成为研究员。很多选择继续深造的学生直接进入了博士项目。数学、物理和化学是哈维•穆德学院最热门的专业。参加克莱尔蒙特联盟职业招聘会的雇主中有 41% 的招聘目标锁定哈维穆德学院的毕业生。微软、太空探索技术公司（SpaceX）、Yakima 环境学习基金会（Yelp）、芬威克和韦斯特律师事务所（Fenwick and West LLP），以及霍尼韦尔公司（Honeywell）等都非常看重训练有素的穆德人。

校园人文环境

独立的宿舍使得学生可以形成自己的集体文化。每个宿舍都有自己的个性特点和派对风格，因此学生间容易形成更亲密的关系。每个学年开始前，学生们都要填写一份 3 页纸的关于宿舍选择的调查问卷，而学校也总能帮助学生们找到匹配的宿舍。校园内饮酒政策比较宽松，在联盟的五个成员学院中，哈维•穆德学院的派对水平名声在外，派对主题非常吸引人。克莱蒙特地区没有太多娱乐项目，因此学生们习惯在校园里找乐子。

对于校园文化多元性方面的缺失，哈维•穆德从来不回避，而且做出许多努力去改善这一状况。校园中大约有 2% 的非洲裔美国人，20% 的亚裔美国人，10% 的西班牙裔，13% 的国际学生和 44% 的白人。学校的整体学习氛围自由，学生在政治上不活跃。女生占 46%，男生占 54%，这对于一个以 STEM 项目见长的大学来说，女生比例算是很高了（从历史上来看，比例也是很高的了）。如果你想要去一个鼓励正式约会文化的学校，那么来哈维 • 穆德吧。传统在校园中遍地开花，在这里不要为学生的奇装异服和古怪性格感到大惊小怪。你会经常邂逅穿裙子的男生，淡定。

录取难度

哈维 • 穆德学院是一所小型的大学，只有 13% 的国际生，因此每年国际学生的招生数量非常有限。女生申请会比男生更容易获得录取，因为哈维 • 穆德学院希望它的学生性别比例更加均衡。成功的申请者需要证明他们深谙小型社区校园文化的价值所在，以及学校特有的联盟成员身份可以为 STEM 学生带来的机遇。

需要考虑的事情

你会喜欢哈维 • 穆德学院，如果……

- 你是一个男生，但经常有尝试穿裙子的想法
- 你喜欢小型社区集体的亲密氛围
- 吸毒和酒精自由对你来说很有吸引力
- 你想从 STEM 的相关研究中得到更多

你会不喜欢哈维 • 穆德学院，如果……

- 你不喜欢也无法认同书呆子
- 相对于通力合作的学习氛围你更喜欢竞争激烈的学习氛围
- 校园优美对你来说至关重要

佳桥校友录取情况

录取比例	22.7%
SAT 阅读成绩中位数	740
SAT 数学成绩中位数	800
SAT 写作成绩中位数	785
SAT 总分中位数	2310
TOEFL 成绩中位数	116

财政情况

全年学费	52383 美元 (2016—2017)
经济资助可能性	低

学生为学校所在地区打分

安全	3
有趣	4
生活成本	3
中国食物	1
交通便利	2
酒吧和俱乐部	2
超市 / 便利店选择	1
周边就业市场	2
是否需要车	3
总评	2

*满分 4 分

气候

年平均气温范围	11℃ ~25℃
年平均降水量	58.7cm
年平均湿度	81.87%
年平均降雪量	0cm

从中国出发的航班

从中国有直达洛杉矶国际机场（LAX，Los Angeles International Airport）的航班，而从机场到哈维 • 穆德学院只需要不到一小时。学生可以选择从香港、北京或者上海出发。

哈弗福德学院

地址：370 W LANCASTER AVE，HAVERFORD，PA 19041
网址：WWW.HAVERFORD.EDU
中国招生官：SONIA GIEBEL
招生官邮箱：SGIEBEL@HAVERFORD.EDU
招生办公室电话：610-896-1350
附近主要城市：费城，学生们可以乘坐 SEPTA 通勤火车到达学校，大概需要 30 分钟

最佳匹配点分析

希望去一个小型并且距离大城市只有通勤距离的文理学院的学生应该考虑哈弗福德学院。从这里乘火车到费城只需要 30 分钟，它距离著名的女子学院布林莫尔学院也非常近。因为距离优势，这两个学院允许学生们在任一学校上课或者选修专业。只有一千多人的校园使得每个精英学生之间都能进行紧密的课堂交流互动，而不会产生竞争的压迫感。因为有非常深厚的贵格会传统（尽管现在学校已经没有宗教倾向），哈弗福德学院对于自身的学术和社会荣誉准则都非常看重。荣誉准则给了学生们许多自律机会，包括可以在家完成的期末考试和未成年饮酒的自我管理等。荣誉准则也不是一成不变的，学生们每年都会对它进行调整。

学术机会

哈弗福德学院一直以自己是文理学院而骄傲，因此学校“拿到学位的要求”或者课

程设置的初衷都是让学生们了解更多的学科。除了第一学年对写作课程以及对除英语外的第二门语言有两个学期的学习要求外，哈弗福德学院的学生还必须在人文学科、社会科学和自然科学领域各修完最少三门课程。哈弗福德学院的优势专业包括生物学、物理学、英语、历史、政治和经济，学生们也可以自己设计跨学科专业。学生到邻近的斯沃斯莫尔学院和宾夕法尼亚大学学习的机会也非常多。学校仍然保持着严格的学术氛围，对成绩膨胀十分抵触。75% 的教授住在校内，你可以容易地接触到教授并且得到他们的个人关注。在这里学生与教授保持着良好的个人关系，而教授也经常鼓励学生们参加本科生研究项目。学校的人文艺术中心（Center for the Arts and Humanities）和 Koshland 综合自然科学研究中心（Koshland Integrated Natural Sciences Center）也会为本科生提供研究补助、暑期研究项目奖学金及旅行研究补助。

信息速览

US News 文理学院排名	12
学校位置	东北
学校类型	私立
周边环境	郊区

本科学生情况

学生总数	1194 (2015)
申请人数	3468 (2015)
录取率	24.6% (2015)
男女学生比例	47/53
国际学生百分比	11.4%
亚裔百分比	14%

你可能还考虑以下学校

阿姆赫斯特学院	布朗大学
斯沃斯莫尔学院	宾夕法尼亚大学
卫斯理大学	塔夫茨大学

职业发展

由于学院本身规模较小，所以哈弗福德学院的校友网也比较小。但是福德人很愿意帮助他们的校友留意和提供相关的招聘信息，特别是在费城、华盛顿特区、纽约、波士顿以及加州地区。费城可以为哈弗福德的毕业生提供非常好的就业市场。2013 届毕业生中，有 53% 的毕业生直接就业，16% 选择继续读研究生。科学和教育领域是该届毕业生就业最多的领域，分别占 22% 和 21%。想要读数学和科学方面研究生的学生在哈弗福德可以占得先机，有 23% 的毕业生选择在数学和科学领域继续读书。尽管哈弗福德学院没有本科生研究项目，但是它与宾夕法尼亚大学有合作的 4+1 工程项目，与加州理工学院有合作的 3/2 工程项目。

校园人文环境

人们通常认为哈弗福德的学生专心学术，但是他们往往忽略了一点：超过三分之一的福德人是大学水准的运动员。不过事实上学校的运动场景相当匮乏，大部分学生都会缺席黑松鼠队（学校运动队）的比赛。但仍然会有很多学生选择校内运动项目来疏解繁重的课业压力。在饮酒和吸毒方面学生们需要自觉遵守荣誉准则，因此相对同类院校要

佳桥校友录取情况

录取比例	20%
SAT 阅读成绩中位数	700
SAT 数学成绩中位数	800
SAT 写作成绩中位数	750
SAT 总分中位数	2250
TOEFL 成绩中位数	113

财政情况

全年学费	48656 美元 (2015—2016)
经济资助可能性	低

学生为学校所在地区打分

安全	3.5
有趣	1.5
生活成本	2.5
中国美食	1
公共交通	1.5
酒吧和俱乐部	2
超市 / 便利店选择	2
周边就业市场	1.5
是否需要车	3
总评	2.5

*满分 4 分

气候

年平均气温范围	-2℃ ~24℃
年平均降水量	117cm
年平均湿度	71.72%
年平均降雪量	49.8cm

从中国出发的航班

当地的国内机场距离学校非常近，而费城国际机场（PHL，Philadelphia International Airport）距离学校有 25 分钟路程。两者都没有来自中国的直达航班，但是到学校的公共交通都很便宜。

自由一些。大部分时候，哈弗福德没有很多派对，但周末晚上通常会有派对，也会有哈弗福德学院、布林莫尔学院和斯沃斯莫尔学院共同举办的一些活动，不过这些都不算是学校有象征性的文化传统。兄弟会和姐妹会也不被学校允许。因为学校太小了，举办派对的人往往会发现进出参加的都是同一拨人。哈弗福德小镇非常安静，也相当安全，但夜生活非常有限。不过，距离学校只有几站火车路程的费城可以为那些想要体验美式城市生活的学生们提供绝佳场所。哈弗福德的学生也向往校外学习的机会，超过 50% 的学生会选择参加国外学习项目。

录取难度

哈弗福德学院在中国的招生录取非常挑剔苛刻。高分从来不会保证被录取。但和其他顶级文理学院相比，哈弗福德学院容易录取一点。

需要考虑的事情

你会喜欢哈弗福德学院，如果……

- 你希望去一个小型的学校，可以得到教授很多关注
- 信任在你的道德准则中是非常重要的一点。哈弗福德学院的荣誉准则非常看重对学生的信任
- 你对数学和自然科学非常感兴趣

你会不喜欢哈弗福德学院，如果……

- 你对学校的运动队抱有很大憧憬
- 你自称是派对达人，并且总是在寻找快节奏的氛围

约翰·霍普金斯大学

地址：3400 N. CHARLES STREET，BALTIMORE，MD 21218
网址：WWW.JHU.EDU
中国招生官：JESSE TOMCZAK
招生官邮箱：JESSE.TOMCZAK@JHU.EDU
招生办公室电话：410-516-8171
附近主要城市：巴尔的摩

最佳匹配点分析

一直以来，约翰·霍普金斯大学都因为拥有全美顶尖的医学预科项目而闻名遐迩，但申请者也应该关注它久负盛名的国际研究项目。约翰·霍普金斯大学不适合那些胆小的人，因为在自然科学方面想要拿到好成绩的竞争异常激烈，学校近年来在成绩评价上也越来越严。一位佳桥校友表示学校的种族多样化程度还是很高的，“20% 的学生是亚裔”，但是“从另一种意义上说又不是那么多样化，因为有一半的学生希望将来成为医生”。除了学校提供的大量独立研究机会之外，巴尔的摩这座城市也为学生们提供了很好的平台，帮助他们得到与自身研究领域相关的宝贵工作经验。

学术机会

约翰·霍普金斯大学意识到学校高强度的学习会给学生造成诸多压力，因此也采取了一些缓和措施，比如学生第一学期的成绩采用“满意”和“不满意”的打分政策，从而帮助新生更好地过渡。学校的生物科学相关专业声名远播，特别是生物学和生物医学

信息速览

US News 大学排名	10
学校位置	中部大西洋
学校类型	私立
周边环境	城市

本科学生情况

学生总数	5299 (2015)
申请人数	24718 (2015)
录取率	13.2% (2015)
男女学生比例	51/49
国际学生百分比	10.4%
亚裔百分比	19.7%

有本科项目的学院

克里格文理学院（Krieger School of Arts and Sciences）
怀廷工程学院（Whiting School of Engineering）
凯里商学院（Carey Business School）
皮博迪音乐学院（Peabody Institute）

你可能还想考虑以下学校

康奈尔大学　宾夕法尼亚大学
布朗大学　哈佛大学
杜克大学

工程专业。那些在国际研究领域有强烈学习欲望的学生可以深入研究一下该校在国际研究方面的交叉学科专业，因为它可以综合约翰·霍普金斯大学多所卫星校园的教学资源和优势，比如华盛顿特区、意大利博洛尼亚和中国南京校园。因为学校非常注重研究生教育，一个佳桥的校友说教授一般都“不是那么容易接近，但是研究生助教都非常友好，他们都愿意跟你交朋友”。即便如此，进行独立研究项目的大量本科生还是会得到教授和研究生的帮助。学校的本科生独立研究可以得到很多项目的资金支持，如院长本科研究奖（Provost's Undergraduate Research Awards）和伍德罗·威尔逊本科研究奖学金计划（Woodrow Wilson Undergraduate Research Fellowship Program）。生物学、生物物理学、化学和工程学的实验室以及约翰·霍普金斯医学院的很多系都会定期向符合条件的本科生开放研究机会。这些研究都有足够的生物学背景，学生们可以由此获得生物学的学分。

职业发展

近年来约翰·霍普金斯大学的毕业生无论是在就业领域还是在继续深造高等教育方面都表现不俗。根据学校网站数据显示，2012 届毕业生中 46% 的学生在毕业后半年内即获得了全职工作，35% 的学生升入研究生院或者专业学院继续深造。2006 年到 2012 年期间，约翰·霍普金斯大学申请美国医学院的毕业生中有 80% 获得了录取；而在 2012 年申请季中，超过 83% 的申请人被一所或多所美国法学院录取，这些数据都远远超过全美平均水平。怀廷工程学院职业中心的工作人员向来以指导其毕业生进入理想的就业领域而闻名，正如学校官网介绍所说，97% 的工程学院毕业生在毕业前都参加过至少一项以就业为导向的指导项目。约翰·霍普金斯大学目前拥有 186000 名在世的校友，所以学生发现在美国东海岸热门城市就业非常容易，特别是在巴尔的摩、华盛顿特区和纽约这几个城市。

校园人文环境

约翰·霍普金斯大学的校园种族多样化还是非常出色的，但是中国留学生的人数却并不很多。一位佳桥校友说:“中国留学生真的非常少，这在某种意义上也算一种优势。但是我的大部分朋友都是美籍华人。”学校的男子长曲棍球队是传统体育强项，一度在校园里掀起体育热潮，但是与其他学校优秀的国家一级篮球和橄榄球校队相比又逊色很多。鉴于学生们都以学习为乐，学校里的“派对场景要比其他学校的小很多，有派对也通常是联谊会举办的”。一个佳桥校友说道。约会也不是那么常见，因为大家都“太忙了”。学校食物的选择和多样化也不太有吸引力，很多中国留学生只能满足于“美式菜肴”。虽然如此，学生们仍然有很多课外活动选择，像划独木舟或者俱乐部休闲运动等。

录取难度

职业目标明确并且有相关经验的学生申请时会更加有利。想要申请工程学院的学生需要付出更多努力。学校还是比较看重 SAT 成绩的，录取的平均分数在 2200 分到 2300 分之间。

需要考虑的事情

你会喜欢约翰·霍普金斯大学，如果……

- 你对健康科学、工程或国际研究感兴趣
- 在竞争的环境里你更容易成功
- 你愿意牺牲自己的社交生活来成全更高的学术追求

你会不喜欢约翰·霍普金斯大学，如果……

- 你视高等教育为一种寻求合作的机会
- 你是美食控！约翰·霍普金斯的餐饮出名地差
- 你对本科研究不感兴趣，因为你的大部分同学将会在这里进行自己的研究项目

佳桥校友录取情况

录取比例	10.1%
SAT 阅读成绩中位数	720
SAT 数学成绩中位数	800
SAT 写作成绩中位数	780
SAT 总分中位数	2190
TOEFL 成绩中位数	115

财政情况

全年学费	48710 美元 (2015—2016)
经济资助可能性	非常低

学生为学校所在地区打分

安全	1
有趣	2
生活成本	2
中国食物	1
交通便利	2
酒吧和俱乐部	1
超市 / 便利店选择	2
周边就业市场	1.5
是否需要车	4
总评	2

*满分 4 分

气候

年平均气温范围	-1℃ ~25℃
年平均降水量	108.6cm
年平均湿度	70.28%
年平均降雪量	56.9cm

从中国出发的航班

假期和年末都有穿梭巴士往返于学校和巴尔的摩华盛顿国际机场（BWI，Baltimore Washington International Airport）之间，从机场搭乘出租车到学校需要 30 美元。从中国没有直飞航班到巴尔的摩。

马卡莱斯特学院

地址：1600 GRAND AVENUE，ST. PAUL，MN 55105
网址：WWW.MACALESTER.EDU
中国招生官：STEVE COLEE
招生办公室邮箱：INTERNATIONALADMISSIONS@MACALESTER.EDU
招生办公室电话：800-231-7974
附近主要城市：明尼阿波利斯，圣•保罗

最佳匹配点分析

马卡莱斯特学院以其较高的国际学生比例而闻名，所以中国学生在这里不用担心找不到可以相处的群体。决定入读这所学校的学生应该带着他们的人造皮毛外套来，众所周知，明尼苏达的气候并不温暖宜人。对于那些期待充实派对生活的学生们来说，马卡莱斯特学院不适合你。但那些寻求小班上课和教授关注的学生们可以来这所优秀的大学。

MACALESTER COLLEGE

学术机会

马卡莱斯特向学生提供38个专业，另外给予学生设计他们自己跨学科项目的机会，但是它的一些学术优势在于与其他学校的良好合作。学校提供给学生很多职业预科培训项目，这些项目是同华盛顿圣路易斯大学合作开展的，允许学生们参加法律预科、医学预科、合作办学的建筑学以及工程学等学科的学习。而且马卡莱斯特学院还是双城大学联盟（Associated Colleges of the Twin Cities Consortium）的成员之一，这意味着该校学生有机会在联盟内其他成员学校学习。大约有 60% 的学生会参加学校的国外学习项目。让学校多元化和培养学生的文化意识一直以来都是学校的办学宗旨。

另外学生们还可以通过学校的马卡莱斯特日本屋项目（Macalester's Japanese House）了解日本文化。这个项目鼓励学生与日语为母语者一起生活，从而培养对日语的熟悉程度。该项目也举办了一些与日本文化相关的活动，比如说电影之夜和烹饪交流会。

佳桥的学生说："想要找到教授真的非常容易。" 平均只有 17 人的小班授课让课堂气氛非常亲密，教授会认识每一位学生。但是说到学校的成绩系统，他们说："大部分课上只有 10% 的学生可以拿到 A，大部分课程不采用百分比记分。" 经济系因为课程挑战性比较大被单独列出。几乎所有的佳桥校友们大部分的时间都花在了学业上，他们中的绝大多数都认为学生之间的竞争非常激烈但同时也非常激励人。社会科学、生物学和外国语言是学校最出色的几个系。

信息速览

US News 文理学院排名	23
学校位置	中西部
学校类型	私立
周边环境	郊区

本科学生情况

学生总数	2,073 (2014)
申请人数	6031 (2015)
录取率	39% (2015)
男女学生比例	39/61
国际学生百分比	14%
亚裔美国人百分比	11.6%

你可能还考虑以下学校

卡尔顿学院	科罗拉多学院
格林尼尔学院	波莫纳学院
明德学院	布朗大学

职业发展

不出所料，在这所以学术资源优势闻名的明尼苏达州的小型院校中，有 60% 的学生在毕业后的 5 年内都继续深造了研究生，因此马卡莱斯特学院素有"研究生工厂"的美誉。很多学生最后会进入非常优秀的研究生院。

每年都会有三分之二的学生完成他们的实习，这些实习机会主要分布在非营利性机构、政府部门、教育行业和艺术机构。很多学生毕业后被 AmeriCorps，瑞士信贷（Credit Suisse）、Clearwater Action、惠普、摩根大通、微软和 Teach for America 聘用。佳桥校友普遍认为学校的校友网很有效，但是也有个别学生表示"学校的校友网不如一些有基督教背景的学院"。

校园人文环境

在马卡莱斯特学院，24% 的学生是有色人种，女性学生占大多数，14% 的学生是国际学生。一个学生说："在这里我交了很多朋友，非洲、欧洲、南美洲和亚洲的都有。" 每

佳桥校友录取情况

录取比例	29.6%
SAT 阅读成绩中位数	690
SAT 数学成绩中位数	790
SAT 写作成绩中位数	690
SAT 总分中位数	2100
TOEFL 成绩中位数	107

财政情况

全年学费	48666 美元 (2015—2016)
经济资助可能性	高

学生为学校所在地区打分

安全	3.5
有趣	2
生活成本	2.5
中国食物	2
交通便利	2
酒吧和俱乐部	2
超市 / 便利店选择	2
周边就业市场	2
是否需要车	2.5
总评	2.5

*满分 4 分

气候

年平均气温范围	−10℃ ~23℃
年平均降水量	80.9cm
年平均湿度	77.60%
年平均降雪量	116.8cm

从中国出发的航班

从中国没有直达的航班。学生们必须先飞到美国的其他机场（例如洛杉矶国际机场），然后再转机到明尼阿波利斯—圣保罗国际机场 (MSP, Minneapolis-Saint Paul International Airport)。从机场搭乘出租车到学校只需 10 分钟。

年学校都会举办一次国际圆桌会议（International Roundtable），与会者会讨论一些国际事件并呼吁人们去关注它们。马卡莱斯特学院有 50% 的学生会做志愿者，这无疑要归功于学校注重提高公民参与度的教学目标。相应地，学校的学生在政治上也非常活跃，一般属于自由派。一位佳桥校友说："马卡莱斯特学院并非非常多样化，因为还是存在'政治正确'。作为一种禁忌，像任何有关反同性恋的表达都是禁止在校园内出现的词汇。"中上层阶级学生是学校的主要群体。一百多个活跃的学生俱乐部给了学生们与同侪分享激情的众多机会。

校园内没有联谊会，这可能是佳桥校友反映学校没有饮酒压力的原因之一。派对是有的，但不是社交生活的主要方式。谈到学校的大学体育场景，佳桥的校友说："人们对于体育活动不是那么疯狂，可能是因为大部分日子都在下雪。在马卡莱斯特学院没有任何一项美国的热门体育运动（篮球、橄榄球或棒球）像在其他学院那样受欢迎，但足球很受欢迎。"马卡莱斯特学院离明尼阿波利斯和圣保罗都很近，这为学校的学生们提供了各种便利。博物馆、剧院、美术馆和音乐会，以及大型专业体育赛事（如明尼苏达维京人橄榄球赛、明尼苏达双城队棒球赛，以及 NBA 赛事中的明尼苏达森林狼队的比赛）都是学生们非常喜欢的。

录取难度

中国学生应该在申请中重点强调他们的国际视野来提高录取的可能性。不论是国际化经历还是能够接受不同背景文化的强有力的适应性都是学校所看重的。SAT 成绩虽然很重要，但不是马卡莱斯特学院录取办公室最为看重的。不过 2100 分以上的成绩将会在录取中比较有优势。

需要考虑的事情

你会喜欢马卡莱斯特学院，如果……

- 你喜欢寒冷的气候
- 你想去一个不是完全脱离社会的文理学院
- 你希望尝试新的不同族裔的食物
- 你想要一个非常强大的国际化社区

你会不喜欢马卡莱斯特学院，如果……

- 你还没有做好远离海滩的准备
- 你希望大学里有非常强的体育氛围

麻省理工学院

地址：77 MASSACHUSETTS AVE，CAMBRIDGE，MA 02139
网址：WEB.MIT.EDU
中国招生官：无
招生办公室邮箱：ADMISSIONS@MIT.EDU
招生办公室电话：617-253-3400
附近主要城市：波士顿

最佳匹配点分析

不论是从所处的地理位置还是从学校自身来说，麻省理工学院都是一所出类拔萃的学校。大多数同学会热爱学校所在的城市，还有其靠近波士顿的有利地理位置，以及该地区众多的著名院校。不介意美国东北部严寒的学生应该会适应这里的环境。毋庸置疑，校园里有“很多书呆子”。另外需要提醒那些想要追求比较均衡大学生活的学生：麻省理工学院的课业负担非常繁重。

学术机会

从众多本科生可以得到的优质研究机遇、灵活的课程，到世界一流的师资和心地坦荡、思维宽广的师生群体，麻省理工学院都没有辜负全美理工大学首冠的美誉。但是，如一位佳桥校友所说，得到好成绩“非常难，学校按照百分比评分，平均成绩是 B”。学业的紧张意味着学生们有时候需要一周学习 80 个小时，但学生之间更多的是通力协作而不是激烈竞争。麻省理工学院的顶级专业包括工程、商科、金融、计算机、数学和物理。学生们还能灵活地选择参加韦尔斯利学院和哈佛大学的课程而不需要另交学费。为缓解大一新生的压力，第一学年的成绩不分等级，而是采用“通过”或者“未通过”的打分体系，这样学生们就不必担心自己会与其他同学有太大差距。本科生研究机遇项目（Undergraduate Research Opportunities Program）允许学生启动或者加入一个研究项目，做研究的同时可以得到学分或者项目津贴。

职业发展

麻省理工学院的全球教育和职业发展组织（GECD，MIT Global Education & Career Development）以及它的职业管理系统——职业桥（CareerBridge），可以帮助在校生和校友们取得联系，在各个领域获取潜在的工作和雇主信息，同时也能帮助学生探索未来发展的道路。2012 届毕业生中，39% 的学生决定继续攻读研究生或职业教育学位，另外有 53% 决定找工作。吸引麻省理工学院毕业生的常见就业领域包括航空航天、国防、计算机技术、咨询和金融业。顶级雇主包括家喻户晓的甲骨文公司（Oracle）、亚马逊、谷歌、苹果、摩根士丹利等。

麻省理工学院毕业生的平均年薪约 66874 美元。麻省理工学院的佳桥校友表示对毕业后找到一份工作并无压力，对学校的校友网充满自信：“正式或者非正式的校友渠道都可用。”麻省理工学院拥有多种校友网络，包括麻省理工学院中国校友网（CAMIT）。

信息速览

US News 大学排名	7
学校位置	东北
学校类型	私立
周边环境	城市

本科学生情况

学生总数	4527 (2015)
申请人数	18306 (2015)
录取率	8% (2015)
男女学生比例	54/46
国际学生百分比	9.7%
亚裔美国人百分比	24.4%

有本科项目的学院

建筑和城市规划学院（School of Architecture and Planning）

工程学院（School of Engineering）

人文、艺术和社会科学学院（School of Humanities, Arts, and Social Sciences）

斯隆管理学院（MIT Sloan School of Management）

理学院（School of Science）

你可能还考虑以下学校

哈佛大学	普林斯顿大学
耶鲁大学	加州理工学院
哥伦比亚大学	康奈尔大学
杜克大学	

校园人文环境

很多理工类院校都面临男女学生比例失调的问题，但麻省理工学院却拥有相对均衡的性别比例，并且学校正努力创造一个多元化的校园环境。学生中大约 25% 是亚裔美国人，国际学生仅占不到 10%（这应该让你意识到麻省理工学院在选择时有多么挑剔）。少

佳桥校友录取情况

录取比例	22.7%
SAT 阅读成绩中位数	740
SAT 数学成绩中位数	800
SAT 写作成绩中位数	800
SAT 总分中位数	2330
TOEFL 成绩中位数	118

财政情况

全年学费

46400 美元 (2015—2016)

经济资助可能性 高

学生为学校所在地区打分

安全	4
有趣	4
生活成本	3
中国食物	3
交通便利	3
酒吧和俱乐部	2
超市 / 便利店选择	2
周边就业市场	4
是否需要车	2
总评	4

*满分 4 分

气候

年平均气温范围	-3℃ ~22℃
年平均降水量	122cm
年平均湿度	67%
年平均降雪量	134.6cm

从中国出发的航班

从北京、上海和香港都有直达波士顿的航班。学生可以乘地铁、往返巴士或出租车从波士顿洛根国际机场（BOS，Logan International Airport）到达校园。

数族裔（非裔美国人和拉丁裔美国人）比例稍多于 20%，而白人相对较多，接近 40%。校园里联谊会生活比较突出，大概 50% 的男生参加兄弟会，27% 的女生参加姐妹会，但这并不是唯一的选择。独立生活小组（Independent Living Groups）是由有相同兴趣的学生所组成的学生团体，也是一种选择。学校有 510 多个学生组织，学生们可以在丰富的资源和可信赖的环境中去寻找自己的圈子。麻省理工学院还有一个独特的"独立活动月"（Independent Activities Period），学生们在这个为期四周的时间段里可以自由选择学校举办的各种课程、研讨会和活动。

学生们热爱学校周边的环境，就像一位佳桥校友提到的，他们体验到了"在波士顿和剑桥间的平衡的生活"。波士顿为学生们提供了观看音乐会、体育赛事、参观历史古迹和博物馆，以及与各种充满激情的人打交道的绝佳机会。

录取难度

一位曾担任过招生办主任的现 MIT 高级官员曾私下里说："在 MIT 的一千多名学生中，国际学生大约有 100 名，他们来自 48 个国家。"祝你好运！

需要考虑的事情

你会喜欢麻省理工学院，如果……

- 你喜欢计算机、技术并且希望周围的人有同样的爱好
- 你希望周围有很多大学生
- 你寻找的学校食堂必须有美食

你会不喜欢麻省理工学院，如果……

- 你期待大型的学校间体育赛事
- 学校的国际学生数量对你非常重要

明德学院

地址：14 OLD CHAPEL RD，MIDDLEBURY，VT 05753
网址：WWW.MIDDLEBURY.EDU
中国招生官：BARBARA MARLOW
招生官电话：802-443-5167
招生官邮箱：MARLOW@MIDDLEBURY.EDU
附近主要城市：波士顿，开车需要大约 3.5 小时

最佳匹配点分析

明德学院位于佛蒙特州乡村，距离附近的几个大城市都有好几个小时车程。它在社交和气候条件方面的不足都被它强大的学术力量、美丽的校园，以及拥有自己的滑雪场地这些优势弥补了。那些对环境不怎么介意、天性自由、以四海为家的学生，以及那些冬季运动爱好者们会尤其喜欢这所顶级文理学院。

学术机会

明德学院在外国语言和国际研究方面堪称学术发电厂，学生们有机会在加利福尼亚州的蒙特雷国际研究院（Monterey Institute of International Studies）进行一个学期的学习。不论专业是什么，大多数学生都愿意利用学校一流的师资力量学习一门新的语言。学校在 40 多个国家设立了国外学习项目，很多学生也会选择其中之一参加。明德学院其他的强势项目还包括环境研究、生物学和英语。学校的 J-term 也很有名，学生在每年 1 月可以选择

信息速览

US News 文理学院排名	4
学校位置	东北
学校类型	私立
周边环境	乡村

本科学生情况

学生总数	2526 (2014)
申请人数	8892 (2015)
录取率	19.9% (2015)
男女学生比例	48/52
国际学生百分比	10%
亚裔美国人百分比	6%

你可能还想考虑以下学校

达特茅斯学院	威廉姆斯学院
耶鲁大学	哈佛大学
阿姆赫斯特学院	布朗大学

参加各种课程、做研究或者进行实习。学生们必须参加两门强化写作的研讨课程，另外还需要在八个学术领域中完成七门课程，涉及四种不同的文化，以保证他们接受综合性的全面教育。明德学院所有的课程都强调写作的重要性，课程设置充满挑战，课业负担也是出名的繁重。但是教授们都非常乐于提供帮助，也时刻准备着为学生们答疑解惑。

职业发展

明德学院的校友网由本科校友、它的语言学校校友以及 Bread Loaf 英语学院（Bread Loaf School of English）的校友共同组成。学校支持他们之间相互联系，从而创造了一个真正国际化的专业校友网。职业和实习中心（CCI，The Center for Careers and Internships）可以帮助学生们获取各种资源、联系以往校友，从而实现他们在理想领域的职业发展。本科校友最热门的应聘行业包括教育、金融、咨询和科学技术领域。很多毕业生也会选择进一步深造。

校园人文环境

明德学院的学生们非常自由开放，有些宿舍甚至曾经投票希望男女共浴。所有的学生都被保证给予校内住宿，97% 的学生会选择住在校内。除了传统的宿舍外，学校还有学术兴趣屋（Academic Interest Houses），一种环保的住宿方式。它是具有联谊会性质的男女共住公寓，这种住宿方式也吸引了 9% 的学生。尽管学校在种族多元化方面有些欠缺，但是明德学院吸引了很多具有国际化思维的学生，他们通过课堂以及国外交流学习加深了对不同文化和社会的认识，从另一个角度为学校创造了一种智识层面的多元化环境。明德学院活动委员会（MCAB，The Middlebury College Activities Board）以及不同的学生组织活跃在校园内，为学生们的社交互动提供了大量机会。尽管很多人可能会选择比较温暖的地方，但是明德学院的学生们很享受这里的严寒和这个冬季圣地提供的大量户外滑雪、滑板滑雪和滑冰活动。同样地，曲棍球和滑雪队也得到了学生们的大力支持。另外，明德户外项目（Middlebury Outdoor Programs）也是学生们乐意参加的。从中学生们可以获得大量户外和露营的技能，包括野外急救。尽管学术负担很重，但是学校并非充满竞争，学生们在一起很少讨论分数。

录取难度

虽然明德学院的录取平均分很高，但学院一直在寻找“璞玉”，例如那些标准化分数低于平均分，但却有天赋的学生。

需要考虑的事情

你会喜欢明德学院，如果……

- 你喜欢户外
- 你对国际研究感兴趣
- 你希望与教授之间保持亲密的联系

你会不喜欢明德学院，如果……

- 你希望学校有就餐计划（meal plan）
- 你寻求种族多元化
- 你希望住在或者靠近一个大城市

佳桥校友录取情况

录取比例	12.5%
SAT 阅读成绩中位数	710
SAT 数学成绩中位数	800
SAT 写作成绩中位数	730
SAT 总分中位数	2240
TOEFL 成绩中位数	113

财政情况

全年学费	47418 美元 (2015—2016)
经济资助可能性	非常低

学生为学校所在地区打分

安全	3
有趣	3
生活成本	4
中国食物	3
交通便利	3
酒吧和俱乐部	4
超市 / 便利店选择	3
周边就业市场	3
是否需要车	2
总评	4

*满分 4 分

气候

年平均气温范围	-7℃ ~21℃
年平均降水量	93.8cm
年平均湿度	74%
年平均降雪量	175.3cm

从中国出发的航班

学生们可以选择乘坐出租车或者往返巴士从纽约或者波士顿的机场前往学校，也可以飞到伯灵顿国际机场（BTV，Burlington International Airport），然后乘坐大巴、往返巴士或者出租车到学校。

纽约大学

地址：70 WASHINGTON SQ S，NEW YORK，NY 10012
网址：WWW.NYU.EDU
中国招生官：NILS SUNDIN
招生办公室邮箱：ADMISSIONS@NYU.EDU
招生办公室电话：212-998-4500
附近主要城市：纽约

最佳匹配点分析

作为一所位于纽约市中心受到高度赞誉的大学学府，纽约大学提供给学生的机遇就像这个城市能提供的一样多。尽管没有传统意义上的大学校园，但是正如一位佳桥校友所说，纽约大学与纽约格林威治镇的融合教会了学生们“如何像一个纽约人那样生活”。

学术机会

为了满足大约25000名本科学生的不同需求，纽约大学提供了大量的学术机会和专业项目供学生选择，其中最为著名的当属蒂施艺术学院（Tisch School of the Arts）和斯特恩商学院（Stern School of Business）了。其他10个本科学院也大都有很多职业导向型的项目，为学生今后进入职场做好准备。同样值得一提的还有学校的加勒廷个性化学习学院（Gallatin School of Individualized Study），允许学生基于自己的兴趣来设计学术项目。无论在哪个学院、学习什么专业，佳桥校友表示虽然课程都很具挑战性，但仍可以把握，尽管一定程度上课程难易取决于“你有什么样的教授”。虽然一些入门的介绍课或者大课是由在读博士生授课，但是教授们通常也都很容易接触到并且愿意提供帮助。纽约大学是全美最大的独立研究型大学，校内拥有超过 130 个机构和中心，因此这里的学生拥有大量在自己专业兴趣领域内开展研究的机会。

职业发展

鉴于其位于纽约市中心的优越位置，佳桥的校友认为在学年内找到工作和实习很容易。2013 届学生中有 94% 的学生一毕业就成功地找到了工作或者继续攻读研究生或职业教育学位。在整个学年中，学校都会举办各种职业招聘会，将学生和来自各行各业的企业联系在一起。纽约大学的沃瑟曼职业发展中心（Wasserman Center for Career Development）在帮助学生们抓住潜在的就业机会方面非常成功：2013 届毕业生中有 73% 的学生称在找工作的时候利用了纽约大学的资源，46% 的学生通过学校提供的渠道成功找到了工作。

校园人文环境

佳桥校友对于纽约大学的规模有比较矛盾的感觉：有的认为没有一个集中的校园使得学校感觉非常大；其他人则觉得学校好像非常小，“因为几乎每天都能撞见朋友”。也就是说，尽管没有一个综合意义上的纽大社区，但是学生们仍可以通过校内外大量的社交圈子找到自己的位置。学校有超过 300 个学生俱乐部和组织，吸引他们加入其中寻找志同道合之友。佳桥校友都同意的一点就是学生群体的多元化，拥有不同的种族、社会经济背景和知识背景的各种学生群体应有尽

信息速览

US News 大学排名	32
学校位置	东北
学校类型	私立
周边环境	城市

本科学生情况

学生总数	25722 (2015)
申请人数	50092 (2015)
录取率	32% (2015)
男女学生比例	43/57
国际学生百分比	19%
亚裔美国人百分比	14.5%

有本科项目的学院

文理学院 (College of Arts & Science); 牙科学院 (College of Dentistry); 护理学院 (College of Nursing); 全球公共卫生学院 (College of Global Public Health); 科朗数学研究所 (Courant Institute of Mathematical Sciences); 加勒廷个性化学习学院 (Gallatin School of Individualized Study); 斯特恩商学院 (Leonard N. Stern School of Business); 专业研究学院 (School of Professional Studies); 西佛社会工作学学院 (Silver School of Social Work); 史丹赫文化、教育和人类发展学学院 (Steinhardt School of Culture, Education and Human Development); 坦登工程学院 (Tandon School of Engineering); 蒂施艺术学院 (Tisch School of the Arts)

你可能还考虑以下学校

哥伦比亚大学　南加州大学
康奈尔大学
加州大学伯克利分校

佳桥校友录取情况

录取比例	37%
SAT 阅读成绩中位数	670
SAT 数学成绩中位数	790
SAT 写作成绩中位数	695
SAT 总分中位数	2155
TOEFL 成绩中位数	106

财政情况

全年学费	46278 美元 (2015—2016)
经济资助可能性	非常低

学生为学校所在地区打分

安全	3
有趣	4
生活成本	3
中国食物	4
交通便利	4
酒吧和俱乐部	4
超市 / 便利店选择	4
周边就业市场	3
是否需要车	1
总评	3

*满分 4 分

气候

年平均气温范围	-2℃ ~24℃
年平均降水量	122cm
年平均湿度	66%
年平均降雪量	38.1cm

从中国出发的航班

从中国可以选择从北京、上海或者香港直飞到肯尼迪国际机场（JFK，John F. Kennedy International Airport）或者纽瓦克自由国际机场（EWR，Newark Liberty International Airport）。

有，尽管一个校友也指出各个群体的学生倾向于与自己人形成圈子而不是与其他群体的人融合在一起。纽约大学的校园与纽约市融为一体，因此学生们得以享受数不清的酒吧、俱乐部、博物馆、百老汇演出、音乐会、体育赛事和其他一切可用资源。大多数项目都会对学生提供折扣。纽约大学的学生们可以说是这座城市本身的缩影，在学习、兼职工作、实习和活跃的社交生活中寻求平衡，他们是一群努力工作、生活节奏飞快的城市个体。

录取难度

申请难度根据申请专业的不同而不同，有时会有很大差别。蒂施艺术学院和斯特恩商学院的许多项目在各自领域里都是极有竞争力的。

需要考虑的事情

你会喜欢纽约大学，如果……

- 你对商科或者艺术感兴趣
- 你寻求多元化程度很高的学校
- 你希望生活在一个大城市里

你会不喜欢纽约大学，如果……

- 你希望要一个传统的大学校园
- 你想要很强的社区归属感
- 你更加喜欢一个安静的环境

西北大学

地址：633 CLARK STREET，EVANSTON，IL 60208
网址：WWW.NORTHWESTERN.EDU
中国招生官：STEPHEN BOWE
招生官邮箱：S-BOW@NORTHWESTERN.EDU
招生办公室电话：847-491-3023
附近主要城市：芝加哥，乘坐往返巴士需要 45 分钟时间

最佳匹配点分析

身处全美排名第 12 的大学里，西北大学的学生会发现他们处于一个高度自我激励又竞争激烈的群体中。在勇敢地挺过了伊利诺伊州相对漫长的寒冷冬季后，学生们可以享受埃文斯顿的宁静。如果你打算学习金融或者学商（或者进入任何其他特色学院），并且自信可以主动冲破自己的舒适区，那么西北大学会是一个最佳选择。对艺术和音乐感兴趣的学生也会在这里有家的感觉，因为充满艺术活力的芝加哥就在附近。

学术机会

佳桥校友透露道："学校的班级规模刚刚好。有大课也有小课。大部分通识性的基础课程人数很多，其他的是小班，这是一种非常合理的安排。"另外一位校友补充道："研究机会也相当多。"一般实行学季制（Quarter System）的学校学生每个学季只需要上三门

信息速览

US News 大学排名	12
学校位置	中西部
学校类型	私立
周边环境	郊区

本科学生情况

学生总数	9001 (2015)
申请人数	32124 (2015)
录取率	13% (2015)
男女学生比例	49/51
国际学生百分比	8.5%
亚裔美国人百分比	17%

有本科项目的学院

文理学院（Judd A and Marjorie Weinberg College of Arts and Sciences）
新闻学院（Medill School of Journalism）
工程学院（Robert R. McCormick School of Engineering）
传媒学院（School of Communication）
音乐学院（Henry and Leigh Bienen School of Music）
教育和社会政策学院（School of Education and Social Policy）

你可能还考虑以下学校

杜克大学　芝加哥大学
宾夕法尼亚大学　哥伦比亚大学
乔治城大学
圣路易斯华盛顿大学

课，但是在西北大学学生们通常会选四门课。学生们觉得课业负担可以接受。西北大学最强势的项目有化学、工程、经济学、新闻学、传媒学、历史、政治科学和音乐，学校提供足够多样化的专业满足勤奋好学的学生们多种多样的兴趣。除了新闻学院外，大一学年转学到其他学院并不太难。

职业发展

所有西北大学的佳桥校友们都表示对自己学校的校友网络非常有自信，相信如果需要帮助的话，学校的校友网络一定能够助他们一臂之力。鉴于学校可以利用全美最大城市之一芝加哥的各种资源，学生们可以方便地接触到很多公司。"大公司也同样认为西北大学是一个很重要的招聘地点。"大多数学生毕业后都倾向于走向职场而不是继续接受教育。咨询和金融类工作是最热门的就职领域。西北大学的学生在大一的时候就会发现学校在就业指导方面的用心。一位佳桥校友说："学校设有专门的办公室和工作人员，可以帮助学生们审阅简历并且提供面试技巧辅导。另外还有在线系统列出各种工作招聘信息，可供学生查询和申请。"

校园人文环境

对于很多西北大学的佳桥校友来说，尽管他们也会深入芝加哥市区寻求各种新鲜事物，但是校园就是他们的家。学校附近的小镇埃文斯顿虽然提供的娱乐项目不多，但是安全又富有情趣。学生们在校园里也不会觉得必须要有辆车，这可以体现校园能够充分满足学生们的各种需求。学生们选择去芝加哥市区的话可以有非常多的娱乐机会，像观看专业的体育赛事、参观博物馆和美术馆、欣赏音乐会等。

佳桥校友的社交圈子通常是这里的中国学生。一位校友说道:“很少看到有人喝酒,不喝酒也不会有压力。但是我猜兄弟会和姐妹会的情况可能不同。”联谊会生活、戏剧和体育组成了学校的三大社交圈子,学生们倾向于按照自己的兴趣爱好在头一两年里就形成自己的交往圈子。

但是整体来说学生群体是开放的,西北大学 49% 的人口是少数族裔。“我们的学校非常多元化。你可以见到来自世界各地的同学和教授,体验到不同的文化。这里的学生也知道在这种多文化环境中相处的技巧。”学校有 500 多个学生组织和俱乐部,因此有足够多的课外活动和机会让你去结识同伴。

录取难度

西北大学每年录取的学生 SAT 成绩介于 2200 分到 2300 分之间。要注意的是一些特色学院,像新闻学院和工程学院的录取会更具有挑战性。

需要考虑的事情

你会喜欢西北大学,如果……

- 你更喜欢过集体生活
- 你喜欢篮球和橄榄球
- 你非常关注志愿者活动并且希望将来可以参与其中(西北大学有很多慈善活动,包括学校最受欢迎的一项活动——舞蹈马拉松)

你会不喜欢西北大学,如果……

- 寒冷的气候让你不想动
- 对于充满竞争的气氛你倾向于羞涩地避开
- 你更喜欢知识导向型而非职业导向型的校园

佳桥校友录取情况

录取比例	12.3%
SAT 阅读成绩中位数	720
SAT 数学成绩中位数	800
SAT 写作成绩中位数	730
SAT 总分中位数	2250
TOEFL 成绩中位数	111

财政情况

全年学费

48624 美元 (2015—2016)

经济资助可能性　非常低

学生为学校所在地区打分

安全	3
有趣	3
生活成本	3
中国食物	2.5
交通便利	2
酒吧和俱乐部	1.5
超市 / 便利店选择	1.5
周边就业市场	2.5
是否需要车	2.5
总评	3

*满分 4 分

气候

年平均气温范围	-6℃ ~23℃
年平均降水量	87cm
年平均湿度	72.46%
年平均降雪量	74.6cm

从中国出发的航班

北京、上海或者香港都有到芝加哥奥黑尔国际机场(ORD, O'Hare International Airport)的直航航班,乘坐往返巴士从机场到学校仅需 45 分钟。

圣母大学

地址：220 MAIN BUILDING，NOTRE DAME，IN 46556
网址：WWW.ND.EDU
中国招生官：MARY DE VILLIERS
招生官邮箱：MDEVILLI@ND.EDU
招生办公室电话：574-631-7505
附近主要城市：芝加哥，开车大约需要 2 小时

最佳匹配点分析

圣母大学位于美国中西部地区，一年之中大部分时候都笼罩在冬季的大风和严寒中。学生以白人为主，且大部分学生有宗教信仰；对于那些相对能够忍受冬天严寒，并且能够很容易适应一个新环境的学生来说，这里将是一个很好的目的地。作为一个相对大型的私立院校，学校鼓励具有高度自我激励能力的学生挑战各种竞争、获得各种发展机会，尤其是在商业和哲学领域。想要寻求一个紧密社区联系的学生在这里也会很活跃，因为圣母大学没有联谊会体系，大部分学生的社交活动都在他们的宿舍楼内进行。追求更有活力的城市气氛的学生可能要另寻他处了，因为圣母大学距离芝加哥有 2 个小时的车程。

学术机会

圣母大学在 *US News & World Report* 上排名第 18，是美国中西部地区的学术重镇。除了一些通识性初级课程学生人数较多外，其他课程都是小班授课。一位佳桥校友说："如果你用心，教授还是很容易接触到的。"圣母大学的学术环境通常被描述为既竞争激烈同时也是通力合作，具体取决于学生选修的课程。学校最热门的专业多是社会科学类专业，包括金融、经济、政治学和心理学。一般来说学校的学术课业负担还是很具挑战性的。

职业发展

圣母大学坚实的校友网络已经成为帮助在校生和毕业生寻找就业机会的良好途径。学校靠近芝加哥，很方便学生们寻找夏季实习机会。但事实上圣母大学在美国东北部的城市中，包括波士顿和纽约，也有着非常出色的校友网络。佳桥校友们说圣母大学的学生非常注重职业生涯规划。该校享誉全球的商学院可以为其校友提供全球商业领域内顶级公司的工作机会。商学院、建筑学院和工程学院的学生毕业后大部分会选择就业而非继续深造。理学院恰恰相反，毕业后会有 57% 的学生选择继续深造。文理学院的比例相对均衡一些，46% 选择进入就业大军，另外的 31% 选择继续深造。

信息速览

US News 大学排名	18
学校位置	中西部
学校类型	私立
宗教联系	罗马天主教
周边环境	郊区

本科学生情况

学生总数	8551 (2014)
申请人数	18157 (2015)
录取率	19.8% (2015)
男女学生比例	52/48
国际学生百分比	4.6%
亚裔美国人百分比	6%

有本科项目的学院

建筑学院（School of Architecture）

文理学院（College of Arts and Letters）

门多萨商学院（Mendoza College of Business）

工程学院（College of Engineering）

理学院（School of Science）

你可能还考虑以下学校

杜克大学　波士顿学院

宾夕法尼亚大学　西北大学

乔治城大学

校园人文环境

圣母大学并不以多元文化而出名，国际学生和中国学生的入学率都相对较低。尽管圣母大学的国际学生群体不是非常强大，但是也由于越来越多的中国学生将该校作为他们入学的首选之一而日益扩大。学校的很多学生是中上层社会的白人，在各自的社区中都非常活跃，具有出众的学术驱动力，他们很多是被学校的天主教背景吸引而来。可以

佳桥校友录取情况

录取比例	25.9%
SAT 阅读成绩中位数	720
SAT 数学成绩中位数	800
SAT 写作成绩中位数	750
SAT 总分中位数	2230
TOEFL 成绩中位数	110.5

财政情况

全年学费	47929 美元 (2015—2016)
经济资助可能性	非常低

学生为学校所在地区打分

安全	3.5
有趣	1.5
生活成本	1.5
中国美食	1.5
公共交通	1.5
酒吧和俱乐部	1
超市 / 便利店选择	1,5
周边就业市场	2.5
是否需要车	2.5
总评	2.5

＊满分 4 分

气候

年平均气温范围	-5℃ ~23℃
年平均降水量	100.4cm
年平均湿度	71.7%
年平均降雪量	153cm

从中国出发的航班

离学校最近的机场是南本德国际机场（SBN，South Bend International Airport）。搭乘出租车到机场需要 20 美元，也可以乘坐往返巴士。没有从中国直达南本德的航班，学生们需要在芝加哥或者纽约转机。

说学校的人口分布很好地反映了美国的整体人口分布。想要留在美国特别是东海岸工作的学生可以在圣母大学开始他们在社交方面的转型。尽管不以派对出名，圣母大学仍然有自己的以“痛饮”为主题的“周四到周六宿舍派对”。社交圈子基本上以宿舍位置划分，但是学生们也可以从学校大量的学生社团组织里找到自己的同类朋友。佳桥校友反映这里的学生对国际学生都非常友好，他们中很多从高中时期开始就是运动员。因此，学生们非常骄傲地拥戴自己的橄榄球队、篮球队和曲棍球队，特别是“爱尔兰斗士”（学校的橄榄球队名称）。球赛当天狂热的爵士乐演奏是校园文化非常重要的一部分。致力于服务精神和奉献精神的培养是圣母大学非常重要的教学目标，学校非常鼓励学生们回馈他们的社区。

录取难度

尽管圣母大学不在全美最难录取的大学之列，但是与类似排名的大学相比，它在中国录取的学生数目相对有限。拿到录取的学生 SAT 成绩一般要在 2200 分以上。

需要考虑的事情

你会喜欢圣母大学，如果……

- 你寻求“努力学习，尽情玩乐”的校园文化
- 你期待大多数社交活动发生在校园内

你会不喜欢圣母大学，如果……

- 你认为社区服务活动是浪费时间的一件事
- 作为一个少数族裔让你觉得被疏远
- 你希望待在美国的一个大城市里

波莫纳学院

地址：333 N COLLEGE WAY，CLAREMONT，CA 91711
网址：WWW.POMONA.EDU
中国招生官：FRANCES NAN
招生官邮箱：FRANCES.NAN@POMONA.EDU
招生办公室电话：909-621-8134
附近主要城市：洛杉矶，在交通高峰期开车或坐巴士需要两个小时。METROLINK 在克莱蒙特市的站点在学校附近，距离学校大约两个街区

最佳匹配点分析

作为公认的美国西海岸顶级的文理学院，波莫纳学院在悠闲而充满阳光的加州为学生提供了享誉盛名的本科教育。作为克莱蒙特学院联盟（Claremont Consortium）的成员之一，波莫纳学院与另外四所本科院校——匹泽学院（Pitzer College）、斯克利普斯学院（Scripps College）、克莱蒙特麦肯纳学院（Claremont McKenna College）和哈维•穆德学院（Harvey Mudd College）一起，为在校生提供了众多课程和研究方面的共享资源。学校八比一的学生 / 老师比例让学生们可以享受非常密切的课堂环境。波莫纳学院庞大的人均校友捐赠有力地促进了学校的资金配置，可以为暑期科研项目以及学生自主开发的项目提供大量的资金支持。尽管波莫纳学院距离洛杉矶市区仅 35 分钟车程，但该地区公共交通的不便和堵车严重的恶名意味着学生们主要会在校园周围活动。

信息速览

US News 文理学院排名	4
学校位置	西海岸
学校类型	私立
周边环境	郊区

本科学生情况

学生总数	1610 (2015)
申请人数	8091 (2015)
录取率	9.76% (2015)
男女学生比例	49/51
国际学生百分比	8.9%
亚裔百分比	12.9%

你可能还想考虑以下学校

威廉姆斯学院　斯坦福大学
加州大学洛杉矶分校
阿姆赫斯特学院
克莱蒙特麦肯纳学院
南加州大学

学术机会

在波莫纳学院，学生可以充分享受相对灵活的课程设置，但是必须参加批判探索研讨课（Critical Inquiry Seminar）——一门鼓励大一新生对一些已知成立的事实和理论提出质疑的课程。同时，学校还要求学生必须在创意表达（Creative Expression）、社会体制与人类行为（Social Institutions and Human Behavior）、历史、价值、道德与文化研究（History，Values，Ethics and Cultural Studies）、物理与生物科学（Physical and Biological Sciences）以及数学逻辑（Mathematical Reasoning）这五个领域内学习通识课程。波莫纳学院的优势专业包括经济学、媒体研究、心理学和英语。虽然学校的自然科学学科如物理学不是特别出名，但是波莫纳学院的学生们可以选择联盟成员哈维•穆德学院的相关课程来弥补这一不足。波莫纳学院的教授对学生项目的参与度非常高，目前大约有 52% 的教授参与学生的研究活动。学校有众多的研究平台供学生们开展相关领域的研究项目，比如暑期本科生研究项目（SURP，Summer Undergraduate Research Program）。学校也会用研究助学金（Research Assistantships）为学生的研究提供资助。学校为 56% 的学生提供在超过 34 个不同国家交换学习的机会。波莫纳学院的学生还有机会学习工程预科项目，通过学校的 3-2 计划，学生可以获得学校与加州理工学院和华盛顿圣路易斯大学联合办学的理学学士和文学学士学位。

职业发展

因其靠近洛杉矶市区的有利位置，大约 150 名学生可以通过波莫纳学院的大学实习项目（PCIP，Pomona College Internship Program）在洛杉矶地区 50 多个不同的机构完成带薪实习。对于想在洛杉矶以外的城市寻找就业机会的学生，学校的寒假招聘项目（Winter Break Recruiting Program）可以为大四学生提供去美国其他城市（波士顿、芝加哥、纽约、旧金山和华盛顿特区）面试的旅行补贴。克莱蒙特联络网（ClaremontConnect）是一个基于网络的就业信息体系，波莫纳学院的校友可以在这里分享或者获取就业信息，从而使学生们受益于来自克莱蒙特大学联盟所有成员在该网站上发布的就业信息。在

2012—2013 学年，克莱蒙特大学联盟成员在该网站发布了 250 多家单位的招聘信息。在 2014 届毕业生中，大约 36% 的学生毕业后就参加了工作，12% 进入研究生院或职业学院继续深造，另有 11% 接受了包括富布莱特奖学金（Fulbright Scholarships）在内的研究奖学金。2014 届毕业生入职的三个最热门的领域是商业 / 金融、教育 / 非营利机构和政府 / 法律行业。

校园人文环境

波莫纳学院向来以自由、开放和包容闻名，它努力促进学校形成一个比东海岸的常春藤名校以及像阿姆赫斯特学院和威廉姆斯学院这样的文理学院更加友好和放松的学术环境。波莫纳学院也不是那种压力过大的大学，这里的学生都愿意相互合作、彼此支持。不像很多其他文理学院的学生，波莫纳学院的学生不用忍受与社会隔绝的苦恼。虽然 98% 的学生住在校园内，但是他们可以享受校园以外的社交生活。他们可以参加社会活动以及克莱蒙特大学联盟的活动，总的来说克莱蒙特学院联盟成员学校之间的学生约会群体是相当可观的。学生们可以与波莫纳学院或者是其他学院联盟成员学校的同学们互动，这里有 200 多个俱乐部和社团组织可供选择。尽管洛杉矶糟糕的交通状况限制了学生们的活动范围，但是波莫纳学院的学生们还是有机会去著名的圣塔莫尼卡海滩游玩，还可以时不时去参观洛杉矶市区的博物馆或去听音乐会。在波莫纳学院较受欢迎的学校传统中，滑雪海滩日（Ski-Beach Day）充分利用了学校在南加州的有利位置。学校早上用大巴将学生们载到当地的滑雪胜地滑雪，午饭后再将学生们送到洛杉矶县或者橙县的海滩放松半天。

佳桥校友录取情况

录取比例	22.2%
SAT 阅读成绩中位数	770
SAT 数学成绩中位数	800
SAT 写作成绩中位数	760
SAT 总分中位数	2330
TOEFL 成绩中位数	114

财政情况

全年学费	47280 美元 (2015—2016)
经济资助可能性	非常低

学生为学校所在地区打分

安全	4
有趣	3
生活成本	2
中国食物	2
交通便利	3
酒吧和俱乐部	1
超市 / 便利店选择	1
周边就业市场	1
是否需要车	3
总评	3

*满分 4 分

气候

年平均气温范围	11℃ ~25℃
年平均降水量	58.7cm
年平均湿度	81.87%
年平均降雪量	0cm

从中国出发的航班

在没有堵车的情况下，洛杉矶国际机场（LAX，Los Angeles International Airport）距离学校 45 分钟车程（因此开车大概需要 1~1.5 小时之间）。从北京、上海或者香港出发有直飞航班到洛杉矶。

录取难度

每年仅有极少数来自中国的幸运儿被波莫纳学院录取。录取学生的 SAT 成绩都在最高分数档里。2013 年秋季入学的学生中，92.4% 的学生高中时成绩都在他们年级排名前 10%。录取的学生必须有领导力和非常高的课外活动参与度。

需要考虑的事情

你会喜欢波莫纳学院，如果……

- 你希望自己身处一个既放松又严格的学术体系中
- 你想去一所种族和地域都非常多元化的学校
- 你梦想成为一个教育家、银行家或者咨询专家

你会不喜欢波莫纳学院，如果……

- 你想去一所四季分明的大学
- 你希望加入一所宗教气息浓厚的大学

普林斯顿大学

地址：WEST COLLEGE BUILDING，PRINCETON，NJ 08544
网址：WWW.PRINCETON.EDU
中国招生官：无
招生办公室邮箱：UAOFFICE@PRINCETON.EDU
招生办公室电话：609-258-3060
附近主要城市：纽约和费城，乘坐新泽西铁路运输（NJ TRANSIT）公司的火车需要一个半小时；开车需要 1 小时

最佳匹配点分析

尽管你可能听说过普林斯顿大学的名字，但是你大概不清楚为何它能成为当今全美排名最高的大学。确实，普林斯顿大学有很大比例的富家子弟学生。很多学生在大三和大四学年会面临是否要花费 2000 美元甚至更多以参加学校独有的饮食俱乐部（Eating Clubs）的选择（尽管近年来普林斯顿大学已经提供一定的资助来缓解这种情况）。另外，不同于其他一些顶级名校，普林斯顿大学不鼓励分数膨胀。这就意味着如果你没有在精神和体力上做好双重准备的话，那么这里可能不适合你。然而，如果你是坚持不懈的 A 型性格并且不介意在毕业之前经历艰辛的漫漫长路的话，普林斯顿大学给你的远非充满激励气氛的校园。拥有全美最高的人均捐赠（这意味着学校在每个学生身上的投资花费是最高的），学生们在这里可以几乎不受限制地充分享受各种资源。

信息速览

US News 大学排名	1
学校位置	中部大西洋沿岸
学校类型	私立
周边环境	郊区
本科学生情况	
学生总数	5402 (2015)
申请人数	27290 (2015)
录取率	7% (2015)
男女学生比例	50.5/49.5
国际学生百分比	11.4%
亚裔百分比	21.5%

有本科项目的学院

工程和应用科学学院（School of Engineering and Applied Science）

伍德罗·威尔逊公共和国际事务学院（Woodrow Wilson School of Public and International Affairs）

建筑学院（School of Architecture）

你可能还考虑以下学校

哈佛大学	哥伦比亚大学
耶鲁大学	杜克大学
达特茅斯学院	宾夕法尼亚大学

学术机会

如果没有准备充分和训练有素的学生，一个顶级学校的声誉就无从谈起。而这两点都需要艰苦的学习过程，这也正是普林斯顿大学的各个学术院系可以提供给学生的。学校提供两种学位：文学学士和工学学士。工学学士学位需要学习计算机科学、自然科学和数学。大三和大四的学生都需要撰写独立论文，很多人文学科课程甚至要求学生每周都要与教授进行讨论。过去几年里普林斯顿大学的成绩紧缩政策导致了学生总体 GPA 的下滑。尽管课业负担很重，但这并不影响学生们保持对课业的诚实和自豪。学校推行“荣誉法则”，考试不设监考，学生们彼此监督。

职业发展

在 2013 届大四学生中，86.6% 的学生已经做好了毕业后的规划。65.4% 的学生会参加工作，19.7% 的学生开始了学术生涯。在毕业之后就开始工作的学生中有 12% 进入专业领域或者科学、技术领域；有 12.2% 进入金融和保险公司；22.62% 选择非营利性机构和政府部门；5% 选择进入信息技术领域。像所有顶级大学的毕业生一样，普林斯顿大学的校友们同样难忘他们美好的大学生活，每年学校举办的各种活动都是联系好友的最佳机会。

校园人文环境

普林斯顿大学的日常生活围绕着学校的 6 个住宿学院展开，每个学院都是一个充满各种生活设施、传统和派对的微观世界，学校里每个学生都是其中一个住宿学院的一员。有的学院甚至资助学生们去纽约观看芭蕾和歌剧。联谊会存在但并没有被学校正式认可，大部分时候它的功用都被饮食俱乐部所取代。作为学校一种独特的体系，饮食俱乐部事实上像是为上层社会学生们提供的一个可以吃喝和社交的场所（更像是一所豪宅）。要想进入这些俱乐部需要经过一系列的筛选，并且成员需要承担一定的义务。大概75%的大三和大四学生认为饮食俱乐部可以很好地替代常规食堂。饮食俱乐部也举办派对，校园外的饮酒机会比较少，也没有多少选择。想要杜绝饮酒的中国留学生在这里不会是唯一。

普林斯顿大学非常多元化，学生群体中有8%的非洲裔美国人，22%亚裔美国人，9%的西班牙裔和11%的国际学生群体。白人则占了45%。普林斯顿大学确实有一定数量的富家子弟。划船、橄榄球和篮球比赛永远不会被忽略。学生们喜欢学校周边城市安全而舒适的环境，但是昂贵的生活方式就不那么令人兴奋了。

录取难度

像哈佛大学、耶鲁大学一样，普林斯顿大学的录取没有规则可循，仅有10%的GPA 4.0和14.5%的SAT超过2300分的学生被录取。独立研究和受到国际认可的高中活动有利于申请。

需要考虑的事情

你会喜欢普林斯顿大学，如果……

◆ 你希望大学生活对你的智力是一种挑战

◆ 你希望积极地参与到社区活动中，并且有为非营利机构和政府部门工作的打算

你会不喜欢普林斯顿大学，如果……

◆ 高成本的生活费用对你来说是个问题

◆ 独立工作对你来说很难适应

◆ 一般意义上的精英主义在这里可能会不适用

佳桥校友录取情况

录取比例	2.6%
SAT阅读成绩中位数	740
SAT数学成绩中位数	800
SAT写作成绩中位数	800
SAT总分中位数	2330
TOEFL成绩中位数	118

财政情况

全年学费	43450美元（2015—2016）
经济资助可能性	高

学生为学校所在地区打分

安全	4
有趣	2.5
生活成本	3
中国食物	2
交通便利	2.5
酒吧和俱乐部	2
超市／便利店选择	2
周边就业市场	2
是否需要车	2
总评	3

*满分4分

气候

年平均气温范围	-2℃~24℃
年平均降水量	125.2cm
年平均湿度	74.25%
年平均降雪量	64.2cm

从中国出发的航班

从中国没有直达的国际航班。学生们必须先飞到纽瓦克自由国际机场（EWR，Newark Liberty International Airport），然后乘坐新泽西火车（NJ Transit）公司的火车或者往返巴士到达新泽西州的普林斯顿。可以选择从香港国际机场、首都国际机场或者浦东国际机场飞往纽瓦克自由国际机场。

莱斯大学

地址：6100 MAIN STREET，HOUSTON，TX 77005
网址：WWW.RICE.EDU
中国招生官：无
招生办公室电话：713-348-7423
招生办公室邮箱：ADMI@RICE.EDU
附近主要城市：休斯敦，乘坐往返巴士从莱斯大学到乔治·布什洲际机场需要1小时

最佳匹配点分析

美丽的莱斯大学坐落在潮湿的得克萨斯州，每年吸引着上千名学生来到这个湿润炎热的地区。尽管只有3900名本科学生，莱斯大学却拥有三十亿的捐赠基金，可以帮助学生们负担一部分学费支出。如果你对STEM（Science科学、Technology技术、Engineering工程、Math数学）领域感兴趣，选择莱斯大学；如果你喜欢和“书呆子”交朋友，并把探索知识当作一种乐趣，那么莱斯也适合你；如果你打算将来成为世界上顶级的技术公司的工程师，那么莱斯大学也会对你有所帮助。但是如果你不确定自己的兴趣是否在STEM领域，或者处在一个很小的社区会让你感到窒息，那么请重新全面地研究莱斯大学后再来决定取舍。

学术机会

莱斯大学有很多专业闻名全球，包括建筑学院、音乐学院和工程学院的一些专业。莱斯大学还提供很多交叉学科，例如，认知科学、管理学、政治学、生命科学和生物工程学以及神经科学。许多项目允许本科生从事与其专业有关的研究。学校课程确实有一定难度，但是教授们亲切友好，愿意在学生探索知识的道路上给予一臂之力。尽管莱斯大学也提供人文学科和社会科学领域的专业，但选择非常少。

职业发展

对 2013 届莱斯大学毕业生去向的年度调查发现，64% 的学生在毕业后几个月内即进入就业大军，36% 选择继续攻读研究生。莱斯大学毕业生的顶级雇主包括埃森哲（Accenture）、贝勒医学院（Baylor College of Medicine）、波士顿咨询集团（Boston Consulting Group）、凯捷（Capgemini）、德勤、埃克森美孚（Exxonmobil）、Teach for America，Epic，谷歌、摩根大通、亚马逊、美国银行（Bank of America）和脸书（Facebook）等。选择继续读研究生的学生一般会入读医学院和工程学院。学校强大的校友网络可以帮助校友们实现未来的计划。

校园人文环境

学校的住宿学院体系可以帮助同学们更早地找到归属感，每个学院都有自己的特点和便利的设施。住宿学院社区的优势使得校内学院之间的体育比赛吸引了众多观众。但是住宿学院社区有时候会很排外。莱斯大学乐于接纳国际学生，就像他们乐于接纳书呆子一样。这里的学生有派对党，也有几乎什么派对都不参加的，还有介于两者之间的。学校没有联谊会，因为这样可以促进社区之间的相互包容。一句话，莱斯大学是一个无论你喜欢怎样形式的放松都能找到朋友的地方。

信息速览

US News 大学排名	18
学校位置	西南
学校类型	私立
周边环境	城市

本科学生情况

学生总数	3879 (2015)
申请人数	17951 (2015)
录取率	16% (2015)
男女学生比例	52/48
国际学生百分比	11.8%
亚裔美国人百分比	22.6%

有本科项目的学院

乔治 • 布朗工程学院（George R. Brown School of Engineering）
人文学院（School of Humanities）
谢波德音乐学院（The Shepherd School of Music）
魏斯自然科学学院（Wiess School of Natural Sciences）
社会学学院（School of Social Sciences）
建筑学院（School of Architecture）

你可能还考虑以下学校

杜克大学　华盛顿圣路易斯大学
西北大学　范德比尔特大学
埃默里大学

佳桥校友录取情况

录取比例	9.9%
SAT 阅读成绩中位数	770
SAT 数学成绩中位数	800
SAT 写作成绩中位数	750
SAT 总分中位数	2230
TOEFL 成绩中位数	112

财政情况

全年学费
41650 美元 (2015—2016)

经济资助可能性 非常低

学生为学校所在地区打分

安全	3
有趣	2.5
生活成本	2
中国食物	2
交通便利	2
酒吧和俱乐部	1.5
超市／便利店选择	2.5
周边就业市场	3
是否需要车	3.5
总评	3

＊满分 4 分

气候

年平均气温范围	11℃ ~29℃
年平均降水量	123.2cm
年平均湿度	73.63%
年平均降雪量	0cm

从中国出发的航班

从中国没有直达的航班。学生们必须转机才能到达霍比机场（HOU，Will P. Hobby Airport）或者乔治•布什洲际机场（IAH，George Bush Intercontinental Airport）。

校园里允许饮酒，年满 21 岁的学生都可以持有酒水，也可以在宿舍喝酒。不同于得克萨斯州，大部分莱斯学生属于自由派，然而有 50% 的学生来自德克萨斯本州。多样化的宗教组织吸引了莱斯大学有着不同宗教兴趣的学生们。没有哪个种族在学校占主体地位。学校有 7% 的非洲裔美国人，22% 的亚裔美国人，15% 的西班牙裔，12% 的国际学生和 42% 的白人。

莱斯大学在校园内给学生提供很多培养领导力的机会以及很多有趣的、独具特色的学校传统。休斯敦市拥有数不清的就餐选择，它可以是危险的、有趣的、喧嚣的或者富有文化气息的，完全由你决定。

录取难度

莱斯大学的录取很难预测。它不看重分数，而是看重多元化。如果你正在申请莱斯大学，记得一定要体现出你能为学校多元化做出贡献。大部分申请者集中在学校的科学和技术相关专业。

需要考虑的事情

你会喜欢莱斯大学，如果……

- 你喜欢夏季的潮湿，或者是害怕冬天
- 你不介意跟朋友外出的时候有些傻点子
- 你不是联谊会生活迷

你会不喜欢莱斯大学，如果……

- 你对科学和技术领域以及这些领域的人几乎没什么兴趣
- 你希望在你所在的社区发现政治行动主义

斯坦福大学

地址：450 SERRA MALL，STANFORD，CA 94305
网址：WWW.STANFORD.EDU
中国招生官：ANTHONY DINH
招生官邮箱：ADINH@STANFORD.EDU
招生办公室电话：650-723-2091
附近主要城市：旧金山，开车或者乘坐大巴大概四五十分钟

最佳匹配点分析

斯坦福大学是由一位想要创建一所西部哈佛的铁路大亨建立的，他确实做到了。今天，斯坦福大学继续吸引着那些聪明和勇敢的人们来到这里，拓展着人类对技术领域的认知。那些想要良好的职前教育、富有企业家精神和非常渴望教育的学生在这里最能获益。在斯坦福诸多专业中，热门的有生物学、国际关系、经济学，但那些对计算机和工程学充满热爱和欣赏的学生最能在这里找到宾至如归的感觉。

学术机会

在自然科学领域，没有任何一所大学可以与斯坦福大学匹敌。数学、物理、化学和计算机都是学校的顶级项目；传媒、经济学和心理学排名也位居全美前十。在大多数工程学领域，斯坦福大学都位居前三，个别位居前五。新生们会在一起学习他们的必修课程，包括写作和人文学科的一些通识教育课程。同时，学校又给予学生们充分的信任，

信息速览

US News 大学排名	4
学校位置	西海岸
学校类型	私立
周边环境	郊区

本科学生情况

学生总数	6994（2015）
申请人数	42497（2015）
录取率	5%（2015）
男女学生比例	53/47
国际学生百分比	8.7%
亚裔美国人百分比	20.6%

有本科项目的学院

文理学院（School of Humanities and Sciences）
工程学院（School of Engineering）
地球、能源与环境科学学院（School of Earth, Energy & Environmental Sciences）

你可能还考虑以下学校

哈佛大学
加州大学洛杉矶分校
加州大学伯克利分校
普林斯顿大学
宾夕法尼亚大学
麻省理工学院

允许他们自己做未来专业的规划，不在专业或者课程要求方面设立太多障碍。学生们有机会上品酒课和骑马课。从教授那里通常可以得到研究机会，教授们也非常愿意为自己的实验室找到成本低廉、热情度高的学生劳动力。仅有 13% 的课程会有超过 50 人同时上课。尽管学术课程艰难，但是同学之间经常在一起学习并且愿意互相协助。教授打分也非常大方。为了拥护真正的硅谷传统，斯坦福大学成为最早采用移动技术的大学，比如教科书已经越来越多地以电子书的形式出现在数字设备上。

职业发展

距离旧金山 35 英里、圣何塞 20 英里的斯坦福大学是众多技术公司招聘的中心。学校的很多学生入学前已经拥有职前培训的倾向，因此毕业即就业对他们来说不成问题，像谷歌、贝恩（Bain）、高盛、微软和甲骨文（Oracle）这样的公司每年都能刷新斯坦福毕业生的录用率。斯坦福校友指导计划（Stanford Alumni Mentoring Program）可以帮助毕业生联系到成功的校友。在斯坦福大学，校友网络是学生们毕业后找到社会立足点的一个普遍途径，大约有 30% 的毕业生通过校友网络成功找到工作。学生们也很适应这样的校友网络，很多企业家通过这样的方式找到公司需要的可靠顾问和最初的投资者。

校园人文环境

白人占了学生总人口的 40%，亚裔美国人占 20%，学校学生群体非常多样，因此对不同的文化和理念都有很好的接受度。大部分学生感到校园规模合适、非常完美；联谊会生活不是非常盛行，仅有不到 15% 的学生参与其中。学校有很多非传统联谊会，像针对喜欢电脑游戏的学生设立的社团。新生们会等到大一春天才决定是否参加某个社团，以便有充足的时间考虑自己的社交圈子。斯坦福大学对于学校的体育传统非常自豪，它的棒球、篮球和橄榄球队闻名全美。对校园内饮酒和药物使用，斯坦福大学持宽松态度，因为学校相信学生们的自制能力和自我管理意识。学生们也不觉得住在校外非常必要，一方面是因为校外住宿的选择大多花费昂贵，另一方面学校的宿舍舒适方便、管理得当。校园里非常适宜骑自行车。短途旅行到帕罗奥图（Palo Alto）是学生们可以选择的一个很好但是偏贵的娱乐项目。那里气候舒适宜人，更是锦上添花，让人更加喜欢。

录取难度

斯坦福大学的录取非常困难，一般来说它从中国招生的数量不多。即便 2400 分的 SAT 也不能保证录取。中国学生们在申请时应该更加注重强调自己的领导力和团队协作能力。录取委员会比较看重申请者的国际项目和奖项。

需要考虑的事情

你会喜欢斯坦福大学，如果……

◆ 你想要探索多元化的专业

◆ 工程和计算机科学是你潜在的就业领域，或者靠近硅谷这点很吸引你

◆ 你希望自己身边有一群成就高、充分做好职前准备的学生。同时，他们悠闲自在、协力合作，并且拥有很有感染力的乐观精神

◆ 季节更替对你来说并不重要

你会不喜欢斯坦福大学，如果……

◆ 你需要一个充满活力的城市环境

◆ 你更希望在美国东海岸有一个较为强大的校友网

◆ 你喜欢寒冷气候的阴郁

佳桥校友录取情况

录取比例	17.4%
SAT 阅读成绩中位数	720
SAT 数学成绩中位数	800
SAT 写作成绩中位数	790
SAT 总分中位数	2260
TOEFL 成绩中位数	115

财政情况

全年学费	45729 美元 (2015—2016)
经济资助可能性	低

学生为学校所在地区打分

安全	4
有趣	4
生活成本	3
中国食物	2
交通便利	1
酒吧和俱乐部	2
超市 / 便利店选择	1
周边就业市场	3
是否需要车	3
总评	3

＊满分 4 分

气候

年平均气温范围	10℃ ~19℃
年平均降水量	61cm
年平均湿度	82.92%
年平均降雪量	0cm

从中国出发的航班

从香港国际机场、首都国际机场或者上海浦东国际机场都有到旧金山国际机场（SFO，San Francisco International Airport）的直达航班。从机场到学校可以选择大巴或者往返巴士。

塔夫茨大学

地址：419 BOSTON AVE.，MEDFORD，MA 02155
网址：WWW.TUFTS.EDU
招生办公室电话：617-627-3170
中国招生官（北京、南京、上海）：JENNIFER SIMONS
招生官邮箱：JENNIFER.SIMONS@TUFTS.EDU
中国招生官（除北京、南京、上海之外的其他城市）：GREG WONG
招生官邮箱：GREG.WONG@TUFTS.EDU
附近主要城市：波士顿，乘坐公交车需要二十分钟

最佳匹配点分析

在波士顿这个孕育了五十多所美国大学的城市里，塔夫茨大学一直是这个“美国大学城”中名列前茅的院校之一。距离哈佛大学和麻省理工学院仅十几分钟路途，塔夫茨的学生们享有这所城市提供给所有学生的机遇和资源。塔夫茨大学张开双臂欢迎世界各地的学生，仅2013级学生就来自全球约五十个国家和地区。一位佳桥校友写道：“国际学生和交换生在这里有他们自己的文化圈子，同时又能与这里的本地学生很好地融合。人们来自不同的地方，兴趣不同、禀赋各异，这对于学校的多元化是至关重要的。”塔夫茨大学的学生们非常具有社会意识，并且将其作为他们身份认同很重要的一部分，他们经常会将自己的社会觉悟同对国际关系的兴趣结合在一起考虑。另外，塔夫茨大学的生物学和健康科学也是非常出名的，这两个专业的毕业生一直都能进入顶尖的医学院或保健公司。

学术机会

塔夫茨大学的学术以难度高出名，但学生们大多都协力合作（除了某些全美顶级的医学预科项目的学生之外）。一位佳桥校友写道：“核心课程，特别是人文学科和社会学，对于一个来自非英语国家的国际学生来说想要拿到 A 是非常难的。至少第一年是这样。”除了有名的医学预科项目之外，塔夫茨大学享有盛誉的专业还有国际关系、环境工程、哲学、社区健康学以及戏剧。本科生参与研究的机会非常多。塔夫茨大学本科生总数只有五千多人，这使得学生们可以很容易地接触到教授。理科有优势的学生应当留意学校的国际研究项目（International Research Program），该项目为文理学院的学生设立，旨在为学生们提供与塔夫茨大学教授一起发展和进行国际化的科学研究项目的机会。每年塔夫茨大学都会举办一场本科研究和奖学金研讨会（Undergraduate Research & Scholarship Symposium），庆祝和奖励为科学研究做出不同贡献的本科生们。

信息速览

US News 大学排名	27
学校位置	东北
学校类型	私立
周边环境	郊区

本科学生情况

学生总数	5126 (2014)
申请人数	19062 (2015)
录取率	16% (2015)
男女学生比例	49/51
国际学生比例	10%
亚裔百分比	12%

有本科项目的学院

文理学院（School of Arts and Sciences）

工程学院（School of Engineering）

你可能还考虑以下学校

布朗大学　宾夕法尼亚大学

康奈尔大学

约翰·霍普金斯大学

西北大学　乔治城大学

职业发展

塔夫茨大学一直为培养学生成为积极的社会公民而骄傲，因此该大学近年来在输出 Peace Corps 志愿者人数上位列中型院校第九名也就不足为奇了。塔夫茨大学的学生毕业后在国外的就业率也超过了全美平均水平，大约 19% 的 2013 届毕业生获得了在国外的就业机会。有数据显示塔夫茨毕业生在一些投资银行、贸易和销售领域的就业率曾经有过高于哈佛和麻省理工的学生或校友的例子。塔夫茨大学的学生也非常热衷投身于教育和新闻领域。

校园人文环境

古怪多变而又机智聪明，塔夫茨的学生们从来不吝啬展现自己奇怪的一面。然而拥有如此多样化的学生群体，你很难精准地概括出一个“典型”的塔夫茨学生是什么样的。

佳桥校友录取情况

录取比例	3.7%
SAT 阅读成绩中位数	690
SAT 数学成绩中位数	800
SAT 写作成绩中位数	720
SAT 总分中位数	2210
TOEFL 成绩中位数	109

财政情况

全年学费

49520 美元 (2015—2016)

经济资助可能性 非常低

学生为学校所在地区打分

安全	3.5
有趣	2
生活成本	2
中国美食	2
公共交通	2.5
酒吧和俱乐部	1
超市 / 便利店选择	1.5
周边就业市场	3.5
是否需要车	2
总评	2.5

*满分 4 分

气候

年平均气温范围	-4℃ ~23℃
年平均降水量	122cm
年平均湿度	68%
年平均降雪量	135.9cm

从中国出发的航班

从首都国际机场、浦东国际机场或者香港国际机场都有直达波士顿洛根国际机场（BOS，Logan International Airport）的航班。在学校和机场之间有往返摆渡车。

"各种各样的人，来自各种不同的背景、不同的种族、持有不同的政治观点、拥有不同的宗教信仰。在塔夫茨再怎么古怪也不足为奇，因为每个人都以某种方式奇特着。"一位佳桥校友这样说。关于塔夫茨的学生生活，另一位佳桥校友提到学校的体育赛事不多见，尽管很多学生努力去运动。虽然兄弟会在塔夫茨已经有一个多世纪的历史了，但是联谊会生活在校园不占压倒性的地位。派对在学校很常见，但没有到难以忍受的疯狂程度。距离波士顿市区较近，波士顿的俱乐部、酒吧和餐馆都是塔夫茨的学生们暂时逃离学习时的选择。

录取难度

SAT 2200 分以上的学生申请塔夫茨大学会比较有竞争优势。塔夫茨大学希望它的学生是积极的社区成员，因此领导职位以及社区服务应该在申请中突出强调。另外不要害怕展现你奇怪的一面，因为塔夫茨就喜欢这样的申请人。

需要考虑的事情

你会喜欢塔夫茨，如果……

- 你有兴趣学习国际关系学或者生物学
- 你自认为是一个奇怪的人并以此为傲
- 你期待一个多元化的大学社区

你会不喜欢塔夫茨，如果……

- 你没有做好同哈佛大学和麻省理工学院的工程学和金融学的学生竞争的准备
- 你很传统保守，在这里需要时刻准备着面对诸多诡异和不同寻常的事情
- 你寻求一个体育项目非常强的学校

加州大学戴维斯分校

地址：1 SHIELDS AVENUE，DAVIS，CA 95616
网址：WWW.UCDAVIS.EDU
中国招生官：无
招生办公室邮箱：学生可以在 HTTPS：//UCDAVIS.ASKADMISSIONS.NET/ASK.ASPX 上提出问题
招生办公室电话：530-752-2971，530-752-3614（国际学生）
附近主要城市：旧金山，坐公交车或火车需要 1.5 小时

最佳匹配点分析

加州大学戴维斯分校不像它的姊妹学校加州大学伯克利分校和加州大学洛杉矶分校那样受欢迎，但是在某些领域，它是伯克利和洛杉矶都望尘莫及的。来到这里的学生会喜欢它慢节奏的校园生活、有趣的传统和宁静浓厚的学习氛围。对于想要生活在城市中的学生来说，戴维斯分校可能并不是理想的选择。来到这里的学生们会发现校园内比校园外更适合活动，因为戴维斯的夜生活很少。萨克拉门托地区的气候不是加州最迷人气候的代表，但是整体上来说，戴维斯常年无雪，是非常适宜居住的城市。来到戴维斯可以体验到脚踏实地的校园环境和卓越的学术氛围，对于周边的环境则不要期待太多。

信息速览

US News 大学排名	41
学校位置	西海岸
学校类型	公立
周边环境	郊区

本科学生情况

学生总数	28384 (2015)
申请人数	64626 (2015)
录取率	38.2% (2015)
男女学生比例	41/59
国际学生百分比	10%
亚裔美国人百分比	37%

有本科项目的学院

文理学院（College of Letters and Science）

工程学院（College of Engineering）

生物科学学院（College of Biological Sciences）

农业和环境科学学院（College of Agriculture and Environmental Sciences）

你可能还考虑以下学校

加州大学欧文分校

加州大学伯克利分校

加州大学圣芭芭拉分校

加州大学洛杉矶分校

学术机会

想要学习生物学、动物学（尤其是那些关注兽医行业的学生）以及工程学的学生可以在这里打下坚实的基础。艺术、葡萄酒酿造和农业工程也是这里的顶级课程。转院系在这里也较为容易。学季制（Quarter System）也让学生们能最大限度地去汲取知识。与很多大型研究型大学不同，戴维斯近 80% 的课堂学生数量都不会超过 50 人，这为学生和教授以及同学之间创造了更多面对面互动的机会。教授对教学的奉献受到高度赞誉和认同。在这里研究机会也很多，学生们从不担心他们对知识的渴求会得不到满足。

职业发展

2009 年，有 37% 的毕业生选择继续深造，另有 52% 选择毕业后工作。80% 选择继续深造研究生教育的学生都被他们的第一志愿和第二志愿录取，这让戴维斯引以为傲。科学或工程领域的学生们在找工作或者实习机会的时候一般都不会遇到困难。但是，商科和会计方向的学生可能需要付出更多的努力才能获得招聘企业的关注。加州大学戴维斯分校的就业服务部门会为学生提供有用的实习机会，并在毕业时帮助他们寻找工作，但对校友的支持不是太多。

校园人文环境

校园内文化活动丰富，有很多有趣和著名的学校传统（如野餐日 Picnic Day，戴维斯分校的开放日），学校有植物园以及种类繁多的俱乐部（如果没有你感兴趣的也可以选择自己新建一个），包括学校自己的广播电台以及学生自己运营的一个公交车站。公共交通为学生们往返戴维斯和伯克利之间、发掘旧金山湾区和萨克拉门托地区提供了方便。周边的城镇都非常小，以至于一两年内就可以认识镇上的大多数面孔。联谊会生活仅仅吸引了 8% 的本科学生，在这里聚会不会占用学生太多时间。

加州大学戴维斯分校的亚裔学生占到学生总数的 37%，你会很容易地在自己身边发现华裔学生。学生们说在学校周围就可以吃到中国食物，吃饭在这里并不贵。寿司自助餐在周边小镇也是非常热门的选择。戴维斯的食堂在加州大学系统里应该是除了洛杉矶分校以外最好的了。

录取难度

加州大学戴维斯分校不像加州伯克利或加州洛杉矶分校那么难录取。SAT 拿到 1950 分或者更高分的学生会比较容易被录取。

需要考虑的事情

你会喜欢加州大学戴维斯分校，如果……

- 你喜欢户外活动
- 你喜欢小镇和小的社区团体
- 你更喜欢周围有大量的亚洲学生
- 你希望将来成为计算机科学家

你会不喜欢加州大学戴维斯分校，如果……

- 你需要一个拥有活力的城市环境
- 你想学习会计和金融

佳桥校友录取情况

录取比例	71%
SAT 阅读成绩中位数	650
SAT 数学成绩中位数	800
SAT 写作成绩中位数	690
SAT 总分中位数	2100
TOEFL 成绩中位数	105

财政情况

全年学费	38659 美元 (2015—2016)
经济资助可能性	非常低

学生为学校所在地区打分

安全	3.5
有趣	3
生活成本	3
中国食物	2
交通便利	4
酒吧和俱乐部	2
超市 / 便利店选择	2
周边就业市场	2.5
是否需要车	1
总评	3

*满分 4 分

气候

年平均气温范围	8.3℃ ~25℃
年平均降水量	57.2cm
年平均湿度	79.94%
年平均降雪量	0cm

从中国出发的航班

学生可以选择从香港国际机场、首都国际机场或者上海浦东国际机场直飞旧金山国际机场（SFO，San Francisco International Airport）。之后可以选择驾车、乘坐大巴或者乘坐火车到达目的地。

加州大学洛杉矶分校

地址：405 HILGARD AVENUE，BOX 951405，LOS ANGELES，CA 90095
网址：WWW.UCLA.EDU
中国招生官：无
招生办公室电话：310-825-3101
招生办公室邮箱：学生可以在 HTTPS: //WWW.ADMISSION.UCLA.EDU/CONTACTFORM/UGADM.ASPX 上提出问题
附近主要城市：洛杉矶，加州大学洛杉矶分校距离洛杉矶市区开车 20~30 分钟路程

最佳匹配点分析

加州大学洛杉矶分校号称自己是全美每年本科申请人数最多的学校，原因显而易见。美丽的校园、无懈可击的气候条件、排名很高的专业项目以及名声在外的学校食堂创造出一个几乎“过分舒适”的大学生活。那些喜欢每个学期班上都充满全新面孔的学生是能够最大程度领略加州大学洛杉矶分校迷人之处的。然而，一些佳桥校友也表示如此众多的学生有时也会令他们感到困扰。

学术机会

在 US News 排名第 23 的加州大学洛杉矶分校曾经是学术声名卓著的加州大学伯克利分校的一部分，后来才发展成为拥有独特优势专业的独立机构。它的优势专业包括语言学、心理学、传媒、电影和戏剧艺术。一位佳桥校友说这里的教授都非常容易接近，“前两年的通识教育课程以讲座和讨论的形式进行。教授负责讲座授课，助教负责课程讨

论。大三、大四两年，大部分的课程则全部由教授执教。”学生们会发现课程进行得很快，这是因为学校将标准的 16 周一个学期缩短到了 10 周一个学期，但这并不是不易掌控的。一位佳桥校友表示：“低年级的课程教授往往会采用百分比评分，但不是所有的课程都这样。不同的教授评分标准也不同。”大部分时候，教授们可以在办公时间为学生们提供帮助。研究机会很多，但是先联系教授从而获得机会是最容易的。护理学院和戏剧电影影视学院在大二或者大三才接受学生。文理学院和工程学院之间的转院通常较为简单。

职业发展

虽然一般来说，“棕熊们”都很自信并以自己的学校为荣（UCLA 的学生在太平洋十二校联盟中被称为 Bruins），但是他们对于利用校友网络的态度却充满了矛盾情绪。作为一个大型院校，学生们更多地倾向于从周边的朋友圈、职业兄弟会（由有着相同的职业目标的学成组建的兄弟会）和职业服务中心寻求就业帮助。然而，洛杉矶地区本身就是一个丰富、灵活和多功能的就业平台。南湾地区的大公司，如霍尼韦尔（Honeywell）和埃克森美孚（Exxon Mobil）等，提供了大量的技术和工程相关的就业岗位。

另外，四大会计师事务所和一些顶级的咨询公司每年都会在洛杉矶分校招聘。拥有雄心壮志、想成为工程、金融、市场和咨询领域专业人士的学生们在这里可以获得取之不尽的资源。

校园人文环境

学校内主要的社交都是围绕各种学生组织进行的，那些想要很快找到归属感的中国学生可以加入学校的中国学生学者联合会（CSSA）。一位佳桥校友说：“大部分的中国学生仍然是和中国学生在一起玩儿。”为了避免这种情况，学生们可以加入职业兄弟会，它们是同样的热门、有效的社交网络。

饮酒主要出现在联谊会活动中，但其他活动场合也会有。大约 30% 的学生参加联谊

信息速览

US News 大学排名	23
学校位置	西海岸
学校类型	公立
周边环境	城市

本科学生情况

学生总数	29585 (2015)
申请人数	92722 (2015)
录取率	17.3% (2015)
男女学生比例	44/56
国际学生百分比	12%
亚裔美国人百分比	32.8%

有本科项目的学院

文理学院（College of Letters and Science）
艺术和建筑学院（School of the Arts and Architecture）
戏剧和影视学院（School of Theater, Film，and Television）
护理学院（School of Nursing）
工程和应用科学学院（School of Engineering and Applied Science）
音乐学院（School of Music）

你可能还考虑以下学校

南加州大学
密歇根大学
斯坦福大学
北卡大学教堂山分校
加州大学伯克利分校
加州大学圣地亚哥分校

佳桥校友录取情况

录取比例	27.8%
SAT 阅读成绩中位数	710
SAT 数学成绩中位数	800
SAT 写作成绩中位数	730
SAT 总分中位数	2220
TOEFL 成绩中位数	109

财政情况

全年学费	37959 美元 (2015—2016)
经济资助可能性	非常低

学生为学校所在地区打分

安全	3
有趣	4
生活成本	3
中国食物	4
交通便利	2
酒吧和俱乐部	3
超市 / 便利店选择	3
周边就业市场	3
是否需要车	4
总评	3

*满分 4 分

气候

年平均气温范围	13℃ ~24℃
年平均降水量	44.9cm
年平均湿度	75.54%
年平均降雪量	0cm

从中国出发的航班

从中国有直达洛杉矶国际机场（LAX，Los Angeles International Airport）的航班。学生们可以选择从香港、北京或者上海飞往洛杉矶。

会，不过联谊会不是垄断性的。随着社交圈子的发展，年龄限制逐渐消失，联谊会派对更多的变成一种可选择性的活动而不是标准活动。“饮酒在我们学校是一件平常的事”。尽管加州大学洛杉矶分校禁止在校园里饮酒，但是学生们觉得偷偷地将酒带进宿舍是件壮举。未成年饮酒现象是存在的，但并不普遍，不会让人觉得受不了。

由于“学校周边公共交通非常糟糕，外出很难，除非你有一辆车”，学生们大学前两年主要是在校园里面活动。所有的佳桥校友都强调拥有一辆车的重要性。校园以外，韦斯特伍德（Westwood）是一个有趣、安全的社区，拥有昂贵而浪漫的餐厅。再向外，就是丰富迷人、辽阔庞大的洛杉矶了。

录取难度

加州大学洛杉矶分校每年的录取标准波动很大，但是一般来说 SAT 超过 2100 分的学生比较有优势。像很多加州大学系统的其他成员一样，洛杉矶分校在审理过程中也非常看重分数和 GPA 这些硬件条件。

需要考虑的事情

你会喜欢加州大学洛杉矶分校，如果……

- 你需要并且想要有实习机会
- “加州大学洛杉矶分校的食物堪称完美！我的一位南加州大学的朋友来到这里在学校餐厅就餐后告诉我他都打算转学到这里了。”
- 你喜欢运动

你会不喜欢加州大学洛杉矶分校，如果……

- 你寻求种族多样化，并且更多的想要体验文化碰撞
- 你想要寻找一种更加紧张和学术化的学校氛围

加州大学圣地亚哥分校

地址：9500 GILMAN DRIVE，LA JOLLA，CA 92093
网址：WWW.UCSD.EDU
中国招生官：无
招生办公室电话：858-534-4831
招生办公室邮箱：INFOINTERNATIONAL@AD.UCSD.EDU
附近主要城市：圣地亚哥，从圣地亚哥国际机场开车 20~25 分钟可达

最佳匹配点分析

通过将本科学生编入 6 个住宿学院，加州大学圣地亚哥分校成为加州大学系统中为学生创造更小校园社区做出最多努力的大学。期待平静和慢节奏校园环境的学生会比喜欢大都市繁华生活的学生更适合来这里。加州大学圣地亚哥分校的生物学和工程学排名很高，强烈推荐想要从事这两个领域工作的学生选择这所学校。这里没有寒冷的气候，中国南方那些厌倦了高温气候、想要拥有不同气候体验的学生可能会对这里失望。圣地亚哥分校不是一个派对盛行的学校，同样地，圣地亚哥这所城市也不属于派对城市，虽然两者都没有小到你会谴责它没有盛大的节日狂欢之类的活动。那些想要在学习之余寻找一个合适的社交生活平衡的学生会在这所加州南部的校园里体验到完美的匹配。

信息速览

US News 大学排名	39
学校位置	西海岸
学校类型	公立
周边环境	城市

本科学生情况

学生总数	26590 (2015)
申请人数	78091 (2015)
录取率	33.9% (2015)
男女学生比例	52/48
国际学生百分比	18%
亚裔美国人百分比	46%

有本科项目的学院

艺术与人文学学院（Division of Arts and Humanities）

数学与物理科学学院（Division of Mathematics and Physical Sciences）

生物科学学院（Divisions of Biological Sciences）

社会科学学院（Division of Social Sciences）

雅各布工程学院（Jacobs School of Engineering）

斯科里普斯海洋学研究所（Scripps Institution of Oceanography）

你可能还考虑以下学校

加州大学洛杉矶分校　迈阿密大学

加州大学圣芭芭拉分校

加州大学戴维斯分校

学术机会

加州大学圣地亚哥分校有许多强大的特色专业，例如，纳米工程、生物工程、行为神经科学、航空航天工程和海洋学等。此外，戏剧和舞蹈、经济学、政治科学以及多媒体 / 视觉传媒排名也非常靠前。除了工程学院（Jacobs School of Engineering）的一些特定专业外，转专业并不难。六个本科住宿学院每个都有自己略为不同的教育理念，这在每个学院不同的毕业要求上得到体现。例如，John Muir 住宿学院注重学术个性，而 Eleanor Roosevelt 住宿学院则关注让学生们成为世界公民。校园里的研究机会非常多，特别是科学领域的研究项目，学生的 GPA 是能否参与到研究项目中的主要衡量标准。一位目前正在学习工程的佳桥校友说课程内容容易掌握，成绩一般采用百分比评分体系。

职业发展

2012—2013 学年完成学业的学生有 73% 找到了自己的工作，最热门的就业专业分布在技术、商业、生命 / 健康科学、人性化服务和艺术 / 传媒领域。剩下的 27% 选择了继续研究生教育和职前培训项目的学习。夏普健康医疗公司（Sharp Healthcare）、高通（Qualcomm）、凯泽永久医疗集团（Kaiser Permanente）和圣地亚哥天然气和电力公司（San Diego Gas & Electric）经常在圣地亚哥分校招聘。一些佳桥校友并不打算将来利用学校的校友网，但学校确实为毕业生们提供了很多校友网络联盟来帮助即将走向职场的毕业生们，为他们将来的就业提供专业的指导服务。

校园人文环境

加州大学圣地亚哥分校的本科住宿学院系统在加州大学系统中独具特色。所有申请该校的学生都要将Revelle、Warren、Muir、ERC、Marshall、Sixth这六个住宿学院按照自己的喜好进行排序。每个学院都是拥有自己不同通识教育课程和课外活动的小社区。很多学生会推荐毕业要求最少的两个学院：Warren学院和Muir学院。但是高中毕业生需要谨记每个学院都有不同的社交活动和学术特色。你的专业可能会被所选的住宿学院特有的社区环境影响，虽然这种影响不是直接的。

圣地亚哥是一个悠闲的城市，附近有美丽的海滩，这为学生们提供了很多户外娱乐活动的机会。佳桥的校友很少提到这所城市会缺少什么东西，中国食物大概是个例外。在圣地亚哥分校只有大概23%的学生参与到了低调的联谊会生活中。该校相对安静的运动场面是一点不足，但运动的多样性弥补了这一遗憾，尽管中国学生可能并不这么认为。学校里大概有46%的亚裔学生，23%的白人学生，12%的墨西哥裔美国人，9%的其他种族学生，2%非裔美国人，3%拉丁裔和5%的菲律宾裔（不计入亚裔）。

录取难度

加州大学圣地亚哥分校的工程学院录取较其他院系稍有难度，但是总体上来说，该校每年都会录取相当大比例的中国学生。SAT和TOEFL成绩在审理过程中比较被看重。

需要考虑的事情

你会喜欢加州大学圣地亚哥分校，如果……

佳桥校友录取情况

录取比例	62.3%
SAT 阅读成绩中位数	670
SAT 数学成绩中位数	800
SAT 写作成绩中位数	710
SAT 总分中位数	2150
TOEFL 成绩中位数	108

财政情况

全年学费	38265 美元 (2015—2016)
经济资助可能性	非常低

学生为学校所在地区打分

安全	4
有趣	3
生活成本	3
中国食品	2.5
交通便利	3
酒吧和俱乐部	3
超市 / 便利店选择	3.5
周边就业市场	3
是否需要车	3
总评	3.5

*满分4分

气候

年平均气温范围	13℃ ~24℃
年平均降水量	32.4cm
年平均湿度	80.89%
年平均降雪量	0cm

从中国出发的航班

从中国没有直达圣地亚哥的航班，学生们需要从其他地方（比如说西雅图）转机才能到达圣地亚哥国际机场（SAN，San Diego International Airport）。

- 你喜欢户外活动
- 你打算将来成为生物学家
- 你有兴趣上一所研究型大学，同时又希望它是一个小型的、文理学院类型的社区

你会不喜欢加州大学圣地亚哥分校，如果……

- 你想要一个忙碌些的大城市环境
- 你想要学习会计或者金融

加州大学圣芭芭拉分校

地址：1210 CHEADLE HALL，UNIVERSITY OF CALIFORNIA，SANTA BARBARA，SANTA BARBARA，CA 93106
网址：WWW.UCSB.EDU
中国招生官：无
招生办公室邮箱：学生可以在 HTTPS：//ADMISSIONS.SA.UCSB.EDU/CONNECT/CONTACT-US 上提出问题
招生办公室电话：805-893-2881
附近主要城市：洛杉矶，乘坐大巴或者 AMTRAK 火车约一个半小时车程

最佳匹配点分析

站在一片悬崖上俯瞰海洋，加州大学圣芭芭拉分校就像童话中的学校。帅气的男生和漂亮的女生每天穿着无袖上衣生活在天堂般的校园中，天空总是散发着金色光芒。理所当然地，在天堂每个人都参加派对。如果酒精、社交文化、只拥有单一季节的美和拥有两万名同学不是你所喜欢的，那么这里不适合你。工程专业的学生们要注意，由于工程学院已有的声望和与声望相匹配的严格要求，在圣芭芭拉分校你有可能从来不会享受到这样的舒适生活。总体来说，加州大学圣芭芭拉分校仍然是一个非常好的学校，拥有工程、生物学以及物理学方面的强势项目。

信息速览

US News 大学排名	37
学校位置	西海岸
学校类型	公立
周边环境	郊区

本科学生情况

学生总数	20238（2015）
申请人数	70565（2015）
录取率	32.7%（2015）
男女学生比例	47/53
国际学生百分比	6%
亚裔美国人百分比	21%

有本科项目的学院

创意研究学院（College of Creative Studies）
工程学院（College of Engineering）
文理学院（College of Letters & Science）

你可能还考虑以下学校

加州大学戴维斯分校
加州大学洛杉矶分校
加州大学伯克利分校
得克萨斯奥斯汀大学
迈阿密大学
加州大学圣地亚哥分校

学术机会

毫无疑问，学校的班级很大。很多大型讲座由教授讲课，小型的讨论课则由在读博士或硕士助教负责。这里的教授都非常博学，他们都是 STEM（Science、Technology、Engineering and Mathematics 自然科学、技术、工程、数学）领域全美最好的教授。除了工程学院以外，加州大学圣芭芭拉分校的另两个学院都不会给学生过多的课业负担。无论专业是否在 STEM 领域，学生都有很多参与最新研究项目的机会。

职业发展

在学术界，加州大学圣芭芭拉分校的工程学院和生物科学相关领域专业是家喻户晓的，但是具有挑战性的课程设置也会减少你的派对时间。对 2013 届大四学生的调查显示，53% 的学生已经找到了全职工作，22% 的学生会在毕业之后马上继续读研究生或者博士，88% 的学生说他们打算在毕业后的几年内继续深造。最热门的就业领域分布在金融、教育、销售和市场、科研、工程、医学和商业管理等领域。经常在圣芭芭拉分校招聘的公司有塔吉特零售（Target）、英特尔、脸书（Facebook）、Peace Corps、BrightRoll 和 Citrix。学校的校友网络不是最强大的，但是学生们都非常热爱他们的母校。

校园人文环境

Isla Vista 拥有非常棒的气候条件，天气温暖干爽。这里总是清风徐徐、非常迷人，是游人们蜂拥而至的度假胜地。拥有如此棒的海滩，学生们可以时常进行冲浪运动，大学四年至少要有那么一次冲浪体验才行。虽然 Isla Vista 算得上是理想的风景城市，但是几乎所有的学生也都同意这里非常昂贵而且城市气息不强。要想去大一些的城市，有车的学生可以用一个多小时开到洛杉矶（如果堵车的话可能会更耗时一些）。

尽管联谊会生活不是很主流，只有 8% 的男生和 13% 的女生参与其中，但是派对却四季常有（几乎每个人都听说过他们的万圣节狂欢会）。加州大学圣芭芭拉分校拥有非常多样化的学生群体，其中有 48% 的白人学生，21% 的亚裔学生，26% 的西班牙裔学生，还有 3% 的非洲裔美国人。可能是由于这样高度多样化的学生群体，校园文化氛围非常自由，并且当属政治最活跃的校园之一。加州大学圣芭芭拉分校每年都会举办一场免费的音乐节，还有至少 700 名学生支持的校内俱乐部运动会，所以在校园里从不缺少活动。女子篮球赛和男子橄榄球赛都是非常有趣且热闹的活动。尽管圣芭芭拉的学生们喝起酒来像是在沙漠中见到水一般疯狂，但毒品在校园里是严格禁止的，只有在看不见的角落里可能存在少数的吸毒现象。

录取难度

加州大学圣芭芭拉分校的录取很大程度上看重申请者的标准化考试成绩和 GPA 水平。中国录取者的 SAT 成绩往往要超过 1900 分，TOEFL 要超过 90 分。

需要考虑的事情

你会喜欢加州大学圣芭芭拉分校，如果……

- 你想一年四季都有太阳晒出的黑白线
- 你期待大部分的社交活动发生在校园内
- 你是忠实的沙滩迷

你会不喜欢加州大学圣芭芭拉分校，如果……

- 你没有意志力。派对和沙滩会让你分心
- 你不喜欢占主导地位的白色沙滩文化
- 你更加喜欢时不时地下点儿雪

佳桥校友录取情况

录取比例	53.3%
SAT 阅读成绩中位数	660
SAT 数学成绩中位数	800
SAT 写作成绩中位数	690
SAT 总分中位数	2110
TOEFL 成绩中位数	106

财政情况

全年学费	36948 美元 (2015—2016)
经济资助可能性	非常低

学生为学校所在地区打分

安全	3
有趣	4
生活成本	3
中国食物	1
交通便利	1
酒吧和俱乐部	2
超市 / 便利店选择	1
周边就业市场	2
是否需要车	4
总评	4

*满分 4 分

气候

年平均气温范围	11℃ ~21℃
年平均降水量	56.2cm
年平均湿度	83.57%
年平均降雪量	0cm

从中国出发的航班

从中国没有直达的航班。学生们必须先飞到洛杉矶国际机场（LAX，Los Angeles International Airport）然后乘坐大巴或者火车到达圣芭芭拉。

芝加哥大学

地址：5801 S ELLIS AVE，CHICAGO，IL 60637
网址：WWW.UCHICAGO.EDU
中国招生官：CAROL LIN，CHRIS DAVEY
招生办公室电话：773-702-8650
招生办公室邮箱：INTERNATIONALADMISSIONS@UCHICAGO.EDU
附近主要城市：芝加哥

最佳匹配点分析

“娱乐已死”这句芝加哥大学的非官方口号被芝加哥大学的学生——一群将学术研究作为自己高等教育核心追求的人，用作标榜自己的标志。位于全美最大城市之一芝加哥南部的海德公园地区，芝加哥大学吸引了众多被标榜为“书呆子”和“知识分子”的学生来到这里。他们中的很多人都计划在本科阶段学习结束后继续追求硕士或者博士学位。英语、政治学以及人类学方面的学科是芝加哥大学的一些最强学科，但是选择了经济学、数学和物理学的佳桥校友也表示这些项目的课程非常有魅力。

学术机会

从本质上来说，芝加哥大学首先是一个研究机构，这里有着无与伦比的研究机会。除了本科学院外，芝加哥大学设有四个研究生院和六所职业学院。学校的这种研究背景让本科生更易于参加到一些高端的研究课题中来，包括像宇宙物理学和材料学研究（Cosmological Physics and Materials Research）这样的由美国国家科学基金会（National Science Foundation）赞助的研究项目。学校的核心课程称为“共同核心”（Common Core），以小班授课为特色，要求学生学习人文学科和社会科学方面的课程，同时需要熟练掌握一门外语，并研究某一特定文明。芝加哥大学在跨领域跨学科方面也取得了很大的进步，创建了像“重大问题”（Big Problems）和“基础知识：问题和文本”（Fundamentals：Issues & Texts）这样的跨学科专业。芝加哥大学的学术严谨是非常出名的，一位佳桥校友说拿到A“真的非常难”，估计“一个八十人的班里面能够拿到A的人不会超过六个”。尽管芝加哥大学的学习颇具挑战，但受益于学校通力合作的氛围，它激发了学生们前进的动力而非相互间的竞争。

信息速览

US News 大学排名	4
学校位置	中西部
学校类型	私立
周边环境	城市

本科学生情况

学生总数	5869 (2015)
申请人数	30188 (2015)
录取率	8.35% (2015)
男女学生比例	53/47
国际学生百分比	10.8%
亚裔百分比	17.4%

有本科项目的学院

芝加哥大学本科学院（The College of the University of Chicago）

你可能还想考虑以下学校

哥伦比亚大学	西北大学
宾夕法尼亚大学	耶鲁大学

职业发展

根据《高校解决方案》（*The College Solution*）的数据显示，在全美高等院校本科毕业生成功申请研究生比例方面，芝加哥大学排名第九。2013届毕业生中约54%进入就业大军，17%直接升入研究生院或者职业学院。在开始全职工作的学生中，有惊人的21%的毕业生进入了教育和研究领域。芝加哥大学校友网络的影响力曾经很弱，但是近来学校在募捐方面做出的努力已经硕果累累，包括一笔对商学院近3亿美元的捐款。芝加哥的校友们也倾向于从他们的母校招聘实习生和全职雇员。

校园人文环境

芝加哥大学并不以发达的社交出名。学生们可以利用学校附近海德公园区域的餐馆和酒吧，有些学生会到芝加哥市区寻求更好的夜生活。运动场景在学校里也不多见。尽管芝加哥大学是众所周知地不举办“盛大派对”，但是仍然有几个年度校园活动承载着学校的骄傲和古怪的校园传统。芝加哥大学寻宝游戏（University of Chicago Scavenger Hunt，Scav）是一个为期四天的寻宝游戏。参与游戏的学生需要找到一系列作为“宝”的物品（有时候会是特别奇怪的东西），像曾经出现过的著名自制核反应堆。夏日微风节

佳桥校友录取情况

录取比例	19.1%
SAT 阅读成绩中位数	720
SAT 数学成绩中位数	800
SAT 写作成绩中位数	790
SAT 总分中位数	2285
TOEFL 成绩中位数	113

财政情况

全年学费	49026 美元 (2015—2016)
经济资助可能性	非常低

学生为学校所在地区打分

安全	2
有趣	2
生活成本	2.5
中国食物	2
交通便利	2.5
酒吧和俱乐部	2
超市 / 便利店选择	2
周边就业市场	2
是否需要车	1.5
总评	3

*满分 4 分

气候

年平均气温范围	-6℃ ~23℃
年平均降水量	93cm
年平均湿度	72.3%
年平均降雪量	82.1cm

从中国出发的航班

芝加哥奥黑尔国际机场（ORD, O' Hare International Airport）距离学校大概半个小时到一个小时车程，学生们可以乘坐摆渡车或者大巴到达机场。北京、上海和香港都有到芝加哥的直飞航班。

（The Summer Breeze festival）帮助校园走出芝加哥寒冷的冬季，节日里有音乐表演和果冻里摔跤比赛这样的狂欢会。芝加哥大学甚至出资举办了深冬北极熊赛跑（Polar Bear Run），活动中学生们赤身裸体飞跑穿越广场。同时，Doc Films 算是全美存在时间最长的由学生主办运营的电影协会了，而艺术节（Festival of the Arts）则是一场由时尚秀、讲座和艺术装饰组成的盛会。尽管有这些节日，学生们仍然保持对学习的严谨和认真，看到他们，你会领悟到芝加哥大学真正的时尚在于用他们自己的方式去“娱乐”。

录取难度

每年申请芝加哥大学的学生量都在递增，这使得录取率越来越低。被录取的学生 SAT 成绩往往都要超过 2200 分。与其他排名前五的学校相比，芝加哥大学算是相对容易录取的。但是它的录取过程却非常具有芝加哥大学自己的风格，而且颇为苛刻。佳桥被录取的学生很少有 SAT 低于 2250 分的，除非有特殊情况。

需要考虑的事情

你会喜欢芝加哥大学，如果……

- 你对乐趣的定义是进行哲学或者学术讨论直到凌晨三点
- 你想要大量的研究机会，或者打算毕业后进入研究生院
- 你想在必修课程中有人文和社会科学方面的经典课程

你会不喜欢芝加哥大学如果……

- 你不喜欢寒冷的天气
- 你不喜欢 T 恤上印有“芝加哥大学的约会——约会不难，但约会的感觉很奇怪”的人

密歇根大学安娜堡分校

地址：515 EAST JEFFERSON STREET，ANN ARBOR，MI 48109-1316
网址：WWW.UMICH.EDU
附近主要城市：底特律，车程 1 小时
中国招生官：SHANELL HAGOOD（北京）
招生官邮箱：SHLEANNA@UMICH.EDU
招生官电话：734-647-8290
中国招生官：JULIE POLLAK（上海、深圳）
招生官邮箱：JPOLLAK@UMICH.EDU
招生官电话：734-615-3161
中国招生官：ALISON WANG（杭州）
招生官邮箱：ALIWANG@UMICH.EDU
招生官电话：734-647-7850
中国招生官：KRISTEN LEMIRE（重庆、大连、天津、无锡）
招生官邮箱：KDLC@UMICH.EDU
招生官电话：734-615-0383
中国招生官：REUBEN KAPP（常州、成都、广州、南京、宁波、青岛、沈阳、苏州、武汉、西安）
招生官邮箱：KAPPREUB@UMICH.EDU
招生官电话：734-936-2426
中国招生官：ERICA DECKER（其他城市）
招生官邮箱：ELDECKER@UMICH.EDU
招生官电话：734-763-9412

最佳匹配点分析

被誉为“公立常春藤”的密歇根大学是一所大型公立大学。它吸引着来自美国和世界各地的学生来这里的19个学院（其中13个学院有本科生项目）学习。学校提供200多个本科学位项目，学生们可以毫无拘束地选择他们想要深造的学术领域。尽管安娜堡冬季的严寒可能让人觉得讨厌，但是作为一个充满活力的大学城，安娜堡在该州高等学府的领军地位让它感到骄傲。众多中国留学生会大谈他们在密歇根大学的经历，在如此多样化的学生群体中，每个人最终都能找到适合自己的位置或者小圈子。不过，请注意那些可以容纳500名学生的基础性课程，这些课程往往为STEM（Science，Technology，Engineering，and Math，美国政府的STEM计划是一项鼓励学生主修科学、技术、工程和数学领域的计划）专业学生所开设，让这些学生之间的竞争十分激烈。

学术机会

很多大一新生往往被淹没在几百人的课堂中，密歇根大学没有忽视这个问题。为了平衡大一新生的班级规模，密歇根大学通过工程、英语等学科的第一年研讨项目（First-Year Seminars）给学生个性化的关注。密歇根大学的课程作业是公认的严格和耗时，所以学校也并不需要刻意创造竞争激烈的环境。一般来讲，学生选修课程的难易程度决定了学习任务的难度和学习量大小。正如一位佳桥校友所说：“有些课程拿到A是很难的，但是并不是所有课程都是如此。很多课程采用百分比计分。”医学预科课程、工程、艺术和设计、建筑、音乐和商业都是密歇根大学的顶级项目。学校文理学院的荣誉项目（Honors Program）为500名本科生提供了大一、大二参加研究项目的机会，这为他们将来在教授指导下完成荣誉毕业论文奠定了基础。在密歇根大学没有哪门课程是要求所有学生必修的，但是文理学院的学生必须参加数理和种族方面的课程，这也是学校以多样化为傲的一个表现。

信息速览

US News 大学排名	29
学校位置	中西
学校类型	公立
周边环境	城市

本科学生情况

学生总数	28312 (2015)
申请人数	51797 (2015)
录取率	26.3% (2015)
男女学生比例	51/49
国际学生比例	7%
亚裔百分比	13.6%

职业发展

密歇根大学 2013 届文理学院的毕业生就业率达到 63.5%，约 30% 的文理学院毕业生选择继续就读研究生或者在专业领域深造，接近 6.1% 的毕业生仍在求职。很多学生毕业后倾向于留在密歇根州，2013 届毕业生中，有 44% 的毕业生在州内找到就业机会。作为学术重镇和最适宜居住的城市之一，安娜堡为毕业生提供了众多的就业选择，包括高科技、健康服务以及生物科技方面的工作。未来的工程师们有机会选择在汽车制造企业如通用汽车（General Motors）或者燃料排放实验室（Fuel Emissions Laboratory）实习。

校园人文环境

尽管 64% 的学生来自密歇根州，密歇根大学仍然以学生多样化程度很高而享有盛誉。少数族裔占了学生总数的四分之一。一位佳桥校友写道："这是个拥有众多学生的大型学校，所以必然很有趣也很多样化。中国学生约有 2000 人，从大一新生到博士都有。想要认识每个人是不可能的。但是你确实可以交到很多朋友，每天都能认识新的人。"在密歇根大学派对是非常普遍的，"最大的派对是俱乐部举办的活动，其次应该是兄弟会的活动，规模最小但却最常见的当属家庭形式的小型宴会了。"学校指南中在列的学生组织就有 1500 个以上，因此在密歇根大学你几乎可以找到任何种类的俱乐部，包括一些像中华创新与创业联盟（China Entrepreneur Network）这样的专门组织。橄榄球是学生们秋季的焦点，每个周末都能吸引成千的密歇根橄榄球迷们聚集在学校的主场，密歇根体育场（Michigan Stadium，也是全美最大的橄榄球运动场）观看比赛。

有本科项目的学院

陶布曼建筑和城市规划学院（A. Alfred Taubman College of Architecture and Urban Planning）
罗斯商学院（Stephen M. Ross School of Business）
牙医学院（School of Dentistry）
教育学院（School of Education）
工程学院（College of Engineering）
信息学院（School of Information）
运动机能学院（School of Kinesiology）
文学、科学与艺术学院（College of Literature, Science, and the Arts（LSA））
音乐、戏剧与舞蹈学院（School of Music, Theatre & Dance）
护理学院（School of Nursing）
药学院（College of Pharmacy）
公共卫生学院（School of Public Health）
福特公共政策学院（Gerald R. Ford School of Public Policy）
艺术设计学院（Penny W. Stamps School of Art & Design）

你可能还考虑以下学校

康奈尔大学
宾夕法尼亚大学
北卡教堂山大学
华盛顿圣路易斯大学
威斯康星麦迪逊大学

佳桥校友录取情况

录取比例	14.1%
SAT 阅读成绩中位数	690
SAT 数学成绩中位数	800
SAT 写作成绩中位数	720
SAT 总分中位数	2190
TOEFL 成绩中位数	111

财政情况

全年学费

43476 美元（2015—2016，大一、大二学生）

46528 美元（2015—2016，大三、大四学生）

经济资助可能性 低

学生为学校所在地区打分

安全	3.5
有趣	2.5
生活成本	2.5
中国美食	2.5
公共交通	2
酒吧和俱乐部	2
超市 / 便利店选择	1.5
周边就业市场	2.5
是否需要车	3.5
总评	3

*满分 4 分

气候

年平均气温范围	-5℃ ~22℃
年平均降水量	83.9cm
年平均湿度	73.7%
年平均降雪量	83.8cm

从中国出发的航班

底特律大都会国际机场（DTW，Detroit Metropolitan Airport）距学校仅半个小时车程，乘坐大巴或者穿梭巴士都能直接到达机场。从北京和上海都有到达底特律的直达航班。

录取难度

近年来，密歇根大学对中国留学生的开放度已经不如之前，录取率已大幅度下降。很多中国学生在提前录取中被延期或者拒绝，只有那些真正展现出对密歇根有兴趣的学生才得到了录取。许多被密歇根大学录取的学生同时也收到了很多其他声名卓越的大学的录取。

需要考虑的事情

你会喜欢密歇根大学，如果……

- 你喜欢有很多中国学生的大学
- 你有兴趣学习商科或工程

你会不喜欢密歇根大学，如果……

- 你喜欢有棕榈树的校园
- 你觉得你可能应付不了第一学年的大型课堂
- 你是一个杜克迷（杜克和密歇根是体育劲敌）

北卡罗来纳大学教堂山分校

地址： CB#9100，103 SOUTH BUILDING，CHAPEL HILL，NC 27599
网址： WWW.UNC.EDU
中国招生官： 无
招生办公室电话： 919-966-3621
招生办公室邮箱： 学生可以在 HTTP：//ADMISSIONS.UNC.EDU/CONTACT-US/ 上提出问题
附近主要城市： 夏洛特市（两个半小时车程）

最佳匹配点分析

作为美国历史上第一所公立大学，北卡大学教堂山分校已经享有长达两个多世纪的学术盛誉，是大家公认的全美最佳公立大学之一。被称为“最理想大学城”的教堂山市环抱北卡教堂山大学校园，孕育出一系列音乐酒吧、电影院、餐馆以及跳舞场所，为学生常年的娱乐活动提供方便。北卡教堂山大学有非常好的传统体育项目，同学校的文化底蕴相融合。该校与车程相隔几站的杜克大学之间的篮球对抗赛有着悠久的历史。如果不介意上大课，以及 80% 的学生来自北卡州内的事实，那么北卡大学教堂山分校可以为你的本科学习提供良多。

信息速览

US News 大学排名	30
学校位置	南部
学校类型	公立
周边环境	郊区

本科学生情况

学生总数	18415 (2015)
申请人数	31953 (2015)
录取率	30% (2015)
男女学生比例	42/58
国际学生百分比	3%
亚裔百分比	11.7%

有本科项目的学院

文理学院（College of Arts and Sciences）
传媒与新闻学院（School of Journalism and Mass Communication）
吉林斯全球公共卫生学院（Gillings School of Global Public Health）
牙科学院（School of Dentistry）
凯南—弗拉格勒商学院（Kenan-Flagler Business School）
信息与图书馆学学院（School of Information and Library Science）
教育学院（School of Education）
护理学院（School of Nursing）

你可能还考虑以下学校

杜克大学　弗吉尼亚大学
加州大学洛杉矶分校　西北大学
加州大学伯克利分校

学术机会

北卡大学教堂山分校的学术水平可以与美国一些顶级的私立大学相媲美，因此该校有“公立常春藤”的美誉。该校最强的学科有生物、化学、英语、国际和区域研究，以及哲学。打算申请该校数学专业的学生应该关注它的跨学科专业——数学决策科学。它可以让本科生学习在管理科学、生物统计学和财务分析等领域所需掌握的概率论、统计学、数据分析和风险分析的知识。佳桥校友表示在北卡教堂山想要拿到 A 是相对困难的，特别是在人文学科。虽然有些本科生课程是由博士生教授的，但是佳桥校友也表示：大多数课程都是由教授亲自上课，如果有问题也可以很容易地找到他们寻求帮助。近来，创业在北卡成为一种时尚。北卡创业计划（Carolina Entrepreneurial Initiative）旨在帮助北卡教授和学生发展创业项目。正是这个项目促成了北卡挑战（Carolina Challenge）的诞生。北卡挑战是一个学生主办，为北卡教授、学生和想要创业的未成年人准备的商业计划挑战活动。北卡教堂山大学鼓励学生投身到“大学研究机遇数据库”（OUR Database of Research Opportunities）提供的研究活动中。与杜克大学和北卡州立大学的学生一样，北卡教堂山大学的学生在三角研究园（Research Triangle Park）中亦享有一席之地。

职业发展

对金融和银行业感兴趣的学生可以在北卡立足落脚，因为该州在美国全国广播公司财经频道（CNBC）“2010 年最具商业价值州”名单中位列第四名。同时，夏洛特市是美国第二大银行中心、美国银行（Bank of America）的发源地，也是美国发展速度最快的城市之一。大约一半的学生毕业后会选择在州内就业，雇主包括彭博（Bloomberg）、高盛、瑞士信贷（Credit Suisse）、安永、Teach for America、德勤等知名大公司。2013 届毕业生中，在毕业前的 6 个月内，59.3% 被全职聘用，24.7% 追求进一步的深造，5.5% 被兼职聘用，8.9% 还在寻求就业。

校园人文环境

“柏油脚跟”是北卡教堂山球队的昵称，它在校园里拥有众多球迷。从一位佳桥校友的评论中可以捕捉到学生们对运动的热情：“加油！柏油脚跟们！冲到杜克大学去！”尽管因为北卡州政府规定本科生必须有 82% 的学生来自本州，但是与东北部学生相比，该校学生是非常友好的。因为拥有庞大的学生群体，所以很容易就可以碰到来自世界各地的人。“多样性是我最喜欢北卡教堂山的一点！因为这里真的是一个非常大的学校，有如此多的机会……我很难用几句话就说清楚。”一位佳桥校友笑着说道。兄弟会和姐妹会在北卡教堂山分校不是非常盛行，但是仍有很多学生组织为其成员举办派对，每个晚上都可以很容易地找到娱乐活动。在教堂山市中心也有两个俱乐部，学生们会在家庭式宴会变得无聊时去逗留光顾。尽管与杜克大学的竞争声名狼藉，学生们仍会乘坐穿梭于两个校园之间的免费便利巴士参加彼此的社交聚会。

录取难度

北卡教堂山分校每年只招收很少的中国学生，特别是它的商学院，录取率甚至低于一些比它排名靠前的大学。一般来说，能被该校录取的学生通常也能得到很多排名前 20 大学的录取。高分是必须。但值得提醒的是北卡教堂山的录取率每年波动很大。

佳桥校友录取情况

录取比例	28.2%
SAT 阅读成绩中位数	680
SAT 数学成绩中位数	800
SAT 写作成绩中位数	700
SAT 总分中位数	2170
TOEFL 成绩中位数	109

财政情况

全年学费	33644 美元 (2015—2016)
经济资助可能性	低

学生为学校所在地区打分

安全	3
有趣	2.5
生活成本	1.5
中国食物	2
公共交通	2
酒吧和俱乐部	2
超市 / 便利店选择	2
周边就业市场	2
是否需要车	3
总评	3

* 满分 4 分

气候

年平均气温范围	3℃ ~26℃
年平均降水量	114.7cm
年平均湿度	76.9%
年平均降雪量	11.2cm

从中国出发的航班

离学校最近的国际机场是罗利—杜罕国际机场（RDU，Raleigh – Durham International Airport），没有从中国出发的直达航班，学生们需要先在芝加哥、华盛顿或者纽约转机一次。

需要考虑的事情

你会喜欢北卡教堂山大学，如果……

- 你相信学校越大越好。拥有大量本科生，在这里有足够的事情去做
- 你在寻找完美的大学城
- 你不喜欢杜克大学

你会不喜欢北卡教堂山大学，如果……

- 你喜欢可以掌控的小班课
- 毕业后你不考虑留在北卡罗来纳州
- 你是个杜克迷

里士满大学

地址：28 WESTHAMPTON WAY，RICHMOND，VA 23173
网址：WWW.RICHMOND.EDU
中国招生官：MARILYN HESSTER
招生官电话：800-700-1662，804-289-8640
招生官邮箱：MHESSER@RICHMOND.EDU
附近主要城市：华盛顿特区，大约两个半小时车程

最佳匹配点分析

里士满大学以其商科和领导力研究学院闻名，学科设置独特。学校的校友网络和学术声誉对想要在金融领域寻求发展的学生们来说帮助很大。然而值得注意的是，这里的学生对于非本土文化可能不是那么了解和熟知，因此国际学生在交朋友和分享自己的一些观点看法时需要积极主动。在里士满大学派对是非常多见的，如果你打算来这里，要做好身处醉酒者和派对文化中的准备（吸毒现象同样存在）。对于追求加州一样舒适气候的学生来说，这里简直是他们的宝地。

学术机会

罗宾斯商学院在全美最好本科商学院名单上排名前 20，也是唯一进入该排名榜的文理学院商学院。它提供的专业有会计、经济学、金融、国际商务、市场营销和管理学。

信息速览

US News 文理学院排名	32
学校位置	中部大西洋地区
学校类型	私立
周边环境	乡村

本科学生情况

学生总数	2990 (2015)
申请人数	9977 (2015)
录取率	31% (2015)
男女学生比例	52/48
国际学生百分比	10%
亚裔美国人百分比	6%

有本科项目的学院

文理学院（School of Arts and Sciences）

杰普森领导力研究学院（Jepson School of Leadership Studies）

罗宾斯商学院（Robins School of Business）

你可能还考虑以下学校

弗吉尼亚大学　波士顿学院

威廉玛丽学院　华盛顿与李大学

乔治城大学

毫无疑问，这些专业和领导力研究学、生物学、会计、国际研究以及政治学都是里士满大学最强的专业。

在里士满大学，所有课程都由教授亲自上课，学生和教授之间的交流十分密切。里士满大学的核心课程要求广泛，包括很多学科，学生需至少掌握一门外语。对数学和科学感兴趣而又干劲十足，并且计划将来在 STEM（Science，Technology，Engineering and Math，美国政府的 STEM 计划是一项鼓励学生主修科学、技术、工程和数学领域专业的计划）领域寻求职业发展的学生可以通过格兰杰计划（Grainger Initiative）获得进行夏季研究和参加学术交流的经济资助。

职业发展

2013 届毕业生的就业率为 94%，并在 2013 年内提高到 95%。毕业生平均年薪在 40000~44999 美元之间。25% 的毕业生有意进一步深造，另有 8% 的毕业生正在准备申请。在择业的毕业生中，最热门的就业分布在教育、金融、市场、咨询、会计、医疗以及科学研究领域。普华永道会计师事务所和摩根大通最受毕业生欢迎。该校的校友网络非常强大，尤其是商学院和领导力研究学院的校友网。

校园人文环境

里士满大学有许多非常有趣的传统，像授勋夜 / 公告夜（Investiture/Proclamation Night，为大一新生举办的入学仪式）、大三女生组织的戒指舞会（Ring Dance），以及每年春天的烤乳猪聚餐。虽然多样化不是里士满大学的优势，但是它仍有 7% 的非洲裔美国学生、亚裔学生和西班牙裔学生各占 6%，白人学生占主体地位。联谊会生活大大促进了学校社交生活的发展，33% 的男生和 44% 的女生活跃其中。考虑到学校周边社区居民不很丰富的夜生活，学校联谊会生活的流行也就不足为奇了。很多派对是在高年级学生的公寓——Lodges 里举办的，大多数有酒的聚会在校园里举办。里士满大学的兄弟会派对并不禁止女生参加，女性会员和男性会员都可以参

佳桥校友录取情况

录取比例	45.9%
SAT 阅读成绩中位数	660
SAT 数学成绩中位数	800
SAT 写作成绩中位数	670
SAT 总分中位数	2140
TOEFL 成绩中位数	109

财政情况

全年学费
48090 美元 (2015—2016)
经济资助可能性　　非常低

学生为学校所在地区打分

安全	4
有趣	3
生活成本	2
中国食物	2
交通便利	3
酒吧和俱乐部	3
超市／便利店选择	2
周边就业市场	2
是否需要车	3.5
总评	3

*满分 4 分

气候

年平均气温范围	2℃ ~26℃
年平均降水量	110.8cm
年平均湿度	72.25%
年平均降雪量	22.7cm

从中国出发的航班

从中国没有直达里士满的航班，学生们一般需要在华盛顿转机才能到达里士满国家机场（RIC，Richmond National Airport）或乘坐快速巴士到达里士满，行程不到三个小时。

加（很多其他大学的兄弟会派对是不向女生开放的）。派对为每个人提供免费的酒水。里士满市中心有更加热闹的深夜欢庆活动，有许多摆渡车和大巴车往返于校园和市区，交通非常便捷。

录取难度

一般来说，里士满大学的商科要比其他专业录取难度大。中国学生申请的时候如果 SAT 成绩超过 2000 分并且能向录取委员会展现出自己在高中积极参加社团活动，录取会相对容易。

需要考虑的事情

你会喜欢里士满大学，如果……

◆ 你想学习商科，同时也想拥有一个紧密的大学社区

◆ 你是一个外向的人

◆ 你憧憬自己在弗吉尼亚州的谢南多厄河谷（Shenandoah Valley）徒步旅行和露营

你会不喜欢里士满大学，如果……

◆ 你寻求的是有响当当名号的名牌大学

◆ 你寻求的是一个非常有地区多样化的文理学院。尽管里士满大学有相当数量的国际学生，但是来自弗吉尼亚本州的学生还是占了很大比例

罗切斯特大学

地址：500 JOSEPH C. WILSON BLVD.，ROCHESTER，NY 14627
网址：WWW.ROCHESTER.EDU
招生办公室电话：585-275-3221
中国招生官：PATRITIA TOPORZYCKI（黑龙江、吉林和中国西部）
招生官邮箱：PTOPORZYCKI@ADMISSIONS.ROCHESTER.EDU
中国招生官：SARAH CANNY（辽宁）
招生官邮箱：SARAH.CANNY@ROCHESTER.EDU
中国招生官：CLAUDIA GONZALEZ SALINAS（河北和天津）
招生官邮箱：CGONZALEZ@ADMISSIONS.ROCHESTER.EDU
中国招生官：ISTHIER CHAUDHURY（北京、青岛和上海）
招生官邮箱：ICHAUDHURY@ADMISSIONS.ROCHESTER.EDU
中国招生官：CHRIS ANTAL（除青岛之外的山东省其他市县）
招生官邮箱：CHRIS.ANTAL@ROCHESTER.EDU
中国招生官：DAMIAN GARCIA（河南、山西、广东、海南和澳门）
招生官邮箱：DAMIAN.GARCIA@ROCHESTER.EDU
中国招生官：ANDRE MCKANZIE（江苏）
招生官邮箱：ANDRE.MCKANZIE@ROCHESTER.EDU
中国招生官：ZACK TASCHMAN（浙江、安徽、广西、贵州、重庆和香港）
招生官邮箱：ZTASCHMAN@ADMISSIONS.ROCHESTER.EDU
中国招生官：KIM CRAGG（福建、江西和湖南）
招生官邮箱：KCRAGG@ADMISSIONS.ROCHESTER.EDU
中国招生官：KARIME NAIME（湖北）
招生官邮箱：KARIME.NAIME@ROCHESTER.EDU
附近主要城市：罗切斯特市

最佳匹配点分析

罗切斯特大学极其严酷的寒冬是人们耳熟能详的。作为一所位于纽约州北部的私立大学，罗切斯特大学为学生提供了既具挑战性又具学术吸引力的独特本科课程。校园内充满文艺复兴风格和乔治亚风格的建筑，但建筑内部是现代化的基础设施。中国学生会喜欢上校园内的住宿环境，也会发现同学间的关系十分密切。虽然学术氛围颇为严格，但是如果你的朋友评价你友好、豁达、愿意寻找生活乐趣，你就会很好地融入到校园中。如果你愿意忍受几个月的大雪和寒冷以换取一份卓越的学术体验，那么罗切斯特大学将会是一个很好的选择。

学术机会

想要探索了解自己真正兴趣所在的学生会喜欢罗切斯特大学不设置核心课程要求的教学体系。学校鼓励学生构思规划自己的专业。罗切斯特大学最引人注目的专业是它的医学预科和伊斯曼音乐学院开设的音乐专业。对有志于申请该校的学生来说，罗切斯特大学课程的一个真正亮点是可以让文理和工程学院的学生们在自然科学、社会科学和人文学科三大方向中选择其中一个方向的一个专业，但学生必须在另两个方向中各选三门相关的课程。佳桥校友称赞该校的教授可以很容易接触到。一位佳桥校友写道："据我所知，所有的本科课程都由教授上课，如果我需要教授的帮助，他们就在那里。教授有专门的办公时间见学生，如果我有问题，也可以通过电子邮件寻求教授的帮助。"如果学生对物理和天文学感兴趣，可以参加物理与天文学本科研究项目（REUs，Research Experience in Physics and Astronomy for Undergraduates）。在罗切斯特大学，超过 75% 的

信息速览

US News 大学排名	33
学校位置	东北
学校类型	私立
周边环境	郊区

本科学生情况

学生总数	6046 (2015)
申请人数	16390 (2015)
录取率	35% (2015)
男女学生比例	49/51
国际学生百分比	16.8%
亚裔美国人百分比	10.3%

有本科项目的学院

文理和工程学院（The College of Arts，Sciences and Engineering）

伊斯曼音乐学院（Eastman School of Music）

你可能还考虑以下学校

布朗大学　塔夫茨大学

康奈尔大学　波士顿大学

华盛顿圣路易斯大学

佳桥校友录取情况

录取比例	34.3%
SAT 阅读成绩中位数	665
SAT 数学成绩中位数	800
SAT 写作成绩中位数	670
SAT 总分中位数	2075
TOEFL 成绩中位数	108.5

财政情况

全年学费	47450 美元 (2015—2016)
经济资助可能性	非常低

学生为学校所在地区打分

安全	3
有趣	2.5
生活成本	3
中国食物	2.5
交通便利	1.5
酒吧和俱乐部	1.5
超市 / 便利店选择	2
周边就业市场	2
是否需要车	3
总评	2.5

*满分 4 分

气候

年平均气温范围	-4℃ ~22℃
年平均降水量	86cm
年平均湿度	75.7%
年平均降雪量	120.2cm

从中国出发的航班

罗切斯特国际机场（ROC, Greater Rochester International Airport）距离学校非常近，搭乘出租车可以很快抵达。但是没有从中国出发的直达航班，学生需要先在芝加哥、华盛顿或其他城市转机。

学生可以参与到本科生研究项目中来。优秀的本科生在拿到商科（REBS）、工程（GEAR）、医学（REMS）或教育学（GRADE）的本科学位后，还可以被保送到研究生院或者职业学院。The Take Five Program 为优秀的学生提供第五学年免费探索本专业以外学术兴趣的机会。

职业发展

罗切斯特大学的毕业生在光学、计算机、医学、金融和音乐领域都非常具有竞争力。2011 届毕业生数据显示该校的学生毕业后都生活得非常好：在毕业一年后，有 12% 的毕业生选择继续深造或者工作，29% 正在攻读或已完成研究生 / 职业教育学位的学习，另有 46% 在他们理想的行业中全职工作或者实习。超过 90% 的罗切斯特学生会参加实习。

校园人文环境

尽管罗切斯特大学 40% 的学生来自纽约州，学校仍以它的多样化而闻名，其中 11% 的学生是亚裔美国人。2018 届的学生中国际学生更是达到了四分之一。“学校并不大，我们有很多的国际学生。在我的德语课总共 16 个学生中就有 9 个是中国学生。”在罗切斯特大学，你不会看到很大的派对场景。联谊会得到学校的认同（大约 40% 的学生参与到联谊会中），在学校占支配地位，并负责每年举办一些大型的校外活动。伊斯曼音乐学院是全美最好的音乐学院之一，每年都榜上有名，为学生们带来了世界一流表演艺术家们精彩的演出。附近的城市安静却并不死气沉沉，为学生们提供了校外娱乐的机会，如在安大略湖畔闲逛或者参观国际摄影博物馆（International Photography Museum）。我们佳桥的一位受访校友强烈建议“买一辆车！”罗切斯特大学因其所培养的学生志愿者在全美所占比例之高获得了全国性的赞誉，这从一年一度的威尔逊日（Wilson Day）中——在这一天学校鼓励新生积极参与到社区事务中去，可见一斑。

录取难度

尽管有着显著的学术声誉，但是罗切斯特大学不算是最挑剔的大学。如果学生 SAT 分数超过 2100 分，同时拥有积极参与社区活动的经历会更容易拿到该校的录取。

需要考虑的事情

你会喜欢罗切斯特大学，如果……

- 校内住宿对你来说真的非常重要。罗切斯特大学有非常好的宿舍设施
- 你打算学习医学预科、音乐或者化学工程
- 课程必须要有灵活性

你会不喜欢罗切斯特大学，如果……

- 雪是你的劲敌。在罗切斯特你需要做好对付到处是厚厚的大雪的准备
- 你想要一个名牌学校。罗切斯特大学并不像一些与它水平相当的大学那样享有国际声誉

南加州大学

地址：UNIVERSITY PARK，LOS ANGELES，CA 90089
网址：WWW.USC.EDU
中国招生官：AARON BROWN
招生官邮箱：AARONBRO@USC.EDU
招生官电话：213-821-1882
最近的主要城市：洛杉矶

最佳匹配点分析

谈及南加州大学的学生，有些人会不屑地产生“运动员、联谊会活跃分子、有钱人的孩子”这样的偏见，但是作为一个拥有19000名本科学生的高等学府，南加州大学足以包含更加多样化的学生群体。位于一个四季无雪城市的中心地带，南加州大学是一个很难挑出毛病的学校。热爱这所大学的学生会欣赏它的大型聚会和运动场景，以及它严谨的学术。

学术机会

南加州大学的排名逐年攀升，现在已经稳居 *US News & World Report* 排名榜第23名。这一数字也反映出它的全国录取率，以及想要成为南加州大学一员的困难程度。然而，一旦被录取，南加州大学就会利用其发达的本科生研究协会项目（Undergraduate Research Associates

Program）将这些充满好奇求知欲望的学子们护于自己的羽翼之下，并为之提供丰富的学术支持。拥有16个专业学院，南加州大学可以毫不受限地为毕业生的工作及毕业后的发展提供各种指导。在众多学院中，尤其值得关注的是安纳伯格传媒学院、马歇尔商学院以及电影艺术学院。转学院并不总是一件容易的事，尤其是转往一些培养艺术思维的学院。有传闻说马歇尔商学院和维特比工程学院的录取会相对容易，但事实并非如此。佳桥的校友算是勤勉不惧繁重学习的了，但有在建筑专业学习的校友仍然会哀叹，“想要在建筑课上拿到A是真的相当困难。”总的来说，学生会觉得南加州大学的氛围是协力合作和激励向上的。

职业发展

南加州大学虽然学生众多，但是它拥有一个紧密如石的校友网络，这在一定程度上弥补了这点不足。佳桥在南加州大学的校友解释道：“南加州大学的校友网络非常强大，尤其是在亚洲的校友群体。”另外一个校友也表示赞同：“在南加州大学，会有校友招聘会为在校生提供工作。”洛杉矶本已是各种公司扎堆的美国著名城市，再加上这样的便利条件，更增强了学生将来就业方面的优势。南加州大学的学生可以获得洛杉矶所有的资源，从投资银行公司如高盛、四大咨询公司到财富管理公司如安盛顾问（AXA Advisors）。此外，由于学校靠近迪士尼一类的大型企业，许多南加州大学的毕业生还能找到娱乐行业的工作。南加州大学马歇尔商学院的商业教育是该地区最好的。如果你想要从事银行和咨询行业方面的工作，你可以在这里得到全面的职业预备教育方面的支持。

信息速览

US News 大学排名	23
地理位置	西海岸
学校类型	私立
周边环境	城市

本科学生情况

学生总数	19000 (2015)
申请人数	51925 (2015)
录取率	18% (2015)
男女学生比例	50/50
国际学生百分比	24%
亚裔美国人百分比	18%

有本科项目的学院

文理学院（Dornsife College of Letters，Arts and Sciences）

建筑学院（School of Architecture）

罗斯基艺术设计学院（Roski School of Art and Design）

马歇尔商学院（Marshall School of Business）

电影艺术学院（School of Cinematic Arts）

奥斯特鲁夫牙科学院（Ostrow School of Dentistry）

安纳伯格传媒学院（Annenberg School of Communication and Journalism）

戏剧艺术学院（School of Dramatic Arts）

维特比工程学院（Viterbi School of Engineering）

戴维斯老年学学院（Davis School of Gerontology）

凯克医学院（Keck School of Medicine）
桑顿音乐学院（Thornton School of Music）
普莱斯公共政策学院（Price School of Public Policy）
考夫曼舞蹈学院（Kaufman School of Dance）
陈谭庆芬职能科学与职能治疗学院（USC Chan Division of Occupational Science and Occupational Therapy）
艾欧文与杨创新学院（Iovine and Young Academy）

你可能还考虑以下学校

杜克大学　　波士顿学院
宾夕法尼亚大学　　西北大学
乔治城大学

佳桥校友录取情况

录取比例	40.4%
SAT 阅读成绩中位数	710
SAT 数学成绩中位数	800
SAT 写作成绩中位数	720
SAT 总分中位数	2180
TOEFL 成绩中位数	108

财政情况

全年学费
49464 美元 (2015—2016)
经济资助可能性　中等

校园人文环境

在校生人数多并没有让南加州大学的学生苦恼多少。例如，佳桥的一个校友观察到，“从学生数量上来说，是有点拥挤，但校园真是棒极了。通常只需要 10~15 分钟就可以步行穿过校园。无论到哪里都在步行距离之内，但是有一辆自行车或者滑板会更方便。”学生们喜欢他们的校园，也同样喜欢周边的环境，“学校里有各种各样的活动，从音乐会到电影放映和座谈等。”但我们调查的每个学生都认为有辆车会对你探索洛杉矶这座城市的奥秘至关重要。南加州大学的学生群体非常开放和多样化，白人是主要群体，但也只占到 40%。今年南加州大学有 3000 名学生来自中国，这也解释了为什么许多佳桥的校友认为他们的朋友大都是中国人。虽然南加州大学以它充满活力、聚会颇多的联谊会生活闻名，然而只有 30% 的学生会参加兄弟会或姐妹会。一位佳桥校友透露，“如果你想喝酒就可以喝到酒；但如果你不想喝，你也完全可以不喝。”

录取难度

南加州大学倾向于录取 SAT 成绩介于 2100 分到 2200 分之间的学生，申请职业预备学院如维特比工程学院和电影艺术学院的学生，建议从高中起就参加一些与申请专业相关的活动。

需要考虑的事情

你会喜欢南加州大学，如果……

- 你希望毕业后仍可利用学校人际网络
- 墨西哥和美国食品能吸引你的味蕾
- 你喜欢橄榄球

◆ 你对电影、建筑、商业或通信传媒感兴趣

你会不喜欢南加州大学，如果……

◆ 你非常讨厌联谊会

◆ 你不喜欢位于大城市的中心

◆ 你需要看冰雪，并不介意在极端寒冷中冻得瑟瑟发抖

学生为学校所在地区打分

安全	2
有趣	3
生活成本	3.5
中国食物	3
交通便利	1.5
酒吧和俱乐部	3
超市／便利店选择	2.5
周边就业市场	3
是否需要车	4
总评	3

*满分 4 分

气候

年平均气温范围	18℃ ~27℃
年平均降水量	44.9cm
年平均湿度	75.54%
年平均降雪量	0cm

从中国出发的航班

学生可以选择从香港国际机场、北京首都国际机场或者上海浦东国际机场飞到洛杉矶国际机场（LAX，Los Angeles International Airport）。在不堵车的情况下，乘坐穿梭巴士从洛杉矶国际机场到南加州大学校园大概需要 30 分钟时间。

弗吉尼亚大学

地址：PEABODY HALL，MCCORMICK ROAD, CHARLOTTESVILLE, VA 22904
网址：WWW.VIRGINIA.EDU
中国招生官：SENEM KUDAT WARD
招生官邮箱：SDO5S@VIRGINIA.EDU
招生办公室电话：434-982-3200
附近主要城市：华盛顿哥伦比亚特区，乘坐飞机、美铁或者大巴（两个多小时）可以到达

最佳匹配点分析

弗吉尼亚大学与加州大学洛杉矶分校、加州大学伯克利分校、密歇根大学和北卡大学教堂山分校一起，始终名列全美顶级公立大学榜单。尽管弗吉尼亚州立法要求本州学生必须占该校本科生的 70%，佳桥的校友们仍然认为该校“非常多样化”，国际学生来自 150 多个国家和地区。学校的强势科目包括商科、英语、外国语（如西班牙语）以及政治学。这些学科都拥有强大的师资力量和学生资源。尽管弗吉尼亚大学位于离华盛顿特区两个多小时车程的郊区小镇，学生们仍然赞美学校的活泼生机和学校精神。弗吉尼亚大学的准学生们需要注意的是该校的派对美誉，“如果你想的话，每天都有参加聚会的机会。”一位佳桥的校友这么说。

学术机会

麦金泰尔商学院的本科项目也许是弗吉尼亚大学最有吸引力的项目之一，该院目前名列 *US News & World Report* 最好本科商学院第五名。大一新生不能直接被录取到麦金泰尔商学院，学生必须要到大二才能申请转到商学院学习。从历史数据来看，能够转到麦金泰尔的学生平均 GPA 都要在 3.8 左右。弗吉尼亚大学从各个方面奖励学术勤勉的学生。文理学院的新生有机会被提名加入爱恰尔斯奖学金项目（Echols Scholar Program），该项目给予学生接触更多课程的权利和更多的自由，学生可以自己设计独特的学习项目。工程和应用科学学院通过罗德曼奖学金项目（Rodman Scholars Program）为每一年的顶级优秀学生提供奖励，允许学生参加为他们专门设置的 1 学分研讨课程，这样学生可以选择发展他们的工程能力和领导才华。因为弗吉尼亚大学为本科生提供了强大的师资力量和丰富多样的课程选择，很多佳桥的校友称在弗吉尼亚大学，是否能够拿到 A“取决于该课程的教授如何评分。如果你努力学习也不会很难。”弗吉尼亚大学的诚信系统非常严格，学生一旦被发现撒谎、欺骗或者是盗窃，即便仅有一次过错，也将会被开除出校园。得益于弗吉尼亚大学可控的学习量和乐于助人的教职人员，学生们可以在学习和生活之间找到很好的平衡。

职业发展

弗吉尼亚大学麦金泰尔商学院的报告称 2013 届本科毕业生中 98% 已经接受了一份工作，其他的或是升入研究生院，或是目前不在求职状态中。该届毕业生年起薪中位数达到了 70000 美元。2013 届毕业生中进入投资银行工作的比例

信息速览

US News 大学排名	26
学校位置	中部大西洋沿岸
学校类型	公立
周边环境	郊区

本科学生情况

学生总数	15669 (2015)
申请人数	31107 (2015)
录取率	29% (2015)
男女学生比例	44/56
国际学生百分比	8.8%
亚裔百分比	12.5%

有本科项目的学院

建筑学院（School of Architecture）
文理学院（College of Arts and Sciences）
柯里教育学院（Curry School of Education）
工程和应用科学学院（School of Engineering and Applied Science）
麦金泰尔商学院（McIntire School of Commerce）
护理学院（School of Nursing）
弗兰克·巴滕领导力与公共政策学院（Frank Batten School of Leadership and Public Policy）

你可能还考虑以下学校

杜克大学
威廉玛丽学院
宾夕法尼亚大学
北卡大学教堂山分校
乔治城大学

佳桥校友录取情况

录取比例	25.7%
SAT 阅读成绩中位数	730
SAT 数学成绩中位数	800
SAT 写作成绩中位数	750
SAT 总分中位数	2230
TOEFL 成绩中位数	112

财政情况

全年学费	40506 美元 (2015—2016)
经济资助可能性	低

学生为学校所在地区打分

安全	3.5
有趣	2.5
生活成本	1.5
中国食物	2.5
交通便利	2
酒吧和俱乐部	2
超市 / 便利店选择	2
周边就业市场	2.5
是否需要车	3.5
总评	3

*满分 4 分

气候

年平均气温范围	1℃ ~24℃
年平均降水量	114cm
年平均湿度	76.3%
年平均降雪量	47.4cm

从中国出发的航班

交通不便，附近只有夏洛茨维尔—雅宝机场（CHO，Charlottesville-Ablemarle Airport）。该机场主要飞美国国内航班，价格昂贵，没有从中国到达的直达航班。从该机场乘坐出租车到校园需花费 30 美元。

达到惊人的 28.4%，另外有 24.8% 选择在咨询公司就业。其他本科学院的毕业生可以通过大学职业协助网（UCAN，University Career Assistance Network）联系自愿担任顾问和联络协助员的校友帮助提供工作机会。工程类毕业生在经济收入方面也表现良好，尤其是在华盛顿特区。据学校网站数据显示，2013 届工程和应用学院本科毕业生年起薪中位数在 66323 美元左右。职业招聘会和职业中心因其规模较大的优势，比校友网络资源更有效。

校园人文环境

尽管始终保持着全美顶级公立大学机构的地位，弗吉尼亚大学的学生们仍然可以从充满活力的校园人文环境中舒缓课业的压力。一位佳桥校友说："弗吉尼亚大学每天都有一些小型的派对。但是像那种超过 200 人的由学校出资举办的大型聚会一般一个月才会有一次。" 弗吉尼亚大学的本科生通常会让人想到典型的"学院派风格"，兄弟会在学校的社交文化中发挥着主要作用。但是学生们告诉我们说："兄弟会组织都非常友好。"学校的男子橄榄球队，即人们熟知的弗吉尼亚骑士（Wahoos）是学生们热衷的竞技体育团体。据一位佳桥校友说橄榄球队现在已经不是那么强大了，但是弗吉尼亚大学的学生们仍然倾向于参加各种体育项目来支持他们的校队。真正的体育爱好者到校后可以考虑曲棍网球（lacrosse）、游泳和篮球项目。一些佳桥校友更加喜欢学校所在的小镇，觉得趣味盎然，一些则更加喜欢学校本身的环境。总而言之，无论是在校内还是校外的小镇，你都会有足够的事情可做。周围的小镇为活跃的学生们提供了很多户外活动，但是如果没有车出行还是很不方便的。弗吉尼亚大学的校园文化非常重视传统：最早的主校区被命名为 Lawn，争夺这里的住宿权是传统之一；学生提及校园必称 Grounds；唱 *The Good Old Song*；参加秘密组织……凡此种种，不胜枚举。此外，学校的荣誉规章（Honor Code）为校园创造出诚信的氛围，学生们在草坪上休息也不用担心值钱的东西会丢失。中国留学生在这里可以很容易地找到大型中国国际学生社团。

录取难度

弗吉尼亚大学的学生应该是高中活跃的社团领袖，接受过严格的课程学习。被录取的学生平均 SAT 成绩在 2100~2300 分之间。

需要考虑的事情

你会喜欢弗吉尼亚大学，如果……

- 你想学习商科
- 兄弟会 / 姐妹会不会让你受到干扰

你会不喜欢弗吉尼亚大学，如果……

- 你想要在大一而不是等到大三才学习商科
- 不能集中力量应对“学院派风格”的生活

威斯康星大学麦迪逊分校

地址：702 W JOHNSON ST #1101，MADISON，WI 53715
网址：WWW.WISC.EDU
中国招生官：无
招生办公室邮箱：ONWISCONSIN@ADMISSIONS.EDU
招生办公室电话：608-262-3961
最近的主要城市：芝加哥，坐大巴或者开车 3~4 小时可以到达麦迪逊

最佳匹配点分析

虽然不像密歇根大学安娜堡分校那般被中国留学生所熟知，威斯康星大学麦迪逊分校和它在安娜堡的邻居还是有许多相似之处的。作为位于美国顶级大学城镇之一的大型公立院校，威斯康星大学的学生务实肯干，对占本科生人数 7% 的国际留学生十分友好。獾州人（Badgers 是对威斯康星州人的昵称，威斯康星大学的学生也会这么自称）不仅在学术上实力突出，在营造活跃的社交氛围方面也是不遗余力。在这里，你会为成为威斯康星州领军大学的一员而感到非常骄傲。但是如果你无法扛过麦迪逊的严酷寒冬，可能你需要重新考虑是否申请这所大学。

学术机会

威斯康星大学有 70 个学科排名全美前十。受学生欢迎的专业包括政治科学、生物学、经济学和历史，而学校最引人注目的研究领域是教育、农业、生物科学、社会研究以及传媒。接近三万人的本科学生数量使得大一和大二的班级往往人满为患，工程类和商科

类项目的火爆程度使得学校不得不设置严格的GPA要求来控制想要入读这些项目的学生数量。威斯康星大学注重本科生在数理逻辑、写作交流和种族研究方面的教育，要求学生在毕业前必须在这三个领域达标。害怕大型研究型大学过分热闹的学生可以申请大一新生兴趣组（First-Year Interest Groups），住在同一宿舍楼的20名学生会组成一个小组一起去注册三门人数稍少的课程。学科的评定标准在该校非常严格，正如一位佳桥校友所说，只有班里前15%的学生可以拿到A。

职业发展

本科学术机会如此众多，威斯康星大学的毕业生遍布各行各业也就不足为奇了。2013届毕业生中大约64%的学生毕业后直接进入全职工作，24%选择全日制研究生。拿到机械工程学位的毕业生有88%找到工作，与此形成显著对比的是英语专业毕业生的就业率仅为61%。威斯康星大学毕业生就职的知名公司包括波音、毕马威、德勤、安永和Facebook等。威斯康星大学的学生终身享有获得学校职业发展方面资源的特权，比如个性化的咨询、研讨工作坊和简历润色。更不用说遍布世界各地，仅在中国就有三个的校友网络了。

校园人文环境

正如所料，威斯康星大学的许多学生都自称是“奶酪大头”（威斯康星州被称为“奶制品之州”，本州出产的奶酪尤其出名。威斯康星州居民很幽默地称自己为cheeseheads），有7%的本科学生是国际公民。“威斯康星大学不能更多样化了，”佳桥一位校友说。与类似的大学相比，威斯康星大学的亚裔美国人并不占压倒性的比例，但是据一位已经入学的佳桥校友评论“大多数的朋友都是中国学生。”麦迪逊作为威斯康星州的人口大市，城镇居民达20万人。

信息速览

US News 大学排名	41
学校位置	中西部
学校类型	公立
周边环境	城市

本科学生情况

学生总数	29580 (2015)
申请人数	32780 (2015)
录取率	49.2% (2015)
男女学生比例	49/51
国际学生百分比	7%
亚裔百分比	6.7%

有本科项目的学院

农业与生命科学学院（College of Agricultural and Life Sciences）
威斯康星商学院（Wisconsin School of Business）
教育学院（School of Education）
工程学院（College of Engineering）
人类生态学院（School of Human Ecology）
文理学院（College of Letters and Science）
护理学院（School of Nursing）
药学院（School of Pharmacy）

你可能还考虑以下学校

西北大学	伊利诺伊香槟分校
密歇根大学	弗吉尼亚大学
波士顿大学	印第安纳大学

佳桥校友录取情况

录取比例	61.2%
SAT 阅读成绩中位数	590
SAT 数学成绩中位数	780
SAT 写作成绩中位数	660
SAT 总分中位数	2010
TOEFL 成绩中位数	104

财政情况

全年学费	29665 美元 (2015—2016)
经济资助可能性	非常低

学生为学校所在地区打分

安全	4
有趣	2.5
生活成本	1.5
中国食物	3
交通便利	2.5
酒吧和俱乐部	2.5
超市／便利店选择	2.5
周边就业市场	2
是否需要车	3.5
总评	3.5

＊满分 4 分

气候

年平均气温范围	-8℃ ~22℃
年平均降水量	89.5cm
年平均湿度	78.24%
年平均降雪量	98.6cm

从中国出发的航班

从中国没有直达麦迪逊的航班。学生可以飞到芝加哥奥黑尔国际机场（ORD，Chicago O'Hare International Airport），之后乘坐大约 4 个小时大巴到达麦迪逊。学生可以选择从香港国际机场、北京首都国际机场或者上海浦东国际机场飞到芝加哥。

该市与安娜堡和教堂山这样的城市同时享有美国最好的大学城之一的美誉，威斯康星大学的学生们可以热情洋溢地享受精彩的夜生活，几乎每天晚上都可以找到酒吧活动和迎合学生的校内派对。周边社区当然都非常支持威斯康星学生的体育项目，学生们脸上涂着油彩，聚集在一起为橄榄球和曲棍球队喝彩助威。一般情况下，运动对于威斯康星学生们来说意义重大。一位佳桥校友写道："人们做运动。有专门冲浪和在米多特湖上（Lake Mendota）划船的体育俱乐部，也有大的场地供人们进行橄榄球、曲棍球和足球运动。"

录取难度

尽管是美国最强的公立大学之一，威斯康星大学的录取并不是难以企及的。每年都有几百名中国学生被该校录取。

需要考虑的事情

你会喜欢威斯康星大学，如果……

- 你想要在校园内外都有一个充满活力的社交生活。威斯康星大学的学生们时刻准备着派对
- 你在寻找一个拥有生物科学领域主要资源的大学
- 啦啦队精神和较强的学校精神对你很重要

你会不喜欢威斯康星大学，如果……

- 你想到零下结冰寒冷的气候会打寒噤
- 你觉得随时随地可以找到乐子的环境会让你分心

瓦萨学院

地址：124 RAYMOND AVENUE，POUGHKEEPSIE，NY 12604
网址：WWW.VASSAR.EDU
中国招生官：SARAH FISCHER
招生办公室电话：845-437-7300
招生办公室邮箱：ADMISSIONS@VASSAR.EDU
附近主要城市：纽约，乘坐大巴约两小时，火车约 1 小时 40 分钟到达

最佳匹配点分析

在波基普西令人苦恼的冬季里，一些学生可能会对自己当初选择瓦萨学院的决定表示质疑。然而，对于那些寻求学术自由，并且清楚自己来到这里是想要挑战知识和在校课程极限的学生们来说，瓦萨学院无可挑剔。它为学生提供多样化的跨系专业，还允许学生自己设计专业。此外，想要一个人际关系密切的大学学习环境的学生们也会发现瓦萨非常具有吸引力。不过，如果你是女性，并且希望在大学里交男朋友，瓦萨可能会因为性别比例失衡以及与其他院校的互动交流不多而让你失望。如果你不需要经常漫步出校园的话，往往也不会介意瓦萨活泼的校园生活与周边城镇之间的反差。

学术机会

瓦萨学院可能不算一个大学校，它并没有工程系。但是如果你可以充分利用它与达

信息速览

US News 文理学院排名	12
学校位置	东北
学校类型	私立
学校环境	郊区

本科学生情况

学生总数	2450 (2015)
申请人数	7567 (2015)
录取率	25.7% (2015)
男女学生比例	44/56
国际学生百分比	14%
亚裔百分比	15%

你可能还考虑以下学校

布朗大学　斯基德莫尔学院
卫斯理大学　巴德学院
哈弗福德学院

特茅斯学院合作的工程双学位项目，你就会拥有和其他大型研究型大学学生同等的机会。此外，学生们可以借由学院与康涅狄格学院的伙伴关系在国家戏剧学院进一步加深对戏剧的了解。在瓦萨，英语、政治科学、心理学、生物学、历史、经济学、电影和戏剧，以及艺术史专业都是受到高度赞誉的专业，但受欢迎的专业远不止这些。尽管对外语和定量分析方面的课程有一定要求，但瓦萨学院并没有核心课程。教授们不仅执教所有课程，也住在校园宿舍里，以增强和学生之间的互动。佳桥校友反映学校的环境氛围是协力合作的，尽管如此，得 A 还是很困难，按照百分比评分（grading curves）并不常见。

职业发展

IBM 位于波基普西，所以它经常在学校招聘。其他顶级雇主还包括 AC 尼尔森、美联储、日本交流与教学（Japan Exchange and Teaching）机构、位于纽约的律师事务所、纽约教育委员会、纽约地区检察官、纽约出版公司，以及美国司法部和和平队（Peace Corps）。根据先前的一次调查显示，64.3% 的毕业生会受到雇佣，有 12% 的毕业生会追求更高的学位。学年期间的校外实习会由学校的实习工作办公室（Field Work Office）帮助协调安排。每年都有大约 500 名的瓦萨学生获得在各个企业、政府机构和社区组织的实习机会，这让他们在著名的纽约夏季实习季来临时比其他同等水平的学生更有竞争力。限于学校的规模，瓦萨学院在校友网络方面无法与达特茅斯学院和布朗大学这样的学校媲美。

校园人文环境

一名佳桥校友说："感觉学校很小，每年中国学生的数量都在增加。" 大多数学生会感觉波基普西受限于周边有限的交通方式（也不是最安全的），但是通往纽约的便捷把这些不足都抵消了。没有宿舍管理员（Residential Assistant，RA）的学生宿舍给了学生极大的自由。尽管没有兄弟会和姐妹会，但瓦萨每年都有 1000 场校园活动。瓦萨同时也拥有 150 多个独特的学生组织，如射箭俱乐部和交谊舞俱乐部。外界通常将瓦萨学生概括为一群自由嬉皮的中产阶级和上层中产阶级的组合，但事实上，瓦萨可能更加多样化。美国学生中，15% 是亚裔美国人，9% 是拉美裔，6% 为非洲裔美国人，只有 24% 是州内学生。

运动场景并不是最大的，但是女子橄榄球和男子棒球都很受欢迎，另外性别比例不均（56% 的女性）可能会令人尴尬。

喜欢古朴典雅的环境和户外运动的学生会在波基普西找到喜欢的娱乐方式。离校园不远处就坐落着卡茨基尔（Catskills）山脉，可以来个周末远足和野营。夜生活的小点缀，比如说 The Chance 音乐联欢会，让学生们可以在一周严格的学术和课外活动后放松心情。

录取难度

瓦萨学院很小，因此，每年只能招收有限的中国学生。ED 申请被录取的可能性最大，而在申请中表示你喜爱瓦萨学院灵活多样的博雅教育课程（Liberal Arts Curriculum）十分有益。

需要考虑的事情

你会喜欢瓦萨学院，如果……

- 你不介意清醒有节制的聚会
- 你期望大多数社交活动在校园举行

你会不喜欢瓦萨学院，如果……

- 你想要去一个大的美国城市
- 你想要离中国国际学生群体近一些
- 你在寻找种族多样性
- 你期待大学生活会有大型的体育盛事和校园集会

佳桥校友录取情况

录取比例	21.4%
SAT 阅读成绩中位数	680
SAT 数学成绩中位数	800
SAT 写作成绩中位数	710
SAT 总分中位数	2190
TOEFL 成绩中位数	110

财政情况

全年学费	50550 美元 (2015—2016)
经济资助可能性	非常低

学生为学校所在地区打分

安全	2
有趣	1
生活成本	3
中国食物	1
交通便利	1
酒吧和俱乐部	1
超市 / 便利店选择	2
周边就业市场	1
是否需要车	4
总评	2

* 满分 4 分

气候

年平均气温范围	–5℃ ~22℃
年平均降水量	125.5cm
年平均湿度	79.9%
年平均降雪量	89.4cm

从中国出发的航班

从中国没有直达波基普西的航班。学生可以从北京、上海或者香港直飞到纽约肯尼迪国际机场（JFK，John F. Kennedy International Airport），然后乘坐公共汽车或火车去波基普西，两个小时之内到达。

韦尔斯利学院

地址：106 CENTRAL STREET，WELLESLEY，MA 02481
网址：WWW.WELLESLEY.EDU
中国招生官：MILENA MAREVA
招生官邮箱：MMAREVA@WELLESLEY.EDU
招生办公室电话：781-283-2270
附近主要城市：波士顿

最佳匹配点分析

韦尔斯利学院是为数不多的在全世界树立了自己声誉的文理学院。位于波士顿近郊，它以美丽的校园以及发展成熟、备受好评的学术院系而闻名。想要在科学领域深造的学生能够在韦尔斯利很快适应，大展拳脚。A 型人格的智慧和野心在韦尔斯利也更容易被激发出来。如果你想在这里见证一场大学聚会，你可能会感到失望；但如果你更看重安静和安全，你会发现大学周围的环境很令人满意。

学术机会

拥有全美第二古老的物理实验室，学校毋庸置疑拥有广受好评的理科项目。韦尔斯利的经济学和艺术史项目也声名在外，鲜有匹敌。同时与麻省理工学院和哈佛大学、巴布森学院、布兰迪斯大学，以及弗兰克欧林理工学院建立的交叉注册项目让韦尔斯利的学生们可以和这些学校的男性同学更好地交流，同时还能以一所学校的费用选修这五所大学的学术课程。作为十二所大学联盟交换生项目（Twelve College Exchange Program）的一员，学生们可以在任一成员大学体验一年交换生项目，而不需要真正的办理转学。佳桥的校友们高度评价该校的教学质量，表示“所有课程都由教授上课，他们真的非常关注学生”。同学都非常优秀，竞争激烈，这偶尔会令人沮丧。另外，学生想要得到 A 必须要付出“很多”努力。每个班通常只有 12~14 名学生。

信息速览

US News 文理学院排名	4
学校位置	东北
学校类型	私立
周边环境	郊区

本科学生情况

学生总数	2474 (2014)
申请人数	4623 (2015)
录取率	30% (2015)
男女学生比例	0/100
国际学生百分比	12%
亚裔美国人百分比	24%

你可能还考虑以下学校

史密斯学院　阿姆赫斯特学院
布林茅尔学院　威廉姆斯学院
哈佛大学

职业发展

学院拥有一个强大的校友网络，这点可以从佳桥校友对学校的赞美之词中得到证实，“我随处可以见到几十年前毕业的校友，他们都非常友好和乐于助人。许多学生在这里也有相似的经历，校友为在校生提供讲座 / 捐款 / 就业机会在这里非常普遍。”通过“影子计划”（The Shadow Program），得益于校友的热情帮助引荐，在校生可以体验不同的职业经历。韦尔斯利强大的校友网络可见一斑。韦尔斯利职业发展服务的另一个亮点是就业和暑期服务津贴项目中心（Center for Work and Service Summer Stipend program），在此学生可以为无薪实习或类似机会得到津贴补助。

大约 80% 的学生在毕业后十年内会继续深造研究生，66% 会被他们的第一志向研究生院录取。约 69% 的学生毕业后直接工作，2012 届毕业生中 17% 的学生直接接受了研究生院录取。Teach for America，美国银行（Bank of America）、美国第一资本金融银行（Capital One）、安诺析思国际咨询公司（Analysis Group）、麻省理工学院林肯实验室（MIT Lincoln Laboratory），以及韦尔斯利学院本身都是毕业生们最常去的地方。

校园人文环境

虽然全是女生的学校可能是建立女子联谊会最完美的地方，然而在韦尔斯利，社团组织已经取代了女子联谊会。这些社团组织有一些排外，因此并非完全受欢迎，但是它们也举办了很多派对和活动，有很多学生参加。许多学生会寻找有更合适男女比例的校外派对或者其他学校的派对。佳桥的校友们说这里的学生群体构成“非常多样化。我们有一个非常大的少数族裔存在，文化氛围是友好和融洽的”，但校园内主流仍是社会经济

佳桥校友录取情况

录取比例	9.3%
SAT 阅读成绩中位数	755
SAT 数学成绩中位数	785
SAT 写作成绩中位数	710
SAT 总分中位数	2245
TOEFL 成绩中位数	112

财政情况

全年学费

46550 美元 (2015—2016)

经济资助可能性 低

学生为学校所在地区打分

安全	4
有趣	2
生活成本	3
中国食物	2
交通便利	1.5
酒吧和俱乐部	2
超市 / 便利店选择	1.5
周边就业市场	2.5
是否需要车	2
总评	3

*满分 4 分

气候

年平均气温范围	-5℃ ~22℃
年平均降水量	121.1cm
年平均湿度	70.17%
年平均降雪量	126.8cm

从中国出发的航班

学生可以从北京、上海或者香港直飞到波士顿洛根国际机场（BOS，Logan International Airport）。从机场乘坐的士、穿梭巴士或者市郊往返列车 40 分钟到达校园。

背景优越的人群。此外，少数学生难以适应和其他国家的同学混在一起。佳桥的校友提醒说在韦尔斯利，饮酒现象是存在的，但并不普遍。当然，校园里不太容易遇见男生，不过韦尔斯利离波士顿其他院校距离很近，校外遇到男生的机会较多，女同性恋和双性恋也不算什么。总体说来，佳桥很多校友都觉得学校“感觉很棒！ 校园足够大而只有 2000 名学生，同学间的联系也非常紧密！”

录取难度

韦尔斯利学院是美国最难录取的女子学院之一。申请的时候要展现你最好的写作技巧和突出的领导角色。SAT 超过 2200 是录取学生的基本分数。

需要考虑的事情

你会喜欢韦尔斯利，如果……

- 你在寻找种族多样性
- 你热衷政治并想做出改变
- 你喜欢周围是一些积极上进、能力十足的女性
- 你不介意饮酒，但也不想因此感到压力

你会不喜欢韦尔斯利，如果……

- 你想有亲密的男性朋友
- 你想要任何形式的运动场景
- 你想要轻而易举地拿到 A

英文版

Amherst College

220 SOUTH PLEASANT STREET, AMHERST, MA 01002
WEBSITE: WWW.AMHERST.EDU
CHINA ADMISSIONS OFFICER: N/A
ADMISSION OFFICE PHONE NUMBER: 413-542-2328
ADMISSION OFFICE EMAIL ADDRESS: ADMISSION@AMHERST.EDU
CLOSEST MAJOR CITIES: BOSTON, 90 MILES AWAY, ACCESSIBLE BY SHUTTLE SERVICES AND BY THE PETER PAN BUS LINE

Best Fit Analysis

Currently ranked Number 2 by *US News* among all liberal arts colleges in the United States, Amherst College has repeatedly swapped places with Williams College as the top LAC in the country in recent decades. Located in a town ninety miles from Boston for which the college was named, Amherst rests among the rolling hills of rural Massachusetts. Though small, the town of Amherst offers students a vibrant scene that includes art shops and restaurants. As a member of the Five College Consortium, students at Amherst can take classes and utilize resources at four other academic institutions, including Mount Holyoke College, UMass Amherst, Smith College, and Hampshire College. Students at Amherst can expect a rigorous academic environment with some of the most qualified instructors in higher learning, many of whom are drawn to Amherst solely for the

At a Glance

US News Rank	#2
Location	Northeast
Type of School	Private
Environment	Rural

Students

Total Undergrad Enrollment (2014)	1785
# Applicants	8478 (2014)
% Accepted	14 (2014)
Male to Female Ratio	51/49
% International Students	10%
% Asian American	14%

You Might Also Consider...

Williams College
Harvard University
Brown University
Princeton University
Dartmouth College
Middlebury College

purpose of teaching and mentoring students. The college has sought to diversify its campus in recent years, both socioeconomically and racially, yet self-segregation is still commonplace on campus.

Academic Opportunities

Students who are looking for prestigious, elite undergraduate education will find a home at Amherst. Classes are generally very small, as Amherst boasts average class size of approximately 16 students. One AIC alum writes, "All the profs I had/have are super accessible. They have at least 4 hours of office hour[s] every week and making appointment[s] with them is very easy." TYPO, or Take Your Professor Out, is a program that Amherst funds to let students meet with professors over dinner at select restaurants. With 38 majors to choose from, many students have gravitated towards Economics (16%), English (11%), and Psychology (11%). Strong majors also include Psychology, Biology, and Law, Jurisprudence, and Social Thought. The Five College Consortium provides Amherst students the chance to earn specialized certificates in special fields such as Sustainability Studies, Buddhist Studies, and Asian/Pacific/American Studies. As Amherst does not have a Core Curriculum or Gen. Ed. requirements, students' schedules are very flexible and open to a host of interdisciplinary courses. Research is common among undergraduates and may be funded by a number of programs like Dean of the Faculty Summer Research Program or the Howard Hughes Fellowship.

Career Development

As Amherst has a small undergraduate student body of less than 2000 students, specialized attention to each individual is a point on which this college prides itself. Every freshman student, upon arriving at Amherst, is assigned a Freshman Advisor, whose purpose is to guide students towards opportunities in their intended major. Major Advisors are assigned to students when they have declared their field(s) of study. Pathways, an Amherst College alumni-student mentoring program, develops partnerships between students and alumni who have similar career trajectories, while ASIP (Amherst Select Internship Program) exclusively caters to Amherst students by facilitating internship opportunities offered by Amherst parents, alumni, and friends. Approximately 80% of Amherst graduates plan to (or considering to) pursue graduate degrees, but Amherst alums also have notable success acquiring employment from competitive firms directly after graduation. The three most popular fields of direct-after-graduation employment for the Class of 2013 were Education (18.5%), Financial Services (16%), and Healthcare (16%). Popular firms at which Amherst alums have worked include McKinsey & Company, Bain & Company, and Cornerstone Consulting Group.

Campus Social Environment

It's entirely possible to meet every student on Amherst's campus, so expect a highly intimate community at this school. An AIC alum says that sometimes Amherst feels "too small" and doesn't attract notable speakers compared "to peer research universities." Getting to know all the Chinese international students at Amherst is commonplace, but they don't necessarily form a separate clique on campus. Students, rather, are known to self-segregate into three groups, the wealthy, the athletes, and the international students and minorities, but obviously there will be exceptions. Students at Amherst tend to be friendly and collegiate but also carry with them a "jock" vibe. For a small school, an AIC alum says that the "party scene is pretty big" and "[Amherst]

AIC Alum Student Score Profiles

% AIC students accepted	14.3%
Median SAT Critical Reading	760
Median SAT Math	800
Median SAT Writing	760
Median SAT Composite Score	2320
Median TOEFL	115

Financial Facts

Annual Tuition
$50562 USD (2015—2016)
Financial Aid Availability
Very Low

What Students Say about the Location

Safe	4
Fun	3
Expensive	2
Good Chinese Food	2
Public Transportation	3
Bars and Clubs	1
Market/Grocery Options	1
Surrounding Job Market	1
Is Car Necessary?	3
Overall	3

*Out of four Stars

Climate

Average Temperature Range
1℃ to 14℃
Average Annual Precipitation
128cm
Average Annual Humidity
75.9%
Average Annual Snowfall
182cm

Transportation from China:

Students can take direct flight from Beijing, Shanghai or Hong Kong to Logan International Airport in Boston. Then taking cab or shuttle for 2 hours will get you to the campus.

will host something official about once a month and students have bigger parties to go to about every other week," in addition to attending social events at one of the Five Colleges. The town of Amherst also hosts a smattering of bars, many of which are walking distance from campus.

Selectivity

Accepted students to Amherst typically have strong leadership capabilities and have been highly involved in extracurricular activities at their respective high schools. With only a handful of spots allocated for Chinese international students, expect fierce competition to earn a place at this school.

Things to Consider

You'll like Amherst if...

- You seek individualized attention from all your professors.
- You wish to exploit all the opportunities included within the Five College Consortium.
- You dream of becoming an educator, banker, or consultant.

Avoid Amherst if...

- You'd prefer a student body that leans away from elitism.
- You aren't ready to battle the biting cold of New England Winters.

Babson College

231 FOREST STREET, BABSON PARK, MA 02457
WEBSITE: WWW.BABSON.EDU
CHINA ADMISSIONS OFFICER: CHERYL BORDEN
AO EMAIL ADDRESS: CBORDEN@BABSON.EDU
AO PHONE NUMBER: 781-239-5522
CLOSEST MAJOR CITY: BOSTON

Best Fit Analysis

As the birthplace of entrepreneurial studies, Babson College has made a name for itself in the realm of business education. Its alumni and faculty include the President and CEO of Toyota, the co-founder of Home Depot, and the Director of Ford. Students with an entrepreneurial spirit striving to succeed in the business world will appreciate the College's hands-on approach to learning both in and out of the classroom—assuming they're willing to brave the cold New England winters and competitive business-like environment.

Academic Opportunities

Babson's flagship undergraduate program is far and away entrepreneurial studies, which has been ranked No. 1 by *US News* for 17 years in a row. While all students major in business

At a Glance

US News Rank	N/A
Location	Northeast
Type of School	Private
Environment	Suburban

Students

Total Undergrad Enrollment	2107 (2014)
# Applicants	6199 (2014)
% Accepted	28 (2014)
Male to Female Ratio	53/47
% International Students	27
% Asian American	15

You Might Also Consider...

University of Pennsylvania
Northeastern
Boston College
New York University
Boston University

and can choose from a range of concentrations, roughly half of their classes are in the liberal arts. Classes are small, all taught by professors, and rigorous. Many also utilize a case-study approach to instruction, having students learn about concepts through various role-playing and simulation activities. Through the required first year class Foundations of Management and Entrepreneurship, groups of student sreceive up to $3000 to develop and implement their own business plans.

Career Development

With Boston a mere 20-minute drive away, Babson students have access to a plethora of internship and work opportunities. In addition, classes are only held from Monday through Thursday, allowing students to pursue career development opportunities during the school year. More than 150 alumni events on campus every year and programs such as Babson Alumni Supporting Entrepreneurs (BASE) provide Babson students with plentiful opportunities to network with an amazing group of alumni.As for post-graduation plans, 93% of the class of 2013 found employment (25% in finance, 19% in marketing, and 14% in business development) and 6% enrolled in graduate programs within 6 months of graduation.

Campus Social Environment

Babson students are stereotyped as preppy rich kids—it's not uncommon to see students going to class in suits. And while many institutions of higher learning tend to have liberal student populations, Fiske jokes that Babson is "the one college in Massachusetts where it is possible to be a Republican with head held high," though students tend not to be politically outspoken. While it is not the most racially diverse school, 85% of undergraduates live on campus, creating a close sense of community. A byproduct of this is an abundance of social events held on campus. Greek life exists but is not pervasive, with only 19% of women, and

17% of men involved. That being said, students often forego these opportunities in favor of taking the free shuttle to Boston on weekends. Despite its small student body, Babson has nearly 100 student clubs and organizations; the Chinese Student Association has nearly 100 members.

Selectivity

Not the toughest from a score perspective, but don't take this school lightly. Babson tends to be picky, so unless you're an over-achiever that can get into a top15 school easily, it may be wise to really go the extra mile of making your case if you want to attend.

Things to Consider

You'll like Babson if...

- You have a strong interest in business.
- You prefer hands-on as opposed to theoretical learning.
- You thrive in competitive environments.

Avoid Babson if...

- You hate cold weather.
- You are looking for ethnic diversity.
- You want to explore other academic fields.

AIC Alum Student Score Profiles

% Accepted	45
Median SAT Critical Reading	610
Median SAT Math	780
Median SAT Writing	670
Median SAT Composite Score	2060
Median TOEFL	105

Financial Facts

Annual Tuition
$46784 USD (2015—2016)

Financial Aid Availability
Very low

What Students say about the Location

Safe	4
Fun	2
Expensive	3
Chinese food	1
Transportation	2
Bars and Clubs	2
Market/Grocery Options	2
Surrounding Job Market	1
Necessity of Car	4
Overall	2

*Out of Four

Climate

Average Temperature Range
-4℃ to 21.7℃

Average Annual Precipitation
121cm

Average Annual Humidity
70%

Average Annual Snowfall
127cm

Transportation from China

There are direct flights from Beijing, Shanghai, or Hong Kong to Logan International Airport in Boston. And students can get to campus from the airport by bus, train, or taxi.

Boston College

140 COMMONWEALTH AVENUE, CHESTNUT HILL, MA 02467
WEBSITE: WWW.BC.EDU
CHINA ADMISSIONS OFFICER: PETER CARUSO
AO PHONE NUMBER: 617-552-4960
AO EMAIL: PETER.CARUSO@BC.EDU
CLOSEST MAJOR CITY: BOSTON

Best Fit Analysis

In 1863, the Society of Jesus (Jesuits) founded Boston College. Since then, its legacy as an institution affiliated with Jesuit and Catholic values continues. Students who come here certainly should not be disturbed by Catholicism, as 70% of the students identify with the religion, but neither do they need to convert. They'll also have to tough it out with the brutal winters that average more than 30 days of snow a year. Students looking for business instruction will find this university particularly gratifying, as it hosts programs that rank in the top ten. In addition, BC has a relatively more demanding Core Curriculum, to encourage its students to be well-rounded in all subjects.

Academic Opportunities

As a religious school, students will be required to take a theology class as part of their Core, but many find this to be useful for understanding the philosophy of religion and never imposing. In addition following its foundation in the Liberal Arts, courses are required in literature, science, history, philosophy, social science, mathematics, arts, and cultural diversity. All freshmen attend a writing workshop and seniors complete the university capstone. In addition, research is available through the Boston College Undergraduate Research Program as well as Summer Research Opportunities. For students that require financial aid, the Undergraduate Research Fellows Program allows students to perform research in exchange for aid.

BC also has four professional schools. Carroll School of Management and Connell School of Nursing are tough to transfer into, while the College of Arts and Sciences tends to have lower entrance requirements. BC's strongest programs are Chemistry, Economics, English, Finance, Political Science, Physics, and History. With 8 different libraries and a plethora of written volumes and e-books there is an abundance of knowledge to be acquired at BC.

Career Development

About 22% of students pursue graduate degrees, 26% of that in education, and another 19% in law. Graduates who begin working full-time after college make up 60% of the student body. Internships are readily available in the nearby

At a Glance

US News Rank	#30
Location	Northeast
Religious Affiliation	Roman Catholic
Type of School	Private
Environment	Urban

Students

Total Undergrad Enrollment	9100 (2015)
# Applicants	29486 (2015)
% Accepted	29 (2015)
Male to Female Ratio	53/47
% International Students	6
% Asian American	10

Schools with Undergraduate Programs

Morrissey College of Arts and Sciences
Lynch School of Education
Carroll School of Management
Connell School of Nursing
Woods School of Advancing Studies

You Might Also Consider...

Tufts University
University of Virginia
William and Mary
Notre Dame
Villanova University
Georgetown

AIC Alum Student Score Profiles

% Accepted	26
Median SAT Critical Reading	680
Median SAT Math	800
Median SAT Writing	725
Median SAT Composite Score	2140
Median TOEFL	109

Financial Facts

Annual Tuition
$46670 USD (2015—2016)

Financial Aid Availability
Very low

What Students say about the Location

Safe	3
Fun	3
Expensive	4
Chinese food	3
Transportation	3
Bars and Clubs	4
Market/Grocery Options	3
Surrounding Job Market	3
Necessity of Car	2
Overall	4

*Out of Four

Climate

Average Temperature Range
-4℃ to 23℃

Average Annual Precipitation
120.7cm

Average Annual Humidity
69.8%

Average Annual Snowfall
125.7cm

Transportation from China

There are direct flights from Beijing, Shanghai, and Hong Kong to Boston Logan International Airport (BOS). Students can take a taxi from Logan International Airport to BC in about 35 minutes.

Boston city. Accounting, financial services, nursing, and Teach for America are the industries that most of the new BC workforce migrate into, and top employers include top 4 accounting firms, as well as banks and Teach for America. The Career Center helps students and alumni connect with employers and other Eagles.

Campus Social Environment

Boston College's isn't the most regionally, ethnically, or religiously balanced school, with 72% of its students coming from Massachusetts, and 70% are Catholic. Only about 141 in the undergraduate class are Chinese students. That means students will have ample room to familiarize themselves with unfamiliar cultures in America's melting pot. There are different student organizations for students to explore and develop their interests and passions with like-minded individuals.

Boston College doesn't allow for Greek Life, and maintains a dry campus, but parties and underage drinking still exists. However, students who are over 21 may seek nightlife within the city or in one of the many schools nearby. That being said, many students find close friends within their dorms and halls as well as through volunteer programs and other extracurricular activities.

Kids at BC are often defined by their two major loves—sports and preppiness. Don't be surprised if you spot a number of students wearing their favorite pro sports teams on their sweatshirts walking around campus, or if you find a lot of your peers here gearing up for intramural competitions.

Although BC isn't in the heart of Boston, there are convenient public transportation options to take people into the city, and Boston city doesn't disappoint as a college town. The city of Boston offers many opportunities for entertainment and enlightenment coming from its place in American history and its passion for sports.

Selectivity

BC students tend to take students with SATs in the 2100-2200 range and have completed a number of volunteer projects in high school. About 82% of freshmen were in the top 10% of their high schools.

Things to Consider

You'll like BC if...

◆ Football, basketball, and hockey are a second language to you or you're looking for a school with a big athletics program.

◆ The finance industry is where you envision yourself in the future.

◆ You want access to a city but don't want to be right in the heart of one.

Avoid BC if...

◆ You're not willing to surround yourself with a considerable number of Catholic students.

◆ You have qualms about being in the minority.

◆ You're not a fan of the snow and harsh winters.

Boston University

233 BAY STATE ROAD, BOSTON, MA 02215
WEBSITE: WWW.BU.EDU
CHINA ADMISSIONS OFFICER SAMANTHA FIFIELD
AO EMAIL ADDRESS: SFIFIELD@BU.EDU
ADMISSION OFFICE PHONE NUMBER: 617-353-2300
CLOSEST MAJOR CITY: BOSTON

Best Fit Analysis

Located in the heart of Boston, students at Boston University provides an ample amount of social and academic opportunities in the cultural capital of Massachusetts (and New England). BU continues to climb the rankings of national universities in the United States, jumping ten spots in US News & World Report rankings in just the past year, and has increasingly become more appealing to Chinese international students. With a vibrant urban backdrop, you should only consider BU if you're willing to forgo a traditional college campus. If you don't mind bundling up for frigid New England winter and have a strong interest in finance, management, education, or film studies, BU can serve to prepare you for limitless opportunities available for international students.

Academic Opportunities

As BU is one of the nation's largest private universities, prospective students might be surprised to find that 90 percent of the classes that first-year students take have 25 students or fewer. With ten different undergraduate schools to choose from—each with their own general education requirements—Boston University offers its students a variety of academic programs and curriculums. One of BU's best known undergraduate schools is the College of Communication, which prepares students for careers in Film & Television, Journalism, and Mass Communication, Advertising, & Public Relations. One study abroad opportunity is the Los Angeles Internship Program in the Film & Television departments, which allows for BU students to spend a semester working alongside filmmakers in Hollywood. In general, the academic environment at BU depends on the fields and career paths that students are aiming to pursue, giving them professional experience that makes it easier to transition to the work force after graduation. BU students majoring in Engineering, Computer Science, and Business often find themselves elbowing each other to earn the top grades, especially in introductory level courses that can have over 300 students.

Career Development

With strong alumni networks on the East Coast, BU remains a good option for students interested in preparing to enter the job market. Nevertheless, BU's circle of influence extends beyond its surrounding

At a Glance

US News Rank	#41
Location	Northeast
Type of School	Private
Environment	Urban

Students

Total Undergrad Enrollment	16496 (2014)
# Applicants	54757 (2015)
% Accepted	32 (2015)
Male to Female Ratio	40/60
% International Students	24.4
% Asian	14.8

Schools with Undergraduate Programs

College of Arts and Sciences
College of Communication
College of Engineering
College of Fine Arts
College of General Studies
College of Health and Rehabilitation Sciences: Sargent College
Frederick S. Pardee School of Global Studies
School of Education
School of Hospitality Administration
School of Management

You Might Also Consider...

Fordham	Northeastern
NYU	Case Western Reserve

AIC Alum Student Score Profiles

% AIC students accepted	39.7
Median SAT Critical Reading	590
Median SAT Math	770
Median SAT Writing	665
Median SAT Composite Score	1995
Median TOEFL	104

Financial Facts

Annual Tuition
$47422 USD (2015—2016)
Financial Aid Availability
Very Low

What Students say about the Location

Safe	3
Fun	3
Expensive	4
Good Chinese food	3.5
Public transportation	4
Bars and Clubs	1.5
Market/Grocery Options	2
Surrounding Job Market	2.5
Is Car Necessary?	2
Overall	3

*Out of four Stars

Climate

Average Temperature Range
-3℃ to 23℃
Average Annual Precipitation
122.4cm
Average Annual Humidity
69.8%
Average Annual Snowfall
129cm

Transportation from China

Logan International Airport. Boston University accessible from airport through shuttles and cabs. Travel time from airport: 15~50 minutes, depending on traffic and mode of transportation.

region, in fact, in 2012, a survey published by the *New York Times* and the *International Herald Tribune* reported that BU was ranked 7th among U.S. schools for employability in global markets, behind only Harvard, Yale, Stanford, MIT, Columbia, and Princeton. The starting salary for BU grads averages $46000, while alumni's mid-career salaries comes in at $90000. The Career Advisory Network, which is managed by Boston University's Alumni Association, is a volunteer program that BU alumni take part in to give career advice to students. Commonly addressed problems include: how they got started in their respective fields, the impact of work on their social lives, and if graduate school is a recommended option. BU boasts 51 international alumni groups and has a very large global alumni presence. The Center for Career Development at BU helps guide undergrads and alumni through the difficult process of starting, or continuing, their internship and job search.

Campus Social Environment

Much of BU's social charm lies in the innumerable opportunities for young people provided by Boston. The rich history of the city provides many exciting sites and museums to explore. The city has strict policies regarding the use of fake IDs to enter bars and clubs, so sometimes the under 21 crowd is left to socialize only at fraternity parties and apartment parties on the weekends. For BU students of legal drinking age, Lansdowne Street is often the spot for clubbers, but more casual venues include the Middle East, Phoenix Landing, Venu, or Rise. The sports scene at BU does not have an overly dominating presence compared to other American institutions of higher education, but one AIC student notes that among BU's Division I sports programs (known collectively as the Terriers), "Hockey is the biggest." The city of Boston provides ample opportunities to see Professional sporting events, with the most prominent sports being Baseball, Football and Basketball. Many AIC alumni at BU tend to find solace in the large proportion of Chinese international students at the university. An AIC student reports that Boston's Chinatown helps quash feelings of homesickness with a number of authentic Chinese restaurants. BU also has over 500 student clubs for students to discover and pursue their interests among like-minded individuals.

Selectivity

As BU's popularity has soared in recent years, its admittance rate has been characterized by sharp declines. The schools within BU vary in admissions competitiveness, but students from China are typically expected to have over a 1900 on their SAT to earn a spot as a Terrier.

Things to Consider

You'll like Boston University if...

- You have a particular interest in management and finance, education, or film.
- You are self-motivated and proactive.
- You thrive in competitive, urban environments.

Avoid Boston University if...

- You want a traditional college campus, not one that meshes directly into a city.
- Prefer small class sizes over everything else.
- You're not willing to put up with cold winter weather.

Brandeis University

415 SOUTH STREET, WALTHAM, MA 02454
WEBSITE: WWW.BRANDEIS.EDU
CHINA ADMISSIONS OFFICER: N/A
ADMISSION OFFICE PHONE NUMBER: 781-736-3500
ADMISSION OFFICE EMAIL ADDRESS: ADMISSION@BRANDEIS.EDU
CLOSEST MAJOR CITY: BOSTON, BUSES AND TRAINS AVIAILABLE (20~30 MINUTES)

Best Fit Analysis

We're tempted to suggest, "If you're not Jewish, don't apply," but the reality is Brandeis students are very liberal, open, and outspoken. So perhaps, we should instead suggest, "If you're not liberal, and politically active, don't apply." You'll need to be adaptable, and outgoing as well, to connect with a student body that is predominantly White and Jewish. In addition, if you want to work hard and play hard, Brandeis might disappoint in helping you fulfill the latter. Come if you want to become a teacher, and come if you love Boston and New York City.

Academic Opportunities

Professors teach classes at Brandeis, a university that aims to help its students experience the best of the university and college environments. The most popular majors at Brandeis include biology, chemistry and economics. With regards to the academic rigor, a Chinese international student shares, "It is actually very difficult." To aid students with their coursework, Brandeis selects a group of Roosevelt Fellows of undergraduate students who excelled in their studies and can counsel classmates on choosing classes. In addition, the BUGS program is a peer tutoring program that students can seek help from. Future teachers, consider Brandeis's highly-ranked education programs.

The Gateway program, recommended to International students as a summer training and facilitates the transition many students have to make. It includes mandatory summer sessions to enhance English proficiency, and writing tutorials every week during the school year.

At a Glance

US News Rank	#34
Location	Northeast
Type of School	Private
Environment	Suburban

Students

Total Undergrad Enrollment	3729 (2014)
# Applicants	10004 (2014)
% Accepted	35 (2014)
Male to Female Ratio	43/57
% International Students	18
% Asian American	12.8

Schools with Undergraduate Programs

College of Letters and Sciences
Brandeis International Business School

You Might Also Consider...

Tufts University
Boston College
Emory University
Boston University
New York University
Brown University

Career Development

Top employers of Brandeis students are Merrill Lynch, Teach for America, Peace Corps, Chase Manhattan, Goldman Sachs, and Deutsche Bank. Within six months of graduating, 58% of seniors were employed, while 36% of them confirmed graduate positions, and another 4% were still seeking employment. Healthcare, education, service, financial services, and consulting were the top fields that attracted students. A plurality of students had had at least 3 internships before graduating, a testimony to the strength of the career center, and the ambition of students. An AIC student brags, "Brandeis has [a] great network in Boston and New York".

Campus Social Environment

It's probably impossible to graduate Brandeis without noticing, as our alum nicely put,

AIC Alum Student Score Profiles

% Accepted	26.5
Median SAT Critical Reading	645
Median SAT Math	785
Median SAT Writing	685
Median SAT Composite Score	2040
Median TOEFL	106

Financial Facts

Annual Tuition
$47702 USD (2015—2016)

Financial Aid Availability Low

What Students say about the Location

Safe	4
Fun	2
Expensive	2
Chinese food	3
Transportation	3
Bars and Clubs	1
Market/Grocery Options	2
Surrounding Job Market	3
Necessity of Car	4
Overall	4

*Out of Four

Climate

Average Temperature Range
-5℃ to 22℃

Average Annual Precipitation
119.4cm

Average Annual Humidity
68.4%

Average Annual Snowfall
129.6cm

Transportation from China

There are direct flights from Beijing, Shanghai, and Hong Kong to Boston's Logan International Airport, which is a short 30-minute drive from Brandeis's campus.

"By the way, Jewish is everywhere..." About 50% of the population is Jewish. 21% of the student body identifies as a minority, 18% are international, and the gender ratio highly favors males. It is useful to note that Brandeis is nonsectarian and exclusivity is scorned, which may explain why the Greek system is banned on campus. Regarding parties, our Chinese international student informant says "60% [of students party]. We are not a party school," adding "we hold parties in [the] library and art museums." Alcohol isn't prevalent, but sports are. The same student notes the scene is "Really big. Big as our science building," in particular, the soccer scene. However, the campus offers a lot of extracurricular activities such as the student-run TV and radio station, and Boston, which can be accessed through free shuttles is a hub of activity. As is custom with the Jewish faith, students at Brandeis highly value social work and community service. Blood drives, volunteer teaching, working with underrepresented minorities, and developing shelter for the homeless are common activities that a number of students on Brandeis's campus engage themselves in. The international Chinese community is definitely not as strong here as compared to some other schools in the Boston area.

Selectivity

Activism and community service are highly valued activities by Brandeis's admissions committee. Admission to Brandeis is competitive, but not nearly as competitive as some other schools in the Boston area like Harvard and MIT. Prospective students should reach for at least a 2100 on the SAT.

Things to Consider

You'll like Brandeis if…

- You're interested in other cultures outside of your own, particularly some that are native to the East Coast.
- You're not lazy and don't mind the short commute outside of the immediate surroundings.

Avoid Brandeis if…

- You view exclusive clubs are a fun part of the college experience.
- You want quick and easy access to a cultural melting pot.
- You are homophobic.

Brown University

75 WATERMAN STREET, PROVIDENCE, RI 02912
WEBSITE: WWW.BROWN.EDU
CHINA ADMISSIONS OFFICER: PANETHA OTT
AO PHONE NUMBER: 401-863-2378
AO EMAIL ADDRESS: PANETHA_OTT@BROWN.EDU
CLOSEST MAJOR CITY: PROVIDENCE, LESS THAN AN HOUR FROM BOSTON AND 3 HOURS FROM NYC

Best Fit Analysis

Of the eight ivies, Brown is known for its liberal atmosphere, both academically and socially. In general, since Brown boasts a population of happiest students in the nation, everyone should fit in. Still, prospective students should consider if they would love the rainy and cold weather that presides most of the year. Those who are looking for more structure in their curriculum may also want to seek it elsewhere, as Brown offers a notoriously boundless program.

Academic Opportunities

In 1969, Brown established the New Curriculum, which introduced interdisciplinary university courses, the option to take any course satisfactory/no credit, dropped distribution requirements, and removed pluses, minuses, and no credit on transcripts. Needless to say, this allows for a lot of flexibility in your academic plans. You can design your own major, and take courses without stressing about fitting in general education requirements. However, it does make choosing classes and getting into popular ones tougher. Students profess that professors are attentive and engaged in teaching. Top programs at Brown are biological studies, history, international relations, English, and political science. Less than 20% of introductory classes have more than 50 students and overall, Brown ensures its undergraduates receive a solid education. Due to its proximity to the Rhode Island School of Design, students can also take classes there. The Brown/RISD Dual Program offers a five-year plan for students who want to be more involved in RISD.

Career Development

About 65% of graduating students find employment directly after school and another 22% follow the path of advanced education. Many students pursue professional degrees in the medical field, with law and education being the runner up choices in popularity. For those who choose the industry route, business, education, medical, arts, government, and communications are the fields graduates most often find themselves in.

Because Providence is the capital of Rhode Island, a lot of students find internships with the government. But even for those who are not so interested in government, companies recruit in Brown for top talent every year. Common employers include Bain, Goldman Sachs, Google, Harvard University, Morgan Stanley, Peace Corps, Teach for America, and Microsoft. Brown has a strong alumni network across the Eastern coast, but its international presence lacks in comparison to powerhouses such as Yale and Harvard.

At a Glance

US News Rank	#14
Location	Northeast
Type of School	Private
Environment	Urban

Students

Total Undergrad Enrollment	6320 (2015)
# Applicants	30396 (2015)
% Accepted	9.5 (2015)
Male to Female Ratio	48/52
% International Students	11.6
% Asian American	12.9

Schools with Undergraduate Programs

The College
School of Engineering

You Might Also Consider...

Harvard University
Princeton University
Cornell University
Tufts University
Dartmouth College

AIC Alum Student Score Profiles

% Accepted	12.6
Median SAT Critical Reading	710
Median SAT Math	800
Median SAT Writing	720
Median SAT Composite Score	2180
Median TOEFL	112

Financial Facts

Annual Tuition
$50224 USD (2016-17)
Financial Aid Availability
Very Low

What Students say about the Location

Safe	3.5
Fun	2
Expensive	3
Chinese food	1
Transportation	2
Bars and Clubs	1.5
Market/Grocery Options	1
Surrounding Job Market	1.5
Necessity of Car	2
Overall	3

*Out of Four

Climate

Average Temperature Range
1℃ to 20℃
Average Annual Precipitation
125.5cm
Average Annual Humidity
76.03%
Average Annual Snowfall
103.2cm

Transportation from China

No direct flights from China. Students must find a layover city before flying into Theodore Francis Green Memorial State Airport, just a 15-minute shuttle ride from Brown University.

Campus Social Environment

Caucasian Americans hold the majority at Brown, with Asians in a distant second at 13%, but most students feel well accepted regardless of their ethnicity or racial identity. 97% of students at Brown are out of state, and 12% of that comes from abroad. Students are generally more collaborative and laid-back compared to peers in similarly selective institutions. In addition, they are also politically active, especially on social justice issues. Greek life barely makes a dent in the population, 12% of men and 4% of women choose to participate. Brown is home to over 400 registered student organizations from intramural basketball to co-ed acapella. Alcohol is still prevalent, and Brown has been known to have some racy parties. Providence isn't the kind of city that could give New York City a run for its money, but it offers cultural events and a safe haven for students to roam.

Selectivity

Brown University is highly selective, and in general it does not take many students from China. International students who are studying in the U.S. have a better shot of getting into this Ivy League school, and it always helps if you can demonstrate your artsy or quirky side in your application. Expect to have a chance only if your SAT is over 2200.

Things to Consider

You'll like Brown if...

◆ You want to explore different academic fields.

◆ Attending medical school is your dream.

◆ You want to go to a Liberal Arts College, but want the national reputation of an Ivy League School.

Avoid Brown if...

◆ You need the dynamic environment of a major American city.

◆ You're not willing to put up with the quirkiness.

Bryn Mawr College

101 N MERION AVE, BRYN MAWR, PA 19010
WEBSITE: WWW.BRYNMAWR.EDU
CHINA ADMISSIONS OFFICER: JENNIFER KEEGAN
AO PHONE NUMBER: 610-526-7877
AO EMAIL ADDRESS: JKEEGAN@BRYNMAWR.EDU
CLOSEST MAJOR CITY: PHILADELPHIA; STUDENTS CAN REACH BYRN MAWR BY COMMUTER RAIL, SETPA, ABOUT 20 MINUTES

Best Fit Analysis

Just a quick train ride away from downtown Philadelphia, Bryn Mawr, whose name Welsh means "Big Hill," is consistently recognized as one of the most beautiful college campuses in the United States. In fact, the college's M. Carey Thomas Library has even been designated a National Historic Landmark. With an undergraduate enrollment of just over 1000 students, young women at Bryn Mawr can expect to get a lot of attention from the college's world-renown faculty. The political climate at Bryn Mawr tend to lean toward the liberal, even radical, side and many students find themselves getting involved in social activism. As over a third of all women at Bryn Mawr major in math or the sciences, prospective students interested in preparing for a career in STEM-related field should consider this all-women's institution.

At a Glance

US News Rank	#25
Location	Northeast
Type of School	Private
Environment	Suburban

Students

Total Undergrad Enrollment	1300
# Applicants	2700 (Average of the last four years)
% Accepted	39.9(Average of the last four years)
Male to Female Ratio	0/100
% International Students	24
% Asian	14

You Might Also Consider...

Barnard College
Haverford College
Wellesley College
Smith College
Swarthmore College
Mt. Holyoke College

Academic Opportunities

Ranked among the top ten of all colleges and universities in the United States for producing graduates who continue their studies to earn a Ph.D., students at Bryn Mawr take their academics quite seriously. As a Quaker institution, however, students are required to uphold a honor code that forbids students to talk about grades. This also cuts down on feelings of competition among the college's undergraduates. Although the Fine Arts departments at Bryn Mawr are noticeably limited compared to other LAC peer institutions, Bryn Mawr excels in hard sciences, and every year about 3 percent of the graduating class consists of physics majors, which is nearly 50 times the national average for women. Bryn Mawr is a member of the Tri-College consortium alongside previously all-male college Haverford and Swarthmore. Students can take classes at the University of Pennsylvania as a part of the Quaker Consortium. Additionally, a 3-2 Program available through Cal Tech gives Bryn Mawr students interested in engineering the chance complete three years of coursework in applied science and finish off their undergraduate careers with two years of engineering at Cal Tech. A new interdisciplinary experience offered at BMC, known as the 360° Program, is a cluster of courses that bridge together two or more courses in the humanities and natural sciences aimed at using multi—faceted approaches to solving real world problems.

Career Development

Bryn Mawr features an Extern Program that gives students options to explore different career paths before deciding to commit to a particular field. During the Winter or Spring breaks, Externs shadow alumnae sponsors in the workplace from anywhere between two days to two weeks. Bryn Mawr's Recruiting Program welcomes employers to campus to interview

AIC Alum Student Score Profiles

% AIC students accepted	35.4
Median SAT Critical Reading	670
Median SAT Math	795
Median SAT Writing	710
Median SAT Composite Score	2115
Median TOEFL	110

Financial Facts

Annual Tuition
$46030 USD (2015—2016)

Financial Aid Availability
Does provide to high performance students

What Students say about the Location

Safe	3.5
Fun	2.5
Expensive	2
Good Chinese food	2.5
Public transportation	3
Bars and Clubs	2
Market/Grocery Options	2.5
Surrounding Job Market	1.5
Is Car Necessary?	2.5
Overall	3.5

*Out of four Stars

Climate

Average Temperature Range
-2℃ to 24℃

Average Annual Precipitation
116.9cm

Average Annual Humidity
71.72%

Average Annual Snowfall
49.8cm

Transportation From China

Students have to have a layover before arriving at Philadelphia International Airport, which is half hour drive or shuttle exists to take you there. No direct flights.

students for post-graduate positions and summer internships. Graduates from Bryn Mawr pursue a number of different fields, particularly in academia and education. Alumni from the Class of 2012 have gone to earn Ph.D.s in the London School of Economics, North Carolina State University, work in San Francisco and Atlanta for Teach for America, and find employment for the Green Corps. The Wall Street Journal ranked Bryn Mawr among its list for the top ten liberal arts schools that feed into the country's top law, medical, and business schools.

Campus Social Environment

Bryn Mawr has an extremely diverse campus and fosters a culture of acceptance and tolerance. "We have a large number of international students and we are also taking big roles at school. There are students from Asia, Europe, Africa, Latin America," writes an AIC alum. Over half the college's student body is made up of individuals who identify either as students of color or international students. Bryn Mawr has a poor athletics scene, as one AIC alum notes, "our teams are usually really small." The town of Bryn Mawr is wealthy and safe, but does not have a lot to offer students aside from shopping at a handful of expensive boutique stores and coffee runs to Starbucks. Philadelphia, however, is only a 22-minute ride from Bryn Mawr on the commuter train to relieve students in need some urban mischief. While nightlife isn't huge at Bryn Mawr, there are options. An AIC remarks, "50% [of] our parties are usually full of tri-college (Bryn Mawr, Haverford and Swarthmore) students…there are some parties, but I don't think it can be as big as the universities'." Traditions are integral component of the college's identity to bring undergraduates together and foster a sense of community. For instance, Parade Night marks the end of the first day of classes, in which freshwomen are paired with "sisters" from the junior class who guide them through the next two years of college life.

Selectivity

Though Bryn Mawr has a small undergraduate enrollment, it has a large percentage of international students and is particularly welcoming to Chinese applicants. Applicants with an SAT score over 2000 tend to fare better.

Things to Consider

You'll like Bryn Mawr if...

- You're a young woman interested in Physics, Math, or Foreign Languages.
- You'd feel more comfortable at a school with lots of international students.
- You are academically oriented and independent-minded.
- You dig traditions.

Avoid Bryn Mawr if...

- You're a guy. Even with a 2400 SAT and a patent on a drug that cures cancer, you won't get in.
- You want to be at a liberal arts school that has well-known Fine Arts Programs.
- You want a lot of social options readily available off campus.

California Institute of Technology

1200 EAST CALIFORNIA BOULEVARD, PASADENA, CA 91125
WEBSITE: WWW.CALTECH.EDU
CHINA ADMISSIONS OFFICER: JANN LACOSS
AO PHONE NUMBER: 626-395-6343
CHINA ADMISSIONS OFFICER EMAIL: JLACOSS@CALTECH.EDU
CLOSEST MAJOR CITY: LOS ANGELES, 20 MINUTES BY CAR OR 2 HOURS BY BUS

Best Fit Analysis

If you want to earn a lot of money, then come here, for Caltech grads have the highest median starting salary of any school in the nation. That's if you think you have the energy, optimism, and persistence to make it through 4 years of grueling academic training. If you plan to go to grad school, then become a PhD in a science field, start at Caltech. Intellectual curiosity and an open empathetic mindset are tools to help you enjoy your time at this very unique institution.

At a Glance

US News Rank	#10
Location	West Coast
Type of School	Private
Environment	Suburban

Students

Total Undergrad Enrollment	1001 (2014)
# Applicants	6507 (2015)
% Accepted	9 (2015)
Male to Female Ratio	54/46
% International Students	7
% Asian American	38

You Might Also Consider...

Stanford University
Harvey Mudd College
MIT
UC-Berkeley
Carnegie Mellon

Academic Opportunities

To fulfill the starving minds of the young geniuses of our generation, Caltech bumps up the rigor of its curriculum to sometimes unbearable levels. This should not be underestimated. With a core of 30 classes, students can often feel stifled at this small institution. At the same time, it rewards students with numerous Academic Opportunities in the form of the popular SURF program (Summer Undergraduate Research Fellowship) in which students can work with professors or conduct their own projects every year and get paid. Our alumni say, "Just email the professor. Research is really easy to find." A majority of students participate every single summer, and many continue these projects over the year as well. An AIC alum shares: "professors are friendly, but busy." Alternatively, graduate students who work and live close to undergraduates often develop close and beneficial relationships with the students they advise. Caltech offers 6 divisions of study (somewhat abbreviated here): Biology, chemistry, engineering, geological and planetary sciences, humanities and social sciences, mathematics, and astronomy. About 20% of students double major. Even without double majoring, students have to deal with high levels of stress from their workload, and Caltech tries to help them transition by making the first-year grading system a pass/no pass system. An AIC alumnus in the school shares, "[The environment is] collaborative. People work together on problem sets and often times offer help even when they are done with their own work." Caltech also has a cooperative agreement with Occidental College and the Art Center College of Design that allows the students to take classes at both while earning Caltech credit.

Career Development

Caltech doesn't release all its postgraduate statistics, but students estimate as many as 50% of the student body chooses higher education after undergraduate study. Many top consulting and technology firms such as Bain, LEK Consulting, Microsoft, Nvidia, Oracle, Pfizer value

AIC Alum Student Score Profiles

% Accepted	22.2%
Median SAT Critical Reading	740
Median SAT Math	800
Median SAT Writing	785
Median SAT Composite Score	2310
Median TOEFL	116

Financial Facts

Annual Tuition

$43710 USD (2015—2016)

Financial Aid Availability Low

What Students say about the Location

Safe	3.5
Fun	3
Expensive	2.5
Chinese food	3
Transportation	1
Bars and Clubs	2
Market/Grocery Options	2
Surrounding Job Market	2
Necessity of Car	4
Overall	3

*Out of four

Climate

Average Temperature Range

13℃ to 25℃

Average Annual Precipitation

59.6cm

Average Annual Humidity

79.9%

Average Annual Snowfall

0cm

Transportation From China

Students can fly directly from China to Los Angeles. Options include: HKG to LAX; PEK to LAX; PVG to LAX. Buses from LA to Pasadena are available.

the skills that Caltech students have. The alumni network is small, but useful. However, one Chinese international Student confides, "Most of them work in the academia, so not a lot of real world opportunities." However, Caltech's TecherLink connects students and alumni to the working world via internships and employment opportunities with notable success. With Silicon Valley located in the same state, Caltech grads can make smooth transitions between life at college and working for a tech startup.

Campus Social Environment

The residential colleges define social life. Each of the 7 houses has its own character, community, architecture, parties, traditions, etc. Students develop undeniably strong bonds with their housemates, and collectively, they help each other brave the harsh academic climate. Cooperation and community is imperative to the wellbeing of students in schools like Caltech. Undergraduate students stay up extremely late talking and hanging out in their house or working on problem sets. While undergrads have the opportunity to move off campus after their first year, 95% choose to stay with their housemates. Chinese international Students do not need to worry about having trouble fitting in. Although Caltech has its share of nerdy, socially awkward students, they can all find a community within the open and unique student body. About 38% of students are Asian, 9% are Hispanic, 2% are African American, 13% International and 34% are white.

Chinese international students say "Caltech parties are lame" and the school has a large share of "Asians and Jewish."

Selectivity

Accepted students are the top crop of science and mathematics students worldwide. International awards, success in competitions, and innovative measures taken in engineering-related projects are important to be considered as a viable applicant.

Things to Consider

You'll like Caltech if...

◆ Small communities where everyone knows your name and your significant other's name sound fantastic.

◆ You've known you wanted to study science and technology since you were 5, or younger.

Avoid Caltech if...

◆ You want to have a wide range of dating opportunities.

◆ You want to be in a large American city.

◆ You're tired of stressful academic environments.

Carleton College

1 N COLLEGE ST., NORTHFIELD, MN 55057
WEBSITE: WWW.CARLETON.EDU
CHINA ADMISSIONS OFFICER: CHARLIE COGAN
AO PHONE NUMBER: 507-222-4190
AO EMAIL ADDRESS: CCOGAN@CARLETON.EDU
CLOSEST MAJOR CITY: MINNEAPOLIS (1.5 HOURS BY CAR)

Best Fit Analysis

One of the premier liberal arts institutions in the Midwest, Carleton College places an extreme amount of focus on its undergraduate student body. A typical "Carl," a nickname given to students at the college, is one who is academic but not particularly cutthroat or competitive. Though it has low grade inflation, as an AIC alum notes that only "around 20% of the class get A's," students are Carleton are characterized by their strong sense of humor and willingness to collaborate and cooperate. Carleton's stronger majors lie in the natural sciences, particularly Biology, Chemistry, and Geology, and if you're interested in one day pursuing a PhD, Carleton ranks sixth among all colleges and universities in the percentage of alum who eventually secure doctorate degrees.

At a Glance	
US News Rank	#8
Location	Midwest
Type of School	Private
Environment	rural
Students	
Total Undergrad Enrollment	2014 (2015)
# Applicants	6722 (2015)
% Accepted	20.6 (2015)
Male to Female Ratio	47/53
% International Students	10.3
% Asian American	8.4
You Might Also Consider...	
Davidson College	
Macalester College	
Williams College	
Tufts University	

Academic Opportunities

Carleton College is run on a trimester schedule with three classes per trimester. As each trimester is only ten weeks long, the courses are typically fast-paced and rigorous. Core curriculum at Carleton is extensive and covers a wide range of subjects, so if you know what you want to study, and have no interest in other subjects, Carleton may be a drag. Though it can be tough to earn A's at Carleton, students benefit from a faculty that is bent on teaching. AIC alum laud Carleton's professors as "very accessible for conversations outside of class about both the academic and personal issues." Professors here are evaluated based on whether they can explain themselves to students and students notice. In tune with many liberal arts colleges across the United States, classes at Carleton are very small, as the school boasts a student-faculty ratio of 9:1. AIC alumni state, "[Classes are] small enough to feel like you have a close-knit community and that you know enough people around you," but sometimes "[Carleton] seems too small in the amount of courses it offers." Though Carleton is not among the most international LACs in the United States, 70% of students participate in some form of off-campus studies program. Researches in Physical Sciences are relatively abundant as 50-60 summer student-faculty research positions are offered by both departments and individual faculty members.

Career Development

Students at Carleton note that it's relatively easy to gain access to research opportunities in their respective fields because of the accessibility of professors. Many students don't find themselves heading towards a consulting or finance track post-graduation. An AIC alumnus heard that, "People don't get fancy jobs after graduation. Lots of Carleton students go to grad schools." The Career Center at Carleton provides several platforms for students to explore their fields of interest. Externships, for instance, allow students to "work with their alumni hosts at

AIC Alum Student Score Profiles

% AIC students accepted	12.9
Median SAT Critical Reading	730
Median SAT Math	800
Median SAT Writing	760
Median SAT Composite Score	2290
Median TOEFL	114

Financial Facts

Annual Tuition
$48987 USD (2015—2016)
Financial Aid Availability Low

What Students say about the Location

Safe	4
Fun	2
Expensive	2
Good Chinese food	2
Public transportation	1.5
Bars and Clubs	2
Market/Grocery Options	1
Surrounding Job Market	2
Is Car Necessary?	2.5
Overall	3

*Out of four Stars

Climate

Average Temperature Range
-10℃ to 23℃
Average Annual Precipitation
80.4cm
Average Annual Humidity
78.28%
Average Annual Snowfall
93.2cm

Transportation From China

The Minneapolis International Airport is an hour away and shuttles and busses are available to help students commute. No direct flight to China available.

their workplaces, allowing for quality observation time as well as hands-on experience." Couches-for-Carls allows current students and alums the chance to find free places to stay in homes of the Carleton network while seeking employment.

Campus Social Environment

Carleton has a reputation of attracting elite students who don't have an "elitist" attitude. One student has noted that Carleton is "diverse in an intellectual sense…[and] everyone is nice." This LAC is not particularly strong or notable for its athletics, however, the men and women's Frisbee teams have had competitive success, winning the National Championship in 2001, 2009, and 2011. Within such a tight-knit community, traditions are an integral component of Carleton's social environment. Among them, playing broomball on the outdoor ice rinks during the winter and a spring festival honoring "Rotblatt," a baseball pitcher, and the Mid-Winter Ball are some of the college's most celebrated. Northfield, MN offers very little for students off campus, so students are dependent upon the college for social outlets. There are no fraternities and sororities at Carleton, and thus partying is not a huge factor of the social scene. "People only party…[on] the weekends and there is not peer pressure to join," reports an AIC alum.

Selectivity

Carleton is selective, but not among the most selective institutions in the United States, and can be friendly to Chinese students compared to its peer institutions. They have, in the past, looked past scores to find individuals with heart and talent, but the admissions process is not so much "easy" as it is "unique."

Things to Consider

You'll like Carleton if...

- Having smaller nurturing classes is crucial to your learning environment.
- You're looking for a creative and quirky environment.

Avoid Carleton if...

- You plan to go into consulting or finance.
- You're not willing to put up with cold winter weather.

Carnegie Mellon University

5000 FORBES AVE, PITTSBURGH, PA 15213
WEBSITE: WWW.CMU.EDU
CHINA ADMISSIONS OFFICER: N/A
ADMISSION OFFICE PHONE NUMBER: 412-268-2082
ADMISSION OFFICE EMAIL ADDRESS: UNDERGRADUATE-ADMISSIONS@ANDREW.CMU.EDU
CLOSEST MAJOR CITY: PITTSBURGH

Best Fit Analysis

A premier research institute, Carnegie Mellon University boasts strong programs in a number of academic fields. From the arts and humanities to biotechnology and computing, students who are able to keep up with the intense workload will receive an education geared towards using classroom knowledge to tackle real-world problems.

Academic Opportunities

CMU is committed to providing students with a "liberal-professional" education: demonstrating the importance of the liberal arts, while emphasizing the development of marketable technical skills. To that end, cross-disciplinary courses are common. AIC alumni report that classes tend to be quite demanding, especially in math- and science-related fields, but "not impossible." They also feel that "class sizes are fine and students can get enough personal care." Professors teach most classes, and are quite accessible through office hours; one AIC alum also mentioned that "TA sessions held by graduate students are very helpful." Some of CMU's strongest programs include Computer Science, Engineering, Music, and Drama. Undergraduate research is supported in all academic fields through grants that cover research expenses, fellowships for summer projects, and awards supporting students presenting at academic conferences; the Meeting of the Minds symposium is held each May, celebrating undergraduate research throughout the campus.

At a Glance

US News Rank	#23
Location	Northeast
Type of School	Private
Environment	Urban

Students

Total Undergrad Enrollment	5800 (2015)
# Applicants	36131 (2015)
% Accepted	16.2 (2015)
Male to Female Ratio	54/46
% International Students	20
% Asian American	31

Schools with Undergraduate Programs

College of Engineering
College of Fine Arts
Dietrich College of Humanities & Social Sciences
Tepper School of Business
Mellon College of Science
School of Computer Science
H. John Heinz Ⅲ College

You Might Also Consider...

Columbia	Cornell
Harvard	Johns Hopkins
MIT	Northwestern

Career Development

Thanks to its proximity to downtown Pittsburgh, students can find internship and work opportunities near campus during the school year and summer, and the career center offers a number of resources for exploring these and other options. In addition, CMU has partnerships with Google, Facebook, IBM, and other companies that provide support to CMU students and alumni in gaining work and internship experience. And though many CMU grads pursue careers in technology, a large portion are also drawn to diverse careers such as education, the arts, consulting and engineering. 27% of the class of 2013 opted to pursue more advance degrees following graduation.

Campus Social Environment

With its strong programs in the arts, humanities, and sciences, CMU attra cts a diverse student

AIC Alum Student Score Profiles

% Accepted	33.6
Median SAT Critical Reading	680
Median SAT Math	800
Median SAT Writing	720
Median SAT Composite Score	2200
Median TOEFL	110

Financial Facts

Annual Tuition
$49610 USD (2015—2016)

Financial Aid Availability
Very low

What Students say about the Location

Safe	3
Fun	2
Expensive	2
Chinese food	2
Transportation	2
Bars and Clubs	2
Market/Grocery Options	2
Surrounding Job Market	3
Necessity of Car	4
Overall	3

*Out of Four

Climate

Average Temperature Range
-3℃ to 23℃

Average Annual Precipitation
93.8cm

Average Annual Humidity
80%

Average Annual Snowfall
45.8cm

Transportation from China

From Pittsburgh International Airport, students can take a taxi, rental car, public bus, or shuttle to campus.

population with a wide variety of interests. But, as one AIC alum points out, "we have as many drama nerds as technology nerds, but they do not hang out with each other." Academically, there is lots of diversity, but little mixing between groups. AIC students also note that "there are many people from different cultural backgrounds," to the extent some do not feel they are a minority. Downtown Pittsburgh, which is 20 minutes away by bus, provides an array of off-campus activities from bars and clubs to musical and theater performances. Due to the strong academic focus of most of the student body, the social scene on campus is somewhat lacking: as one AIC student puts it, "[we] don't really party in the middle of the semester." That said, 11% of male and 12% of female students are part of Greek life.

Selectivity

Not an easy school to get admitted, especially for their popular majors like computer science, but on the positive, CMU gives you ample space to make your case. A good university to consider for those who are not the best test-takers and have more to offer than meets the eye.

Things to Consider

You'll like Carnegie Mellon if…

◆ You want an education that emphasizes job preparation.

◆ You're interested in engineering, computer science, music, or drama.

- You want a variety of off-campus social activities.

Avoid Carnegie Mellon if...

- You want an active social scene on-campus.
- You are looking for an integrated student body.
- You do not want to focus solely on academics.

Case Western Reserve University

10900 EUCLID AVE, CLEVELAND, OH 44106
WEBSITE: WWW.CASE.EDU
CHINA ADMISSIONS OFFICER: DREW CRAWFORD, MEGAN GOODMAN
AO EMAIL ADDRESSES: DREW.CRAWFORD@CASE.EDU, MEGAN.GOODMAN@CASE.EDU
ADMISSION OFFICE PHONE NUMBER: 216-368-4450
CLOSEST MAJOR CITY: CHICAGO, ROUGHLY 4 HOURS AWAY BY CAR.

Best Fit Analysis

Born from the merging of Case Institute of Technology and Western Reserve University, Case Western University is known for its strong technical education and solid programs in the humanities. Though not as renowned as Carnegie Mellon, Case Western provides a comparable education, but has historically had more relaxed admissions.

Academic Opportunities

All students participate in the Seminar Approach to General Education and Scholarship program, taking smaller seminar classes that focus on critical thinking and writing skills, throughout their four years. According to one AIC alum, classes tend to be rigorous but manageable, and professors are readily accessible through office hours. Especially noteworthy majors include Biomedical Engineering, Polymer Science, Nursing, and Music; the Pre-professional Scholars Program also grants qualified students conditional acceptance to Case Western's law, social work, medical, or dental graduate schools. In terms of undergraduate research, Case Western's SOURCE program offers a cornucopia of options from on-campus projects assisting faculty, to individual projects that take advantage of the numerous nearby institutions such as the Cleveland Museums of Art, Natural History, and the Botanical Gardens.

At a Glance

US News Rank	#37
Location	Midwest
Type of School	Private
Environment	Urban

Students

Total Undergrad Enrollment	5121 (2015)
# Applicants	22821 (2015)
% Accepted	36 (2015)
Male to Female Ratio	55/45
% International Students	11
% Asian American	20

Schools with Undergraduate Programs

Case School of Engineering
College of Arts and Sciences
Frances Payne Bolton School of Nursing Weatherhead School of Management

You Might Also Consider...

Ohio State University
Carnegie Mellon
University of Michigan
Johns Hopkins
Washington University in St. Louis

Career Development

Students have little trouble finding internships thanks to Cleveland's strong local industry in both engineering and medicine, though the proximity to the arts and historic districts provides opportunities in other fields as well. The Practicum Program allows students in the College of Arts and Sciences and School of Management to engage in a 14-week long full-time professional experience. A staggering 42% of the class of 2013 is pursuing an advanced degree. Graduates who pursue immediate employment fall largely in the areas of engineering, information technology, business and nursing. Though not particularly well known for its alumni network, CWRU students and alums have the opportunity to receive advice from alumni through the Alumni Career Network.

Campus Social Environment

Case Western's intense academic atmosphere is complemented by a very cooperative environment: whether it's working together on problem sets or expressing solidarity through the Midnight Scream during finals week, there is great emphasis placed on collaboration. Students are

AIC Alum Student Score Profiles

% Accepted	19.3
Median SAT Critical Reading	640
Median SAT Math	800
Median SAT Writing	690
Median SAT Composite Score	2130
Median TOEFL	106

Financial Facts

Annual Tuition
$44156 USD (2015—2016)
Financial Aid Availability
Very low

What Students say about the Location

Safe	2
Fun	2
Expensive	2
Chinese food	2
Transportation	1
Bars and Clubs	2
Market/Grocery Options	1
Surrounding Job Market	3
Necessity of Car	4
Overall	2

*Out of Four

Climate

Average Temperature Range
-3℃ to 23℃
Average Annual Precipitation
106.2cm
Average Annual Humidity
78.48%
Average Annual Snowfall
151cm

Transportation from China

There is no direct flight from China to Cleveland. Students have to have a layover at Chicago. After flying to Cleveland Hopkins International Airport, students must take a short train followed by a bus to get to campus.

generally considered "nerdy," though AIC alumni report their interests are quite diverse. Being situated in Cleveland means Case Western students have access to a variety of off-campus events, though between Greek groups (which attract 28% of men and 31% of women) and other student organizations there are usually activities taking place on-campus. Though students can get cheap bus service around Cleveland, AIC alumni note that having a car would be more convenient, especially for travelling to Chicago and other cities. The student body is also fairly physically active, with 55% participating in intramurals; while sporting events generally do not receive much attention, the football game against Carnegie Mellon rallies a sizeable following.

Selectivity

Students treated this excellent school like a punching bag since it never required a supplement and offered an Early Action option. CWRU responded to the mass influx of Early Action by holding a tighter grip on acceptance letters. Competitive students, don't be surprised by receiving a Deferral at best or a Rejection.

Things to Consider

You'll like Case Western if...

- You want to do undergraduate research.
- You are interested in engineering or pre-med.
- You enjoy a collaborative environment.

Avoid Case Western if...

- You prefer working individually.
- You want a strong collegiate sport culture.
- You do not want to be in an urban setting.

Claremont McKenna College

500 E 9 STREET; CLAREMONT, CA 91711
WEBSITE: WWW.CMC.EDU
CHINA ADMISSIONS OFFICER: CONOR FRITZ
AO EMAIL ADDRESS: CFRITZ@CMC.EDU
ADMISSION OFFICE PHONE NUMBER: 909-621-8088
CLOSEST MAJOR CITY: LOS ANGELES (40 MINUTES BY CAR)

Best Fit Analysis

CMC is best suited for students with ambitions in business leadership and public affairs, but also looking for a well-rounded liberal arts education. Students uncomfortable around alcohol may want to stay away from CMC. While they will not be pressured to drink, partying is extremely prevalent and a big part of the social scene. As a member of the 5C consortium, CMC combines intimate school setting and plentiful resources. Come here if you want to experience intellectual LAC atmosphere while pursuing a business-oriented career track.

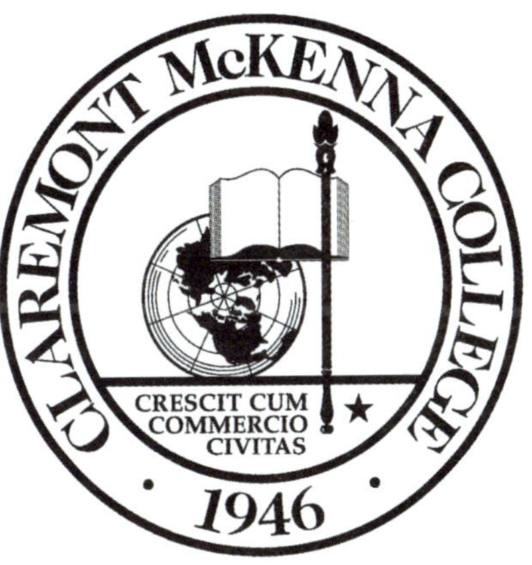

Academic Opportunities

Consider CMC if you want a "pragmatic" liberal arts education, as the *Wall Street Journal* listed CMC as a top ten best "feeder" into grad schools for law, business, and medicine.

At a Glance

US News Rank	#9
Location	West Coast
Type of School	Private
Environment	Suburban

Students

Total Undergrad Enrollment	1328 (2015)
# Student Applicants	7152 (2015)
% Accepted	9.8 (2015)
Male to Female Ratio	51/49
% International Students	16.6
% Asian American	10.3

You Might Also Consider...

Pomona College
Pitzer College
Occidental College
Stanford University
Scripps College

Nearly 30% of students are economics majors and other top programs include government, business, and international relations. Claremont provides the AISS program, which allows freshmen to take an accelerated science track, however the program is only for the truly passionate as it requires a 13 hours of class every week (5 on Friday). In general, students say science is not CMC's strength, and shares their science program with Scripps and Pitzer.

Students are generally cooperative and rarely compare grades, though one AIC student believes that CMC-ers are actually "extremely competitive."

72% of students conduct research with faculty, so research opportunities are more than available. All classes are taught by professors, who according to one AIC alum are all "really accessible." While CMC is a small school, it has big school resources, due to its membership in the 5C consortium: aside from CMC's 33 majors and 8 sequences, students have the opportunity to choose from over 2,000 course offerings available at CMC's sister schools.

Career Development

According to the AIC students surveyed, CMC students are focused and career oriented. 87% of C'13 participated in at least one internship during their college career, and CMC supported 146 summer internships in 2013 (largely in the non-profit sector). 48% of graduates surveyed had found full-time employment within six months of graduation, and another 13% were pursuing graduate school. Common career tracks for C'13 include: consulting (21%), investment banking (13%), accounting (13%), finance (10%), science/technology (10%), and education/nonprofits (10%). Business and Govt./Law combined for another 15%. CMC students don't lack for idealism either, as 9 students in the Class of 2013 received Fulbright Scholarships.

Campus Social Environment

CMC students party. Really. Hard. Despite there being no Greek organizations on campus, lax alcohol policies and plentiful, often themed parties (e.g. Monte Carlo, Superheroes) have given CMC a reputation for hosting the biggest and most elaborate parties of the 5Cs. Social life revolves around campus (94% of students live on-campus), as Claremont Village, though home to a variety of boutiques, restaurants, movie theaters, and yogurt shops, is not really vibrant or big enough to be considered a college town. While CMC students are very politically aware, they are far from pretentious and very accepting of each other. CMC is pretty racially diverse (3% African American; 8% Hispanic; 10% Asian American) and very politically diverse, but sexual and religious diversity is lacking. International students make up 17% of the student body: Chinese students (22 Chinese students, from China, enrolled in the class of 2018), numbering over 50, make up the largest contingent, so they will not feel alone, but CMC students generally do a good job of intermixing with those of different backgrounds. The Marion Minor Cook Athenaeum brings in speakers four days a week, and allows students to have intellectual debates over gourmet dinners.

Selectivity

Claremont McKenna, like the rest of the Claremont Consortium is tough to get into. Few ever get in with scores under 2280, and students with leadership and balanced profiles enjoy more preference.

Things to Consider

You'll like CMC if...

AIC Alum Student Score Profiles

% AIC students accepted	15.2
Median SAT Critical Reading	710
Median SAT Math	800
Median SAT Writing	680
Median SAT Composite Score	2170
Median TOEFL	105

Financial Facts

Annual Tuition
$48800 USD (2015—2016)
Financial Aid Availability
Very Low

What Students say about the Location

Safe	4
Fun	3
Expensive	2
Good Chinese food	2
Public transportation	3
Bars and Clubs	1
Market/Grocery Options	1
Surrounding Job Market	1
Is Car Necessary?	3
Overall	3

*Out of four Stars

Climate

Average Temperature Range
11℃ to 25℃
Average Annual Precipitation
58.7cm
Average Annual Humidity
81.87%
Average Annual Snowfall
0cm

Transportation From China

LAX is an hour's drive from Claremont. There are multiple airports nearby. Direct flights available to LAX.

- You want to go to a Liberal Arts College, but want a more pre-professional atmosphere.
- You'd enjoy t-shirt/flip-flops weather year-round.
- You are comfortable interacting with students from many backgrounds.

Avoid CMC if…

- You're looking for the Greek community experience.
- You prefer not to spend most of your time on campus.

College of William and Mary

116 JAMESTOWN ROAD, WILLIAMSBURG, VA 23187-8795
WEBSITE: WWW.WM.EDU
CHINA ADMISSIONS OFFICER: DEBORAH BASKET
AO PHONE NUMBER: 757-221-4223
AO EMAIL ADDRESS: DLBASK@WM.EDU
CLOSEST MAJOR CITY: WASHINGTON, D.C., ABOUT 2 HOURS BY AMTRAK TRAIN

Best Fit Analysis

If you are coming to the second oldest school in the nation, you'd better be prepared for academic rigor that has been carefully attended to and cultivated for more than 300 years. Known for greying the boundary between public and private school, the College of William and Mary is a haven for students who are serious about academic study. If you're looking for rowdier fun, your search should not necessarily stop here. Research opportunities, especially in the STEM fields (science, technology, engineering, mathematics), are abundant for aspiring researchers. Students who hope to meet other Chinese international Students or just international students in general may find their hopes dashed here. However, if American history is something you want to live in, there may be few better places than Williamsburg.

At a Glance

US News Rank	#34
Location	Mid Atlantic
Type of School	Public
Environment	Suburban

Students

Total Undergrad Enrollment	6301 (2015)
# Applicants	14952 (2015)
% Accepted	34.5 (2015)
Male to Female Ratio	44/56
% International Students	5.7
% Asian American	8.2

Schools with Undergraduate Programs

Programs in Arts and Sciences
Mason School of Business
School of Education

You Might Also Consider...

Georgetown University
Tufts University
Boston College
University of Virginia
UNC-Chapel Hill

Academic Opportunities

William and Mary, unlike some universities, places a lot of emphasis on its undergraduate four-year education, observable in the small classes and tough curriculum it serves. The most popular majors at William and Mary are business, management, marketing, biology and psychology. AIC students weigh on the subject: "All courses are taught by professors, and they are pretty accessible," and "I am rarely graded on curve, and it's not hard to get an A on math and science, but really hard on humanities courses." Take it with a grain of salty subjectivity, but students agree the reputation the school has for being rigorous is not unfounded. Still, students don't find the atmosphere depressing, "students are pretty smart here and collaborative. We sometimes form study groups to go over materials before tests." As a renowned research university, it provides opportunities for students to participate in top-notch projects.

Career Development

The Mason School of Business has a great reputation, with as many as 87% of graduating students finding jobs within a few months of graduation. Overall, 64% of students go into industry straight after graduation with employers like AmeriCorps, Bloomberg, Booz Allen Hamilton, CIA, IBM, MediaVest, Peace Corps, Teach for America, Deloitte, KPMG, Ernst and Young, PWC. The alumni network isn't as strong as many east coast private schools, and our AIC insiders tell us that the majority of William and Mary alumni are either from the DC/Government area or from Virginia. The school boasts that its students earn doctorates at a higher rate than any other public university.

Campus Social Environment

As a public school, William and Mary primarily caters to Virginia students, so most students hail from within state. Only 6% come from other countries, and 60% of the students are Caucasian. What it doesn't provide in diversity, it makes up for with a lenient alcohol policy, perhaps to facilitate socializing of different cultures. Students never abuse this though, and AIC students reveal, "no pressure at all [to drink], there are some people [who] drink at my school, but not too many." Greek life encompassed around 25% of the male population, 29% of the female population, and is not an imposing presence. Drugs are very restricted on campus.

Off campus, Williamsburg is a rather expensive touristy town, with not too much to do after hours. AIC alums recommend having a car, and prefer activities on campus.

Selectivity

As a public university, William and Mary doesn't take a significant number of students from out of state and internationally. Score average range from 2000-2250; admitted students are active leaders in their high schools.

Things to Consider

You'll like William and Mary if...

- You want to make friends with Caucasian Americans.
- You're looking for a bar scene.
- You want to intern or work in Washington DC.
- Studying, taking tests, academic exploration is very important to you.

Avoid William and Mary if...

- You aspire to meet many people around the world.
- You're not willing to engage in the traditions that help define this school.

AIC Alum Student Score Profiles

% Accepted	29
Median SAT Critical Reading	675
Median SAT Math	800
Media SAT Writing	725
Median SAT Composite Score	2140
Median TOEFL	109

Financial Facts

Annual Tuition

$35122 USD (2015—2016)

Financial Aid Availability

Very Low

What Students say about the Location

Safe	4
Fun	1.5
Expensive	1.5
Chinese food	2
Transportation	2
Bars and Clubs	1.5
Market/Grocery Options	1.5
Surrounding Job Market	1.5
Necessity of Car	4
Overall	2.5

*Out of four

Climate

Average Temperature Range

3℃ to 26℃

Average Annual Precipitation

114.7cm

Average Annual Humidity

74.65%

Average Annual Snowfall

22.9cm

Transportation from China

There are no direct flights from China. Students typically fly into Washington, DC and then take the Amtrak train to Williamsburg.

Columbia University

1130 AMSTERDAM AVENUE, NEW YORK, NY 10027
WEBSITE: WWW.COLUMBIA.EDU
CHINA ADMISSIONS OFFICER: EDWARD
AO EMAIL ADDRESS: ET2416@COLUMBIA.EDU TRUONG
ADMISSION OFFICE PHONE NUMBER: 212-854-2522
CLOSEST MAJOR CITY: NEW YORK CITY (COLUMBIA IS LOCATED IN MANHATTAN)

Best Fit Analysis

We have been hard-pressed to find a student who doesn't like Columbia University, especially its diversity and prime location. In general, the only complaint has been that the surrounding areas can be a little dangerous and noisy. Most students have faith in their abilities to handle and conquer the invigorating fast-paced life of NYC, but it isn't for everyone. Those who are serious about their studies, who are not too sure what they want to major in yet, will find Columbia to be a good fit, but if you already have a clearly defined academic focus, Columbia's Core Curriculum can slow you down.

Academic Opportunities

As the fourth most selective university in the nation, Columbia University makes sure that its students are well adjusted to life after college. It excels in the departments of English, History, Political Science, Economics, Biology, Music, Drama, and Mechanical Engineering and maintains a firm stance on an extensive set of core curriculum requirements. It takes 2 years to finish the requirements, which include 2 semesters of science, an understanding of contemporary civilization, literature, and humanities. The Ivy League school houses its own professor rating system, and provides many research opportunities. The atmosphere is, as our AIC Alum put it, "Intellectual rather than pre-professional." Columbia maintains an intimate learning sphere, and Chinese students also say, "Grad students only teach recitation sessions. My professors for small seminar classes are incredibly accessible and warm-hearted, they maintain office hours and they are very happy to talk to you whenever." The School of Engineering is famous for its interdisciplinary research in areas such as bioengineering and nanotechnology, and while Columbia charges a hefty price for the privilege to be educated there, it makes the money count.

At a Glance

US News Rank	4
Location	Northeast
Type of School	Private
Environment	Urban

Students

Total Undergrad Enrollment	8613 (2015)
# Applicants	36250 (2015)
% Accepted	6.1 (2015)
Male to Female Ratio	53/47
% International Students	16
% Asian American	17

Schools with Undergraduate Programs

Columbia College
Columbia School of Engineering and Applied Sciences

You Might Also Consider...

Harvard University
Princeton University
New York University
UPenn
Dartmouth College

Career Development

Despite its generally intellectual emphasis, Columbia also provides its students with ample opportunities to focus on their futures with networking secessions and on campus interviews with top companies such as JP Morgan and LinkedIn. For those who are interested in the academic world, New York City's research institutes are easily accessible for internships. In the class of 2013, 58.3% of the students were employed, while 20% had confirmed placements in graduate school within 6 months of graduation. Of the employed, 55.7% had an annual salary above $50000, and 30.8% had starting offers over $70000. Students sought graduate positions all over the top 10 schools in the world. Those employed chose industry jobs in financial services, consulting, computers, education, research, legal services, internet and ecommerce,

AIC Alum Student Score Profiles

% Accepted	17.3
Median SAT Critical Reading	740
Median SAT Math	800
Median SAT Writing	795
Median SAT Composite Score	2310
Median TOEFL	115

Financial Facts

Annual Tuition	$50526 (2015—2016)
Financial Aid Availability	Low

What Students say about the Location

Safe	3
Fun	4
Expensive	3
Chinese food	3
Transportation	4
Bars and Clubs	4
Market/Grocery Options	4
Surrounding Job Market	2.5
Necessity of Car	1
Overall	4

*Out of four

Climate

Average Temperature Range	-2℃ to 24℃
Average Annual Precipitation	122cm
Average Annual Humidity	66%
Average Annual Snowfall	38.1cm

Transportation from China

Direct flights are available from China to JFK International Airport in New York. Public transportation can get you from the airport to Columbia's campus in about 40 minutes.

and media and top recruiting companies included Accenture, JP Morgan, Citigroup, Google, Columbia and Bank of America. Columbia has one of the most powerful alumni networks in the USA, and offers a wide range of services to alumni including access to the Columbia Career Coaches Network.

Campus Social Environment

Our AIC Alum shares, "it's big in the sense that you can always meet new people at classes (lectures) and parties and all kinds of student activities. But it's also small as you begin to realize that all your friends are somehow connected in certain ways." So at the end of the day, Columbia feels pretty small and the Chinese international students feel that Columbia is so diverse (the most diverse of all the Ivies) that it can't help but be accepting of all. 52% of the student body is of a minority group.

There is plenty to do in the city, as one might expect with the Big Apple, although Chinese International Students intimate, "We are still a bit close to Harlem." About 10% women and 10% men go Greek, and it's not necessary to pay attention if that's not your scene. Columbia has many of its own traditions, such as Orgo night where the marching band go to the library during Finals Week and disrupts all seriousness for about an hour. In addition, Columbia's CORE club helps generate entrepreneurial seeds by hosting events and competitions every year.

Selectivity

Competition is incredibly tight, as Columbia is known for being one of the toughest schools to get into in the entire country. Scores above 2300 don't provide any guarantees, and students should make a point to provide an intense interest in studying in New York City in their applications.

Things to Consider

You'll like Columbia if...

- You want to expose yourself to cultures around the world.
- Artsy activities like museums and plays appeal.
- You want to go into finance.

Avoid Columbia if...

- Any amount of danger frightens you.
- Exploring curriculums outside of your major seems like a waste of time.

Cornell University

144 EAST AVENUE, ITHACA, NY 14853
WEBSITE: WWW.CORNELL.EDU
CHINESE ADMISSION OFFICER: N/A
ADMISSIONS OFFICE PHONE NUMBER: 607-255-5241
ADMISSION OFFICE EMAIL ADDRESS: ADMISSIONS@CORNELL.EDU
CLOSEST MAJOR CITY: NEW YORK CITY, ABOUT A FOUR-HOUR BUS RIDE

Best Fit Analysis

Cornell is a versatile school with a lot to offer Chinese international students with its 7 undergraduate colleges. Students who would be able to make the most out of the campus should be proactive, socially and academically. Campus is large, so finding organizations to expand and develop social networks is important. There's something here for everyone, whether you are interested in sports, making international friends or love to part. Keep in mind academic workload can be overwhelming at times, and procrastinating can take a toll. AIC Students reports, "Ithaca is at least 2 hours away from other cities. So it does lack anything you would expect in a big city. But it is a beautiful place." Cornell also experiences extremely cold winters, so be prepared with your warmest apparel.

Academic Opportunities

Ranked Number 15 by US News & World Report, Cornell University offers challenging academics and has the reputation of killer finals. Introductory classes are often taught with the help of graduate students, but students report professors are "pretty accessible." Popular majors at Cornell include Biology, Hospitality Management and Economics. While some AIC alumni feel the campus is too big, those in more specialized schools report the faculty-student ratio is perfect. Within the College of Arts and Sciences, students take full advantage of Cornell's broad range of offerings and distribution requirements, taking 2/3 of their curriculum outside of their major. While it has been known for having a high suicide rate, Cornell students also have access to excellent counseling services. Many resources are available to students who hope to plan their own research project.

Career Development

A majority of students in Cornell graduate with job offers, and of these, many find their first stepping stones in the finance industry. According to the career website, 54% of students began professional careers directly after college, while 30% chose to seek higher levels of education. Students report that it is rather easy to find jobs during the year, and Cornell's career center does a good job of helping its students locate jobs, with separate job posting networks for the local community and outside of it. AIC Students say: "Students are all connected, and alumni always offer job opportunities for us."

At a Glance

US News Rank	#15
Location	Northeast
Type of School	Private
Environment	Suburban

Students

Total Undergrad Enrollment	14315 (2015)
# Applied	41907 (2015)
% of Applicants Accepted	14.9 (2015)
Male to Female Ratio	48/52
% International Students	10
% Asian American	16

Schools with Undergraduate Programs

College of Agriculture and Life Sciences
College of Architecture, Art, and Planning
College of Arts and Sciences
College of Engineering
School of Hotel Administration
College of Human Ecology
School of Industrial and Labor Relations

You Might Also Consider...

Duke	Harvard
Princeton	Stanford
Yale	UPenn

AIC Alum Student Score Profiles

% Accepted	12
Median SAT Critical Reading	730
Median SAT Math	800
Media SAT Writing	770
Median SAT Composite Score	2290
Median TOEFL	114

Financial Facts

Annual Tuition
$49116 USD (2015—2016)
Financial Aid Availability
Very Low

What Students say about the Location

Safe	3.5
Fun	3
Expensive	3
Chinese food	2.5
Transportation	2
Bars and Clubs	2
Market/Grocery Options	2
Surrounding Job Market	3
Necessity of Car	3
Overall	3

*Out of four

Climate

Average Temperature Range
-6℃ to 21℃
Average Annual Precipitation
94.8cm
Annual Average Humidity
77.99%
Average Annual Snowfall
124.1cm

Transportation from China

There are direct flights from China. Students can fly into NYC's JFK International Airport and proceed to take a four-hour bus from the city to Ithaca, NY.

Campus Social Environment

Cornell has a diverse ethnic distribution, and Chinese international students will have no trouble finding students from their country and foreign nations to bond with. In 2012, there were 341 undergraduate students from China. Many AIC students report around half of their friends are from China. One student recounts, "We have people from everywhere in the world, tons of believing, and diverse opportunities for majors and minors." There's widespread LGBT support, which speaks to the open-mindedness of the community. In general, AIC students say, "There are lots of [parties], and they are always held on weekends." Ice hockey and football have a large following in Cornell. There are more than 500 student organizations on Cornell, and activities on campus everyday. Twenty to twenty-five percent of students are involved in Greek organizations, but they don't define the social scene. "Food options are pretty diverse" in general due to the culinary school but few Chinese food options exist.

Selectivity

Cornell's College of Engineering is one of the more selective schools on campus. Other schools in Cornell accept a wider range of scores from low 2100's to high 2200's being the norm.

Things to Consider

You'll like Cornell if...

- You like football and hockey.

◆ You're interested in business, hotel management, industrial relations, engineering, or human ecology.

◆ You expect most social events to be on campus.

◆ You want to be close to an international Chinese student community.

◆ You are looking for ethnic diversity.

Avoid Cornell if…

◆ You hate cold weather.

◆ You want to be in a large American city.

◆ You want to attend a school with intimate class sizes.

◆ You dislike a pre-professional atmosphere.

Dartmouth College

6016 MCNUTT HALL HANOVER, NH 03755
WEBSITE: WWW.DARTMOUTH.EDU
CHINA ADMISSIONS OFFICER: BECKY SABKY
ADMISSION OFFICE PHONE NUMBER: 603-646-1216
ADMISSION OFFICE CONTACT: HTTPS://ADMISSIONS.DARTMOUTH.EDU/CONTACT-US
CLOSEST MAJOR CITY: BOSTON (2.5 HOURS BY CAR)

Best Fit Analysis

For students looking for Ivy League prestige, but an LAC-like environment, Dartmouth is just the place. Nestled in a town of 11000 people on the border of New Hampshire and Vermont, the undergraduate-focused Dartmouth combines intimate classroom settings with plentiful research opportunities, and extensive core requirements with flexible schedule options. Facing bitter winters and a lacking local social scene, students are unified by their love for academic exploration, Mother Nature and lots and lots of beer (pong).

Academic Opportunities

Dartmouth is most known for its distinctive D-Plan, an innovative quarter system which guides both the pace and academic spirit of the school. While students are required to stay on campus for certain quarters, they can choose when they want to enroll for the rest of their college career. This flexibility allows students to potentially take an entire year gaining work experience in an internship, volunteering on a service project, or conducting field research. On the flip side, courses move quickly—Finals rear their ghastly head every three months. Students gain a well-rounded education through the extensive General Requirements, and the most popular majors include economics, government, history, and engineering. In terms of the learning environment, Dartmouth offers a very cooperative atmosphere. According to one AIC alum, "professors are usually very approachable" and the students surveyed all felt that classes were just the right size. Dartmouth students are very passionate and dedicated to what they do, so whatever pizzazz the city of Hanover lacks, Dartmouth more than makes up for with an intellectually vibrant and supportive student body.

At a Glance

US News Rank	#12
Location	Northeast
Type of School	Private
Environment	Rural

Students

Total Undergrad Enrollment	4307 (2015)
# Applicants	20507 (2015)
% Accepted	10.9 (2015)
Male to Female Ratio	51/49
% International	8.9
% Asian	14.9

Schools with Undergraduate Programs

Undergraduate College

Thayer School of Engineering

You Might Also Consider...

Duke	Boston College
UPenn	Northwestern
Georgetown	

Career Development

The Dartmouth name is storied, but lively as ever: 170 graduates have served in Congress and it is also ranked fourth in its production of Fortune 500 CEOs. With an extremely active alumni network and a professional emphasis, it is no surprise that over 60% of the Class of 2012 was employed within six months of graduating, most commonly in finance, education, and consulting. Health/sciences, arts/communication and technology combined for another quarter of graduates pursuing full-time work. Most of these graduates found themselves remaining in the Northeast/Mid-Atlantic, but many also found jobs in D.C., Chicago and popular metro locations in California and Texas. Graduate school was a common option as well, with 11% currently enrolled in programs and 64% intending to apply within five years of graduation. Meanwhile, Dartmouth students don't lack in idealism either as the school consistently ranks among the Top 20 small schools producing Peace Corps volunteers.

AIC Alum Student Score Profiles

% AIC students accepted	10.3
Median SAT Critical Reading	735
Median SAT Math	800
Median SAT Writing	780
Median SAT Composite Score	2310
Median TOEFL	118

Financial Facts

Annual Tuition
$48120 USD (2015—2016)
Financial Aid Availability
Very Low

What Students say about the Location

Safe	3
Fun	2
Expensive	3
Good Chinese food	1
Public transportation	1
Bars and Clubs	1
Market/Grocery Options	1
Surrounding Job Market	2.5
Is Car Necessary?	2.5
Overall	2

*Out of four Stars

Climate

Average Temperature Range
−9℃ to 20℃
Average Annual Precipitation
104.1cm
Average Annual Humidity
81.06%
Average Annual Snowfall
182cm

Transportation from China

Convenient shuttle to airport is provided; buses to Logan Airport and Manchester Airport are also available. Logan is 2.5 hours away; Manchester is 1.5 hours away. Logan has direct flights to China but Manchester does not.

Campus Social Environment

Although the Dartmouth of old was the inspiration for "Animal House," the classic American movie depicting collegiate debauchery and mischief at its best (or worst), in recent years it has toned down its reckless partying reputation. That said, because the alcohol policy is lax and the sleepy town of Hanover offers little in terms of entertainment, Greek Life continues to reign supreme. For those tired of or uninterested in partying, the DOC (Dartmouth Outing Club) also has a huge presence on campus and acts as a social scene in itself

Students are sometimes stereotyped as white, preppy, party-hard "bros" and beneficiaries of conservative old boy networks, but in reality, Dartmouth of today is a progressive and diverse place (though self-segregating is common). You can find students of all kinds, but they are commonly outdoorsy, down-to-earth, "work hard-play hard" types. All of the AIC students surveyed said that less than 30% of their friends were Chinese Internationals, and with less than ten Chinese students matriculating every year, AIC students interested in Dartmouth should be ready and willing to mix and mingle with a wide variety of people

Selectivity

Dartmouth rarely takes Chinese students. Without a 2200, you may have little opportunity to make it into Dartmouth. Perhaps what would be more beneficial is spending a few years in American high schools, as that would legitimize any academic accolades.

Things to Consider

You'll like Dartmouth if…

- You love activities outdoors.
- You are focused on developing your career.

Avoid Dartmouth if…

- The city life is what you look forward to the most in America.
- Exclusive Greek life intimidates you.
- Communities where everyone knows your name feel stifling.

Davidson College

209 RIDGE ROAD, DAVIDSON, NC 28035
WEBSITE: WWW.DAVIDSON.EDU
CHINA ADMISSIONS OFFICER: KAYE-LANI LAUGHNA
AO EMAIL ADDRESS: KALAUGHNA@DAVIDSON.EDU
ADMISSION OFFICE PHONE NUMBER: 800-768-0380
CLOSEST MAJOR CITY: CHARLOTTE, (20 MIN BY BUS OR CAR)

Best Fit Analysis

With deep Presbyterian roots, Davidson puts a strong emphasis on service and integrity. This manifests itself in an Honor System featuring self-scheduled, un-proctored exams or "reviews." The Honor System dictates both the academic and social life as well as 85% participation rate in community service. Students looking for an excellent and well-rounded education will find comfort in Davidson's Liberal Arts Core, a cornerstone of the undergraduate curriculum. Unfortunately, Davidson's location doesn't offer many advantages. Those looking for a school where they don't have to explain themselves every time they mention where they're being educated certainly won't enjoy their experience.

Academic Opportunities

Davidson students pride themselves on being hard workers. That said, intimate classes, accessible professors, and a well-respected honor code creates an atmosphere of intellectual curiosity and mutual trust. Davidson's Liberal Arts Core requires one course each in Literature, Fine Arts, history, Religion, Philosophy, as well as three in math or sciences and two in the social sciences. Research opportunities are readily available to students who choose to seek them out and are often imbedded into the curriculum. In 2012, 243 students engaged in semester-long independent research. Campus is pretty balanced academically, as popular majors include political science, English, and psychology, but also natural sciences like biology and chemistry. In addition, Davidson also offers combined BA-BS programs in engineering with Columbia and WUSTL. Generally, 70%-80% of students long to taste the world outside North Carolina and participate in study abroad programs before graduation. One drawback is that many students have complained about grade deflation problems in recent year, which leads to a demanding academic environment.

At a Glance

US News Rank	#9
Location	Mid-Atlantic
Religious Affiliation	Presbyterian
Type of School	Private
Environment	Rural

Students

Total Undergrad Enrollment	1950 (2015)
# Applicants	5382 (2015)
% Accepted	22.2 (2015)
Male to Female Ratio	49/51
% International	5.9
% Asians	6.2

You Might Also Consider...

St. John's College
Wake Forest University
Dartmouth University
Vanderbilt University

Career Development

Davidson Wildcats are students at heart, as 80% of graduates eventually go on to get a graduate degree. Of recent graduates, around 44% are pursing full-time work, 18% are involved in a fellowship or service opportunity, and 20% are pursuing graduate school. With an alumni giving rate of over 60%, Wildcats are loyal to and proud of their alma mater. Over a quarter of graduates stay in North Carolina, though 12% are now living abroad.

Campus Social Environment

To this day, Davidson is still largely white, upper-middle class and Southern (46.5% from Southeast US) and is characterized as having a more conservative flavor. Racial diversity is one of the hottest topics on campus, often popping up in the school newspaper and campus discussions. That said, campus is inclusive and welcoming: international students only make up

AIC Alum Student Score Profiles

% AIC students accepted	23.1
Median SAT Critical Reading	660
Median SAT Math	790
Median SAT Writing	700
Median SAT Composite Score	2150
Median TOEFL	110

Financial Facts

Annual Tuition
$46966 USD (2015—2016)
Financial Aid Availability
Very Low

What Students say about the Location

Safe	4
Fun	2
Expensive	3
Good Chinese food	2
Public transportation	2.5
Bars and Clubs	1
Market/Grocery Options	1
Surrounding Job Market	1.5
Is Car Necessary?	3
Overall	2.5

*Out of four Stars

Climate

Average Temperature Range
4℃ to 26℃
Average Annual Precipitation
113.8cm
Average Annual Humidity
78.13%
Average Annual Snowfall
9.7cm

Transportation from China

Charlotte Douglas International Airport is 30 minutes away and can be reached by taxi. No direct flight available.

6% of the student body (24 Chinese), but they tend to mix well with students from all over the US.

Fraternities for males and eating houses for females (35 and 40% participation respectively) set the tone for the social scene. Davidson students also know how to let loose on the weekends, whether it's through parties or (for the non-drinkers) participating in activities organized by the Union Board. Social life almost entirely revolves around campus: with a population of 7100, the town itself is the epitome of "quaint." As a result, some students complain that the party scene is repetitive. For the rest, Charlotte is relatively close and can offer more exciting opportunities. In addition, Myrtle Beach and ski slopes are both several hours away.

Selectivity

Davidson is not the most famous school in China, which means few apply. Similarly, few get in. Still, we know that admissions are certainly competitive, and Davidson values extracurricular achievement and the ability to critical think and reflect.

Things to Consider

You'll like Davidson if...

◆ You're looking for a close-knit community and caring faculty.

◆ You don't know how to do laundry. (only school with free laundry service!)

Avoid Davidson if...

◆ You will be offended if people ask, "what's Davidson?"

◆ You are looking for a school with a large Chinese student body (and will easily miss Chinese food).

Duke University

2138 CAMPUS DRIVE, DURHAM, NC 27708
WEBSITE: WWW.DUKE.EDU
CHINA ADMISSIONS OFFICER: SOLOMON ENOS
AO PHONE NUMBER: 919-684-0175
AO EMAIL ADDRESS: SOLOMON.ENOS@DUKE.EDU
CLOSEST MAJOR CITY: RALEIGH (30 MINUTES; FREE BUSES PROVIDED BETWEEN DUKE AND UNC)

Best Fit Analysis

Consistently ranking in the Top 10 slots of National Universities, Duke contends as the reining champion of "School Spirit" among the most selective institutions. Located within the "Research Triangle" of North Carolina, Duke provides students unparalleled Academic Opportunities through its two undergraduate schools, the Trinity College of Arts and Sciences and the Pratt School of Engineering. With an incredibly strong fraternity culture and Division I basketball fervor present on campus, "Dukies" are typically considered to be high-achieving, practical individuals who are also highly competitive and ambitious.

At a Glance

US News Rank	#8
Location	South
Type of School	Private
Environment	Suburban

Students

Total Undergrad Enrollment	6485 (2015)
# Applicants	31186 (2015)
% Accepted	11 (2015)
Male to Female Ratio	50/50
% International	10
% Asian	22

Schools with Undergraduate Programs

Trinity College of Arts and Sciences

Pratt School of Engineering

You Might Also Consider...

UNC-Chapel Hill	Harvard
Princeton	Rice
UVA	

Academic Opportunities

Duke's Electrical and Biomedical Engineering majors are particularly strong, as well as its liberal arts degrees in Biology, Neuroscience, Economics, and Public Policy. As the spirit of competition engulfs Duke's national title-winning basketball culture, it is not surprising that Duke's academic atmosphere can be relatively cutthroat. An AIC alum at the Pratt School of Engineering notes that getting A's at Duke is "very difficult." The competitive nature of Duke is a driving force that motivates students to have particularly rigorous academic schedules, and 83% of undergraduates seek a double major, minor, or certificate. The university also offers many unique interdisciplinary majors and the opportunity to design a new major for students with diverse interests. With particularly strong cores in life sciences and engineering, Duke offers students a wide range of research opportunities available both on campus with world-renown faculty in a highly academic atmosphere. Students interested in health sciences should take note of Duke because opportunities for medical research abound in the area surrounding Duke's campus. Students have opportunities to have their research funded by Duke-operated initiatives including the TGen-Duke Biomedical Futures Program and the Howard Hughes Research Fellows.

Career Development

Duke's nearby Medical Center provides career opportunities for pharmacology and biochemistry students. Though Duke boasts a strong pre-medical and health sciences track in addition to its well-known engineering programs, Duke students find themselves in the competitive fields of financial services and consulting. The 2012 Duke Senior Survey reports that 15.5% and 12.1% of the graduating class entered financial services and consulting, respectively, with almost one-fourth of the Class of 2012 settling in New York City following graduation. Duke holds a Diversity Networking Dinner for undergraduates to cater towards employers who are seeking to diversify their organizations, inviting financial giants like BlackRock, RBC Capital Markets, and J.P. Morgan to the table. The Fannie Mitchel Expert-in-Residence series encourages accomplished professionals to provide knowledge and counseling to Duke students by establishing mentor-mentee relationships.

Campus Social Environment

Duke is considered to have a highly diverse international and domestic student body, with just over 50% of the student body self-identifying as "Caucasian." One AIC student reports that Duke is "pretty diverse. [There are] so many international students from different countries and areas," Yet students from different backgrounds tend to self-segregate. Socially speaking, Duke embraces the "Work Hard, Play Hard" mentality that is evident in the school's "Culture of Champions." The two major social highlights of Duke's atmosphere revolve around the men's basketball team, the Blue Devils, and the noticeable presence of Greek life. Many students camp out at the notorious "K-ville", a plot of land designated for students to pitch tents in hopes of gaining access to some high-profile basketball matches. Unlike some other elite national universities, the party scene at Duke is incredibly strong, with opportunities to attend drinking events up to "4 days a week." Approximately 27% of men join fraternities and 42% of women are in sororities.

AIC Alum Student Score Profiles

% AIC students accepted	12
Median SAT Critical Reading	730
Median SAT Math	800
Median SAT Writing	765
Median SAT Composite Score	2275
Median TOEFL	115.5

Financial Facts

Annual Tuition
$49498 USD (2015—2016)
Financial Aid Availability
Very Low

What Students say about the Location

Safe	2.5
Fun	2
Expensive	3
Good Chinese food	2
Public transportation	3
Bars and Clubs	2
Market/Grocery Options	2
Surrounding Job Market	2.5
Is Car Necessary?	3.5
Overall	3

*Out of four Stars

Climate

Average Temperature Range
3℃ to 26℃
Average Annual Precipitation
115.4cm
Average Annual Humidity
77.87%
Average Annual Snowfall
10.6cm

Transportation from China

Raleigh-Durham International Airport is 25 minutes away, and Duke provides shuttles during holiday season. The airport is also reachable by taxi. No direct flight to China available.

Selectivity

Numbers have grown throughout the years. Duke takes approximately over 30 Chinese international students into their freshman class. We wouldn't be surprised if they re-ceive approximately 1000+ applications from Chinese internationals these days.

Things to Consider

You'll like Duke if…

- You thrive from the heat of intense academic competition.
- You have a strong desire to study health sciences and engineering.

Avoid Duke if…

- You prefer an intimate, cooperative learning environment.

Emory University

201 DOWMAN DR, ATLANTA, GA 30322
WEBSITE: WWW.EMORY.EDU
CHINA ADMISSIONS OFFICER: SCOTT ALLEN
AO EMAIL ADDRESS: SCOTT.ALLEN@EMORY.EDU
ADMISSION OFFICE PHONE NUMBER: 404-727-6036 (EMORY COLLEGE), 770-784-8328 (OXFORD COLLEGE)
CLOSEST MAJOR CITY: ATLANTA

Best Fit Analysis

Emory has long been a popular choice for Chinese international students as a mid-sized university with a spattering of pre-professional paths. Located on the outskirts of Atlanta, one of the U.S.'s fastest growing urban hubs, Emory provides its students a blend of on-and-off campus opportunities socially, academically, and professionally. Though Emory traditionally draws many students from the southern part of the United States, the school is known to be relatively diverse and politically active, with a high awareness of and engagement with world events.

Academic Opportunities

Emory is separated into nine colleges, each with its own admissions process. Students

At a Glance

US News Rank	#21
Location	South
Type of School	Private
Environment	City

Students

Total Undergrad Enrollment	7803 (2015)
# Applicants	20462 (2015)
% Accepted	23.6 (2015, Emory College) 37.5% (2015, Oxford College)
Male to Female Ratio	44/56
% International Students	18.5
% Asian	19

Schools with Undergraduate Programs

Emory College of Arts and Sciences
Oxford College
Goizueta Business School
Nell Hodgson Woodruff School of Nursing

You Might Also Consider...

Duke
University of Virginia
Northwestern University
Vanderbilt
Washington University in St. Louis

interested in business should highly consider Emory, as enrolled students can opt to apply for a two year program at the Goizueta Business School after their sophomore year and intern at one of the many financial firms located in downtown Atlanta. Students who do intend on trying to gain admittance to the Goizueta School of Business should know that it typically has the reputation of being Emory's toughest undergraduate track. An AIC alum studying business at Emory says to get an A, "It is really difficult and in business, [there] is a curve on the grade. 10% [of students get an] A." After their sophomore year, students can additionally apply to transfer into the Nell Hodgson Woodruff School of Nursing, whose students, along with Chemistry and Biology majors, can take advantage of the close relationship Emory has established with the Center for Disease Control. Students applying to Emory can either apply to the university's main campus in Atlanta or opt to complete their first two years at Oxford College, a two-year liberal arts campus about forty miles away from Emory's downtown location that offers students a more intimate learning environment before continuing on to the main university. Professional disciplines like Premed and Prelaw at Emory are typically considered to have a strong reputation, and students interested in engineering can enroll in the dual degree program with Georgia Tech that lets students earn a bachelor's degree at Emory and either a bachelor's or master's in engineering at Georgia Tech.

Career Development

In general, students at Emory are known to be very career-oriented. An AIC alum states that at Emory, "It is very easy to find [a] job search if you go to the career center on campus."

Emory's partnerships with many organizations within the greater Atlanta area are on the greatest draws to the university for prospective students. In addition to offering work-studies, internships, and volunteer opportunities at the Center for Disease Control, the Global Health Scholars program gives a chance to intern in global health fields abroad. Furthermore, students at Emory can intern abroad for credit if they meet certain criteria outlined by the Center for International Programs Abroad. The Scholarly Inquiry and Research at Emory (SIRE) program provides grants for students interested in research projects, and the Summer Undergraduate Research Experience (SURE) gives students the chance to research under a faculty mentor and create a presentation of their work at the end-of-the-summer formal research symposium. A recent survey of Emory's Class of 2013 reports that 43% of the class is currently enrolled at graduate and professional schools, while 26% entered directly into the work force. Other students are volunteering abroad or participating in postgraduate internships.

Campus Social Environment

One of the more notable qualms that students have about Emory is its lack of "school spirit." With "sports…not really big on campus," according to an AIC alum, the undergraduate student body doesn't have a focal point to ground itself on. Nevertheless, some AIC students have found Emory to be "a party school" as "you can find any kinds of party." About a fourth of men and women participate in Greek life at Emory that help create a vibrant social scene on-campus with several large events hosted on fraternity row during the school year, but students also take

AIC Alum Student Score Profiles

% AIC students accepted	13.4
Median SAT Critical Reading	670
Median SAT Math	795
Median SAT Writing	690
Median SAT Composite Score	2130
Median TOEFL	111

Financial Facts

Annual Tuition

$45700 USD (2015-2016, Emory College)

$41000 USD (2015-2016, Oxford College)

Financial Aid Low

What Students say about the Location

Safe	3
Fun	2.8
Expensive	2.5
Good Chinese food	2.5
Public transportation	2
Bars and Clubs	2
Market/Grocery Options	2
Surrounding Job Market	2
Is Car Necessary?	4
Overall	2.8

*Out of four Stars

Climate

Average Temperature Range 5℃ to 26℃

Average Annual Precipitation 133.4cm

Average Annual Humidity 76.12%

Average Annual Snowfall 2.5cm

Transportation from China

Cab or public bus will get you to Hartsfield-Jackson international airport in 30 minutes to 1 hour. No direct flight available.

advantage of throwing parties in off-campus residences and head to downtown Atlanta to enjoy the cities extensive bar and club scene that are easily accessible via Emory's network of shuttles. While students in the business school are known for the intense sense of competitiveness, Emory students are stereotypically labeled as laid-back but "clean-cut" and "career-oriented." In addition, sustainability and environmental protection initiatives are big here, with many students focused on enacting lifestyle changes that benefit the environment.

Selectivity

Emory is known to be the easiest school to get into of all national universities ranked 20 and above by US News & World Report. Oxford College (a 2-year campus nearby) can be easier to get into, where lower-scoring students can still exit with a degree at Emory. It's recommended that students opt for the option to apply to both.

Things to Consider

You'll like Emory if…

- You enjoy delicious foods! Atlanta has an excellent variety of amazing restaurants to choose from.
- You want the best of both worlds for on-campus and off-campus opportunities.
- You'd prefer a school with a high percentage of racial diversity.

You should avoid Emory if...

- You're looking for an institution with a lot of school pride.
- You want a school with strong networks in other regions of the US.

Georgetown University

37th AND O STREETS, NW, WASHINGTON, DC 20007
WEBSITE: WWW.GEORGETOWN.EDU
CHINA ADMISSIONS OFFICER: VANESSA J. KREBS
ADMISSION OFFICER EMAIL ADDRESS: VJK5@GEORGETOWN.EDU
ADMISSION OFFICE PHONE NUMBER: 202-687-3600, LOCATED WITHIN WASHINGTON, DC

Best Fit Analysis

Located in one of the more affluent neighborhoods of the American capital, Washington, DC, Georgetown University features a unique college experience with campus that has limitless access to arguably one of the most influential cities in the world. Georgetown students often take advantage of various internships for government institutions, NGOs and business firms in the greater DC metropolitan area. With one of the premier undergraduate schools of foreign service in the country, Georgetown attracts highly qualified students from across the globe interested in diplomacy and politics, with especially strong language programs to match. Likewise, the campus itself resonates with political discussion and activity. Unfortunately, though, recent years have indicated that it is extremely difficult for students studying in Mainland China to earn a spot at Georgetown.

At a Glance

US News Rank	#21
Location	Mid-Atlantic Region
Type of School	Private
Religious Affiliation	Roman Catholic
Environment	Urban

Students

Total Undergrad Enrollment	7595 (2014)
# Applicants	19478 (2015)
% Accepted	17 (2015)
Male to Female Ratio	45/55
% International Students	13.7
% Asian	9.2

Schools with Undergraduate Programs

Georgetown College
Walsh School of Foreign Service
McDonough School of Business
School of Nursing and Health Studies

You Might Also Consider...

Duke University
Boston College
UPenn
Cornell University
Notre Dame
University of Virginia

Academic Opportunities

Georgetown University has been climbing *US News & World Report's* rankings in recent years, and it's not surprising why. Currently ranked at Number 21, Georgetown prides itself as the academic powerhouse of Washington, DC Because of it's location, Georgetown is able to recruit top-notch professors across various fields, especially as it relates to foreign affairs, international development, and business. Furthermore, the university is able to attract diplomats and heads of state, including former alumnus Bill Clinton, to speak on campus throughout the school year. The Rafik B. Hariri Building, completed in 2009 as the latest addition to the McDonough School of Business, features state of the art facilities and lecture halls that are open to both undergraduate and graduate students and has facilitated the business school's rise in rankings over the past several years. Many introductory courses, such as Intro to Chemistry or Microeconomics, tend to be overcrowded with first year students, but sophomore, junior, and senior level courses are often formatted as tight-knit discussion groups.

Career Development

Georgetown's strongest pockets of alumni networks exist on the East Coast, particularly in the Washington, DC and New York City metropolitan areas, as well as San Francisco and Los Angeles. Many students across all of Georgetown's four undergraduate schools have found themselves securing jobs in consulting and financial sectors after graduation. As is common with many mid-sized national universities, Georgetown hosts on-campus recruit sessions for top banking firms such as Citibank and Goldman Sachs, and the Cawley Career Center provides students the opportunities to give it their best go through a series of mock interviews provided by the career services professionals. In addition, many alumni head to professional schools after graduation.

Campus Social Environment

Although Jesuit in origin, Georgetown is accepting of students from all faiths, but does consider religious affiliation during the admissions process. In addition, as a Jesuit institution, Georgetown is banned from hosting and recognizing fraternities on-campus. As a result, students often find their friend groups through a combination of whom they meet in their freshmen year dorms in addition to more than 200 co-curricular clubs and activities that exist to meet students' needs.

Among the more prominent and well-known student organizations that host social events are The Corps, a student-run company, the Georgetown University Alumni & Student Federal Credit Union, and the large number of intramural, club, and varsity teams that infiltrate the sport-conscious campus. During the winter and spring, students rally behind the Division I Men's Basketball Team, the Georgetown Hoyas, which has over the years produced several NBA professionals.

With proximity to the hustle-and-bustle and downtown Washington, students take advantage of a variety of bars and restaurants in the surrounding neighborhoods, of which many are within a short walking distance from student residences.

While Georgetown is known for its international student body, it has recently developed a reputation for breeding circles of snootiness. Many students boast wealthy students from the Northeast United States, and some students have insisted that

AIC Alum Student Score Profiles

% AIC students accepted	27
Median SAT Critical Reading	770
Median SAT Math	800
Median SAT Writing	710
Median SAT Composite Score	2200
Median TOEFL	109

Financial Facts

Annual Tuition
$48048 USD (2015—2016)

Financial Aid Availability
Very Low

What Students say about the Location

Safe	2.5
Fun	3
Expensive	4
Good Chinese food	2.5
Public transportation	3.5
Bars and Clubs	3
Market/Grocery Options	3
Surrounding Job Market	3
Is Car Necessary?	1.5
Overall	3

*Out of four Stars

Climate

Average Temperature Range
0℃ to 25℃

Average Annual Precipitation
107cm

Average Annual Humidity
76.56%

Average Annual Snowfall
44.5cm

Transportation from China

Dulles International Airport is accessible, but not easy to reach via public transport.

these elitists ultimately dominate the social scene with exclusive parties and bar events.

Selectivity

Georgetown University is not always trusting of credentials Chinese students boast (past scandals of manipulated report cards), and thus, few Chinese students ever get in. In recent years, they've begun to take a few more per year, but there is no evidence to believe this will continue.

Things to Consider

You'll like Georgetown if…

- You want a school with a lot of pride, especially as it relates to basketball.
- You have an interest in international relations, foreign affairs, or diplomacy.
- You're interested in having internships during the school year.

Avoid Georgetown if…

- The thought of "preppiness" makes you cringe.
- You'd prefer a quiet, rural campus. While it's not New York City, DC can get a bit rowdy.

Georgia Institute of Technology

225 NORTH AVE NW, ATLANTA, GA 30332
WEBSITE: WWW.GATECH.EDU
CHINA ADMISSIONS OFFICER: ANDREA JESTER
AO EMAIL ADDRESS: ANDREA.JESTER@ADMISSION.GATECH.EDU
ADMISSION OFFICE PHONE NUMBER: 404-894-4154
CLOSEST MAJOR CITY: ATLANTA

Best Fit Analysis

Though also offering classes in the humanities and solid architecture and management programs, Georgia Institute of Technology is most well-known for its strong engineering programs. Set squarely in Atlanta, students willing to endure sweltering summers, an intense workload, and the not-entirely safe urban environment will receive a stellar technical education here.

Academic Opportunities

Georgia Tech has a reputation for being academically challenging, to the point that many students take five years to complete their degrees. AIC alumni agree that classes can be difficult, but are manageable "as long as you work hard." They also note that some classes are taught by TAs, and certain intro classes such as Calculus and Computer Science have very large enrollment, but between office hours, email, and even Skype, "there are no troubles in approaching professors." Due to the prevalence of grading on a curve, classes tend to be extremely competitive, adding to the academic pressure. Undergraduates have access to a number of research opportunities, especially through the Georgia Tech Research Institute, which sponsors roughly 40% of all research. Students at Georgia Tech also have access to ten interdisciplinary programs, and cooperative programs with nearby schools, including a 3-2 program with Emory.

At a Glance

US News Rank	#36
Location	South
Type of School	Public
Environment	Urban

Students

Total Undergrad Enrollment	15142 (2015)
# Applicants	27270 (2015)
% Accepted	32 (2015)
Male to Female Ratio	65/35
% International Students	11
% Asian American	19.8

Schools with Undergraduate Programs

College of Architecture
College of Computing
College of Engineering
College of Sciences
Scheller College of Business
Ivan Allen College of Liberal Arts

You Might Also Consider...

Duke University
Emory University
University of Michigan
Virginia Tech

Career Development

A well-known school located in a metropolitan area, Georgia Tech provides students with a number of internship and work opportunities. Especially noteworthy is the Undergraduate Cooperative Education Program—a five-year program wherein students alternate semesters between classes at Georgia Tech and full-time employment, earning valuable work experience while completing their undergraduate studies. Georgia Tech alums also enjoy a strong alumni network with local organizations based both around region and around shared interests, as well as life-long access to career services.

Campus Social Environment

Georgia Tech students tend to adopt a work-hard, play-hard mentality, taking the weekends to unwind and relieve some of their stress. According to AIC alumni, "there are many parties" on-campus hosted by the Greek organizations (which attract 23% of men and 29% of women). Sporting events also attract a lot of student attention, especially Georgia Tech's football and basketball teams. Thanks to its location in the city of Atlanta, there is an abundance of activities and venues students can explore off-campus; however, students should take special care to ensure their personal safety, as some of the neighborhoods near campus are questionable, with vehicular theft and armed robbery being relatively frequent occurrences. That said, AIC alumni say they still feel mostly safe. As for diversity, AIC alumni agree that campus feels very diverse, and they often work with people from different countries and cultural backgrounds on class projects.

Selectivity

Many students who don't get into stellar engineering programs like Rice, Cornell, MIT, Johns Hopkins used to treat GIT as a solid or safety school. Beware, GIT has started rejecting increasingly talented students, and may now be a reach for you!

Things to Consider

You'll like Georgia Tech if...

- You want a school with lots of team spirit.
- You're interested in engineering.
- You want an urban setting.

Avoid Georgia Tech if…

- You hate hot weather.
- You want close relationships with professors.
- You do not want a competitive environment.

AIC Alum Student Score Profiles

% Accepted	19
Median SAT Critical Reading	640
Median SAT Math	800
Median SAT Writing	695
Median SAT Composite Score	2135
Median TOEFL	106

Financial Facts

Annual Tuition
$45972 USD (2015—2016)

Financial Aid Availability None

What Students say about the Location

Safe	2
Fun	3
Expensive	1
Chinese food	3
Transportation	2
Bars and Clubs	2
Market/Grocery Options	3
Surrounding Job Market	3
Necessity of Car	4
Overall	3

*Out of Four

Climate

Average Temperature Range
5℃ to 26℃

Annual Average Precipitation
133.4cm

Annual Average Humidity
76%

Annual Average Snowfall
2.5cm

Transportation from China

There is no direct flight from China to Atlanta. Students have to have a layover before arriving at Atlanta. After flying into Hartsfield-Jackson International Airport, students can get to campus by taking either a train or taxi.

Harvard University

86 BRATTLE STREET, CAMBRIDGE, MA 02138
WEBSITE: WWW.HARVARD.EDU
CHINESE ADMISSION OFFICER: N/A
ADMISSION OFFICE PHONE NUMBER: 617-495-1551
ADMISSION OFFICE CONTACT: HTTPS://COLLEGE.HARVARD.EDU/CONTACT-US
CLOSEST MAJOR CITY: BOSTON, JUST A 10 MINUTE TAXI OR METRO RIDE FROM DOWNTOWN

Best Fit Analysis

Harvard is where the best of minds meet the most eager of minds. Students who just want to have the privilege of meeting celebrities in the academic fields should absolutely come here, but those who want more personal attention with professors might want to look elsewhere. Money and exclusive clubs are everywhere in Harvard, and students should be ready to look beyond that, or engage with it readily. Students who want to go into finance will find the Harvard alumni network exceptionally useful.

Academic Environment

At Harvard, it's hard not to be motivated when you're surrounded by some of the smartest minds of the century. Students are awed by the amount of achievement that is embodied by their professors, and even their teaching assistants, but often have trouble getting ahold of their venerable professors. Academic advising bridges that distance between faculty and students. Some grade inflation may be present, and students can get B+'s rather easily, but find C's and A's harder to come by.

Harvard's East Asian studies program is praised by many, but is definitely not the only major with a wide breadth of offerings and innovative classes. Many departments have state of the art facilities, and provide many resources for their students. For example, the Visual Arts department dispenses free art supplies; studio space is available to students all the time. Students interested in Biology will find Harvard offers 5 different concentrations in the field, allowing students more focus in their studies. Also, the university provides the Math 55 class, which condenses 4 years of math into one, and reveals the wide breadth of options the school offers its intellectually thirsty students. Cross-registration empowers students to take classes at MIT. The learning process is designed for adventurous students; there is a one-week shopping period before they have to register for classes, and the Q-guide provides past student evaluations. University endowment is the largest at Harvard of any other school (although Princeton trumps Harvard in per capita endowment), which means there is no end to the resources offered to students.

At a Glance

US News Rank	#2
Location	Northeast
Type of School	Private
Environment	Urban

Students

Total Undergrad Enrollment	6700 (2014)
# Applicants	37307 (2015)
% Accepted	5.6(2015)
Male to Female Ratio	53/47
% International Students	12.2
% Asian American	21.3

Schools with Undergraduate Programs

School of Engineering and Applied Sciences
Harvard College

You Might Also Consider...

Princeton University
Dartmouth College
Yale University
UPenn
Columbia University

Career Development

From the survey of graduating 2013 seniors, we learn that 61% will be employed after school, with 18% opting for graduate studies/continued education instead. Of those employed, a plural majority (16%) chose consulting, and 15% chose finance. So although Harvard doesn't have business majors, students have no trouble breaking into the field. Chinese international

AIC Alum Student Score Profiles

% Accepted	4.8%
Median SAT Critical Reading	770
Median SAT Math	800
Media SAT Writing	800
Median SAT Composite Score	2370
Median TOEFL	116

Financial Facts

Annual Tuition	$45278 USD (2015—2016)
Financial Aid Availability	Low

What Students say about the Location

Safe	3.5
Fun	3
Expensive	3
Chinese food	3
Transportation	4
Bars and Clubs	3
Market/Grocery Options	3
Surrounding Job Market	3.5
Necessity of Car	1
Overall	4

*Out of four

Climate

Average Temperature Range	–3℃ to 23℃
Average Annual Precipitation	122cm
Average Annual Humidity	69.8%
Average Annual Snowfall	129cm

Transportation from China

Students can fly directly from China to Boston. Options include: PEK to BOS; PVG to BOS; HKG to BOS. The campus is just a 15 minutes' taxi ride from Boston Logan International Airport.

students who want to stay in the east coast can expect to find a good handful of Harvard students there. Engineering and technology sectors were also lucrative and popular majors.

When asked where they saw themselves in 10 years, 20% wanted to be in health, 11% in the arts and entertainment field, and 9% in government. The average salary for Harvard graduates was $60000. Alumni are very accessible and come back every 5 years for reunions.

Campus Social Environment

Few find fault with the cultural and stimulating streets of Boston, which is only 10 minutes away from Cambridge. Students from 80 schools leak into Boston on the weekends so there is typically much to do in the surrounding towns of Boston. However, drinking laws are strict in the State of Massachusetts, so don't bring your fake ID. In addition, in the winters, it can be hard to see rays of the sun.

Harvard's housing system is atypical, but formulates strong bonds between students. Freshmen are assigned dorms initially, but in their sophomore year, they get to find a group of 8 people with whom to spend the next three years living with. Everyone loves living on campus, and everyone does, but houses and facilities can be a bit older.

Although Harvard isn't a party school compared to some state schools, drinking is a popular activity. Of the polled 2013 seniors, 25% said they drank more than twice a week, while only 9% never drink, and 7% drink less than a month. Of this same group, 38% have done marijuana, and 25% do it at least occasionally. 16% have tried more intense perception-altering chemicals. Harvard doesn't recognize Greek Council, and while some unofficial groups exist, Finals Clubs take the spotlight in Cambridge. They are very exclusive clubs that invite sophomores and freshmen to take part in a "punch season" process, whereby individuals attend events and are evaluated for admission into the club by existing members. These clubs hold parties that the rest of the school can attend (sometimes), and members make up about 10% of the male population, 5% of the female population. Exclusivity is a trait common to many Harvard clubs, not the Finals Clubs. Diversity isn't a big problem on campus, as 6% of students are African American, 21% are Asian, 8% Hispanic, and 12% international, and students are mostly pretty liberal and open-minded.

Selectivity

As one of the top schools in the nation (or so claimed by US News every year, less than 6% of applicants are admitted every year. Only a couple Chinese students are admitted annually. No magic formula will get you in.

Things to Consider

You'll like Harvard if…

- You can be an independent learner when professors are too busy.
- You love the surrounding area of Boston.
- Academic achievers > Entertainment Celebrities for you.

Avoid Harvard if…

- You're for a social scene that is more inclusive.
- Mild weather is a factor in your decision.
- You don't like cold weather.

Harvey Mudd College

KINGSTON HALL, 301 PLATT BOULEVARD, CLAREMONT, CA 91711
WEBSITE: WWW.HMC.EDU
CHINA ADMISSIONS OFFICER: PETER OSGOOD
ADMISSION OFFICE PHONE NUMBER: 909-621-8011
AO EMAIL ADDRESS: POSGOOD@HMC.EDU
CLOSEST MAJOR CITY: LOS ANGELES, HMC IS ABOUT A 45 MINUTE TRAIN RIDE FROM LAX INTERNATIONAL AIRPORT

Best Fit Analysis

Harvey Mudd College is the kind of school that accepts everyone but not everyone accepts. People of all different habits, dispositions, weirdness can find a home here, but if you're not the open-minded type, then don't attend. Their goal is to develop mathematicians, scientists, and engineers that will understand their impact on the world through a comprehensive education that includes a focus on humanities and social sciences. Whether you want to pursue science through academic or professional career paths, HMC will not disappoint, but if you are not that serious about studying the STEM fields, do not linger on this page.

Academic Opportunities

With 7 departments (physics, science, math, engineering, chemistry, biology, computer science, and humanities) as well as one mathematical biology interdisciplinary program, and ISP (independent Study Program), HMC's academics are simple enough to memorize in a minute's time. It's deceptively simple, given the discipline it will require from the average Mudder to graduate. The Core curriculum requires 1/3 of the classes go towards fulfilling math, science, engineering requirements, and another 1/3 of the classes to go toward satisfying humanities, arts, and social sciences requirements. The entire history of HMC has only seen 7 students with the perfect 4.0, and grade inflation does not exist. Everyone at HMC has participated in research, most have utilized the clinic program or write senior theses. The Clinic program, most concentrating on engineering, computer science, physics, and math fields, gathers students to work on a project suggested by a company. Often these companies later hire from these groups. Due to the size of the HMC population, or the lack thereof, all professors know your name by heart, whether or not you're in their class, and possibly many other things about you. 200 students pursue research projects every summer. Because HMC is part of the Claremont Consortium, students can freely take classes in any of the other colleges.

At a Glance

US News Rank	#14
Location	West Coast
Type of School	Private
Environment	Suburban

Students

Total Undergrad Enrollment	815 (2015)
# Applied	4119 (2015)
% Accepted	13 (2015)
Male to Female Ratio	54/46
% International Students	13
% Asian American	20

You Might Also Consider...

MIT	Rose-Hulman
Caltech	Rice University
Carnegie Mellon	Olin

Career Development

HMC students reportedly have some of the highest starting salaries in the nation. About 63% end up in the industry, 30% in graduate school, 4% in fellowships. Many of the students pursuing higher education choose and get into PhD program. Mathematics, physics, chemistry are the top fields of study that Mudders choose. 41% of employers who attend the Consortium career fairs target HMC. Companies like Microsoft, SpaceX, Yelp, Fenwick and West LLP, Honeywell appreciate the well-trained Mudders.

AIC Alum Student Score Profiles

% Accepted	22.7%
Median SAT Critical Reading	740
Median SAT Math	800
Media SAT Writing	785
Median SAT Composite Score	2310
Median TOEFL	116

Financial Facts

Annual Tuition
$52383 USD (2016—2017)

Financial Aid Availability Low

What Students say about the Location

Safe	3
Fun	4
Expensive	3
Chinese food	1
Transportation	2
Bars and Clubs	2
Market/Grocery Options	1
Surrounding Job Market	2
Necessity of Car	3
Overall	2

*Out of four

Climate

Average Temperature Range
11℃ to 25℃

Average Annual Precipitation
58.7cm

Average Annual Humidity
81.87%

Average Annual Snowfall
0cm

Transportation from China

There are direct flights from China to get to Los Angeles International Airport, which is less than an hour from Harvey Mudd's campus. Options include: HKG to LAX; PEK to LAX; PVG to LAX

Campus Social Environment

The individual dormitories allow for communities that students can identify with. Each has its own personality, and parties, so as to develop stronger shared bonds. Students fill out a 3-page survey to determine their dorms in the beginning of the school year and the college does a good job of finding a fit. The alcohol policy is very flexible. Of the five colleges in the consortium, HMC has the reputation of hosting the best parties, with elaborate themes. There's not much to do in Claremont, so students find ways to enjoy themselves on campus.

HMC acknowledges its lack of diversity, but makes an effort to improve. It is comprised of 2% African Americans, 20% Asian Americans, 10% Hispanic, 13% International, and 44% White. In general, students are liberal leaning but politically dormant. Women make up 46%, and males 54%, which is a ratio that could certainly be much skewed at a STEM-heavy institution (and historically, has been). If you want to go to a school that encourages serious dating culture, join the Mudders. Eccentricities in fashion and character, traditions are common on campus, and don't be surprised to see guys walking around in skirts.

Selectivity

Mudd is a small institution, and with only 13 percent of the student body identifying as international, it only accepts a select few for admission every year. Women will have a better shot applying than men, as Mudd tries to balance its gender ratio. Successful applicants demonstrate their understanding of the values associated with small communities, in addition to the opportunities the Consortium provides STEM students.

Things to Consider

You'll like Harvey Mudd if…

- You're a boy and you have always wanted to try on a skirt.
- You like the warmth and intimacy of small communities.
- Drug and Alcohol freedom sounds amazing.
- You can't get enough of STEM research.

Avoid Harvey Mudd if…

- You can't identify with nerdiness.
- You prefer competitive learning to collaborative learning.
- The way a campus looks aesthetically is a top priority for you.

Haverford College

370 W LANCASTER AVE, HAVERFORD, PA 19041
WEBSITE: WWW.HAVERFORD.EDU
CHINA ADMISSIONS OFFICER: SONIA GIEBEL
AO EMAIL ADDRESS: SGIEBEL@HAVERFORD.EDU
ADMISSION OFFICE PHONE NUMBER: 610-896-1350
CLOSEST MAJOR CITY: PHILADELPHIA;, STUDENTS CAN REACH HAVERFORD BY COMMUTER RAIL, SETPA, ABOUT 30 MINUTES

Best Fit Analysis

Prospective students interested in a very small liberal arts college within commuting distance of a major U.S. city should take Haverford College into consideration. Just thirty minutes by train to Philadelphia, Haverford also rests within close proximity to the all-women's Bryn Mawr College, with which Haverford shares a Bi-College relationship that allows students to enroll in classes or pursue a major at either school. With a student body of just over a thousand students, members of this elite LAC can expect intense classwork interactions and discussions but without the feeling of competition among peers. With strong roots in Quaker heritage (though the college is currently nonsectarian), Haverford College takes its academic and social Honor Code very seriously. The Honor Code provides students a notable amount of autonomy, ranging from take-home final exams to self-policing underage drinking and is modified by the students every year.

Academic Opportunities

Haverford prides itself on being a liberal arts institution, and thus its "Requirements for the Degree," or curriculum, is designed to expose students to a wide array of disciplines. In addition to a first year writing requirement and the equivalent of studying a language other than English for two semesters, Haverford students must also complete a minimum of three course credits in each of the three divisions of the humanities, social sciences, and natural sciences. Strong majors at Haverford include Biological and Physical Sciences, English, History, Political Science, and Economics, but students are also granted the freedom to design their own interdisciplinary major. Opportunities for study at nearby institutions like Swarthmore and U Penn are numerous as well. Resistant to grade inflation, academic rigor at Haverford remains relatively tough. However, as 75% of professors live on campus, they are highly accessible and able to give students plenty of individual attention. Students at the Ford often develop personal relationships with their professors, who often encourage them to participate in undergraduate research initiatives. Both the Center for the Arts and Humanities and the Koshland Integrated Natural Sciences Center fund research stipends, summer research fellowships, and research travel for undergraduate students.

At a Glance

US News Rank	#12
Location	Northeast
Type of School	Private
Environment	Suburban

Students

Total Undergrad Enrollment	1194 (2015)
# Applicants	3468 (2015)
% Accepted	24.6 (2015)
Male to Female Ratio	47/53
% International	11.4
% Asian	14

You Might Also Consider...

Amherst College	Brown University
Swarthmore College	UPenn
Wesleyan University	Tufts University

Career Development

Haverford's alumni network is small, as expected, but Fordies are willing to help fellow alumni fish out opportunities for employment, especially in Philadelphia, Washington, D.C., NYC, Boston and California. Philadelphia itself offers a good market for job seekers after graduation. For the Class of 2013, 53 percent headed directly into the work force while 16 percent opted for graduate school programs. Science and education were the top two industries

AIC Alum Student Score Profiles

% AIC students accepted	20
Median SAT Critical Reading	700
Median SAT Math	800
Median SAT Writing	750
Median SAT Composite Score	2250
Median TOEFL	113

Financial Facts

Annual Tuition
$48656 USD (2015—2016)

Financial Aid Availability — Low

What Students say about the Location

Safe	3.5
Fun	1.5
Expensive	2.5
Good Chinese food	1
Public transportation	1.5
Bars and Clubs	2
Market/Grocery Options	2
Surrounding Job Market	1.5
Is Car Necessary?	3
Overall	2.5

*Out of four Stars

Climate

Average Temperature Range
-2℃ to 24℃

Average Annual Precipitation
117cm

Average Annual Humidity
71.72%

Average Annual Snowfall
49.8cm

Transportation

The local domestic airport is close by, but the Philadelphia International Airport is about 25 min away. Neither have direct flights from China, but public transportation does allow students to get to Haverford without breaking the bank.

that employed graduates from Class of 2013 funneled into, representing 22 percent and 21 percent of the class, respectively. Students interested in pursuing graduate studies in the mathematics and the sciences can jumpstart their careers at the Ford, as 23 percent of those enrolled in graduate programs upon leaving Haverford find themselves engaging these fields. Though Haverford doesn't have an undergraduate research program on campus, it sponsors a 4+1 engineering program with UPenn and a 3/2 engineering program with Caltech.

Campus Social Environment

Haverford students are often considered academically-oriented, but what many outsiders forget to recognize is that over a third of all Haverford students are varsity-level athletes. The sports scene, however, is seriously lacking and most students fail to show up to cheer on the Black Squirrels varsity teams. There are, however, a good amount of students who participate in intramural sports as a way to relieve themselves from the academic grind. Students handle the drug and alcohol policies as part of the Honor Code, so students experience relative freedom in relation to peer institutions. For the most part, Haverford doesn't have much of a party scene. Parties can be found on weekend nights and there are events coordinated between Haverford, Bryn Mawr and Swarthmore, but they're not a defining part of the school's culture, and fraternities and sororities are not allowed on campus. Those who do party are likely to see the same people out and about as the school is incredibly small. The town of Haverford is quaint and incredibly safe, but doesn't offer much in the way of nightlife. Philadelphia, however, is only a short train ride away for students interested in exploring urban America. Haverford students are also looking outward for learning opportunities, with over 50% of students choosing to study abroad.

Selectivity

Haverford is highly selective and critical of Chinese students. High scores are never a guaranteed in. Compared to other LAC's in the top tier, it can be slightly easier to get into Haverford.

Things to Consider

You'll like Haverford if…

◆ You want a small school with lots of attention from professors.

◆ Trust is an important component of your moral code. Haverford puts so much trust in its students via the honor code.

◆ You're interested in math or the sciences.

Avoid Haverford if…

◆ You're looking to cheer on athletic teams.

◆ You're a self-proclaimed party animal, who looks forward to fast-paced surroundings.

Johns Hopkins University

3400 N. CHARLES STREET, BALTIMORE, MD 21218
WEBSITE: WWW.JHU.EDU
CHINA ADMISSIONS OFFICER: JESSE TOMCZAK
AO EMAIL ADDRESS: JESSE.TOMCZAK@JHU.EDU
ADMISSION OFFICE PHONE NUMBER: 410-516-8171
CLOSEST CITY: BALTIMORE, M.D.

Best Fit Analysis

Johns Hopkins University has consistently been known as one of the top "pre-med" institutions in the United States, but prospective students should also be aware of its prestigious International Studies programs. JHU isn't for the faint of heart, as competition thrives on campus for students wishing to excel in rigorous science courses and grade deflation has been common in recent years. An AIC alum notes that the racial make-up of the school is relatively diverse as, "20%...[of] people on campus" are Asian, but not "diversified because pretty much half of the population wants to become doctors." In addition to the numerous opportunities for independent research that is available to students through the university, Baltimore provides a platform for students to engage in valuable work experience geared towards their fields of study.

Academic Opportunities

Johns Hopkins is aware that the university cultivates an academic pressure cooker environment and has thus adopted a policy that marks students' first semester grades as "satisfactory" or "unsatisfactory" to assist freshmen with the transition into college life. As its reputation suggests, JHU provides its students with premier educational opportunities in the biological sciences, particularly for Biology and Biomedical Engineering majors. Students who are strongly considering an education in International Studies, however, can exploit JHU's interdisciplinary major in International Studies (IS), which draws strength from its satellite campuses in Washington, D.C., Bologna, Italy, and Nanjing, China. As Johns Hopkins places a high degree of emphasis on its graduate-level programs, one AIC alum remarks that professors are generally, "Not so accessible, but grad students are always so friendly and want to make friends with you." Nevertheless, both the presence of professors and graduate students contribute to the high number of undergraduate students that participate in independent research, which can be funded by programs such as the Provost's Undergraduate Research Awards and the Woodrow Wilson Undergraduate Research Fellowship Program. "Laboratories in Biology, Biophysics, Chemistry, and Engineering as well as departments at Johns Hopkins Medical Institutions, regularly have openings for qualified undergraduates to participate in research that is sufficiently biological in nature to receive biology credit".

At a Glance

US News Rank	#10
Location	Mid-Atlantic
Type of School	Private
Environment	Urban

Students

Total Undergrad Enrollment	5299 (2015)
# Applicants	24718 (2015)
% Accepted	13.2 (2015)
Male to Female Ratio	51/49
% International	10.4
% Asians	19.7

Schools with Undergraduate Programs

Krieger School of Arts and Sciences
Whiting School of Engineering
Carey Business School
Peabody Institute

You Might Also Consider...

Cornell University
UPenn
Brown University
Harvard University
Duke University

AIC Alum Student Score Profiles

% AIC students accepted	10.1
Median SAT Critical Reading	720
Median SAT Math	800
Median SAT Writing	780
Median SAT Composite Score	2190
Median TOEFL	115

Financial Facts

Annual Tuition
$48710 USD (2015—2016)
Financial Aid Availability
Very Low

What Students Say about the Location

Safe	1
Fun	2
Expensive	2
Good Chinese food	1
Public transportation	2
Bars and Clubs	1
Market/Grocery Options	2
Surrounding Job Market	1.5
Is Car Necessary?	4
Overall	2

*Out of four Stars

Climate

Average Temperature Range
-1℃ to 25℃
Average Annual Precipitation
108.6cm
Average Annual Humidity
70.28%
Average Annual Snowfall
56.9cm

Transportation from China

Shuttle offered on holidays and at the end of the year; taxis to Baltimore Washington International Airport cost $30. No direct flights from China.

Career Development

Recent Johns Hopkins graduates have found success in both finding employment in the work force and applying to competitive graduate school programs. According to the Johns Hopkins website, 46% of the Class of 2012 were employed full-time six months after graduation and 35% were enrolled in graduate or professional school six months after graduation. Exceeding far beyond national averages, 80% of JHU graduates who applied to US medical school were admitted for the application years between 2006 and 2012, and over 83% of JHU graduates were accepted to one or more US law schools for the 2012 application season. Johns Hopkins Whiting School of Engineering Career Center staff is notable for guiding its students to their intended career fields, as the JHU website cites that 97% of graduates participated in at least one career-oriented program before graduation. With more than 186000 current living JHU alumni, graduates have found it particularly easy to network in some of the urban hubs of the East Coast, particularly Baltimore, Washington, D.C., and New York City.

Campus Social Environment

Johns Hopkins University boasts a racially diverse campus but doesn't particularly have a large Chinese population. An AIC alum states, "There are really few [international Chinese students], so it's kind of an advantage to reach out. However, most of my friends are ABC." The Johns Hopkins Men's Varsity Lacrosse Team has been a historically powerful program that creates some sports buzz on campus, but it pales in comparison to elite Division I basketball and football programs that generate hype on other college campuses. As students are often consumed in their studies, JHU's "Party scene is smaller than other schools, [and they take place] mostly at frat houses," says a former AICer. Dating is also not so common as "people are too busy." The selection and diversity of food at the university is not particularly enticing, and many international Chinese students settle for "American" cuisines. With this said, students can still engage themselves in a range of extracurricular activities such as kayaking and club sports.

Selectivity

Students who have a pre-determined career path and related experiences will fare better when applying to JHU. Those seeking the engineering school will have a hard time. Average SAT scores fall within the 2200~2300 range and can be a very important part of your application.

Things to Consider

You'll like Johns Hopkins University if...

- You are interested in health sciences, engineering, or international studies.
- You need competition to thrive.
- You're willing to sacrifice your time socializing for the sake of academics.

Avoid Johns Hopkins if...

- You view higher education as an opportunity to collaborate.
- You're a foodie! JHU is known for having weak dining facilities.
- You're not interested in undergraduate research, as most of your peers will be conducting their own.

Macalester College

1600 GRAND AVENUE, ST. PAUL, MN 55105
WEBSITE: WWW.MACALESTER.EDU
CHINA ADMISSIONS OFFICER: STEVE COLEE
ADMISSION OFFICE EMAIL ADDRESS: INTERNATIONALADMISSIONS@MACALESTER.EDU
ADMISSION OFFICE PHONE NUMBER: 800-231-7974
CLOSEST MAJOR CITY: MINNEAPOLIS/ST. PAUL

Best Fit Analysis

Macalester is famously known for its large proportions of international students, so Chinese students don't have to worry too much about not finding a crowd to fit in with. Students who decide to matriculate here should bring their faux fur jackets, as Minnesota is not known to have hospitable weather. For those looking for a fulfilling party scene, Macalester is not for you. On the flip side, those students who dream of small classes and caring professors should come to this prestigious college.

MACALESTER COLLEGE

Academic Opportunities

Macalester offers 38 majors, and the option to design your own interdisciplinary program, but some of its academic assets lie in its cooperation with other schools. Students here are offered many pre-professional training programs through an agreement with Washington University that allows them to take prelaw, premed, cooperative architecture, and engineering programs with the similarly renowned Washington University. In addition, it is part of the Associated Colleges of the Twin Cities Consortium, which means students have the added option of studying courses at nearby colleges, also part of the consortium. About 60% of Macalester students study abroad, as cultivating diversity and cultural awareness is considered one of the university's main tenets.

Students can also get a taste of Japanese culture through Macalester's Japanese House, which encourages several students to live with a native speaker of Japanese to hone proficiency in the language, in addition to hosting Japanese-related activities such as movie nights and recipe swaps.

AIC students say it's "really easy to find the professors." With class sizes at an average of 17 students, classes are intimate and professors get to know their students. But in regards to school grading policies, they say "10% A in most of my classes. Most not curved." Economics, in particular, is singled out for its challenging curriculum. Almost all AIC students spend most of their time on school work and most regard the student body as competitive but also motivating. Social sciences, biological sciences and foreign languages are some of the stronger departments at Macalester.

At a Glance

US News Rank	#23
Location	Midwest
Type of School	Private
Environment	Suburban

Students

Total Undergrad Enrollment	2073 (2014)
# Applicants	6031 (2015)
% Accepted	39 (2015)
Male to Female Ratio	39/61
% International Students	14
% Asian American	11.6

You Might Also Consider...

Carleton College
Colorado College
Grinnell College
Pomona College
Middlebury College
Brown University

Career Development

Unsurprisingly, 60% of students at this small school in Minnesota known for its excellent academic resources find themselves in grad school 5 years after college. Macalester has, as a result, earned a reputation for being a grad school factory. Many students end up at top graduate schools.

Two-thirds of students complete internships every year, often in nonprofit organizations,

AIC Alum Student Score Profiles

% Accepted	29.6
Median SAT Critical Reading	690
Median SAT Math	790
Media SAT Writing	690
Median SAT Composite Score	2100
Median TOEFL	107

Financial Facts

Annual Tuition

$ 48666 USD (2015—2016)

Financial Aid Availability High

What Students say about the Location

Safe	3.5
Fun	2
Expensive	2.5
Chinese food	2
Transportation	2
Bars and Clubs	2
Market/Grocery Options	2
Surrounding Job Market	2
Necessity of Car	2.5
Overall	3.5

*Out of four

Climate

Average Temperature Range

−10℃ to 23℃

Average Annual Precipitation

80.9cm

Average Annual Humidity

77.60%

Average Annual Snowfall

116.8cm

Transportation from China

No direct flights from China. Students must fly into another American airport (e.g. LAX), before flying into Minneapolis-St. Paul International airport, which is just a 10-minute taxi ride away from campus.

government, education, and the arts.

Many students are recruited by AmeriCorps, Credit Suisse, Clearwater Action, Hewlett Packard, JP Morgan, Microsoft, and Teach for America after they graduate. AIC students find their alumni network to be available, but one students notes, "the network is not bad but not as good as at some Christian academies."

Campus Social Environment

At Mac, about 24% are students of color, with a denser female population, and 19% of students are international. One student shares, "I made a lot of friends from Africa, Europe, South America, and Asia." Every year, Mac hosts the International Roundtable, a forum to discuss and spread awareness about global issues. About 50% of Macalester students volunteer, no doubt encouraged by the institution's goal to increase civic engagement. Correspondingly, students are known to be politically active and generally liberal. An AIC alumni notes, "Macalester is not perfectly diverse since there is something 'politically-correct', a taboo, in the college, like any anti-homo expressions are forbidden." Upper-middle class students are the socioeconomic majority. With over 100 active student clubs there are opportunities for students to pursue common passions with their peers.

There is no Greek life on campus, which may or may not be a contributing factor to AIC students reporting little to no pressure to drink. Parties exist, but do not define social life. Pertaining to the collegiate sports scene, AIC students say, "people are not crazy in sports probably due to the fact that it is snowing most school days...none of popular American sports (basketball, football, and baseball) are popular in Macalester as in other colleges. Instead, soccer is universal." Macalester's close proximity to the Twin-Cities (Minneapolis and St. Paul) offers a variety of opportunities for students to explore. Museums, theatre, art galleries, and concerts are popular attractions, as well as the large professional sports scene for the Vikings (NFL), Twins (MLB), and Timberwolves (NBA).

Selectivity

Chinese students should emphasize their international perspectives on their applications to better their chances at Mac. Both international experience and the demonstrated ability to accept others from different backgrounds is encouraged. SAT scores, though important, are not of the greatest concern to the Mac admissions office, but students with scores over 2100 tend to have better results in earning admittance.

Things to Consider

You'll like Macalester if...

- You like cold weather.
- You want to go to an LAC that isn't totally isolated from civilization.
- You want to try new ethnic foods.
- You want a strong international community.

Avoid Macalester if...

- You're not prepared to be hundreds upon hundreds of miles away from the beach.
- You're looking for a strong collegiate athletics presence.

Massachusetts Institute of Technology

77 MASSACHUSETTS AVE, CAMBRIDGE, MA 02139
WEBSITE: WEB.MIT.EDU
CHINA ADMISSIONS OFFICER: N/A
ADMISSION OFFICE PHONE NUMBER: 617-253-3400
ADMISSION OFFICE EMAIL ADDRESS: ADMISSIONS@MIT.EDU
CLOSEST MAJOR CITY: BOSTON

Best Fit Analysis

MIT is a versatile school with a lot in terms of both location and internal network. Most students love the city and its proximity to Boston as well as other schools in the area. Students who don't mind the cold should have no problem adjusting to the surroundings. Unsurprisingly, there are "a lot of nerdy kids on campus." Another thing to keep in mind is the heavy coursework at MIT, for students who want a more balanced college lifestyle.

Academic Opportunities

Between accessible quality research opportunities for undergraduates, flexible curriculum, attentive world-class teachers, and a community of big-hearted big-minded individuals, MIT lives up to its reputation as the #1 polytechnic institute in the U.S. The downside is, as one AIC alum put it, grading is "very difficult, graded on a curve with center on B." Academic intensity means students sometimes study up to 80 hours a week, but environment is not as competitive as it is collaborative. Top majors at MIT include Engineering, Business, Finance, Computer Science, Mathematics, and Physics. Students also have the flexibility to take courses at Wellesley or Harvard without additional fees. To ease the transition for freshmen, first-years are put on a pass—no pass system, so they don't have to worry about overreaching to differentiate themselves. The undergraduate research opportunities program allows students to initiate and join research while earning academic credit or a stipend for it.

At a Glance

US News Rank	#7
Location	Northeast
Type of School	Private
Environment	Urban

Students

Total Undergrad Enrollment	4527 (2015)
# Applicants	18306 (2015)
% Accepted	8 (2015)
Male to Female Ratio	54/46
% International Students	9.7
% Asian American	24.4

Schools with Undergraduate Programs

School of Architecture and Planning
School of Engineering
School of Humanities, Arts, and Social Sciences
MIT Sloan School of Management
School of Science

You Might Also Consider...

Harvard	Princeton
Yale	Cal Tech
Columbia	Cornell
Duke	

Career Development

MIT Global Education & Career Development (GECD) and its CareerBridge interface help students and alumni connect to potential jobs and employers in various fields, as well as help them explore their future paths. For the 2012 graduates, 39% decided to go on to graduate and professional education, while 53% decided to take on industry jobs. Common industry fields that capture MIT students included aerospace, defense, computer technologies, consulting, and finance, and top employers included household names such as Oracle, Amazon, Google, Apple, Morgan Stanley, etc.

Average salary for MIT graduates was around $66874. AIC alumni at MIT feel no pressure

AIC Alum Student Score Profiles

% Accepted	22.7
Median SAT Critical Reading	740
Median SAT Math	800
Median SAT Writing	800
Median SAT Composite Score	2330
Median TOEFL	118

Financial Facts

Annual Tuition	$46400 USD (2015—2016)
Financial Aid Availability	High

What Students say about the Location

Safe	4
Fun	4
Expensive	3
Chinese food	3
Transportation	3
Bars and Clubs	2
Market/Grocery Options	2
Surrounding Job Market	4
Necessity of Car	2
Overall	4

*Out of Four

Climate

Average Temperature Range	–3℃ to 22℃
Average Annual Precipitation	122cm
Average Annual Humidity	67%
Average Annual Snowfall	134.6cm

Transportation from China

There are direct flights from Beijing, Shanghai and Hong Kong to Boston. From Logan International Airport, students can reach campus by subway, shuttle, or taxi.

about getting a job after college, and showed confidence in the alumni network, noting that "formal and informal network channels are available." MIT has a variety of Alumni networks including the Chinese Alumni/ae of MIT (CAMIT).

Campus Social Environment

While some polytechnic schools suffer from uneven gender ratios, MIT has relatively equal proportions of men and women, and has striven to create diverse environments. About 25% of its population is Asian American, only about 10% International (which should give you an idea how selective it is) and a little over 20% of African Americans and Hispanic/Latino. Caucasians comprise a plurality at just under 40%. Greek life is salient on campus, with 50% of men in fraternities, 27% of women associated, but not overbearing and students report that Independent Living Groups, which support communities of similar interests, are a viable alternative. With over 510 student organizations students have a rich and supportive environment to find their niche. MIT also has a unique "Independent Activities Period," a four-week long period where optional classes, seminars, activities are held.

Students love the surrounding environment, with AIC alumni noting that they experienced "balanced life between Boston and Cambridge." Boston offers fantastic opportunities to see concerts, sporting events, historical sites, museums, and more, and to interact with a diverse group of passionate people.

Selectivity

A former Dean and current high-ranking MIT official said in private "Among MITs 1,000+ student body, approximately 100 students are international students hailing from 48 countries". Good luck!

Things to Consider

You'll like MIT if…

- You like computers/technology and want to be around people similarly intrigued.
- You want to be around many college students.
- You're looking for school with good food.

Avoid MIT if…

- You're looking for a big collegiate sports scene.
- An international student population is important to you.

Middlebury College

14 OLD CHAPEL RD, MIDDLEBURY, VT 05753
WEBSITE: WWW.MIDDLEBURY.EDU
CHINA ADMISSIONS OFFICER: BARBARA MARLOW
AO PHONE NUMBER: 802-443-5167
AO EMAIL ADDRESS: MARLOW@MIDDLEBURY.EDU
CLOSEST MAJOR CITY: BOSTON. BOSTON IS ABOUT 3.5 HOURS AWAY BY CAR

Best Fit Analysis

Located in rural Vermont, hours away from any large cities, what Middlebury lacks in social opportunities and good weather, it makes up for with strong academics, a beautiful campus, and its own ski mountain. Students who are environmentally unconscious, liberal, cosmopolitan, and winter sport enthusiasts will especially enjoy this top Liberal Arts College.

Academic Opportunities

Middlebury is an academic powerhouse when it comes to foreign languages and international studies, with students having the opportunity to spend a semester studying at the Monterey Institute of International Studies in California. Most students take advantage of the world-class faculty to learn a new language, regardless of their major, with many also participating in one of the many study abroad programs available in more than 40 different countries. Other strong programs include Environmental Studies, Biology, and English. Also notable is Middlebury's J-term, during which students can spend the month of January taking classes, doing research, or interning. Students take two writing-intensive seminar courses and must satisfy distribution requirements in seven of eight academic areas spanning four different cultures, ensuring a comprehensive education. At Middlebury there is an emphasis on writing in all courses, classes are challenging, and the workload famously intense; however, professors are very supportive and readily accessible.

At a Glance	
US News Rank	#4
Location	Northeast
Type of School	Private
Environment	Rural
Students	
Total Undergrad Enrollment	2526 (2014)
# Applicants	8892 (2015)
% Accepted	19.9 (2015)
Male to Female Ratio	48/52
% International Students	10
% Asian American	6
You Might Also Consider...	
Dartmouth	Williams
Yale	Harvard
Amherst	Brown

Career Development

Middlebury bolsters its alumni network by connecting alumni of the undergraduate college, its Language Schools, and the Bread Loaf School of English, creating a truly international professional network. The Center for Careers and Internships (CCI) helps students connect to resources and alumni to pursue a future in their desired field. The most popular fields of employment for undergraduate alumni are education, finance, consulting, and science and technology; many graduates also go on to pursue more advanced degrees.

Campus Social Environment

Midd Kids tend to be quite liberal, to the point that some dorms have voted for co-ed showers in the past. All students are guaranteed on-campus housing, and 97% take advantage of this. In addition to more traditional dorms, there are also academic interest houses, an environmental house, and Greek-like co-ed social houses that attract 9% of students. Though sorely lacking in ethnic diversity, Middlebury attracts internationally-minded students, many of whom deepen their understanding of different cultures and societies both in the classroom and through studying abroad, creating an intellectually diverse environment that is sensitive to other perspectives. The Middlebury College Activities Board (MCAB) and different student

AIC Alum Student Score Profiles

% Accepted	12.5
Median SAT Critical Reading	710
Median SAT Math	800
Median SAT Writing	730
Median SAT Composite Score	2240
Median TOEFL	113

Financial Facts

Annual Tuition
$47418 USD (2015—2016)
Financial Aid Availability Very Low

What Students say about the Location

Safe	3
Fun	3
Expensive	4
Chinese food	3
Transportation	3
Bars and Clubs	4
Market/Grocery Options	3
Surrounding Job Market	3
Necessity of Car	2
Overall	4

*Out of Four

Climate

Average Temperature Range
−7℃ to 21℃
Average Annual Precipitation
93.8cm
Average Annual Humidity
74%
Average Annual Snowfall
175.3cm

Transportation from China

Students have the choice of taking a taxi or shuttle from one of the airports in New York City and Boston, or can fly to Burlington International Airport and then take a bus, shuttle, or taxi to campus.

organizations on campus provide an array of opportunities for student engagement and social interactions. And while many people might opt for warmer climates, Middlebury students relish in the plethora of outdoor skiing, snowboarding, and ice skating opportunities living in a winter wonderland provides. Similarly, the hockey and ski teams enjoy strong support from the student body. Also available to students are the Middlebury Outdoor Programs, wherein students can acquire a variety of outdoor and camping skills, including wilderness first aid. Despite the arduous academics, the environment is not competitive, and students rarely ever discuss grades.

Selectivity

Despite high score averages, Middlebury continues to keep their eyes open for the "diamonds in the rough" i.e. talent that may have scores below their average.

Things to Consider

You'll like Middlebury if...

- You enjoy the outdoors.
- You are interested in international studies.
- You want close relationships with faculty.

Avoid Middlebury if...

- You want a meal plan.
- You are looking for ethnic diversity.
- You want to be in or near a large city.

New York University

70 WASHINGTON SQ S, NEW YORK, NY 10012
WEBSITE: WWW.NYU.EDU
CHINA ADMISSIONS OFFICER: NILS SUNDIN
ADMISSION OFFICE PHONE NUMBER: 212-998-4500
ADMISSION OFFICE EMAIL ADDRESS: ADMISSIONS@NYU.EDU
CLOSEST MAJOR CITY: NEW YORK CITY

Best Fit Analysis

A highly-regarded university set in the heart of the Big Apple, New York University offers students about as many opportunities as the city it calls home. Though lacking a traditional campus, NYU's integration into New York City's Greenwich Village teaches students, as one AIC alum put it, to "live like a New Yorker."

Academic Opportunities

To satisfy its roughly 25000 undergraduate students, NYU offers a plethora of academic opportunities and programs; those with the most notoriety are probably the Tisch School of the Arts and the Stern School of Business. Many of the 11 undergraduate schools also offer career-based programs, tailoring students' education to prepare them for entering the workforce. Also noteworthy is the Gallatin School of Individualized Study, wherein students are allowed to develop their own programs based on their personal interests. Regardless of the specific school

At a Glance

US News Rank	#32
Location	Northeast
Type of School	Private
Environment	Urban

Students

Total Undergrad Enrollment	25722 (2015)
# Applicants	50092 (2015)
% Accepted	32 (2015)
Male to Female Ratio	43/57
% International Students	19
% Asian American	14.5

Schools with Undergraduate Programs

College of Arts & Science
College of Dentistry
College of Nursing
College of Global Public Health
Courant Institute of Mathematical Sciences
Gallatin School of Individualized Study
Leonard N. Stern School of Business
School of Professional Studies
Silver School of Social Work
Steinhardt School of Culture, Education and Human Development
Tandon School of Engineering
Tisch School of the Arts

You Might Also Consider...

Columbia	USC
Cornell	Berkeley

or program, AIC alumni report that classes are generally challenging but manageable, though to some extent it depends on "what kind of professor you have." Though some introductory or larger lectures are taught by graduate students, professors are usually readily accessible and helpful. As the largest independent research university in the U.S. with over 130 institutes and centers on-campus, students at NYU also have abundant opportunities to pursue projects in their fields of academic interest.

Career Development

Given its placement in the heart of New York City, it is unsurprising AIC alumni feel it is easy to find jobs and internships during the school year. 94% of the class of 2013 successfully found employment or entered a graduate or professional degree program following graduation. NYU hosts a variety of career fairs throughout the academic year to connect students with employers from diverse industries. NYU's Wasserman Center for Career Development is very helpful in connecting students with potential job opportunities: 73% of students from the class of 2013 reported using NYU resources in their job search, and 46% found employment through them.

Campus Social Environment

AIC alumni have mixed feelings about the size of the NYU: some feel the lack of a centralized campus makes the school very large, while others note it seems pretty small "because you can run into friends almost every day." That said, while there is not much in the way of an overarching NYU community, students can find their niche in the abundance of social circles available both on- and off-campus. There are over 300 student clubs and organizations that interested students can join to pursue common passions and pursuits among likeminded peers. One thing AIC alumni do agree on is the diversity of the student body, with numerous ethnic, socioeconomic, and intellectual backgrounds represented—though one alum points out these groups tend to form groups more than intermingle. Central to NYU's social environment is its city setting, and students often take advantage of the myriad of bars, clubs, museums, Broadway performances, concerts, sporting events, and other opportunities readily available to them. Many of these offer student discounts. Students at NYU tend to represent the city itself, balancing academics, part-time jobs, internships, and robust social lives, making them a hard-working and fast-moving group of individuals.

Selectivity

Selectivity varies tremendously by the program you apply. Tisch and Stern remain some of the most competitive programs in the nation for their respective fields.

Things to Consider

You'll like New York University if...

- You are interested in business or the arts.
- You are looking for lots of diversity.
- You want to be in a large city.

Avoid New York University if...

- You want a traditional college campus.
- You want a strong sense of community.
- You prefer a quieter environment.

AIC Alum Student Score Profiles

% Accepted	37
Median SAT Critical Reading	670
Median SAT Math	790
Median SAT Writing	695
Median SAT Composite Score	2155
Median TOEFL	106

Financial Facts

Annual Tuition
$46278 USD (2015—2016)

Financial Aid Availability
Very Low

What Students say about the Location

Safe	3
Fun	4
Expensive	3
Chinese food	4
Transportation	4
Bars and Clubs	4
Market/Grocery Options	4
Surrounding Job Market	3
Necessity of Car	1
Overall	3

*Out of Four

Climate

Average Temperature Range
-2℃ to 24℃

Average Annual Precipitation
122cm

Average Annual Humidity
66%

Average Annual Snowfall
38.1cm

Transportation from China

Coming into New York, students can fly directly to JFK and Newark International Airports form Beijing, Shanghai or Hong Kong.

Northwestern University

633 CLARK STREET, EVANSTON, IL 60208
WEBSITE: WWW.NORTHWESTERN.EDU
CHINA ADMISSIONS OFFICER: STEPHEN BOWE
AO EMAIL ADDRESS: S-BOW@NORTHWESTERN.EDU
AO PHONE NUMBER: 847-491-3023
CLOSEST MAJOR CITY: CHICAGO, 45 MINUTES BY SHUTTLE

Best Fit Analysis

Students at the number 12 ranked university in the nation will find themselves part of a highly motivated and competitive crowd, braving the longer winters of Illinois, and enjoying the quietude of Evanston. If you're looking to go into finance, or business (or any of the other specialized schools), and you're confident about taking the initiative to breach your comfort zone, Northwestern's a prime option. Students interested in art or music may also find a home at Northwestern, in which the vibrant Chicago art scene is immediately available.

Academic Opportunities

AIC Alumni reveal, "[Class sizes are] just right. There are big classes and small classes. Most general intro level courses are big and others are small, which is a reasonable arrangement." Another adds to the picture, "Research opportunities are abundant as well." Students in schools that run on a quarter system generally take 3 classes a quarter, but at Northwestern, students tend to take 4. Curves exist to aid these determined individuals. Students find work manageable. Northwestern's strongest programs are Chemistry, Engineering, Economics, Journalism, Communication Studies, History, Political Science, and Music, providing just enough variety to satisfy multifaceted interests of their diligent students. Transferring between colleges is reportedly not too difficult in freshman year, unless your goal is Medill.

Career Development

All Northwestern AIC alumni report confidence in their school's alumni network, and believe it could be helpful if they needed a boost. Given that the school has easy access to one of the biggest cities in the country, students are conveniently in direct line of sight for many companies. "Big firms also think of Northwestern as an essential destination for job fairs." The majority of students share an aspiration for industry professions after graduation over continued education, and consulting/finance jobs tend to be the paths most taken. Even freshman at Northwestern are aware of the faculties of their campus. One AIC alumni shares, "There's a dedicated office at school with staff ready to review your resumes and train your interviewing skills. There's an online system where you can find job listings and apply."

At a Glance

US News Rank	#12
Location	Midwest
Type of School	Private
Environment	Suburban

Students

Total Undergrad Enrollment	9001 (2015)
# Applicants	32124 (2015)
% Accepted	13 (2015)
Male to Female Ratio	49/51
% International Students	8.5
% Asian American	17

Schools with Undergraduate Programs

Judd A and Marjorie Weinberg College of Arts and Sciences
Medill School of Journalism
Robert R. McCormick School of Engineering
School of Communication
Henry and Leigh Bienen School of Music
School of Education and Social Policy

You Might Also Consider...

Duke University
University of Chicago
UPenn
Columbia University
Georgetown
WUSTL

AIC Alum Student Score Profiles

% Accepted	12.3
Median SAT Critical Reading	720
Median SAT Math	800
Media SAT Writing	730
Median SAT Composite Score	2250
Median TOEFL	111

Financial Facts

Annual Tuition

$48624 USD (2015—2016)

Financial Aid Availability Very Low

What Students say about the Location

Safe	3
Fun	3
Expensive	3
Chinese food	2.5
Transportation	2
Bars and Clubs	1.5
Market/Grocery Options	1.5
Surrounding Job Market	2.5
Necessity of Car	2.5
Overall	3

*Out of four

Climate

Average Temperature Range

-6℃ to 23℃

Average Annual Precipitation

87cm

Average Annual Humidity

72.46%

Average Annual Snowfall

74.6cm

Transportation from China

There are direct flights from China to Chicago O'Hare International Airport, which is just a 45-minute shuttle ride from NU's campus. Flight options include: HKG to ORD; PEK to ORD; PVG to ORD.

Campus Social Environment

Campus is home, to many Northwestern AIC students, although they do trek into the city to explore and recruit. Evanston, the nearby town, provides less in form of entertainment, but is nonetheless, safe and nurturing. Students don't necessarily feel the need for a car on campus, and that's telling how fulfilled they feel by their immediate resources. Students that choose to go into the city of Chicago are met with a plethora of entertainment opportunities including professional sporting events, museums, art galleries, and concerts.

AIC's alumni often form social circles from the Chinese student population there. One states, "Seldom saw anybody drunk. Not pressured at all. I guess it'll be a different scene in sororities/ fraternities, though." The Greek system, theater, and athletics cut out three large parts of pie of socializing, and students tend to form cliques based on their interests within the first few years. However, the population is open-minded and 49% of Northwestern is comprised of minorities.

"Our school is very diverse. You get to meet students and professors from all over the world and get a taste of different cultures. The students here also know well of how to handle this multicultural environment." With over 500 student organizations and clubs there are many extracurricular activities and opportunities to connect with your peers.

Selectivity

Northwestern University is a school that selects students with STA scores upwards of 2200-2300's every year. Note, the specialty schools, especially Medill and McCormick are particularly challenging.

Things to Consider

You'll like NU if...

◆ You have a preference for corporate life.

◆ You love basketball and football.

◆ Volunteering is something that you care about deeply and hope to participate in the future. (NU hosts many charity events, including Dance Marathon, one of its most popular.)

Avoid NU if...

◆ Cold weather immobilizes you.

◆ You shy away from competitive atmospheres.

◆ You favor an intellectual campus over a career-oriented campus.

University of Notre Dame

220 MAIN BUILDING, NOTRE DAME, IN 46556
WEBSITE: WWW.ND.EDU
CHINA ADMISSIONS OFFICER: MARY DE VILLIERS
AO EMAIL ADDRESS: MDEVILLI@ND.EDU
ADMISSION OFFICE PHONE NUMBER: 574-631-7505
CLOSEST MAJOR CITY: CHICAGO

Best Fit Analysis

Notre Dame is in the Midwest, and most of the school year is ensconced in winter winds and chills. Students who would thrive here are those who are relatively resistant to cold, and easily adaptable in new social settings, as Notre Dame is composed primarily of religious individuals and those of paler skin color. A relatively large private school, highly motivated students are encouraged to challenge the competition to access its numerous opportunities, especially in Business and Philosophy. Students looking for a close community may thrive here, since ND has no Greek system and most people socialize in their dorms. For those looking for a more dynamic city atmosphere, look elsewhere, as ND is hours away from Chicago.

Academic Opportunities

Ranked Number 18 by US News & World Report, the University of Notre Dame is one of the academic powerhouses of the Midwest. Classes are generally on the smaller side with the exception of common introductory courses. An AIC student reports that professors are very "accessible if you make the effort to find them." The academic environment at Notre Dame is defined as both competitive and collaborative depending on the course work that a student takes. The most popular majors here are definitely more social science based and include finance, economics, political science and psychology. Generally speaking, the academic course load can be relatively challenging.

Career Development

Notre Dame's cemented alumni network serves as a tool to help current students and recent graduates find employment. Though many students exploit Notre Dame's proximity to Chicago as a mean of finding summer internships, the university also has significant alumni networks in cities in the Northeast, including Boston and New York. AIC students report that Notre Dame students are extremely career focused. Notre Dame's reputable business school lends alumni the chance to work at top firms throughout the scope of the business world. Students in the Business, Architecture, and Engineering Schools have a professional focus after college, with the majority choosing industry over schooling. The School of Science is the opposite, with 57% choosing further schooling. The College of Arts and Sciences has a more even split, with 46% choosing to go into the workforce, and 31% choosing further education.

At a Glance

US News Rank	#18
Location	Midwest
Type of School	Private
Religious Affiliation	Roman Catholic
Environment	Suburban

Students

Total Undergrad Enrollment	8551 (2014)
# Applicants	18157 (2015)
% Accepted	19.8 (2015)
Male to Female Ratio	52/48
% International Students	4.6
% Asian American	6

Schools with Undergraduate Programs

School of Architecture
College of Arts and Letters
Mendoza College of Business
College of Engineering
School of Science

You Might Also Consider...

Duke
Boston College
UPenn
Northwestern
Georgetown

AIC Alum Student Score Profiles

% AIC students accepted	25.9%
Median SAT Critical Reading	720
Median SAT Math	800
Median SAT Writing	750
Median SAT Composite Score	2230
Median TOEFL	110.5

Financial Facts

Annual Tuition
$47929 USD (2015—2016)
Financial Aid Availability
Very Low

What Students say about the Location

Safe	3.5
Fun	1.5
Expensive	1.5
Good Chinese food	1.5
Public transportation	1.5
Bars and Clubs	1
Market/Grocery Options	1.5
Surrounding Job Market	2.5
Is Car Necessary?	2.5
Overall	2.5

*Out of four Stars

Climate

Average Temperature Range
-5℃ to 23℃
Average Annual Precipitation
100.4cm
Average Annual Humidity
71.7%
Average Annual Snowfall
153cm

Transportation from China

Taxi from South Bend Regional Airport costs $20; shuttles are also available. No direct flight from China.

Campus Social Environment

Notre Dame is not necessarily known for it's diverse student body and has a relatively low number of both international and Chinese students who enroll. Although the international community at ND is not extremely strong, it does exist as more and more Chinese students are selecting ND as one of their top choices. Many students are "upper-middle class" and "white," are relatively active in their respective communities and are characterized by their prominent academic drive. Many are also drawn to the school's Catholic roots. We would like to note that the demographics mirror the overall American population's very well, and students who want to work in America, especially the east coast could begin their transition socially at ND. Though not known for its party scene, Notre Dame typically has "dorm parties from Thursdays to Saturdays" that feature "heavy drinking." Social circles are generally defined by the location of the dorms, but students may also find friends among their peers at the university's large pool of student organizations. AIC alum have found students to be friendly to international students and many were athletes in high school. With that said, the student body proudly rallies behind Notre Dame's Division I football, basketball and hockey teams (called the "Fighting Irish") and tailgating on game days is a critical piece of campus culture. Dedication to service is crucial to Notre Dame's educational goals, and students are encouraged to give back to their community.

Selectivity

Although Notre Dame is not among the most selective of schools in the US, it offers very limited space to Chinese students compared to universities in the same ranking bracket. Students who get enrolled usually have an SAT score in the upper 2200's.

Things to Consider

You'll like Notre Dame if...

- You're looking for that "work hard, play hard" ethic in college.
- You expect most social events to be on campus.

Avoid Notre Dame if...

- You find community service to be in general, a waste of time.
- Being a minority makes you feel alienated.
- You want to be in a large American city.

Pomona College

333 N COLLEGE WAY, CLAREMONT, CA 91711
WEBSITE: WWW.POMONA.EDU
CHINA ADMISSIONS OFFICER: FRANCES NAN
AO EMAIL ADDRESS: FRANCES.NAN@POMONA.EDU
ADMISSION OFFICE PHONE NUMBER: 909-621-8134
CLOSEST MAJOR CITY: LOS ANGELES, UP TO TWO HOURS BY CAR OR SHUTTLE DURING PEAK TRAFFIC. ALSO A METROLINK STOP IN THE CITY OF CLAREMONT, ABOUT TWO BLOCKS FROM CAMPUS (162)

Best Fit Analysis

Often accredited as the most elite liberal arts college on the West Coast, Pomona College provides its students a prestigious education in a relaxed, sunny California setting. As part of the Claremont Consortium with Pitzer College, Scripps College, Claremont McKenna College, and Harvey Mudd College, Pomona offers students a variety of combined resources for courses and research. Students can expect intimate classroom environments with a student/faculty ratio of 8 to 1. Pomona's large per-capita endowment contributes to the large amount of funding that its administration allocates towards summer research and student-initiated projects. Though the Pomona Colleges lies only 35 minutes by car east of downtown Los Angeles, the area's notorious reputation for poor public transportation and traffic means that many students stay around campus.

Academic Opportunities

Students at Pomona benefit from a relatively flexible curriculum but are required to take a Critical Inquiry Seminar, which challenges first year students to interrogate established truths and theories, and a number of Breadth and Study requirements in areas labeled Creative Expression, Social Institutions and Human Behavior, History, Values, Ethics and Cultural Studies, Physical and Biological Sciences, and Mathematical Reasoning. Strong majors at Pomona include Economics, Media Studies, Psychology and English, though the school is not particularly well-known for "hard science" fields such as Physics. However, Pomona students can take classes at Harvey Mudd College to make up for this identified "weakness." Professors at Pomona tend to get highly involved with their students, as about 52% of faculty are currently working with students on research initiatives. There exist several different research platforms through which Pomona students can lead research in their fields of study, including SURP (Summer Undergraduate Research Program) and funding through the college's Research Assistantships. As far as study abroad goes for Pomona, 56% of its students study abroad with a choice of over 34 different countries to choose from. Pomona also offers students the chance to enroll in Pre-Engineering Programs, such as the 3-2 Plan, to earn a B.S. and B.A. through partnerships with the California Institute of Technology and Washington University in Saint Louis.

At a Glance

US News Rank	#4
Location	West Coast
Type of School	Private
Environment	Suburban

Students

Total Undergrad Enrollment	1610 (2015)
# Applicants	8091 (2015)
% Accepted	9.76 (2015)
Male to Female Ratio	49/51
% International	8.9
% Asian	12.9

You Might Also Consider...

Williams College
Stanford University
UCLA
Claremont McKenna College
USC
Amherst College

Career Development

With close proximity to downtown Los Angeles, approximately 150 students complete paid internships at over 50 different organizations in the Greater LA area through the Pomona College Internship Program (PCIP). For students interested in seeking employment outside of Los Angeles, the Winter Break Recruiting Program provides funding for seniors to travel to five

AIC Alum Student Score Profiles

% AIC students accepted	22.2
Median SAT Critical Reading	770
Median SAT Math	800
Median SAT Writing	760
Median SAT Composite Score	2330
Median TOEFL	114

Financial Facts

Annual Tuition
$47280 USD (2015—2016)
Financial Aid Availability Very Low

What Students say about the Location

Safe	4
Fun	3
Expensive	2
Good Chinese food	2
Public transportation	3
Bars and Clubs	1
Market/Grocery Options	1
Surrounding Job Market	1
Is Car Necessary?	3
Overall	3

*Out of four Stars

Climate

Average Temperature Range
11℃ to 25℃
Average Annual Precipitation
58.7cm
Average Annual Humidity
81.87%
Average Annual Snowfall
0cm

Transportation From China

LAX is 45 minutes away by car without traffic (but can be 1-1.5 hours away with traffic). Direct flights are available from China.

other cities across the U.S. (Boston, Chicago, New York City, San Francisco, and Washington, D.C.) to interview for jobs. ClaremontConnect is a web-based career information system for Pomona alumni to share, connect, and benefit from career opportunities posted by all alumni from the Claremont Colleges. Across all the Claremont Colleges, over 250 employer informational events were hosted in the 2012—2013 school year alone. About 36% of members of the Class of 2014 are working after graduation, while 12% will be attending graduate or professional school directly after graduation from Pomona, and 11% have accepted research fellowships including Fulbright Scholarships. Of those from the Class of 2014 who are employed, the three most popular professional fields are Business/Finance, Education/Nonprofits, and Government/Law.

Campus Social Environment

Pomona has a reputation for being liberal, open and tolerant, promoting a more welcoming and relaxed atmosphere than the Ivies and its LAC counterparts on the East Coast such as Amherst and Williams. Pomona is not known to be a pressure cooker, with many students willing to collaborate with and support their peers. Unlike many other liberal arts colleges, Pomona doesn't suffer from unbearable isolation from the rest of civilization. With this said 98% of students live on campus. Students can enjoy social circles beyond their own campus, by engaging in social events and activities at the other Claremont Colleges, to the point that there seems to be a significant amount of inter-college dating across the Consortium. If students wanted to interact with their peers at Pomona and the rest of the Consortium, to pursue common passions, there are more than 200 clubs and organizations with which to do so. Though awful LA traffic can limit the prevalence of students venturing far from campus, those at Pomona have the chance to hang out at Santa Monica beach and frequent the various museums and concerts in downtown LA. Among the more popular of Pomona's traditions, Ski-Beach Day takes advantage of the school's Southern California location. Pomona buses its students to a local ski resort to hit the slopes in the morning, and after lunch are moved to a Los Angeles County or Orange County beach for the rest of the day.

Selectivity

Only a lucky few applicants are admitted to Pomona across China every year. SAT scores for admitted students are in the top tier, and for the class entering Fall 2013, 92.4% of students came from the top 10% of their classes. Leadership and a high degree of extracurricular involvement are musts.

Things to Consider

You'll like Pomona if...

- You envision yourself in a relaxed but rigorous academic setting.
- You want a school with racial and geographic diversity.
- You dream of becoming an educator, banker, or consultant.

Avoid Pomona if...

- You want to experience a college with all seasons.
- You want a very religious university.

Princeton University

WEST COLLEGE BUILDING, PRINCETON, NJ 08544
WEBSITE: WWW.PRINCETON.EDU
CHINA ADMISSION OFFICER: N/A
ADMISSIONS OFFICE EMAIL ADDRESS: UAOFFICE@PRINCETON.EDU
ADMISSIONS OFFICE PHONE NUMBER: 609-258-3060
CLOSEST MAJOR CITY: NEW YORK AND PHILADEPHIA, BOTH ABOUT A 1- HOUR DRIVE OR 1.5 HOURS BY NJ TRANSIT

Best Fit Analysis

Though you may have heard of the name, you may not know what makes Princeton the top ranking school in America this year. Still, Princeton has a large proportion of wealthy kids. During their junior and senior year, many students are faced with the choice of spending $2000 or more to join the exclusive eating clubs (although in recent years, Princeton has offered aid to mitigate the situation). In addition, unlike some top schools, grade inflation is discouraged, which means if you're not ready to be challenged mentally and physically, this might not be your place. However, if you have that consistent A-type personality and don't mind the arduous journey towards graduation, Princeton offers much more beyond its inspiring campus. With the largest per capita endowment (meaning it has the most to spend on each student), Princeton's students are unlikely to find many limitations on the resources they have access to.

Academic Opportunities

Where would a top school earn its reputation if not from well-prepared and adequately trained students? Both of these traits require a tough learning process, which is exactly what Princeton's academic departments offer. Two types of academic degrees are offered, the AB (Bachelor of Arts) and the BSE (Bachelor of Science in Engineering). The BSE imposes computer science, science and math requirements. Juniors and seniors are required to complete individual papers, and many humanities courses have required weekly preceptorial sessions with faculty. Princeton's grade deflation policy has resulted in a drop in GPA in the last few years. Despite their demanding workload, students maintain a lot of integrity and pride in their work. The school promotes the "Honor Code," where faculty does not proctor exams, and students keep each other in check.

At a Glance

US News Rank	#1
Location	Mid Atlantic
Type of School	Private
Environment	Suburban

Students

Total Undergrad Enrollment	5402 (2015)
# Applicants	27290 (2015)
% Accepted	7 (2015)
Male to Female Ratio	50.5/49.5
% International Students	11.4
% Asian	21.5

Schools with Undergraduate Programs

School of Engineering and Applied Science

Woodrow Wilson School of Public and International Affairs

School of Architecture

You Might Also Consider...

Harvard	Columbia University
Yale University	Duke University
Dartmouth College	UPenn

Career Development

Of the class of 2013 seniors, 86.6% had determined their plans after college, with 65.4% taking up positions in the workforce, and 19.7% beginning their academic careers. Of the ones who had chosen employment as their first step out of Princeton, 12% found themselves in professional, scientific, technical services, with another 12.2% in finance and insurance companies, 22.62% in nonprofit and government sectors, and 5% information technology. Alumni, as is expected of a top school, never forget their beautiful college days, and make trips to reunite with old friends for various events that Princeton hosts every year.

AIC Alum Student Score Profiles

% Accepted	2.6%
Median SAT Critical Reading	740
Median SAT Math	800
Median SAT Writing	800
Median SAT Composite Score	2330
Median TOEFL	118

Financial Facts

Annual Tuition
$43450 USD (2015—2016)

Financial Aid Availability High

What Students say about the Location

Safe	4
Fun	2.5
Expensive	3
Chinese food	2
Transportation	2.5
Bars and Clubs	2
Market/Grocery Options	2
Surrounding Job Market	2
Necessity of Car	2
Overall	3

*Out of four

Climate

Average Temperature Range
–2℃ to 24℃

Average Annual Precipitation
125.2cm

Average Annual Humidity
74.25%

Average Annual Snowfall
64.2cm

Transportation from China

No direct international flights from China. Students must fly into Newark Liberty International Airport before taking NJ transit or shuttle to Princeton, NJ. Flight options include: HKG to EWR; PEK to EWR; PVG to EWR.

Campus Social Environment

Princeton's daily life revolves around its 6 residential colleges, each a microcosm of amenities, traditions, and parties. 100% of campus students identify with one of these. Individual colleges will even sponsor trips to see ballets and operas in New York. Greek life exists but is not formally recognized by the school, and is mostly substituted by Eating Clubs. A unique system, Eating Clubs actually offer upperclassmen a place (more like a mansion) where students can eat and socialize. There is a selection process for the clubs, as well as eating member dues. About 75% of juniors and seniors find eating clubs to be a good alternative to regular dining halls. Eating clubs host parties, and drinking off-campus is less accessible with fewer options. Chinese international students who want to avoid the alcohol scene can, and will not be the only ones.

Princeton is diverse, a home to student body of 8% African Americans, 22% Asian Americans, 9% Hispanics, and 11% international students. Caucasians just barely miss holding the majority at 45%. Princeton does have its fair share of wealthy inheritors as well. Rowing, football, and basketball games are never ignored. Students like the surrounding city for its safe, comfortable environment, but not the expensive lifestyle it requires of its residents.

Selectivity

There's no one formula to get into Princeton, as expected from the HYP schools. Only 10%

and 14.5% of students are accepted with a 4.0 GPA and an SAT score over 2300, respectively. Independent research and/or international recognition for high school activities suggested for prospective applicants.

Things to Consider

You'll like Princeton if...

◆ You hope that college will be a challenge for you intellectually.

◆ You want to actively participate in the community, and have plans to work in the nonprofit and government sectors.

Avoid Princeton if...

◆ High cost of living could be a problem.

◆ Independent work is hard for you to adapt to.

◆ The general sense of elitism will prove to be a turn-off.

Rice University

6100 MAIN STREET, HOUSTON, TX 77005
WEBSITE: WWW.RICE.EDU
ADMISSIONS OFFICE TELEPHONE: 713-348-7423
ADMISSIONS OFFICE EMAIL ADDRESS: ADMI@RICE.EDU
CLOSEST MAJOR CITY: HOUSTON; RICE IS A 1-HOUR SHUTTLE RIDE FROM BUSH INTERCONTINENTAL AIRPORT

Best Fit Analysis

A beautiful campus in the humid state of Texas, Rice University continues to attract thousands of students to the damp and hot region every year. Despite the small 3900 undergraduate population, Rice University has an endowment of 3 billion USD, and uses the money to help provide affordable tuition to students. If you have a passion for the STEM fields, choose Rice. If you enjoy being friends with "nerds" and intellectual exploration is a hobby, then the community of Rice is for you. If you have plans to become an engineer in some of the largest technology firms in the world, Rice will help you. But if you have doubts about your interest in STEM, or a very small community (residential housing) confined within another small community seems stifling, then research Rice more thoroughly to make sure it is worth the tradeoff.

Academic Opportunities

Many programs at Rice University are highly respected around the world, including their architecture, music, and engineering schools. Rice offers interdisciplinary studies in cognitive sciences, managerial studies, policy studies, biosciences and bioengineering, and neuroscience as well. Numerous programs allow undergraduate students to engage in research pertaining to their major. A difficult curriculum is expected, but warm and helpful professors ease the tough trek to mastery. Though Rice offers majors in humanities and social sciences, the options are far fewer.

Career Development

64% of 2013 Rice graduates polled in an annual survey entered the workforce within months of leaving college, while 36% chose grad school. Top employers at Rice include Accenture, Baylor College of Medicine, Boston Consulting Group, Capgemini, Deloitte, Epic, ExxonMobil, Teach for America, Facebook, Google, JP Morgan Chase, Amazon, Bank of America, and many more. Students who chose grad school typically go into medicine and engineering. A strong alumni network facilitates any future plans Owls have.

At a Glance

US News Rank	#18
Location	Southwest
Type of School	Private
Environment	Urban

Students

Total Undergrad Enrollment	3879 (2015)
# Applied	17951 (2015)
% Accepted	16 (2015)
Male to Female Ratio	52/48
% International Students	11.8
% Asian American	22.6

Schools with Undergraduate Programs

George R Brown School of Engineering
School of Humanities
Shepherd School of Music
Wiess School of Natural Sciences
School of Social Sciences
School of Architecture

You Might Also Consider...

Duke University
WUSTL
Northwestern
Vanderbilt University
Emory University

Campus Social Environment

The residential college system helps students find that sense of belonging early, each with its own character and amenities. Due to the strength of the residential college communities, intramural sport games between colleges attract a large audience. Residential college communities can be clique-y at times. Rice students are as receptive to international students

AIC Alum Student Score Profiles

% Accepted	9.9
Median SAT Critical Reading	770
Median SAT Math	800
Median SAT Writing	750
Median SAT Composite Score	2230
Median TOEFL	112

Financial Facts

Annual Tuition
$41650 USD (2015—2016)
Financial Aid AvailabilityVery Low

What Students say about the Location

Safe	3
Fun	2.5
Expensive	2
Chinese food	2
Transportation	2
Bars and Clubs	1.5
Market/Grocery Options	2.5
Surrounding Job Market	3
Necessity of Car	3.5
Overall	3

*Out of four

Climate

Average Temperature Range
11℃ to 29℃
Average Annual Precipitation
123.2cm
Average Annual Humidity
73.63%
Average Annual Snowfall
0cm

Transportation from China

There are no direct flights from China. Students must have a layover before arriving at Will P. Hobby Airport (HOU) or George Bush Intercontinental Airport (IAH).

as they are to nerds. There are students who party a lot, and those who hardly attend any parties, and a few in-between as well. There is no Greek system in Rice, to promote the inclusivity of the community. Suffice to say, Rice is home to a myriad of individuals who can find partners in crime no matter what their preferred form of relaxation is. The campus is a "wet" campus, meaning students over 21 can carry alcohol around and drink in the dorms. Unlike its home state, most Rice students are liberal, but 50% of the students are from Texas. Plenty of religious organizations appeal to the varied interests of the Owls. No one ethnic group holds a majority and the breakdown is as follows: 7% African Americans, 23% Asian, 15% Hispanic, 12% international, 42% Caucasian.

Rice provides students with a lot of leadership opportunities on campus and many fun idiosyncratic traditions. The city of Houston has tons of dining choices, and can be dangerous, fun, rowdy, cultural, depending on what you're looking for.

Selectivity

Rice is a difficult school to predict in terms of acceptance. It does not look at scores, but places more importance on diversity. If you're applying to Rice, make sure you demonstrate how you can contribute to Rice's diversity. Most applicants have a science or technology focus.

Things to Consider

You'll like Rice if…

◆ You enjoy humidity in the summer, or are afraid of winter.

- You don't mind a bit of silliness while hanging out with friends.
- You're not a fan of the Greek system.

Avoid Rice if...

- You have little interest in science and technology or people who have strong interest in these fields.
- Political activism is something that you seek from your community.

Stanford University

450 SERRA MALL, STANFORD, CA 94305
WEBSITE: WWW.STANFORD.EDU
CHINA ADMISSIONS OFFICER: ANTHONY DINH
ADMISSION OFFICE PHONE NUMBER: 650-723-2091
AO EMAIL ADDRESS: ADINH@STANFORD.EDU
CLOSEST MAJOR CITY: SAN FRANCISCO, ABOUT A 40-50 MINUTE BUS RIDE OR CAR RIDE

Best Fit Analysis

Stanford University was created by a railroad magnate who desired to build a Harvard of the West. He did. Stanford today continues to attract bright and courageous individuals and change the scope of technology. Students who would do best here are those with a pre-professional bent, an entrepreneurial spirit and a thirst for education. While Stanford has popular programs in biology, international relations, economics among others, those with a love and appreciation for computers and engineering may most immediately feel at home here.

Academic Opportunities

In the natural sciences, Stanford loses to no one. Math, Physics, Chemistry, Computer

Science, are all top ranked programs, and communications, economics, and psychology are in the top 10. In most engineering specialties, it claims a spot within the top 3, if not the top 5. Initially freshmen stick together and take all their required classes first, which include extensive general education courses in writing and the humanities. At the same time, Stanford trusts its students to make fair decisions about their academic futures, and doesn't impose too many requirements on majors, or prerequisites on classes. Students have the opportunity to take classes on wine tasting and horseback riding. Research opportunities usually come by connecting with the professor first, and professors are always willing to take on cheap, enthusiastic labor for their labs. Only about 13% of classes have more than 50 students in a room. Although academics are tough, students often study together and assist each other. Professors are also generous with grading. In true Silicon Valley tradition, Stanford is an early adopter in mobile technologies; textbooks, for example, are found increasingly on digital tablets rather than on paper.

At a Glance

US News Rank	#4
Location	West Coast
Type of School	Private
Environment	Suburban

Students

Total Undergrad Enrollment	6994 (2015)
# Applicants	42497 (2015)
% Accepted	5 (2015)
Male to Female Ratio	53/47
% International Students	8.7
% Asian American	20.6

Schools with Undergraduate Programs

School of Engineering
School of Humanities and Sciences
School of Earth, Energy & Environmental Sciences

You Might Also Consider...

Harvard	UCLA
UC-Berkeley	Princeton
Univ. of Pennsylvania	MIT

Career Development

Located 35 miles from San Francisco and 20 from San Jose, Stanford is a hub for technology firm recruitment. Many students coming in already have a pre-professional bent, and finding a job on graduation isn't a huge problem for them, since firms like Google, Bain, Goldman Sachs, Microsoft, and Oracle refresh their ranks with Stanford grads every year. The Stanford Alumni Mentoring Program helps students to network with successful alumni, and networking is a very common way for students to find their footing after college. About 30% of students are able to find jobs through networking. Students are comfortable with their alumni network, and many entrepreneurs find mentors and starting investors through it.

AIC Alum Student Score Profiles

% Accepted	17.4
Median SAT Critical Reading	720
Median SAT Math	800
Median SAT Writing	790
Median SAT Composite Score	2260
Median TOEFL	115

Financial Facts

Annual Tuition	$45729 USD (2015—2016)
Financial Aid Availability	Low

What Students say about the Location

Safe	4
Fun	4
Expensive	3
Chinese food	2
Transportation	1
Bars and Clubs	2
Market/Grocery Options	1
Surrounding Job Market	3
Necessity of Car	3
Overall	3

*Out of four

Climate

Average Temperature Range	10℃ to 19℃
Average Annual Precipitation	61cm
Average Annual Humidity	82.92%
Average Annual Snowfall	0cm

Transportation from China

Students can fly directly into San Francisco. Options include: HKG to SFO; PEK to SFO; PVG to SFO. There are several travel options from the airport to Stanford, including buses and shuttles.

Campus Social Environment

Caucasians make up about 40% of the population; Asians occupy approximately 21% of the group, coming out to a pretty diverse student body that is very accepting of different cultures and ideas. Most students feel the campus size is perfect, and Greek life doesn't mean much here; fewer than 15% of students associate themselves with Greek letters. There are a lot of non-traditional Greek groups as well, such as those for students who like computer games. Students don't rush until spring of their freshman year, giving them a lot of space to contemplate their options and mingle. Stanford is also rightly proud of its athletic traditions, which have made the school a powerhouse in baseball, basketball and football. Stanford campus has a loose alcohol and drug policy because they believe in the level-headedness of their students. Stanford students don't feel the need to move off campus, in part because off-campus options are expensive, but also because the dorms on campus are comfortable and well-run. Campus is very bike-able, as is the short jaunt to Palo Alto, which provides a nice, if overpriced, place to hang out. Weather, of course, helps everyone enjoy Palo Alto's amenities all year round.

Selectivity

Stanford is highly selective, and in general it does not take many students from China. A 2400 SAT score does not guarantee admission. Students from China should emphasize their leadership skills and ability to work well with others in their applications. The admissions committee values international programs and awards.

Things to Consider

You'll like Stanford if...

◆ You want to explore diverse majors.

◆ Engineering and Computer Science are your potential career fields, and/or the proximity of Silicon Valley is appealing to you.

◆ You're looking to surrounding yourself with high-achieving, pre-professional students who are laid back, collaborative, and infectiously optimistic.

◆ Seasons aren't something you really care for.

Avoid Stanford if...

◆ You need the dynamic environment of a city.

◆ You'd prefer a strong alumni network on the East Coast.

◆ You enjoy the doom and gloom of colder climates.

Tufts University

419 BOSTON AVE., MEDFORD, MA 02155
WEBSITE: WWW.TUFTS.EDU
ADMISSION OFFICE PHONE NUMBER: 617-627-3170
CHINA ADMISSIONS OFFICERS: GREG WONG (OTHER CITIES) AND JENNIFER SIMONS (BEIJING, NANJING, AND SHANGHAI)
AO EMAIL ADDRESSES: JENNIFER.SIMONS@TUFTS.EDU AND GREG.WONG@TUFTS.EDU
CLOSEST MAJOR CITY: BOSTON (20MIN, BUS, SHUTTLES)

Best Fit Analysis

As a member of one of over fifty colleges that call Boston, Massachusetts their home, Tufts consistently ranks among the top institutions in "America's College Town." Just minutes away from Harvard and MIT, Tufts students share access to many of the same opportunities that students from these institutions have in Boston. Tufts opens its arms to students from around the world, recruiting from about 50 countries for last year's Class of 2017 alone. An AIC alum writes, "International students and exchange students have their own cultural groups and at the same time mingle naturally with domestic students. And more importantly for diversity, people come with a great variety of interest[s] and talent." Students at Tufts are generally socially aware and consider it an important part of their identity, often coupling their

social awareness with their interest in international relations. Tufts also has well-known Biology and Health Science programs that consistently place graduates in top medical schools and health care firms.

Academic Opportunities

The academic environment at Tufts is known to be arduous, but students are mostly collaborative (except for some in the university's premed track, which is one of the best in the country). An AIC alum writes, "For Core [Requirements], especially humanities and sociology, it's extremely hard to get A's as an international student from a non-English speaking country, or at least in the first year." Along with its notable premed track, Tufts boasts reputable programs in International Relations, Environmental Engineering, Philosophy, Community Health, and Drama. Opportunities for undergraduate research are abundant at Tufts; students can access professors with ease given that Tufts' student body totals just over 5000. Students with a knack for science should take note of Tufts' International Research Program, designed for students in the School of Arts and Sciences to develop and conduct scientific research internationally with Tufts faculty. Every year, Tufts hosts an Undergraduate Research & Scholarship Symposium, which celebrates the many different contributions that Tufts undergrads have made towards scientific research.

At a Glance

US News Rank	#27
Location	Northeast
Type of School	Private
Environment	Suburban

Students

Total Undergrad Enrollment	5126 (2014)
# Applicants	19062 (2015)
% Accepted	16 (2015)
Male to Female Ratio	49/51
% International Students	10
% Asian	12

Schools with Undergraduate Programs

School of Arts and Sciences
School of Engineering

You Might Also Consider...

Brown University
UPenn
Cornell University
Johns Hopkins
Northwestern
Georgetown University

Career Development

As Tufts prides itself on shaping its students to become active citizens, it comes as no surprise that the university currently ranks ninth among medium-sized schools that produce Peace Corps volunteers. In the same vein, Tufts students exceed the national average for finding

AIC Alum Student Score Profiles

% AIC students accepted	3.7
Median SAT Critical Reading	690
Median SAT Math	800
Median SAT Writing	720
Median SAT Composite Score	2210
Median TOEFL	109

Financial Facts

Annual Tuition
$49520 USD (2015—2016)

Financial Aid Availability Very Low

What Students say about the Location

Safe	3.5
Fun	2
Expensive	2
Good Chinese food	2
Public transportation	2.5
Bars and Clubs	1
Market/Grocery Options	1.5
Surrounding Job Market	3.5
Is Car Necessary?	2
Overall	2.5

*Out of four Stars

Climate

Average Temperature Range
-4℃ to 23℃

Average Annual Precipitation
122cm

Average Annual Humidity
68%

Average Annual Snowfall
135.9cm

Transportation from China

Shuttles are offered to Logan International Airport, which has direct flights from PEK, PVG, and HKG.

employment outside of the United States following graduation; about 19 percent of the Class of 2013 secured international work opportunities. Tufts students have noted that there are instances where they beat out students/alumni from both Harvard and MIT for investment banking, trade, and sales positions. Tufts students also gravitate towards the fields of education and journalism.

Campus Social Environment

Quirky and intellectual, students at Tufts aren't afraid to let their nerdy side on the loose. Yet with so much diversity on campus, it's hard to pinpoint the defining features of the "typical" Tufts student. "All kinds of people, all kinds of race[s] from all kinds of background[s], holding all kinds of political [beliefs], following all kinds of religion[s]. You will not be considered weird in any way [at Tufts], because everyone is a little bit weird in some way," says a former AIC student. One aspect of Tufts' student life that AIC's Tufts alumni identify is that the university generally lacks a sports scene, though many students make an effort to exercise. While fraternities have existed at Tufts for over a century, Greek life doesn't have an overbearing presence on campus, and parties are available but not over-the-top crazy. With close proximity to downtown Boston, Tufts students have plenty of outlets to escape their academic lives and explore Boston's club, bar, and restaurant scenes.

Selectivity

Applicants to Tufts have better chances for admission if their SAT scores are above 2200. As

Tufts expects its students to be active members in the community, leadership positions and community service should be highlighted in applications to this school. Don't be afraid to show your quirky side, as well. Tufts feeds on it!

Things to Consider

You'll like Tufts if…

- You're interested in studying International Relations or Biology.
- You're weird. And you embrace it.
- You're expecting a diverse college community.

Avoid Tufts if…

- You're not ready to compete for engineering or finance students from Harvard or MIT.
- You're traditional or conservative; prepare for a lot of quirkiness at this school.
- You're looking for a school with strong athletics programs.

University of California–Davis

1 SHIELDS AVENUE, DAVIS, CA 95616
WEBSITE: WWW.UCDAVIS.EDU
CHINESE ADMISSION OFFICER: N/A
ADMISSIONS OFFICE PHONE NUMBER: 530-752-2971, 530-752-3614 (INTERNATIONAL STUDENTS)
ADMISSION OFFICE CONTACT: HTTPS://UCDAVIS.ASKADMISSIONS.NET/ASK.ASPX
CLOSEST MAJOR CITY: SAN FRANCISCO, DAVIS IS ABOUT 1.5 HOURS BY BUS OR TRAIN

Best Fit Analysis

UC Davis isn't as popular as its sister schools, Berkeley and UCLA, but it has strengths in areas UCLA and Berkeley can only admire from afar. Students who come here will enjoy the laid-back campus adorned with bikes, fun traditions, and a quiet, studious environment. For students who are looking for a city, UC Davis may not be the ideal academic setting. Students coming here may be looking for more of a community within the campus, rather than outside of it, as Davis provides little nightlife. The Sacramento area isn't the part of California that is memorialized for its weather, but in general, Davis is a stranger to snow, and is typically very livable. Come to Davis for its down-to-earth community and excellent academics, and try not to expect too much in its surrounding environment.

At a Glance

US News Rank	#41
Location	West Coast
Type of School	Public
Environment	Suburban

Students

Total Undergrad Enrollment	28384 (2015)
# Applicants	64626 (2015)
% Accepted	38.2 (2015)
Male to Female Ratio	41/59
% International Students	10
% Asian American	37

Schools with Undergraduate Programs

College of Letters and Sciences
College of Engineering
College of Biological Sciences
College of Agriculture and Environmental Science

You Might Also Consider...

UC-Irvine	UC-Berkeley
UC-Santa Barbara	UCLA

Academic Opportunities

Students with an interest in biological and animal sciences (especially those with an eye on the veterinarian industry), and engineering will be laying a strong foundation at this university. Art, wine, agricultural engineering also share the spotlight as top curriculums here. Switching between schools is generally not a problem. The quarter system pushes students to absorb material as fast as they can. With near 80% of classes having fewer than 50 students, Davis gives students more face-to-face time with professors and classmates than many large research universities. Professors are applauded for their dedication towards their students. Research opportunities are not rare treasures here, and students never need to worry about their thirst for knowledge going unquenched.

Career Development

In 2009, 37 percent of student graduated and opted for more school, while 52% had paid job offers. Davis boasts the 80% of their students who apply to grad schools get into their first and second choices. Students who aspire to have a science/engineering related profession generally don't have a difficult time being employed or finding internships. However, students in business and accounting concentrations may have to work harder to gain the attention of employers. Though career services at UC Davis has provides useful internships and help finding jobs immediately after graduation, they do not lend much support to alumni.

AIC Alum Student Score Profiles

% Accepted	71
Median SAT Critical Reading	650
Median SAT Math	800
Median SAT Writing	690
Median SAT Composite Score	2100
Median TOEFL	105

Financial Facts

Annual Tuition
$38659 USD (2015—2016)

Financial Aid Availability Very Low

What Students say about the Location

Safe	3.5
Fun	3
Expensive	3
Chinese food	2
Transportation	4
Bars and Clubs	2
Market/Grocery Options	2
Surrounding Job Market	2.5
Necessity of Car	1
Overall	3

*Out of four

Climate

Average Temperature Range
8.3℃ to 25℃

Average Annual Precipitation
57.2cm

Average Annual Humidity
79.94%

Average Annual Snowfall
0cm

Transportation from China

There are no direct flights from China. Students must first fly into San Francisco. Options include: HKG to SFO; PEK to SFO; PVG to SFO.

Campus Social Environment

Internal school culture is rich, with fun and famous traditions like Picnic Day, their Arboretum, and a large catalogue of clubs (which are easy to start if you can't find any to meet your interests) including their own radio station and a student-run bus station. In addition, public transportation enables students to travel between Davis and Berkeley conveniently and explore most of the space between the Bay Area and Sacramento.

The town nearby is small enough that you can recognize most faces by the end of a year or two.

Greek life engages 8% of the undergraduate population, and partying doesn't eat up students' time.

With a 37% Asian population at UC Davis, it'll be easy to find yourself among ethnically Chinese peers. Students note that there are some Chinese food options nearby and food isn't that expensive in Davis. Sushi buffets are also popular spots in the surrounding town. The dining options at Davis are supposed to be the best in the UC system outside of UCLA.

Selectivity

UC-Davis is not nearly as selective at UCB and UCLA. Students applying from China have better results getting into UC-Davis when their SAT scores are 1950 or higher.

Things to Consider

You'll like Davis if…

- You're an outdoorsy person.
- You like small towns and communities.
- You'd prefer to be surrounded by a largely Asian student body.
- You're a budding computer scientist.

Avoid Davis if…

- You need the dynamic environment of a city.
- You want to pursue accounting and finance.

University of California–Los Angeles

405 HILGARD AVENUE, BOX 951405, LOS ANGELES, CA 90095
WEBSITE: WWW.UCLA.EDU
CHINA ADMISSIONS OFFICER: N/A
ADMISSION OFFICE PHONE NUMBER: 310-825-3101
ADMISSION OFFICE CONTACT: HTTPS://WWW.ADMISSION.UCLA.EDU/CONTACTFORM/UGADM.ASPX
CLOSEST MAJOR CITY: LOS ANGELES; UCLA IS ABOUT A 20-30 MINUTE DRIVE FROM DOWNTOWN LA

Best Fit Analysis

The University of California – Los Angeles boasts that it is the school that receives the largest number of applicants every year, and it's not difficult to see why. The beautiful campus, impeccable weather, highly ranked programs, and reputed dining halls make for almost too-comfortable college life. Students that will find UCLA the most charming are the ones who enjoy having the opportunity to have classes every quarter comprised of entirely unfamiliar faces. However; AIC students have noted that an extremely large campus population tended to bother them.

Academic Opportunities

Ranked Number 23 by US News & World Report, UCLA was once a part of the academically prestigious Berkeley, later developing into a separate institution with unique strengths in linguistics, psychology, communications, film, and theater arts. An AIC student reports that professors are very accessible, "We have lectures and discussions for general education courses during first two years. Professors teach lectures and TA teaches discussions. In junior and senior year, most of classes are taught by professors." Students find the curriculum fast due to the quarter system, which shortens the standard education cycle of 16 weeks to 10, but not unmanageable. One AIC student notes: "For lower division courses, usually professors grade students on a curve but not all of them. The curves vary for different professors." For the most part, professors are accessible during the office hours they shell out for assistance. Research opportunities are plentiful, but it's easiest to reach out to professors first. Schools like the School of Nursing, or Theater, Film and Television accept students in their sophomore/ junior year. Transferring between Letters and Sciences and the School of Engineering is usually pretty easy.

At a Glance

US News Rank	#23
Location	West Coast
Type of School	Public
Environment	Urban

Students

Total Undergrad Enrollment	29585 (2015)
# Applicants	92722 (2015)
% Accepted	17.3 (2015)
Male to Female Ratio	44/56
% International Students	12
% Asian American	32.8

Schools with Undergraduate Programs

College of Letters and Science
School of the Arts and Architecture
School of Theater, Film, and Television
School of Nursing
School of Engineering and Applied Science
School of Music

You Might Also Consider...

USC	University of Michigan
Stanford	UNC-Chapel Hill
UC-Berkeley	UC-San Diego

Career Development

Although in general, Bruins are spirited and proud of their school, the general attitude towards the utility of the alumni network is ambivalent. As a large school, students are more likely to look for help within immediate circles, professional fraternities, and career center services. However, the greater Los Angeles area provides a flexible and versatile job-hunting platform. The South Bay area provides plentiful tech and engineering related jobs with large

AIC Alum Student Score Profiles

% Accepted	27.8
Median SAT Critical Reading	710
Median SAT Math	800
Median SAT Writing	730
Median SAT Composite Score	2220
Median TOEFL	109

Financial Facts

Annual Tuition

$37959 USD (2015—2016)

Financial Aid Availability Very Low

What Students say about the Location

Safe	3
Fun	4
Expensive	3
Chinese food	4
Transportation	2
Bars and Clubs	3
Market/Grocery Options	3
Surrounding Job Market	3
Necessity of Car	4
Overall	3

*Out of four

Climate

Average Temperature Range

13℃ to 24℃

Average Annual Precipitation

44.9cm

Average Annual Humidity

75.54%

Average Annual Snowfall

0cm

Transportation from China

There are direct flights from China to LAX. Options include: HKG to LAX; PEK to LAX; PVG to LAX.

companies such as Honeywell and Exxon Mobil.

Additionally, the Big 4 in accounting and top consulting firms recruit at UCLA every year. For the ambitious, there is no end to the resources for aspiring engineering, finance, marketing, and consulting professionals this school supplies.

Campus Social Environment

The primary social scene on campus revolves around student organizations and CSSA is recommended for Chinese students who want to find that sense of belonging quickly. One AIC alumnus noted "Still, most Chinese students hang out with other Chinese students." To avoid this, professional frats, CAC are also popular and useful networks.

Greek life dominates the drinking scene, with about 30% of students with letters, but doesn't monopolize it, and as social circles develop, age restrictions vanish, and Greek parties become more of an alternative activity than a norm. "Drinking is a general thing in our school." Although UCLA is a dry campus, and sneaking alcohol into dorms can be a tactical feat, underage drinking persists, but not in pervasive and suffocating way.

Students hang out on campus their first two years due to "terrible transportation around the campus. Hard to get out unless you have a car." All AIC alumni stress the importance of a car. Outside of campus, Westwood is a quaint, safe neighborhood with expensive, but romantic restaurants. Outside of that is the diverse, expansive playground of Los Angeles.

Selectivity

UCLA's selectivity fluctuates each year, but is generally friendly to students in the upper 2100-2200's. UCLA, like many of the other schools in the University of California system, heavily weigh scores and GPA as part of their admissions process.

Things to Consider

You'll like UCLA if...

◆ You need and want internships!

◆ "Food in UCLA is perfect! One of my USC friends came to my school and told me he was about to transfer to UCLA after eating at our dining hall."

◆ You love sports!

Avoid UCLA if...

◆ You are looking for ethnic diversity, and more of a culture shock.

◆ You are looking for a more intense academic atmosphere.

University of California–San Diego

9500 GILMAN DRIVE, LA JOLLA, CA 92093
WEBSITE: WWW.UCSD.EDU
CHINA ADMISSION OFFICER: N/A
ADMISSIONS OFFICE PHONE NUMBER: 858-534-4831
ADMISSIONS OFFICE EMAIL ADRESS: INFOINTERNATIONAL@AD.UCSD.EDU
CLOSEST MAJOR CITY: SAN DIEGO, UCSD IS A 20-25 MIN DRIVE FROM THE SAN DIEGO INTERNATIONAL AIRPORT

Best Fit Analysis

UCSD does the best job among the UCs of creating a smaller community among its students by splitting up the undergraduate population into 6 residential colleges. Students looking for a peaceful and slow-paced environment as opposed to the active liveliness of a metropolis would do well here. Biology and Engineering are highly ranked at UCSD, and highly recommended to students who hope to enter these fields. Cold weather is a stranger to the campus, and high schoolers from southern parts of China who are looking for seasonal changes may be disappointed here. UCSD is not a party school, nor is San Diego a party city, though neither is small enough to be accused of being devoid of festive revelry options, which means students who are looking for a balance in their social life may find a perfect fit in this southern California school.

Academic Opportunities

UCSD has many strong specialty majors such as nanoengineering, bioengineering, behavioral neuroscience, aerospace engineering, oceanography, etc. In addition, it has highly ranked departments in Theater & Dance, Economics, Political Science, Multimedia/Visual Communication. Aside from certain majors in the Jacobs School of Engineering, it is not difficult to transfer between majors. Each of the 6 undergraduate schools have a slightly different education philosophy which is reflected in the differing graduation requirements each maintains. For example, Muir emphasizes academic individualization, while Roosevelt focuses on global citizenship. Research is plentiful on this campus known for its science programs and GPA is the primary screening factor for getting involved. One AIC student currently studying engineering finds that the curriculum is rather easy and tends to be graded on a curve.

Career Development

For students who completed their coursework in the 2012-2013 school year, 73% found work in a variety of fields, the most popular being Technology, Business, Life/health sciences, Human Services, and Arts/Communication. The remaining 27% ended up in graduate and pre-professional programs. Companies that often recruit at UCSD include Sharp Healthcare, Qualcomm, Kaiser Permanente and San Diego Gas & Electric. While some AIC alumni don't plan to use the college's alumni network in the future, UCSD does provide many alumni network alliances to help career professionals develop their futures.

At a Glance

US News Rank	#39
Location	West Coast
Type of School	Public
Environment	Urban

Students

Total Undergrad Enrollment	26590 (2015)
# Applicants	78091 (2015)
% Accepted	33.9 (2015)
Male to Female Ratio	52/48
% International Students	18
% Asian American	46

Schools with Undergraduate Programs

Division of Arts and Humanities
Division of Mathematics and Physical Sciences
Divisions of Biological Sciences
Division of Social Sciences
Jacobs School of Engineering
Scripps Institution of Oceanography

You Might Also Consider...

UCLA	University of Miami
UC-Berkeley	UCSB
UC-Davis	Stanford University

AIC Alum Student Score Profiles

% Accepted	62.3
Median SAT Critical Reading	670
Median SAT Math	800
Median SAT Writing	710
Median SAT Composite Score	2150
Median TOEFL	108

Financial Facts

Annual Tuition
$38265 USD (2015—2016)

Financial Aid Availability Very Low

What Students say about the Location

Safe	4
Fun	3
Expensive	3
Chinese Food	2.5
Transportation	3
Bars and Clubs	3
Market/Grocery Options	3.5
Surrounding Job Market	3
Necessity of Car	3
Overall	3.5

*Out of four

Climate

Average Temperature Range
13℃ to 24℃

Annual Average Precipitation
32.4cm

Annual Average Humidity
80.89%

Annual Average Snowfall
0cm

Transportation from China

There are no direct flight from China to San Diego. Students have to layover elsewhere.

Campus Social Environment

UCSD is unique about the UC schools in its 6 undergraduate residential college setup. All students seeking admission must rank their favorite from these choices: Revelle, Warren, Muir, ERC, Marshall, Sixth. Each school provides a small community environment with varying general education classes and extracurricular activities. Many students recommend the ones with the least demanding graduation requirements: Warren and Muir, but prospective seniors should keep in mind each school has a different social scene as well as academic focuses. However, your specific major is not directly affected by the school you choose, though it may be influenced by the community you will be surrounded by.

San Diego is a laid-back city with beautiful beaches nearby, providing for a lot of outdoors entertainment for students. AIC Students rarely noted anything lacking in the city, except perhaps Chinese food. Only about 23% of students are involved in the low-key Greek scene at UCSD. What UCSD lacks in its relatively quiet sports scene, it makes up for in diversity, although Chinese students may not think so. About 45% of its students are Asian, 23% Caucasian, 12% Mexican American (counted separately from other Latinos), 9% other or undeclared, 2% African American, 3% Latinos and 5% Filipinos (counted separately from Asian Americans).

Selectivity

Engineering at UCSD is slightly harder to get

into than the rest of the school, but overall UCSD accepts a high percentage of Chinese students every year. SAT and TOEFL scores are weighted heavily into admissions consideration.

Things to Consider

You'll like UCSD if...

- You're an outdoorsy person.
- You're going to be a future biologist.
- You're interested in attending a research university, but are also looking for a small, liberal arts-style community.

Avoid UCSD if...

- You want a busier, type-A city scene.
- You want to pursue accounting or finance.

University of California–Santa Barbara

1210 CHEADLE HALL, UNIVERSITY OF CALIFORNIA, SANTA BARBARA, SANTA BARBARA, CA 93106
WEBSITE: WWW.UCSB.EDU
CHINA ADMISSION OFFICER: N/A ADMISSION OFFICE CONTACT: HTTPS://ADMISSIONS.SA.UCSB.EDU/CONNECT/CONTACT-US
ADMISSIONS OFFICE PHONE NUMBER: 805-893-2881
CLOSEST MAJOR CITY: LOS ANGELES, ABOUT 1.5 HOURS BY BUS OR AMTRAK TRAIN

Best Fit Analysis

On a cliff overlooking the sea, UCSB is one of those schools you hear about in fairytales. Beautiful men and women wearing tanks everyday in a paradise where skies are always radiant and luminous. And of course, in paradise, everyone parties. All the time. If alcohol, hook up culture, mono-seasonal beauty, having nearly 18000 other "classmates" is not your cup of tea, please turn the page. Engineers, beware, due to the levels of prestige and equally high levels of rigor of the professional school, you may never experience of the aforementioned perks of UCSB. With this said, UCSB is still overall a great school with strong programs in engineering and the biological and physical sciences.

Academic Opportunities

It goes without saying that classes will be large, with many large lectures taught by professors and small discussions led by graduate students. However, the professors are very knowledgeable and in many of the STEM fields, they are the best in the nation. Aside of the College of Engineering, UCSB doesn't overload its students with work. Students both within and on the outside of the STEM fields have lots of opportunities to work on leading research of contemporary times.

At a Glance

US News Rank	#37
Location	West Coast
Type of School	Public
Environment	Suburban

Students

Total Undergrad Enrollment	20238 (2015)
# Applicants	70565 (2015)
% Accepted	32.7 (2015)
Male to Female Ratio	47/53
% International Students	6
% Asian American	21

Schools with Undergraduate Programs

College of Creative Studies
College of Engineering
College of Letters & Science

You Might Also Consider...

UC-Davis
UCLA
UC-Berkeley
UT-Austin
University of Miami
UC-San Diego

Career Development

UCSB's College of Engineering and Biological Sciences fields are household names in academia, but a challenging course load zaps partying time. Of the polled 2013 seniors, 53% had found full-time employment and 22% planned to go to grad school directly after graduation. 88% say they plan to continue their education within the next years of graduating. The most popular industries were the finance sector, education, sales and marketing, science and research, engineering, medicine and business management. Companies that often recruit from UCSB include Target, Peace Corps, Intel, Facebook, BrightRoll, and Citrix. Alumni networks are not the strongest, but students do love their alma mater.

Campus Social Environment

Isla Vista has a great climate, one of those amazing, dry, warm, but always breezy locations that people flock to for vacation. Being right on the beach, students usually experiment with

AIC Alum Student Score Profiles

% Accepted	53.3
Median SAT Critical Reading	660
Median SAT Math	800
Media SAT Writing	690
Median SAT Composite Score	2110
Median TOEFL	106

Financial Facts

Annual Tuition
$36948 USD (2015—2016)
Financial Aid Availability Very Low

What Students say about the Location

Safe	3
Fun	4
Expensive	3
Chinese food	1
Transportation	1
Bars and Clubs	2
Market/Grocery Options	1
Surrounding Job Market	2
Necessity of Car	4
Overall	4

*Out of four

Climate

Average Temperature Range
11℃ to 21℃
Average Annual Precipitation
56.2cm
Average Annual Humidity
83.57%
Average Annual Snowfall
0cm

Transportation from China

No direct flights from China. Students must fly into LAX and then take a bus or train to get to Santa Barbara.

surfing at least once in their 4 years of study. Isla may be an idyllic landscape, but almost all students agree that is it very expensive and sponsors very little city life. To get to larger cities, students with cars can zoom into LA within an hour (only to be hassled by traffic perhaps.)

Although Greek life isn't thriving, with only 8% of men and 13% of women involved, but parties are always in season (Most everyone has heard of their famous Halloween festivities. UCSB has a very diverse population, as it is comprised of 48% Caucasian, 21% Asian, and 26% Hispanic, and 3% African American. Possibly as a result of this highly diverse student body, the campus is rather liberal and one of the more politically active schools. UCSB hosts an annual free music festival, and at least 700 students support intramural club sports, so there's never a lack of anything to do on campus. Women's basketball games and men's soccer games are fun, rowdy affairs. However, although UCSB students drink like they live in the desert when it comes to alcohol, drugs are highly restricted and hide in very discreet corners few are aware of.

Selectivity

Admission to UCSB relies heavily upon applicants' test scores and GPA. Admitted applicants from China often have SATs over 1900 and TOEFL scores over 90.

Things to Consider

You'll like UCSB if…

- You want to have tan lines all year round.
- You expect most social events to be on campus.
- You're a bookish beach bum.

Avoid UCSB if…

- You don't have willpower. The party scene and beach can be problematic for some.
- You are not a fan of the dominant American beach-oriented culture.
- You'd prefer a little snow in the mix from time to time.

University of Chicago

5801 S ELLIS AVE, CHICAGO, IL 60637
WEBSITE: WWW.UCHICAGO.EDU
CHINA ADMISSIONS OFFICER: CAROL LIN, CHRIS DAVEY
ADMISSION OFFICE PHONE NUMBER: 773-702-8650
ADMISSION OFFICE EMAIL ADDRESS: INTERNATIONALADMISSIONS@UCHICAGO.EDU
CLOSEST BIG CITY: CHICAGO

Best Fit Analysis

"Where Fun Comes to Die," the unofficial slogan of University of Chicago, was playfully adopted by University of Chicago students who place academics at the centre of their higher education experience. UChicago, located in Hyde Park on the South Side of one of the U.S.'s largest cities, attracts students who label themselves as "nerdy" and "intellectual," as many plan to pursue graduate degrees following their undergraduate tenure. Though some of UChicago's strongest programs are in English, Political Science, and Anthropology, AIC alumni who have opted for Economics, Mathematics, and Physics have found the coursework to be particularly engaging.

Academic Opportunities

At the heart of it all, the University of Chicago is a premier research institution with unparalleled graduate opportunities. Aside from the undergraduate College, UChicago hosts four divisions of graduate research, and six professional schools. The research-oriented backdrop of the school means undergraduate students are prone to take part in high profile initiatives, including those in Cosmological Physics and Materials Research that are sponsored by the National Science Foundation. The Core Curriculum, known as the "Common Core," features small classes and requires courses in the humanities and social sciences, as well as proficiency in a foreign language and study of a specific civilization. The U of C has also made huge strides in interdisciplinary studies, creating such majors as "Big Problems" and "Fundamentals: Issues & Texts". The academic rigor of UChicago is notably high, and an AIC alum reports that getting an A is "really hard" and estimates that "less than 6 students in a 80 [person] class get [an] A." Though the academics at UChicago are difficult, students benefit from the collaborative environment that promotes motivation among peers rather than competition.

At a Glance

US News Rank	#4
Location	Midwest
Type of School	Private
Environment	Urban

Students

Total Undergrad Enrollment	5869 (2015)
# Applicants	30188 (2015)
% Accepted	8.35 (2015)
Male to Female Ratio	53/47
% Asian	10.8
% International	17.4

Schools with Undergraduate Programs

The College of the University of Chicago

You Might Also Consider...

Columbia University
Northwestern
Univ. of Pennsylvania
Yale University

Career Development

According to *The College Solution*, the University of Chicago ranks 9th among all institutions of higher education in the United States that produce the highest percentage of undergrads who end up heading off to graduate school. For the Class of 2013, approximately 54% of grads headed into the work force while 17% went directly into graduate or professional school.

Of those who accepted full-time jobs at the time of graduation, a stunning 21% entered

AIC Alum Student Score Profiles

% AIC students accepted	19.1
Median SAT Critical Reading	720
Median SAT Math	800
Median SAT Writing	790
SAT Composite Score	2285
Median TOEFL	113

Financial Facts

Annual Tuition
$49026 USD (2015—2016)
Financial Aid Availability Very Low

What Students say about the Location

Safe	2
Fun	2
Expensive	2.5
Good Chinese food	2
Public transportation	2.5
Bars and Clubs	2
Market/Grocery Options	2
Surrounding Job Market	2
Is Car Necessary?	1.5
Overall	3

*Out of four Stars

Climate

Average Temperature Range
-6℃ to 23℃
Annual Average Precipitation
93cm
Annual Average Humidity
72.3%
Annual Average Snowfall
82.1cm

Transportation from China

O'Hare International Airport is 30 minutes to 1 hour away. Shuttles and buses exist to get to the airport. Direct flights from China are available.

into the fields of education and academia. Although the U of C once had a reputation for a weak alumni network, recent efforts at fundraising have yielded generous dividends, including a $300 million donation to the top-ranked business school. U of C alumni are prone to recruit for interns and full-time employees from their alma mater

Campus Social Environment

The University of Chicago is not particularly known for its developed social scenes. Students can take advantage of the local eateries and bars in the Hyde Park neighborhood, but some students venture into downtown Chicago for better nightlife options. The sports scene at UChicago is limited, Though UChicago is known to not have "great parties," several annual on-campus events engage the university's proud and quirky traditions. "Scav," short for the University of Chicago Scavenger Hunt, fosters a four-day competition among students to find an array of (sometimes bizarre) items, which have famously included such items as a homemade nuclear reactor. The Summer Breeze festival helps to thaw out campus after frigid Chicago winters by featuring musical performers and carnival fare like Jello-O wrestling. UChicago even sponsors a mid-winter Polar Bear Run, in which students openly streak across the quad. Meanwhile, Doc Films is the country's longest running student film society, and the Festival of the Arts features a fashion show, lectures, and art installations. Despite these festivities, students remain serious about their studies—seeing them, in true U of C fashion, as being "fun" in their own way.

Selectivity

Every year the University of Chicago receives more applications and boasts a lower admissions rate. Students who are accepted to this university generally score over 2200 on the SAT. Compared to other top five schools, Chicago can be relatively easier, but the admissions process can be self-selecting as it is one of the most demanding. We have barely had any students get accepted without a 2250+ score, or special circumstances.

Things to Consider

You'll like the University of Chicago if...

- Your idea of fun is having philosophical or academic debates until 3 in the morning.
- You want a plethora of opportunities for research, or plan on heading to graduate school.
- You want required courses which teach classic texts in the humanities and social sciences.

Avoid the University of Chicago if...

- You don't like the cold.
- You don't like people who wear T-shirts saying "Chicago Dating—the odds are good, but the goods are odd".

University of Michigan–Ann Arbor

515 EAST JEFFERSON STREET, ANN ARBOR MI 48109-1316
WEBSITE: WWW.UMICH.EDU
CLOSEST MAJOR CITY: DETROIT (1 HOUR BY CAR)
CHINA ADMISSION OFFICER: SHANELL HAGOOD (BEIJING)
AO EMAIL ADDRESS: SHLEANNA@UMICH.EDU
AO PHONE NUMBER: 734-647-8290
CHINA ADMISSION OFFICER: JULIE POLLAK (SHANGHAI, SHENZHEN)
AO EMAIL ADDRESS: JPOLLAK@UMICH.EDU
AO PHONE NUMBER: 734-615-3161
CHINA ADMISSION OFFICER: ALISON WANG (HANGZHOU)
AO EMAIL ADDRESS: ALIWANG@UMICH.EDU
AO PHONE NUMBER: 734-647-7850
CHINA ADMISSION OFFICER: KRISTEN LEMIRE (CHONGQING, DALIAN, TIANJIN, WUXI)
AO EMAIL ADDRESS: KDLC@UMICH.EDU
AO PHONE NUMBER: 734-615-0383
CHINA ADMISSION OFFICER: REUBEN KAPP (CHANGZHOU, CHENGDU, GUANGZHOU, NANJING, NINGBO, QINGDAO, SHENYANG, SUZHOU, WUHAN, XI' AN)
AO EMAIL ADDRESS: KAPPREUB@UMICH.EDU
AO PHONE NUMBER: 734-936-2426
CHINA ADMISSION OFFICER: ERICA DECKER (OTHER CITIES)
AO EMAIL ADDRESS: ELDECKER@UMICH.EDU
AO PHONE NUMBER: 734-763-9412

Best Fit Analysis

The University of Michigan is a public university powerhouse, attracting students from every corner of the U.S. and world to study undergraduate and graduate programs offered through nineteen schools. With over 200 undergraduate degree programs, there are few limitations as to what field of academia students can pursuc at Michigan. Ann Arbor tends to get blasted by artic waves of cold during winter but serves as a vibrant college town that prides itself on hosting the state's flagship institution of higher learning. There are plenty of Chinese international students who rave about their experiences at Michigan, and ultimately anyone can find their niche or clique within the diverse student body. Beware, however, of introductory-level lectures that can house up to 500 students, creating stiff competition among STEM students.

Academic Opportunities

Michigan isn't blind to the fact that many first year students can get overwhelmed in massive lectures with hundreds of other students. In order to balance class sizes for freshmen, Michigan offers students individual attention through the First Years Seminars Program, which includes subjects such as engineering and English. The coursework at the University of Michigan is known to be rigorous and time-consuming, but the university doesn't necessarily foster a cutthroat atmosphere. Typically, though, the toughness and workload for students depends on the classes that a student takes. As one AIC alum puts it, "It is difficult for some classes [to get A's], but not so difficult for other classes…many classes are graded on a curve." Premed, engineering, art and design, architecture, music and business are among the top programs at the University of

At a Glance	
US News Rank	#29
Location	Midwest
Type of School	Public
Environment	Urban
Students	
Total Undergrad Enrollment	28312 (2015)
# Applicants	51797 (2015)
% Accepted	26.3 (2015)
Male to Female Ratio	51/49
% Asian	7
% International Students	13.6

Schools with Undergraduate Programs

A. Alfred Taubman College of Architecture and Urban Planning
Stephen M. Ross School of Business
School of Dentistry
School of Education
College of Engineering
School of Information
School of Kinesiology
College of Literature, Science, and the Arts (LSA)
School of Music, Theatre & Dance
School of Nursing
College of Pharmacy
School of Public Health
Gerald R. Ford School of Public Policy
Penny W. Stamps School of Art & Design

Might Also Consider...

Cornell University UPenn
University of North Carolina – Chapel Hill
WUSTL
University of Wisconsin-Madison

Michigan. The school's Honors Program for the School of Literature, Arts and Sciences gives 500 undergraduates the opportunity to participate in research during their first two years that formulates the foundation for pursuing independent research under the guidance of a faculty member for the Honors senior thesis. There are no courses required for all students at Michigan, but students in the School of Literature, Science, and the Arts must take classes in quantitative reasoning and race and ethnicity, a testament to the school's pride as a diverse community.

Career Development

The University of Michigan Class of 2013 graduates from the School of Literature, Science, and the Arts have an employment rate of 63.5 percent after graduation. About 30 percent of graduates from the LSA continued their education in graduate or professional studies, and approximately 6.1% are still seeking employment. Many graduates from Michigan tend to stay in the state of Michigan after graduation, as 44% of the Class of 2013 found employment in-state. The town of Ann Arbor hosts a number of options where students can work after graduation, including high tech, health services, and biotechnology firms. Prospective engineers may opt for internships at automobile manufacturers like General Motors or the Fuel Emissions Laboratory.

Campus Social Environment

Though about 64% of students at Michigan hail from the state of Michigan, the campus has a reputation of being incredibly diverse. One-fourth of total students enrolled at Michigan identify themselves as minorities. An AIC alum writes, "It is a big school with lots of students. So definitely it is fun and diverse. There are around 2000 Chinese students from freshmen to

Ph.D. here. It is impossible for you to know each of them. But you do make a lot of friends and know new people [everyday].” Parties are part of the norm at Michigan. “The biggest would be those events in clubs, secondly would be...[frat] parties and the smallest but most common are house parties.” With over 1500 organizations listed in the school directory, you can find just about any sort of club out there, including specialized organizations like the China Entrepreneur Network. Football is a focal point for students in the fall, bringing thousands of Wolverine fans together at Michigan Stadium on the weekends.

Selectivity

In recent year, Michigan has been less open regarding Chinese students, and acceptance rates have dropped significantly. Many Chinese students will be deferred or rejected during EA, and only those who truly demonstrate their interest in Michigan will get in, ever. Many who get into Michigan also receive offers from multiple prestigious schools.

Things to Consider

You'll like Michigan if...

◆ You'd like to be at a school with many Chinese students.

◆ You're interested in studying business or engineering.

Avoid Michigan if...

◆ You want a campus with palm trees. Bundle up for the harsh winters.

◆ You don't think you can handle the size of first year lectures.

AIC Alum Student Score Profiles

% AIC students accepted	14.1
Median SAT Critical Reading	690
Median SAT Math	800
Median SAT Writing	720
SAT Composite Score	2190
Median TOEFL	111

Financial Facts

Annual Tuition

$43476 USD (2015—2016 Freshman and Sophomore)

$46528 USD (2015—2016, Junior and Senior)

Financial Aid Availability Low

What Students say about the Location

Safe	3.5
Fun	2.5
Expensive	2.5
Good Chinese food	2.5
Public transportation	2
Bars and Clubs	2
Market/Grocery Options	1.5
Surrounding Job Market	2.5
Is Car Necessary?	3.5
Overall	3

*Out of four Stars

Climate

Average Temperature Range -5℃ to 22℃

Average Annual Precipitation 83.9cm

Average Annual Humidity 73.7%

Average Annual Average Snowfall 83.8cm

Transportation From China

Detroit Metropolitan airport is just half an hour from the school, and buses and shuttles are usually available to get to the airport. Direct flights are available from China.

University of North Carolina–Chapel Hill

CB#9100, 103 SOUTH BUILDING, CHAPEL HILL, NC 27599
WEBSITE: WWW.UNC.EDU
CHINA ADMISSION OFFICER: N/A
ADMISSION OFFICE PHONE NUMBER: 919-966-3621
ADMISSION OFFICE CONTACT: HTTP://ADMISSIONS.UNC.EDU/CONTACT-US/
CLOSEST MAJOR CITY: CHARLOTTE (2.5 HR DRIVING)

Best Fit Analysis

The first public university opened in the United States, UNC-Chapel Hill has maintained more than two centuries of academic excellence and is celebrated for being one of the best public institutions in the country. Dubbed the "Ideal College Town," Chapel Hill embraces the UNC community and has sprouted a series of local music bars, movie theatres, restaurants, and dancing venues that keep students entertained year round. UNC has excellent sports programs that play into the school's culture, especially the historical basketball rivalry between UNC and Duke, which is just a short bus ride away. UNC has a lot to offer its undergraduates if you can get past the large lectures and the fact that about 80 percent of students come from the state of North Carolina.

Academic Opportunities

UNC's academics compete with some of the most prestigious private universities in the U.S., earning the school the title as one of the "Public Ivies." Among UNC's stronger majors are Biology, Chemistry, English, International and Area Studies, and Philosophy. Prospective students interested in studying mathematics should take note of UNC's interdisciplinary major in Mathematical Decision Sciences, giving undergrads a background in probability, statistics, data analysis, and risk analysis for fields such as management science, biostatistics, and financial analysis. One AIC alum suggests that it's relatively hard to get an A at UNC, especially in the humanities. Though it's not uncommon for undergraduates at UNC to have some graduate students as instructors, an AICer writes, "Most of my classes are taught by professors. They are easily accessible if I have questions for them." Recently, entrepreneurship has become a buzzword at Chapel Hill. The Carolina Entrepreneurial Initiative (CEI) was created for the purpose of developing entrepreneur programs for both faculty and students. The initiative has been responsible for establishing the Carolina Challenge, a student-led business plan competition for UNC staff and students, and the entrepreneurship minor. UNC encourages its students engage themselves in research presented in the OUR Database of Research Opportunities. As is common with Duke and NC State students, students at UNC have readied access to positions at the Research Triangle Park.

At a Glance

US News Rank	#30
Location	Midwest
Type of School	Public
Environment	Suburban

Students

Total Undergrad Enrollment	18415 (2015)
# Applicants	31953 (2015)
% Admitted	30 (2015)
Male to Female Ratio	42/58
% International	3
% Asian	11.7

Schools with Undergraduate Programs

College of Arts and Sciences
School of Journalism and Mass Communication
Gillings School of Global Public Health
School of Dentistry
Kenan-Flagler Business School
School of Information and Library Science
School of Education
School of Nursing

You Might Also Consider...

Duke University
University of Virginia
UCLA
University of California – Berkeley
Northwestern

AIC Alum Student Score Profiles

% AIC students accepted	28.2
Median SAT Critical Reading	680
Median SAT Math	800
Median SAT Writing	700
SAT Composite Score	2170
Median TOEFL	109

Financial Facts

Annual Tuition
$ 33644 USD (2015—2016)
Financial Aid Availability Low

What Students say about the Location

Safe	3
Fun	2.5
Expensive	1.5
Good Chinese food	2
Public transportation	2
Bars and Clubs	2
Market/Grocery Options	2
Surrounding Job Market	2
Is Car Necessary?	3
Overall	3

*Out of four Stars

Climate

Average Temperature Range
3℃ to 26℃
Average Annual Precipitation
114.7cm
Average Annual Humidity
76.9%
Average Annual Snowfall
11.2cm

Transportation from China

Closest international airport nearby-Raleigh-Durham International Airport (20-minute drive). Unfortunately, no direct flights are available from China.

Career Development

Students interested in finance and banking can ground themselves in North Carolina, as the state ranked fourth in CNBC's list of "Top States for Business 2010." In the same vein, Charlotte, NC is the second largest banking center in the United States, the home of Bank of America, and one of the faster growing hubs in the country. About half of UNC's graduates end up finding employment in-state with organizations such as Bloomberg, Goldman Sachs, Credit Suisse, Ernst & Young, Teach for America, Deloitte Consulting, and many others. Within six months of graduation, 59.3% of the Class of 2013 were employed full-time, 24.7% were pursuing further education, 5.5% were employed part-time, and 8.9% were seeking employment.

Campus Social Environment

The Tar Heels, the name of UNC's sports teams, have a huge presence on campus. An AIC alum's comment captures the school's passion for athletics: "GO TAR HEELS! and go to [bleep] Duke University." As mandated by state law, 82% of UNC undergraduates must come from the state of North Carolina, but are generally considered friendly compared to students from the Northeast. But with a large student body, it's easy to find students who come from all over the world. "DIVERSITY is the top thing I like about UNC! Because this is a really huge school, there's so many opportunities for me... it's hard to describe in a few sentences," beams an AIC alum. Greek life isn't huge at UNC, but many organizations throw parties for their members and it's quite easy to find entertainment any night of the week. There are also two clubs in downtown Chapel Hill that students frequent if house parties start to become monotonous. Though there remains an infamous rivalry between Duke and UNC, students mingle and attend social gatherings at both schools via the convenience of a free shuttle that runs between the two campuses.

Selectivity

UNC accepts very few Chinese students each year, especially to their business school, even in comparison with colleges that are higher up in rank. Generally, students who can get into UNC, should also be able to get into many top 20 schools. High scores are a must. However, note that UNC's acceptance fluctuates year to year.

Things to Consider

You'll like UNC if...

- Bigger is better. With a large undergraduate student body, there's plenty to do here.
- You're looking for the perfect college town.
- You dislike Duke.

Avoid UNC if...

- You want small classes from the get go.
- You wouldn't consider staying in NC after graduation.
- You're a Duke fan.

University of Richmond

28 WESTHAMPTON WAY, RICHMOND, VA 23173
WEBSITE: WWW.RICHMOND.EDU
CHINA ADMISSIONS OFFICER: MARILYN HESSTER
AO PHONE NUMBER: 800-700-1662, 804-289-8640
AO EMAIL ADDRESS: MHESSER@RICHMOND.EDU
CLOSEST MAJOR CITY: WASHINGTON, DC., ABOUT A 2.5 HOURS DRIVE AWAY

Best Fit Analysis

Known for its business and leadership schools, the University of Richmond is unique in its academic offerings. Those who seek opportunities in finance sectors will benefit from the alumni network and reputation here. Still, students should be forewarned that their peers at Richmond may not be very knowledgeable about foreign cultures, and should be proactive about seeking friendships and sharing their perspectives. Partying is no stranger to UR, and if you plan to come here, be prepared to be exposed to inebriated people and party culture (Richmond also is considered a campus with a strong drug presence). Also, students who seek comfortable weather west of California, here is your holy grail.

Academic Opportunities

Robins School of Business ranks in the top 20 of undergraduate business schools and is the only one of that bracket that is part of an LAC. It offers majors in accounting, economics, finance, international business, marketing, and management. Unsurprisingly, these are some of the strongest programs at Richmond along with leadership studies, biology, accounting, international studies, and political science.

At Richmond, professors are the ones who teach the classes, allowing for very intimate scholastic settings. In addition, the Core at Richmond is sweeping set of requirements, encompassing multiple disciplines and requiring proficiency in at least one other language. Highly motivated students interested in math and the sciences and planning to pursue a career in the STEM disciplines can, through the Grainger Initiative, receive financial support for summer research projects and travel to conferences and symposiums to present their research.

At a Glance

US News Rank	#32
Location	Mid Atlantic
Type of School	Private
Environment	Suburban

Students

Total Undergrad Enrollment	2990 (2015)
# Applicants	9977 (2015)
% Accepted	31 (2015)
Male to Female Ratio	52/48
% International Students	10
% Asian American	6

Schools with Undergraduate Programs

School of Arts and Sciences
Jepson School of Leadership Studies
Robins School of Business

You Might Also Consider...

University of Virginia
Boston College
William and Mary
Washington and Lee
Georgetown

Career Development

Richmond had a 94% employment rate within the 2013 seniors, which increases to 95% within the year. The average salary is about 40000-44999. 25% of the population looked to further education, with another 8% planning on applying. Of those who chose industry, the most popular sectors were education, finance, marketing, consulting, accounting, healthcare, and science and research. PricewaterhouseCoopers and JP Morgan Chase are popular clients of Richmond students. The alumni network is reportedly very strong, especially those who hail from the business and leadership schools.

AIC Alum Student Score Profiles

% Accepted	45.9
Median SAT Critical Reading	660
Median SAT Math	800
Median SAT Writing	670
Median SAT Composite Score	2140
Median TOEFL	109

Financial Facts

Annual Tuition
$48090 USD (2015—2016)
Financial Aid Availability Very Low

What Students say about the Location

Safe	4
Fun	3
Expensive	2
Chinese food	2
Transportation	3
Bars and Clubs	3
Market/Grocery Options	2
Surrounding Job Market	2
Necessity of Car	3.5
Overall	3

*Out of four

Climate

Average Temperature Range
2℃ to 26℃
Average Annual Precipitation
110.8cm
Average Annual Humidity
72.25%
Average Annual Snowfall
22.7cm

Transportation from China

There are no direct flights from China to Richmond. Students will likely have to catch a layover before arriving at Reagan National Airport in Washington, D.C. They may then opt to fly to Richmond National Airport or take a Greyhound bus, which will get them to the city in under three hours.

Campus Social Environment

Richmond has a plethora of fun traditions, such as Investiture/Proclamation Night, a night of reflection for freshmen, as well as Ring Dance, held by junior women, and the Pig Roast in the Spring. Diversity is not a strength at Richmond, with African Americans representing 7% of the student population, Asian Americans and Hispanics each claim 6%, with white, Caucasian students as the majority. Greek life facilitates social life on campus, with 33% of men and 44% of women involved. Its prevalence becomes logical once you consider how little nightlife the surrounding neighborhood offers its residents. Many parties happen in senior apartments called "lodges", and most alcoholic gatherings occur on campus. UR fraternity parties are not exclusive to members (restrictions that exist in fraternities at many other colleges), and provide free alcohol for everyone. Downtown Richmond allows for more rowdy late-night festivities, and numerous shuttles and buses simplify the commute.

Selectivity

The business programs at Richmond are typically harder to get into than others. Applicants from China often fare better if their SAT scores are over 2000 and have demonstrated to the admissions committee that they were active in their high school communities.

Things to Consider

You'll like University of Richmond if…

- You want to study business, but also hope to have a close college community.
- You are an outgoing individual.
- You could see yourself hiking and camping in the beautiful Shenandoah Valley of Virginia.

Avoid University of Richmond if…

- You're looking for an institution with a prominent brand name.
- You're looking for an LAC with regional diversity. Though UR has a number of international students, there are a solid percentage of students who come from the state of Virginia.

University of Rochester

500 JOSEPH C. WILSON BLVD., ROCHESTER, NY 14627
WEBSITE: WWW.ROCHESTER.EDU
ADMISSION OFFICE PHONE NUMBER: : 585-275-3221
CHINA ADMISSION OFFICER: PATRITIA TOPORZYCKI (HEILONGJIANG, JINLIN, AND WESTERN PROVINCES)
AO EMAIL ADDRESS: PTOPORZYCKI@ADMISSIONS.ROCHESTER.EDU
CHINA ADMISSION OFFICER: SARAH CANNY (LIAONING)
AO EMAIL ADDRESS: SARAH.CANNY@ROCHESTER.EDU
CHINA ADMISSION OFFICER: CLAUDIA GONZALEZ SALINAS (HEBEI AND TIANJIN)
AO EMAIL ADDRESS: CGONZALEZ@ADMISSIONS.ROCHESTER.EDU
CHINA ADMISSION OFFICER: ISTHIER CHAUDHURY (BEIJING, QINGDAO, AND SHANGHAI)
AO EMAIL ADDRESS: ICHAUDHURY@ADMISSIONS.ROCHESTER.EDU
CHINA ADMISSION OFFICER: CHRIS ANTAL (CITIES IN SHANDONG OTHER THAN QINGDAO)
AO EMAIL ADDRESS: CHRIS.ANTAL@ROCHESTER.EDU
CHINA ADMISSION OFFICER: DAMIAN GARCIA (HENAN, SHANXI, GUANGDONG, HAINAN AND MACAU)
AO EMAIL ADDRESS: DAMIAN.GARCIA@ROCHESTER.EDU
CHINA ADMISSION OFFICER: ANDRE MCKANZIE (JIANGSU)
AO EMAIL ADDRESS: ANDRE.MCKANZIE@ROCHESTER.EDU
CHINA ADMISSION OFFICER: ZACK TASCHMAN (ZHEJIANG, ANHUI, GUANGXI, GUIZHOU, CHONGQING, AND HONGKONG)
AO EMAIL ADDRESS: ZTASCHMAN@ADMISSIONS.ROCHESTER.EDU
CHINA ADMISSION OFFICER: KIM CRAGG (FUJIAN, JIANGXI, AND HUNAN)
AO EMAIL ADDRESS: KCRAGG@ADMISSIONS.ROCHESTER.EDU
CHINA ADMISSION OFFICER: KARIME NAIME (HUBEI)
AO EMAIL ADDRESS: KARIME.NAIME@ROCHESTER.EDU
CLOSEST MAJOR CITY: ROCHESTER, NY

Best Fit Analysis

The University of Rochester, known for its particularly brutal winters, is a private university located in Upstate New York and offers students a unique undergraduate curriculum that's both challenging and academically engaging. With a campus that combines modern infrastructure with Greek revival and Georgian Colonial styles, Chinese students will love on-campus housing and find a tight residential community here. Despite the rigorous academic environment you'll fit right in if your friends tell you that you're kind, open-minded, laid-back and willing to have fun. If you're willing to put up with months of snow and frigid temperatures for an exceptional academic experience, then Rochester might be an option for you.

Academic Opportunities

Students who want to explore their options will appreciate that Rochester doesn't actually have a system for general education course requirements and encourages students to design their own majors. Among Rochester's most notable programs are its premedical track and Music major, offered through the Eastman School of Music. The Rochester Curriculum, a true selling point for prospective students, has students in Arts, Sciences, and Engineering select a major in one of three divisions of learning in natural science, social science, and humanities. Students then must complete a "cluster," or a series of three related courses, in each of the two other divisions. Former AIC students praise the school's professors for their availability. One writes,

At a Glance

US News Rank	#33
Location	Northeast
Type of School	Private
Environment	Suburban

Students

Total Undergrad Enrollment	6046 (2015)
# Applicants	16390 (2015)
% Accepted	35 (2015)
Male to Female Ratio	49/51
% International	16.8
% Asian	10.3

Schools with Undergraduate Programs

College of Arts, Sciences & Engineering
Eastman School of Music

You Might Also Consider...

Brown University
Tufts University
Cornell University
Boston University
Washington University in St. Louis

AIC Alum Student Score Profiles

% AIC students accepted	34.3
Median SAT Critical Reading	665
Median SAT Math	800
Median SAT Writing	670
SAT Composite Score	2075
Median TOEFL	108.5

Financial Facts

Annual Tuition
$47450 USD (2015—2016)
Financial Aid Availability Very Low

What Students say about the Location

Safe	3
Fun	2.5
Expensive	3
Good Chinese food	2.5
Public transportation	1.5
Bars and Clubs	1.5
Market/Grocery Options	2
Surrounding Job Market	2
Is Car Necessary?	3
Overall	2.5

*Out of four

Climate

Average Temperature Range
-4℃ to 22℃
Average Annual Precipitation
86cm
Average Annual Humidity
75.7%
Average Annual Snowfall
120.2cm

Transportation from China

Greater Rochester International Airport is very close by, just a short cab ride away. No direct flights available.

"As far as I know, all the undergraduate classes are taught by professors. And I can get a hold of my professors if I need them. There are office hours available and I can email them with my questions." If you're interested in Physics and Astronomy, you can take part in the Research Experience in Physics and Astronomy for Undergraduates (REUs), one of the many research options. Over 75 percent of students are involved in undergraduate research at Rochester. Rochester additionally offers the most competitive undergraduate candidates guaranteed admission to professional or graduate school after completion of the bachelor's degree in business (REBS), engineering (GEAR), medicine (REMS) or education (GRADE). The Take Five program lets stellar students explore interests outside their major in a tuition-free fifth year.

Career Development

Students who graduate from Rochester with career interests in Optics, Computer Science, Medicine, Finance, and Music often have a competitive edge. Statistics from the Class of 2011 indicate that Rochester alumni fare well in life after graduation. One report reveals that one year after commencement for the Class of 2011, 12% were attending graduate/professional school and working, 29% were attending or had completed graduate/professional schools, and 46% were employed or interning within their desired career field. Over 90% of Rochester students participate in internships.

Campus Social Environment

Despite the fact that about 40 percent of

Rochester students hail from New York State, the campus is known for its diverse student body, with about 11% of students identifying as Asian American. The class of 2018 is very diverse with about a 1/4th of its students being international. "The school is not big at all and we have a lot of international students. In my German class there are only 16 students...and we have 9 Chinese students." Rochester doesn't have a huge party scene, but there is a dominant Greek life presence that the university recognizes (around 40% of the student body is involved) and is responsible for hosting some of the larger off-campus events year round. Every year, the Eastman School of Music, consistently ranked as one of the best graduate school of music in the country, brings in world-renowned performers that students can enjoy viewing. The surrounding city isn't the most exciting, generally described as being quiet but not dead, it offers students opportunities for off-campus recreation, such as hanging out on beaches of Lake Ontario or visiting the International Photography Museum. Our AIC correspondent vehemently shares "GET A CAR!!!" Rochester has been nationally lauded for the high percentage of student volunteers it cultivates, represented by the annual Wilson Day that encourages new and incoming students to participate in community-related events.

Selectivity

Rochester isn't the most selective of schools, even with its notable academic reputation. Prospective students tend to have better success gaining admittance to Rochester with an SAT over 2100 and many instances of community involvement.

Things to Consider

You'll like Rochester if...

- On-campus housing is really important to you. Rochester has some great facilities.
- You are intending on studying premed, Music, or Chemical Engineering.
- Flexibility of curriculum is a must.

Avoid Rochester if...

- Snow is your kryptonite. Get ready for meters upon meters of it at Rochester.
- You want a name brand school. Rochester doesn't carry the international reputation of other schools in its tier.

University of Southern California

UUNIVERSITY PARK; LOS ANGELES, CA 90089
WEBSITE.USC.EDU
CHINA ADMISSIONS OFFICER: AARON BROWN
AO PHONE NUMBER: 213-821-1882
AO EMAIL ADDRESS: AARONBRO@USC.EDU
CLOSEST MAJOR CITY: LOS ANGELES, CA

Best Fit Analysis

Although some scorn the University of Southern California for its "athlete, Greek, rich kid" stereotype, with 18000 students, it's really big enough to encompass a much wider range of profiles. Nestled in the heart of a city that never sees snow, USC is a school that's hard to find fault in. Students who love USC learn to appreciate the large party and sport scene as well as the academic rigor.

Academic Opportunities

USC has slowly climbed the rankings and today rests firmly at number 23 in US News & World Report's books. It's a number that also reflects its nationwide acceptance rate, and how tough it is to earn the right to be a Trojan. However, once accepted, USC takes students under its wing and offers nourishment for the curious intellectual soul, with the well-developed Undergraduate Research Associates Program. With 15 professional schools, there's no limit to the kinds of training that prepare USC grads for the workforce and beyond. In fact, USC plans to open up a new school for dancing in a year. Particularly worth noting are the Annenberg School for Communications, Marshall School of Business, and School of Cinematic Arts. Transferring between schools is not always an easy task, especially for the schools that train the artistic mind. The Marshall School of Business and the Viterbi School of Engineering are rumored to be easier to matriculate into. AIC Students don't mind the workload, but those in architecture programs lament, "It is pretty hard to get A in architecture classes." In general, students find the environment collaborative and motivating.

Career Development

Although USC isn't the smallest of private schools, it makes up for size with an ironbound alumni network. AIC Trojans explain, "[USC] alumni...[are] quite strong, especially in Asia." Another agrees, "Also, there are alumni career fairs when alumni give jobs to students." It's a resource that enhances the advantage students already have from being in a distinguished American city which companies from all industries claim territory in. USC students have access to all the resources that Los Angeles country offers from investment banking firms such as Goldman Sachs, the Big Four Consulting firms and wealth management companies such as AXA Advisors. Additionally, many USC

At a Glance

US News Rank	#23
Location	West Coast
Type of School	Private
Environment	Urban

Students

Total Undergrad Enrollment	19000 (2015)
# Applied	51925 (2015)
% Accepted	18 (2015)
Male to Female Ratio	50/50
% International Students	24
% Asian American	18

Schools with Undergraduate Programs

Dornsife College of Letters, Arts and Sciences
School of Architecture
Roski School of Art and Design
Marshall School of Business
School of Cinematic Arts
Ostrow School of Dentistry
Annenberg School for Communications and Journalism
School of Dramatic Arts
Viterbi School of Engineering
Davis School of Gerontology
Keck School of Medicine
Thornton School of Music
Price School of Public Policy,
Kaufman School of Dance
USC Chan Division of Occupational Science and Occupational Therapy
Iovine and Young Academy

You Might Also Consider...

Duke	Boston College
UPenn	Northwestern
Georgetown	

AIC Alum Student Score Profiles

% Accepted	40.4
Median SAT Critical Reading	710
Median SAT Math	800
Media SAT Writing	720
Median SAT Composite Score	2180
Median TOEFL	108

Financial Facts

Annual Tuition
$49464 USD (2015—2016)
Financial Aid Availability Medium

What Students say about the Location

Safe	2
Fun	3
Expensive	3.5
Chinese food	3
Transportation	1.5
Bars and Clubs	3
Market/Grocery Options	2.5
Surrounding Job Market	3
Necessity of Car	4
Overall	3

*Out of four

Climate

Average Temperature Range
18℃ to 27℃
Average Annual Precipitation
44.9cm
Average Annual Humidity
75.54%
Average Annual Snowfall
0cm

Transportation from China

Flights from China: HKG to LAX; PEK to LAX; PVG to LAX. Shuttles from LAX take about 30 minutes without traffic to reach USC's campus.

grads take up jobs in the entertainment industry due to the school's close proximity to large companies such as Disney. In the area, USC's Marshall School of Business is the best in business training. There is a general pre-professional outlook and expect to find healthy support if you hope to join corporate ranks in banking and consulting industries.

Campus Social Environment

The large numbers of students doesn't bother USC students much. For example, one of our AIC alumni observed, "In terms of student body, it is kind of crowded, but the campus size is just awesome. It usually takes 10-15 minutes to walk through the campus. Everywhere is within walking distance, but a bike/skateboard is preferred." Students love the surrounding city as much as the actual campus, stating, "School offers various events, from concerts to film screenings and panels," but everyone we polled believed that a car was vital to explore all the options that Los Angeles has to offer. The student body is open-minded and diverse, with the greatest racial majority being Caucasian but only representing 40% of the demographics chart. There are 3000 students at USC from China this year, and that helps to explain why many AIC alumni estimate their friend circle to be mostly Chinese. Although USC is known for its' vibrant Greek life, as this is a fundamental source for partying, only about 30% of students participate in fraternities or sororities. One AIC student discloses, "You can always get alcohol if you want to, but you don't really have to if you don't want to."

Selectivity

USC students tend to take students with SAT's in the 2100-2200 range. Student applying to the pre-professional schools, such as the Viterbi School of Engineering or School of Cinematic Arts, are advised to get involved in activities related to their intended major during high school.

Things to Consider

You'll like USC if...

- You hope to utilize school networks after graduation.
- Mexican and American food appeal to your taste buds.
- You love football.
- You're interested in Cinema, Architecture, Business, or Communications.

Avoid USC if...

- You have a strong aversion to Greek life.
- You don't like being situated in the center of a big city.
- You need to see snow, ice, and wouldn't mind shivering from extreme cold from time to time.

University of Virginia

PEABODY HALL, MCCORMICK ROAD, CHARLOTTESVILLE, VA 22904
WEBSITE: WWW.VIRGINIA.EDU
CHINA ADMISSIONS OFFICER: SENEM KUDAT WARD
AO EMAIL ADDRESS: SDO5S@VIRGINIA.EDU
ADMISSION OFFICE PHONE NUMBER: 434-982-3200
CLOSEST MAJOR CITY: WASHINGTON, D.C.; FROM THERE CHARLOTTESVILLE IS ACCESSIBLE VIA AIRPORT, AMTRAK OR BUS (2+ HOURS)

Best Fit Analysis

Along with UCLA, UC Berkeley, UMichigan, and UNC—Chapel Hill, the University of Virginia consistently ranks among the most prestigious public institutions of higher education in the United States. Though state law requires that the University of Virginia build 70% of its undergraduate student body from Virginia, AIC students have labeled the school as "very diverse," with international students hailing from more than 150 countries. Housing strong academic programs in business, English, foreign languages such as Spanish, and Political Science all boast strong faculty and student resources. Although the University of Virginia is located in a suburban town more than two hours away from Washington, D.C., students praise the campus for its liveliness and school spirit. Prospective students of UVA should be aware of the school's party reputation, as you'll have the chance to "party everyday if you want," according to a AIC alum.

Academic Opportunities

Perhaps one of UVA's greatest draws is its undergraduate business school, known as the McIntire School of Commerce, currently ranked as the 5th best undergraduate business school by U.S. News & World Report. Direct admission to McIntire as an incoming freshman, however, is not an option. Prospective students must apply to transfer into the business school during their sophomore year. Historically, the GPA average for students accepted into McIntire hovers around 3.8. UVA rewards academic diligence in a myriad of ways. Incoming freshmen in the College of Arts and Sciences have the opportunity to be nominated for the Echols Scholar Program, which permits students to have greater access to courses and have special freedom from some requirements so that they may design unique programs. The School of Engineering and Applied Sciences offers the Rodman Scholars Program to the top students of each engineering class and places students in a unique curriculum of 1-credit seminars that students may choose to develop their engineering and leadership skills. Because of UVA's large selection of professors and classes that are available to the undergraduate student body, many AIC alum claim that getting A's at the university, "Depends on [how] the professors grade. It's not hard if you work hard." The honor system at UVA is strict—students who are caught lying, cheating, or stealing may be dismissed from campus with just a single infraction. Students find a good work-life balance at UVA between the manageable workload and helpful faculty.

At a Glance

US News Rank	#26
Location	Mid-Atlantic
Type of School	Public
Environment	Suburban

Students

Total Undergrad Enrollment	15669 (2015)
# Applicants	31107 (2015)
% Accepted	29 (2015)
Male to Female Ratio	44/56
% International	8.8
% Asian	12.5

Schools with Undergraduate Programs

School of Architecture
College of Arts and Sciences
Curry School of Education
School of Engineering and Applied Science
McIntire School of Commerce
School of Nursing
Frank Batten School of Leadership and Public Policy

You Might Also Consider...

Duke
College of William and Mary
UPenn
UNC-Chapel Hill
Georgetown University

AIC Alum Student Score Profiles

% AIC students accepted	25.7
Median SAT Critical Reading	730
Median SAT Math	800
Median SAT Writing	750
Median SAT Composite Score	2230
Median TOEFL	112

Financial Facts

Annual Tuition	$40506 USD (2015—2016)
Financial Aid Availability	Low

What Students say about the Location

Safe	3.5
Fun	2.5
Expensive	1.5
Good Chinese food	2.5
Public transportation	2
Bars and Clubs	2
Market/Grocery Options	2
Surrounding Job Market	2.5
Is Car Necessary?	3.5
Overall	3

*Out of four Stars

Climate

Average Temperature Range	1℃ to 24℃
Average Annual Precipitation	114cm
Average Annual Humidity	76.3%
Average Annual Snowfall	47.4cm

Transportation from China

Inconvenient; only a small airport nearby with some expensive domestic fares. Charlottesville-Ablemarle Airport has no direct flights to China. Take a cab from there for $30 to get to campus.

Career Development

UVA's McIntire School of Commerce reports that 98% of the undergraduate Class of 2013 had indicated that they'd accepted a job offer, were enrolled in graduate school, or were currently not in the job market, and the median base salary for the class was estimated to be $70000 USD. A staggering 28.4% of 2013 alums entered the work force with employment at investment banks, while 24.8% of the class opted for jobs at consulting firms. Students in other undergraduate schools can connect with university alumni who have volunteered to serve as mentors and networking assistants through the University Career Assistance Network, otherwise known as UCAN. Engineering alumni also fare well financially, especially in the Washington, D.C. area. The median starting salary for the undergraduate Class of 2013 for the School of Engineering and Applied Sciences is listed at $66323 by the university website. The career fairs and center resources are more useful than the alumni network, especially since it is so large.

Campus Social Environment

Though UVA remains one of the most prestigious public institutions in the United States, students find relief from their workload through UVA's energetic social scene. According to an AIC alumnus, "UVA...[does] have small parties everyday. But for large [school-sponsored] parties, say larger than 200 people, like once a month." Undergraduate students at UVA are typically associated with preppiness, and fraternities play a major role in the school's social culture but students tell us "The community is very nice." Students at UVA rally around the school's Division I Men's Football team, known colloquially as the "Wahoos", but one AIC alum laments that the football program is currently not very strong. Still, UVA students often attend games just to support and serious sports enthusiasts can consider the lacrosse, swimming, or basketball scene. Some AIC alumni prefer the fun town, some prefer the campus vibe instead; suffice to say, there is enough to do in both locations. The surrounding town offers many outdoors nature activities for the active, but it's not easy to get places without a car. Traditions at UVA are an important component of the school's culture, and range from calling the main quad the "Lawn" and vying for housing options on it, referring to the university campus as the "Grounds," singing "The Good Old Song," participating in secrete societies, among many, many others. In addition, the Honor Code creates a community of trust at UVA, where students feel comfortable leaving their valuables lying around in plain sight. Chinese students will easily find a large community of international Chinese students at the school.

Selectivity

Students should be active community leaders in high school and have taken a rigorous curriculum. Average SAT scores fall within the 2100-2300 range.

Things to Consider

You'll like UVA University if...

◆ You intend on studying business.

◆ Greek life doesn't faze you.

Avoid UVA if...

◆ You intend on studying business but want to start in your first year rather than waiting till your third year.

◆ Can't muster the strength to deal with all the preppiness.

University of Wisconsin–Madison

702 W JOHNSON ST #1101, MADISON, WI 53715
WEBSITE: WWW.WISC.EDU
CHINA ADMISSION OFFICER: N/A
ADMISSIONS OFFICE EMAIL ADDRESS: ONWISCONSIN@ADMISSIONS.EDU
ADMISSIONS OFFICE PHONE NUMBER: 608-262-3961
CLOSEST MAJOR CITY: CHICAGO, A 3-4 HOUR BUS RIDE OR CAR RIDE TO MADISON, WI

Best Fit Analysis

Though its not as familiar to Chinese international students as the University of Michigan, the University of Wisconsin-Madison feels very much like its neighbor in Ann Arbor. A large public university located in one of the best college towns in the United States, students at Wisconsin are considered down to Earth and welcoming to international students, who make up 7% of the undergraduate student body. Badgers, or Wisconsin students, are academically capable but put just as much effort into fostering a lively social scene. Students here feel a lot of pride in attending the flagship university of the state of Wisconsin, but if you can't handle the blistering chill of Madison winters, you might want to reconsider your applications.

Academic Opportunities

Seventy programs at Wisconsin rank in top ten lists nationally. Popular majors include political science, biology, economics and history, while the schools most notable fields of study are education, agriculture, biological sciences, social studies, and communication. With almost 30000 undergrads, classes can be overcrowded for first- and second-year students, and popularity among programs in engineering and business have led the university to limit the number of students wishing to enter these fields with strict GPA requirements. Emphasizing Wisconsin's commitment to educating its undergraduates in quantitative reasoning, communication, and ethnic studies, students are required to fulfill requirements in all three fields prior to graduation. Students who fear the chaos of a large research university can apply to First-Year Interest Groups that pairs 20 students together in the same residence hall and has them enroll in a cluster of three smaller classes together. Grading at Wisconsin can be tough in the sciences, as an AIC alum notes that only the top 15% of the class receives As on the curve.

At a Glance

US News Rank	#41
Location	Midwest
Type of School	Public
Environment	Urban

Students

Total Undergrad Enrollment	29580 (2015)
# Applicants	32780 (2015)
% Accepted	49.2 (2015)
Male to Female Ratio	49/51
% International Students	7
% Asian	6.7

Schools with Undergraduate Programs

College of Agricultural and Life Sciences
Wisconsin School of Business
School of Education
College of Engineering
School of Human Ecology
College of Letters & Science
School of Nursing
School of Pharmacy

You Might Also Consider...

Northwestern	UIUC
UMichigan	University of Virginia
Boston University	Indiana

Career Development

With so many undergraduate academic opportunities at Wisconsin, it's not a surprise that students feed into a wide variety of career paths after graduation. About 64% of graduates from the Class of 2013 worked full time directly after graduation, while 24% of the class attended graduate school full-time. Among those who graduated with degrees in Mechanical Engineering, 88% went directly into the work force, a significant contrast from the 61% of English majors who gained employment upon graduating. Some top employers for Wisconsin grads include Boeing, KPMG, Deloitte, Ernst & Young,

AIC Alum Student Score Profiles

% AIC students accepted	61.2
Median SAT Critical Reading	590
Median SAT Math	780
Median SAT Writing	660
Median SAT Composite Score	2010
Median TOEFL	104

Financial Facts

Annual Tuition
$29665 USD (2015—2016)
Financial Aid Availability Very Low

What Students say about the Location

Safe	4
Fun	2.5
Expensive	1.5
Good Chinese food	3
Public transportation	2.5
Bars and Clubs	2.5
Market/Grocery Options	2.5
Surrounding Job Market	2
Is Car Necessary?	3.5
Overall	3.5

*Out of four Stars

Climate

Average Temperature Range
–8℃ to 22℃
Average Annual Precipitation
89.5cm
Average Annual Humidity
78.24%
Average Annual Snowfall
98.6cm

Transportation from China

There are no direct flights from China. Students can fly into Chicago O'Hare International Airport. Flight options include: HKG to ORD; PEK to ORD; PVG to ORD. Buses from Chicago to Madison take about four hours.

Facebook, among many others.

Badgers have life-long access to career development resources such as individual consultations, workshops and resume reviews, not to mention access to a vibrant alumni community with 3 active chapters in China and dozens more spread across the world.

Campus Social Environment

As expected, many of Wisconsin's students are Cheeseheads (e.g.: they hail from Wisconsin). But with seven percent of the undergraduate student body identifying as international citizens, "[Wisconsin] can not be more diverse," according to an AIC alum. Compared with peer institutions, Wisconsin does not have an overwhelming presence of Asian Americans on campus, but former AIC students who are now Badgers remark that "most friends are Chinese students." Madison, WI packs a lot of punch for its size of 200000 people. Located in one of the greatest college towns in America (alongside other staples such as Ann Arbor and Chapel Hill), students at Wisconsin rave about the nightlife and can find bar events and on-campus parties that cater to students almost every night of the week. It, of course, helps that the surrounding community is highly supportive of the Wisconsin Badgers sports programs, in which students with painted faces crowd together to cheer on the football and hockey teams. Sports, in general, are big at Wisconsin. An AIC alum writes, "People play sports. There are sports clubs surfing and boating on the lake of Mendota. There are huge courts for people to play football, lacrosse and soccer."

Selectivity

Despite being one of the strongest public institutions in the United States, admission to Wisconsin is not highly selective. Hundreds of Chinese students are admitted every year.

Things to Consider

You'll like Wisconsin if...

- You want a vibrant social life both on and off campus. Prepare to party at Wisconsin.
- You're looking for a university with prime resources for the biological sciences.
- The "Rah-Rah-Rah"ing associated with strong school spirit is important to you.

Avoid Wisconsin if...

- Thinking about below freezing weather gives you the chills.
- You think you'll get distracted from your academics by the all the opportunities to have fun.

Vassar College

124 RAYMOND AVENUE, POUGHEPSIE, NY 12604
WEBSITE: WWW.VASSAR.EDU
CHINA ADMISSIONS OFFICER: SARAH FISCHER
ADMISSION OFFICE PHONE NUMBER: 845-437-7300
ADMISSION OFFICE EMAIL ADDRESS: ADMISSIONS@VASSAR.EDU
CLOSEST MAJOR CITY: NEW YORK CITY, UNDER TWO HOURS BY BUS OR ABOUT 1 HOUR AND 40 MINUTES BY TRAIN

Best Fit Analysis

Students at Vassar may find themselves questioning their choice during the abrasive winter periods of Poughkeepsie. But aside from that, those who are looking for academic freedom, and know they want to test the limits of their knowledge and the curriculum they are provided with, should find few bones to pick with Vassar, which provides multiple inter-department majors, and allows students to define their own majors. Additionally, those looking for a closer knit college learning environment will find Vassar very appealing. However; if you are a female and hoping for a college boyfriend, Vassar can disappoint with an unfair sex ratio and little interaction with other colleges. In addition, those who don't need to wander off campus too often will not mind the contrast between Vassar's vivacious campus life with that of its surrounding town.

Academic Opportunities

Vassar may not be a large school and has no engineering department, but if students take advantage of the engineering dual-degree program with Dartmouth, they will have the same opportunities as other students from large research universities. In addition, students can further their understanding of drama at the National Theatre Institute via a partnership with Conn College. Within Vassar, English, Political Science, Psychology, Biology, History, Economics, Film and Theater, and Art History are highly acclaimed majors, but not the only ones. There is no core in Vassar, although there are a few requirements in foreign language and quantitative analysis. Professors not only teach all classes, but also live in the dorms, providing a lot of interaction between students and their teachers. AIC students find the environment cooperative, yet nonetheless, getting A's can be difficult and grading curves are unusual.

At a Glance

US News Rank	#12
Location	Northeast
Type of School	Private
Environment	Suburban

Students

Total Undergrad Enrollment	2450 (2015)
# Applicants	7567 (2015)
% Accepted	25.7 (2015)
Male to Female Ratio	44/56
% International Students	14
% Asian	15

You Might Also Consider...

Brown University	Skidmore
Wesleyan University	Bard College
Haverford College	

Career Development

IBM is located in Poughkeepsie, so it often recruits there. Other top employers are AC Nielsen, Federal Reserve, Japan Exchange and Teaching, many NYC law firms, NY Board of Education, NYC District Attorney, NY Publishing firms, US Department of Justice, and Peace Corps. 64.3% of students are employed, while 12% pursued advanced degrees after college according to a previous survey. Outside internships during the academic school year are coordinated through the Field Work Office. Every year, about 500 Vassar students place themselves in various opportunities in businesses, government agencies, and community organizations, giving them a leg up on students with similar profile for prestigious summer internships in New York City. As a result of the school's size, the Vassar alumni network fails in comparison to the networks of schools such as Dartmouth and Brown.

AIC Alum Student Score Profiles*

% Accepted	21.4
Median SAT Critical Reading	680
Median SAT Math	800
Median SAT Writing	710
Median SAT Composite Score	2190
Median TOEFL	110

Financial Facts

Annual Tuition
$50550 USD (2015—2016)

Financial Aid Availability Very Low

What Students say about the Location

Safe	2
Fun	1
Expensive	3
Chinese food	1
Transportation	1
Bars and Clubs	1
Market/Grocery Options	2
Surrounding Job Market	1
Necessity of Car	4
Overall	2

*Out of four Stars

Climate

Average Temperature Range
-5℃ to20℃

Average Annual Precipitation
125.5cm

Average Annual Humidity
79.90%

Average Annual Snowfall
89.4cm

Transportation from China

There are no direct flights from China. Students can fly into New York City's JFK International Airport and then take a bus or train to Poughkeepsie, which will take under 2 hours.

Campus Social Environment

One student says "it feels a bit small, with more Chinese students every year." In addition, most students find Poughkeepsie limiting (also not the safest) with few transportation options to get around, but this is offset by easy access to New York City. There are no RA's so students have a lot of freedom in the dorms. Greek life doesn't exist, but there are 1000 registered campus events every year. Vassar is also home to over 150 unique student organizations such as archery and ball-room dancing. Outsiders generalize Vassar students as a mix of liberal, hippie middle class and upper middle class students, and the truth is, Vassar could be more diverse. Of its American students, 15% are Asian American, 9% are Hispanic, and 6% are African Americans. Only 24% are In-State. The sports scene isn't the largest, but women's rugby and men's baseball are popular, and the uneven sex ratio (56% women) can be disconcerting.

Students interested in quality quaint and outdoor activities can find means of entertainment in Poughkeepsie. The Catskills, a mountain range not far from campus, opens up the possibilities for hiking and camping on the weekends. Smaller nightlife options, such as The Chance music joint, allow students to unwind after a week of rigorous academic and extracurricular demands.

Selectivity

Vassar is small, and as such, only invites several Chinese international students to join its freshman class every year. Getting in ED is likely your best shot and indicating Vassar's flexible liberal arts curriculum doesn't hurt, either.

Things to Consider

You'll like Vassar if…

- You don't mind sober partying.
- You expect most social events to be on campus.

Avoid Vassar if…

- You want to be in a large American city.
- You want to be close to an international Chinese student community.
- You are looking for ethnic diversity.
- You want the full college experience of huge sporting events and campus wide rallies.

Wellesley College

106 CENTRAL STREET, WELLESLEY, MA 02481
WEBSITE: WWW.WELLESLEY.EDU
CHINA ADMISSIONS OFFICER: MILENA MAREVA
ADMISSION OFFICE PHONE NUMBER: 781-238-2270
AO EMAIL ADDRESS: MMAREVA@WELLESLEY.EDU
CLOSEST MAJOR CITY: BOSTON

Best Fit Analysis

Wellesley is one of the few Liberal Arts Colleges that has nurtured a reputation for itself globally. Located just outside of Boston, it is known for its beautiful campus as well as highly acclaimed and well-developed academic departments. Students looking to train in the science fields will find Wellesley to be both accommodating and enabling. Type A personalities would be motivated by the intellect and ambition of the Wellesley admits. Students who might want to test out the college party scene will be disappointed here, but those who value quiet and safety more will find the nearby town satisfying.

Academic Opportunities

With the second oldest physics lab in the nation, it's a no brainer that the school sports a recognized science program. Its strength in the sciences is matched by that of its economics and art history programs, which have reputations few can compete with. Wellesley has an established cross registration program with MIT and Harvard, as well as Babson, Brandeis, and Olin College, where Wellesley's women can come in contact with male peers as well as have access to academic courses at 5 other colleges for the price of one. As part of the Twelve College Exchange Program, students can experience a year at one of the participating colleges without actually transferring. AIC students praise quality of teaching, stating classes are "all taught by professors and they do really care," while observing their peers can be competitive, which can be occasionally depressing. In addition, students who want to receive an A will have to put in "a lot" of effort. Classes are usually only 12-14 students.

At a Glance

US News Rank	#4
Location	Northeast
Type of School	Private
Environment	Suburban

Students

Total Undergrad Enrollment	2474 (2014)
# Applicants	4623 (2015)
% Accepted	30 (2015)
Male to Female Ratio	0/100
% International Students	12
% Asian American	24

You Might Also Consider...

Smith College
Amherst College
Bryn Mawr College
Williams College
Harvard University

Career Development

The college boasts a strong alumni network, backed by testimonials from AIC alumni, "I have met alums elsewhere who graduated decades ago and they are friendly and helpful. Many students here have similar experiences too. It's very common for alums to come back and provide lectures/donations/job opportunities to current students." The Shadow Program, allows students to experience different careers through alumni hospitality. This is indicative of Wellesley's strong alumni network. One of the highlights of Wellesley career development offerings is the Center for Work and Service Summer Stipend program where students can receive a stipend for unpaid internships and opportunities.

About 80% of students go on to grad school within 10 years of graduation, and 66% are accepted into their first choice for grad school. About 69% usually work directly after graduation and 17% of students from Class of 2012 had accepted graduate school offers directly after graduation. Teach for America, Bank of America, Capital One, Analysis Group, MIT Lincoln Laboratory, Wellesley College are the most common employers for students.

Campus Social Environment

Although an all-girl's school might be the perfect breeding spot for sororities, Wellesley

AIC Alum Student Score Profiles

% Accepted	9.3
Median SAT Critical Reading	755
Median SAT Math	785
Median SAT Writing	710
Median SAT Composite Score	2245
Median TOEFL	112

Financial Facts

Annual Tuition	$46550 USD (2015—2016)
Financial Aid Availability	Low

What Students say about the Location

Safe	4
Fun	2
Expensive	3
Chinese food	2
Transportation	1.5
Bars and Clubs	2
Market/Grocery Options	1.5
Surrounding Job Market	2.5
Necessity of Car	2
Overall	3

*Out of four

Climate

Average Temperature Range	-5℃ to 22℃
Average Annual Precipitation	121.1cm
Average Annual Humidity	70.17%
Average Annual Snowfall	126.8 cm

Transportation from China

Students can fly directly from Beijing, Shanghai, or Hong Kong to Logan International Airport in Boston. Campus can be reached from the airport by taxi, shuttle, or commuter train in about 40 minutes.

has replaced sororities with societies. Societies are viewed as somewhat exclusive, and therefore, not extremely popular, but host parties and events a lot of students attend. Many students seek parties off campus and at other schools with more even gender ratios. AIC students find the student body "VERY diverse. We have a very large minority presence and the cultural atmosphere is friendly and accepting," but primarily of a similar privileged socioeconomic bracket. In addition, few students have trouble fitting in and intermingling with peers of other nationalities. Wellesley AIC students note that drinking exists, but is not pervasive. Unsurprisingly, boys are not that easy to meet, but opportunities exist due to Wellesley's proximity to other Boston schools, and there is a visible presence of lesbian and bi-sexual individuals. In general, many AIC students agree that the school "just feels right! Big campus for 2000 students but quite a closely-knit community!"

Selectivity

Wellesley is notoriously one of the toughest all-women colleges to earn admittance to in the United States. Demonstrate your finest writing skills while applying to this college and highlight leadership roles. Scores above 2200 are the norm for admitted students.

Things to Consider

You'll like Wellesley if...

- You are looking for ethnic diversity.
- You are politically engaged and want to make a difference.

- You'd like to be surrounded by motivated and empowered women.
- You don't care for drinking and don't want to be pressured into it.

Avoid Wellesley if…

- You want to have close male friends.
- You want any sort of sports scene.
- You need the easy A.

附录 1　分数换算表

旧 SAT Old SAT	新 SAT New SAT	ACT
2390	1600	36
2370	1590	35
2350	1580	35
2300	1540	34
2250	1490	32
2230	1480	32
2200	1470	32
2150	1490	32
2050	1440	31
2020	1420	31
1970	1390	30
1950	1370	29
1910	1330	29
1890	1340	28
1850	1320	28
1800	1290	27
1750	1250	26
1700	1220	25

旧 SAT 阅读 + 写作 Old SAT Reading + Writing	新 SAT 阅读 / 写作 New SAT Reading / Writing	ACT 英语 / 写作 ACT English / Writing
1600	800	35/36
1580	800	34
1560	790	34
1500	770	33
1460	750	33
1430	750	33
1410	740	32
1400	730	31
1350	710	30
1330	710	30
1310	700	30
1280	690	29
1260	680	28
1240	670	28
1220	660	27
1190	650	26
1160	640	25
1130	620	24
1100	610	24

旧 SAT 数学 Old SAT Math	新 SAT 数学 New SAT Math
800	800
790	800
770	780
740	760
710	740
680	710
650	670
630	650
610	630
600	620
580	600
550	570
530	560
500	530

来源：美国大学委员会

附录 2　大学之最

最鼓励学生探索不同兴趣的大学
Most Engaged in Exploring Diverse Interests

埃默里大学 Emory University
卡尔顿学院　Carleton College
西北大学 Northwestern University
加州大学洛杉矶分校 University of California at Los Angeles
密歇根大学安娜堡分校 University of Michigan-Ann Arbor
韦尔斯利学院 Wellesley College
纽约大学 New York University
卡内基梅隆大学 Carnegie Mellon University
芝加哥大学 University of Chicago
加州大学圣地亚哥分校 University of California at San Diego

最关注学生职业发展的大学
Most Career-Oriented Student Population

卡内基梅隆大学 Carnegie Mellon University
加州大学伯克利分校 University of California at Berkeley
杜克大学 Duke University
威廉玛丽学院 College of William & Mary
埃默里大学 Emory University
西北大学 Northwestern University
韦尔斯利学院 Wellesley College
卡尔顿学院 Carleton College
弗吉尼亚大学 University of Virginia
康奈尔大学 Cornell University
圣母大学 University of Notre Dame
宾夕法尼亚大学 University of Pennsylvania
莱斯大学 Rice University
加州大学洛杉矶分校 University of California at Los Angeles
加州理工学院 California Institute of Technology

最方便找到酒吧和俱乐部的大学
Best for Bars and Clubs

密歇根大学安娜堡分校 University of Michigan-Ann Arbor
埃默里大学 Emory University
西北大学 Northwestern University
加州大学洛杉矶分校 University of California at Los Angeles
莱斯大学 Rice University
康奈尔大学 Cornell University
加州大学伯克利分校 University of California at Berkeley
纽约大学 New York University

最方便找到 KTV 的大学
Best for KTVs

埃默里大学 Emory University
密歇根大学安娜堡分校 University of Michigan—Ann Arbor
西北大学 Northwestern University
纽约大学 New York University
加州大学伯克利分校 University of California at Berkeley

有最好快餐的大学
Best for Fast Food

卡尔顿学院 Carleton College
西北大学 Northwestern University
马卡莱斯特学院 Macalester College
杜克大学 Duke University
埃默里大学 Emory University
卡内基梅隆大学 Carnegie Mellon University
加州理工学院 California Institute of Technology
纽约大学 New York University
加州大学伯克利分校 University of California at Berkeley

有最好餐厅的大学
Best Restaurants

加州理工学院 California Institute of Technology
卡尔顿学院 Carleton College
卡内基梅隆大学 Carnegie Mellon University
杜克大学 Duke University
埃默里大学 Emory University
密歇根大学安娜堡分校 University of Michigan-Ann Arbor
圣母大学 University of Notre Dame
加州大学洛杉矶分校 University of California at Los Angeles
韦尔斯利学院 Wellesley College
哥伦比亚大学 Columbia University
纽约大学 New York University
西北大学 Northwestern University
加州大学伯克利分校 University of California at Berkeley
宾夕法尼亚大学 University of Pennsylvania
南加州大学 University of Southern California

最方便选择超市 / 便利店的大学
Best Market/Grocery Options

卡尔顿学院 Carleton College
卡内基梅隆大学 Carnegie Mellon University
杜克大学 Duke University
埃默里大学 Emory University
韦尔斯利学院 Wellesley College
密歇根大学安娜堡分校 University of Michigan-Ann Arbor
西北大学 Northwestern University
芝加哥大学 University of Chicago
马卡莱斯特学院 Macalester College
哥伦比亚大学 Columbia University
弗吉尼亚大学 University of Virginia
纽约大学 New York University
加州大学洛杉矶分校 University of California at Los Angeles

最方便找到购物中心的大学
Best for Shopping Malls

卡尔顿学院 Carleton College
杜克大学 Duke University
埃默里大学 Emory University
韦尔斯利学院 Wellesley College
西北大学 Northwestern University
密歇根大学安娜堡分校 University of Michigan-Ann Arbor
卡内基梅隆大学 Carnegie Mellon University
马卡莱斯特学院 Macalester College
加州理工学院 California Institute of Technology
加州大学洛杉矶分校 University of California at Los Angeles
哥伦比亚大学 Columbia University
纽约大学 New York University

最方便在学校周边找到旅游景点（博物馆、海滩等）的大学
Best for Touristy-type Venues (Museums, Beaches etc.)

埃默里大学 Emory University
密歇根大学安娜堡分校 University of Michigan-Ann Arbor
威斯康星大学麦迪逊分校 University of Wisconsin-Madison
卡内基梅隆大学 Carnegie Mellon University
杜克大学 Duke University
哥伦比亚大学 Columbia University
纽约大学 New York University
加州大学洛杉矶分校 University of California-Los Angeles

交通最便捷的大学
Best Transportation

韦尔斯利学院 Wellesley College
卡内基梅隆大学 Carnegie Mellon University
杜克大学 Duke University

密歇根大学安娜堡分校 University of Michigan-Ann Arbor
埃默里大学 Emory University
西北大学 Northwestern University
卡尔顿学院 Carleton College
纽约大学 New York University
波士顿大学 Boston University

最安全的大学
Most Safety

韦尔斯利学院 Wellesley College
埃默里大学 Emory University
密歇根大学安娜堡分校 University of Michigan-Ann Arbor
卡尔顿学院 Carleton College
西北大学 Northwestern University
威斯康辛大学麦迪逊分校 University of Wisconsin-Madison
加州大学洛杉矶分校 University of California-Los Angeles
加州大学圣地亚哥分校 University of California-San Diego
马卡莱斯特学院 Macalester College
威廉玛丽学院 College of William & Mary

最好玩的大学
Most Fun

埃默里大学 Emory University
加州大学洛杉矶分校 University of California-Los Angeles
哥伦比亚大学 Columbia University
纽约大学 New York University

对学生最友好的大学
Most Friendly

埃默里大学 Emory University
西北大学 Northwestern University

加州大学圣地亚哥分校 University of California-San Diego
弗吉尼亚大学 University of Virginia
韦尔斯利学院 Wellesley College
威斯康星大学麦迪逊分校 University of Wisconsin-Madison
密歇根大学安娜堡分校 University of Michigan-Ann Arbor
卡尔顿学院 Carleton College
马卡莱斯特学院 Macalester College
卡内基梅隆大学 Carnegie Mellon University

在校期间最容易找兼职 / 实习的大学
Easiest to Find a Part-time Job/Internship during the School Year

埃默里大学 Emory University
纽约大学 New York University

校园附近有最好中餐厅的大学
Best Chinese Food

埃默里大学 Emory University
纽约大学 New York University
西北大学 Northwestern University
加州大学伯克利分校 University of California at Berkeley
弗吉尼亚大学 University of Virginia
加州大学洛杉矶分校 University of California at Los Angeles

最多元化的大学
Most Diverse

密歇根大学安娜堡分校 University of Michigan-Ann Arbor
加州大学洛杉矶分校 University of California-Los Angeles
卡内基梅隆大学 Carnegie Mellon University
韦尔斯利学院 Wellesley College
康奈尔大学 Cornell University

有大型体育赛事的大学
Biggest Sports Scene

密歇根大学安娜堡分校 University of Michigan-Ann Arbor
西北大学 Northwestern University
杜克大学 Duke University
弗吉尼亚大学 University of Virginia
圣母大学 University of Notre Dame

最容易找到老师的大学
Where Teachers Are Most Available

密歇根大学安娜堡分校 University of Michigan-Ann Arbor
杜克大学 Duke University
圣母大学 University of Notre Dame
西北大学 Northwestern University
韦尔斯利学院 Wellesley College
加州大学洛杉矶分校 University of California-Los Angeles
埃默里大学 Emory University
莱斯大学 Rice University
卡内基梅隆大学 Carnegie Mellon University
纽约大学 New York University
马卡莱斯特学院 Macalester College
卡尔顿学院 Carleton College
威廉玛丽学院 College of William & Mary

生活花费最高的大学
Highest Cost of Living

韦尔斯利学院 Wellesley College
西北大学 Northwestern University
埃默里大学 Emory University
加州大学洛杉矶分校 University of California-Los Angeles
密歇根大学安娜堡分校 University of Michigan-Ann Arbor

纽约大学 New York University
波士顿大学 Boston University
康奈尔大学 Cornell University

最吵闹的大学
Most Noisy

纽约大学 New York University
埃默里大学 Emory University
马卡莱斯特学院 Macalester College
波士顿大学 Boston University
卡尔顿学院 Carleton College
哥伦比亚大学 Columbia University

最需要车的大学
Where A Car Is Most Necessary

加州大学洛杉矶分校 University of California-Los Angeles
埃默里大学 Emory University
南加州大学 University of Southern California
密歇根大学安娜堡分校 University of Michigan-Ann Arbor
卡内基梅隆大学 Carnegie Mellon University
杜克大学 Duke University
乔治亚理工学院 Georgia Institute of Technology
加州理工学院 California Institute of Technology
威斯康星大学麦迪逊分校 University of Wisconsin-Madison